Politics in

JAPAN

*The Little, Brown Series
in Comparative Politics*

Under the Editorship of
GABRIEL A. ALMOND
JAMES S. COLEMAN
LUCIAN W. PYE

A COUNTRY STUDY

Politics in
JAPAN

Bradley M. Richardson
The Ohio State University

Scott C. Flanagan
Florida State University

Boston   Toronto
LITTLE, BROWN AND COMPANY

Library of Congress Cataloging in Publication Data

Richardson, Bradley M.
   Politics in Japan.

   (The Little, Brown series in comparative politics.
A Country study)
   Includes index.
   1. Politics and government — 1945–   .
2. Political planning — Japan.   3. Japan — Political
sociology.   4. Functional analysis (Social sciences)
I. Flanagan, Scott C.   II. Title.   III. Series: Little,
Brown series in comparative politics.   Country study.
JQ1624.R53 1984   320.952   84–4338
ISBN 0–316–74432–8

Library of Congress Catalog Card No. 84–4338

ISBN 0-316-74432-8

9 8 7 6 5 4 3

ALP

Published simultaneously in Canada
by Little, Brown & Company (Canada) Limited

Printed in the United States of America

For Barbara
and Rita

Preface

JAPAN IS an important country in the world economy and in world politics. Since its population is roughly that of Germany and France combined, Japan is important in terms of sheer size alone. Japan is also wealthy: current per-capita income levels in Japan hover close to those of the richest countries in the world. Japan has achieved this advanced level of economic wealth very rapidly after a period of expansion in which the world's highest levels of economic growth have been recorded. Not only has Japan recently surpassed the United States in the production of automobiles, it has also in recent years produced more steel than any other non-Communist country with the exception of the United States. Among all countries of the world, Japan ranks third in economic importance after the United States and the Soviet Union. Since economic power is one of the important sources of influence in international affairs, Japan is an important world power.

Japan's current economic and political importance is in part a continuation of trends begun in its historical experience over the past century. Japan was the first country outside Europe and North America to modernize both its political institutions and its economy, having introduced constitutional government and popular elections in 1890, long before other non-Western countries did. These political innovations were accompanied by industrialization more like that of the West than Japan's non-Western location and cultural background might have seemed to encourage. Indeed, around the beginning of the twentieth century Japan came to resemble the major nations of the West more than did any other Asian country. Some of Japan's dynamism of that period was reflected in its involvement in foreign wars and in the extension of its political and economic influence into major portions of neighboring China and the Korean peninsula. While Japan has eschewed a major military commitment and geopolitical role since the end of World War II, the dynamism and drive of Japan's century of modernization continue in many forms.

To study the politics of Japan is to examine the political experiences, institutions, and processes of a major world country that is exceptionally dynamic. Japan is thus in many senses a special case. But Japan's politics also have much in common with those of other large, industrialized nations. Consequently, we come to the study of Japanese politics with some general questions that might be asked about any nation's government. It is impossible to name all of our concerns here. But such issues as the degree to which the government was seen as legitimate in the eyes of citizens and groups, the extent to which power was centralized in the hands of a political elite or decentralized among contending and plural centers of influence, the ways and degree to which citizen interests are represented in political processes, and the roles of different government institutions in making laws and formulating policy have each been examined in our analysis along with other important traditional questions from comparative political science.

While this book focuses appropriately on important general questions asked by political scientists in many countries, concerns suggested by the very nature of Japanese politics itself are not neglected. Since Japan had new political institutions and a new party system in the postwar era, it is natural that we investigate how these parameters of politics affected various kinds of political processes. The fact that one party or political movement has been dominant throughout most of the period since World War II is also of paramount importance to our analysis, as was the presence in Japan of a tradition of strong bureaucratic ministries. Some of Japan's recent dynamism is itself of special interest, since economic and social change in recent decades clearly affect many aspects of politics, including, among others, how people make their voting choices and the substance of political issues.

The results of our investigation are framed in the language of the structure-functional approach to politics, as developed by Gabriel Almond and Bingham Powell, Jr. All countries are assumed to perform the same political functions, such as political recruitment, interest articulation, interest aggregation, and policy making, and it is important to see how political structures perform in each functional area in a specific political system. The structure-functional approach also pays special attention to the interaction between politics and society by stressing the importance of political culture, which is the aggregate of political values and attitudes in a particular system. We have dealt with this subject in great detail because Japan is an interesting example of a non-Western cultural tradition in the process of modernization and change. Outputs, outcomes and capabilities, which are concepts pertaining to the quality of the politics-society interface, are also a central concern of the structure-functional approach in its most recent formulation, and these are given special attention in this book.

Politics in Japan can be conveniently divided into two parts. The first part of the book (Chapters 1–6) focuses on system characteristics — the social and political setting and patterns of political behavior. The first three chapters in this section successively treat Japan's historical background, the postwar reforms and political structure, and the contemporary context of political competition and the parties which structure that competition. The last three chapters in the first half of the book look at Japan's distinct cultural tradition and how that tradition has influenced contemporary political attitudes and behavior on both the mass and elite levels. In this extended treatment of Japan's political culture, evidence of both continuity and change is presented in a discussion of such topics as mass involvement in politics, electoral behavior, patterns of conflict and consensus, and political corruption.

The second part of the book (Chapters 7–11) turns to the heart of the structural-functional paradigm, focusing on system process and performance. Individual chapters deal sequentially with three central process functions — political recruitment, interest articulation and aggregation, and policy-making. The last two chapters in this second part conclude the book with a study of system performance, analyzing system outputs, outcomes, and capabilities. The primary author of each chapter is identified on the first page of each chapter, in footnote form. Of course in each case the primary author received many comments and suggestions from his co-author and in particular it should be noted that Bradley Richardson drafted several pages of material that were incorporated into Chapter 2.

Many persons have helped in the preparation of this book. We are especially indebted to Kurt Steiner, James White, Lucian Pye, Terry MacDougall, Haruhiro Fukui, Chalmers Johnson and Ellis Krauss for their reading of the entire manuscript or portions thereof and for helpful suggestions and comments. As is inevitably the case, we alone are responsible for the final product. We are also greatly indebted to Aiji Tanaka, doctoral candidate in political science at Ohio State University, for his enthusiastic support and extensive assistance in the compilation of new data on Diet processes and outputs, political recruitment, party issue positions and other topics. We are also indebted to Akira Kubota, formerly of the Cabinet Legislative Bureau and currently in the Ministry of International Trade and Industry, for help in identifying important statistics on legislative processes in Japan. Portions of the data gathering and analysis were supported by a gift from the Japan Oil Transportation Company to the Project on Japanese Politics at Ohio State University; this gift is gratefully acknowledged.

B.M.R.
S.C.F.

Contents

Politics in

JAPAN

CHAPTER 1

The Legacies
of the Past

A LITTLE OVER A CENTURY AGO, Japan was an agrarian, feudal society at roughly the same stage of socioeconomic development as
the Tudor England of four hundred years ago. By 1980, Japan
had emerged as a modernized industrial power with an economy
nearly three times as large as Britain and one that ranked third
throughout the entire world, behind only the United States and
the Soviet Union. Much has been written about Japan's phenomenal success story, and a great deal of attention has been focused
on identifying those economic, institutional, and cultural factors
that have contributed to the Japanese miracle in three short
decades following World War II. We will discuss some of these
factors in a later chapter.

The period of rapid Japanese economic development, however,
did not begin with the conclusion of World War II. The more
amazing success story is the speed with which Japan transformed
itself from an agrarian feudal society to a major industrial and
military power in the years between the Meiji Restoration in 1867
and the outbreak of the Second World War in the late 1930s. In
this chapter we will focus on this seventy-year period of modernization in Japan. The question we will primarily be concerned
with, however, is not that of how Japan was able to come so far
so fast, but rather what were the hidden costs of this accelerated

* Scott C. Flanagan

1

pace of change for Japan's political development? In other words, what were the implications of the developmental formula adopted by the Meiji modernizers on the development and democratization of Japan's political institutions? A second related question will be dealt with in the following two chapters; that is, what has been the effect of this prewar experience on Japanese politics in the post-World War II period?

The Meiji Restoration was an historic turning point in the socioeconomic and political development of Japan. It marked the end of feudalism and the beginnings of a modern nation state. The forced opening of Japan to foreign trade by the American Commodore Matthew C. Perry, following the arrival of his naval fleet in Tokyo Bay in 1853, demonstrated the weakness of the Tokugawa Shogunate and set off a movement to return power to the emperor and expel the foreign barbarians. With Japan perched on the brink of civil war, the Shogun was persuaded to resign his office in the fall of 1867, and administrative authority was symbolically restored to the emperor in January of the following year. Thereupon the new leadership, far from expelling the Western barbarians, sought to learn the secrets of their power and to emulate them by adopting many of their economic and political institutions. Thus in a few short years following the Restoration, Japan embarked on an ambitious industrialization program and instituted a political structure modeled after Western constitutional monarchies.

The speed and success of the Japanese modernization program were in part made possible by a number of important changes that took place during the Tokugawa period of high feudalism and that uniquely prepared Japanese society for modernization. First, the Tokugawa house had unified the country by military force in 1603, and their peaceful reign of over two hundred and fifty years coupled with Japan's insularity and enforced isolation fostered the development of a sense of national unity and national identity. A second important change was that early in the Tokugawa era, the warrior class was removed from the land and transformed into a largely urbanized class of salaried administrators. Power came to be exercised through office, and the political system was increasingly bureaucratized. By the late eighteenth century the idea that recruitment to office should be based on knowledge and ability rather than lineage, family rank, or wealth appears to have been widely accepted, at least in theory. As a class, the warriors' esteem for education, professional experience, habits of frugality, cult of action, and social idealism together with the new ideology of merit well prepared them for their new roles as the managers of modern government and industry.[1]

A third development was the emergence of a new innovative elite in the countryside, a class of rural capitalists. In many rural areas by the mid-nineteenth century, handicraft industries (the production of raw cotton, textiles, dyeing, silk, sake, sugar, and paper) rivaled agriculture in economic importance. The surplus capital that this development injected into the countryside gave rise to a new landlord-entrepreneurial class with the wealth to acquire land from poorer peasants who, in turn, could subsist on smaller plots or as landless tenants by supplementing their income through wage labor. This development not only prepared the lower peasantry economically and psychologically for the transition to the urban factory, but it also made entrepreneurial skills an important criteria for mobility within the village socio-economic structure. Finally, a fourth factor was that the emphasis placed on knowledge and merit by various Confucian scholars and literati permeated society and stimulated the diffusion of education such that by the Meiji Restoration, 40–50 percent of Japanese boys received some formal schooling.[2]

Despite all these changes, the Japanese feudal system in its twilight years still imposed severe restrictions on economic activities and occupational mobility. The bulk of the warrior class, which were living on fixed stipends, were becoming increasingly impoverished by inflation. Towards the end of the Tokugawa period, the warrior class, the rising class of rural entrepreneurs, and the wealthy urban merchants found the feudal socioeconomic structure increasingly constraining and disadvantageous. This is one reason why the abolition of the feudal system by the Meiji modernizers met with so little opposition.

[1] Reinhard Bendix, "Preconditions of Development: A Comparison of Japan and Germany," in Ronald P. Dore, ed., *Aspects of Social Change in Modern Japan* (Princeton: Princeton University Press, 1967), pp. 27–68.

[2] Thomas C. Smith, *The Agrarian Origins of Modern Japan* (New York: Atheneum, 1966), p. 212; Ronald P. Dore, "The Legacy of Tokugawa Education," in Marius B. Jansen, ed., *Changing Japanese Attitudes Towards Modernization* (Princeton: Princeton University Press, 1965), pp. 100–1.

Nevertheless, the sociopolitical changes that were instituted in the two decades from the Meiji Restoration in 1867–68 to the promulgation of the Meiji Constitution in 1889 were truly revolutionary in their scope and magnitude. These changes laid the foundation for Japan's economic takeoff, which is usually set around 1900 or at the conclusion of the Russo-Japanese War in 1905.[3] This revolutionary set of Meiji reforms included the abolition of the privileges of the warrior class, the breaking up of the feudal domains and the lords' control of the land, and the abolition of legal class distinctions; an end to restrictions on the cropping and sale of land and on commercial pursuits; the establishment of universal education and free choice of occupation; the creation of a modern centralized bureaucracy and military and institutions of higher learning along Western lines; an emphasis on educational achievement and examination scores as the principal criteria for recruitment into the new national political and economic elites; the wholesale borrowing of Western legal, educational, and monetary systems; and the embarking on an ambitious government initiated and subsidized industrialization program.

The very magnitude of these changes suggests that, notwithstanding the deteriorating circumstances of the warrior class, substantial resistance should have been encountered. There was in fact some resistance, which came to a head in the abortive Saigo Rebellion of 1877. This resistance was minimized, however, by the Meiji modernizers' strategy of easing the acceptance of the dramatic changes they were introducing by cloaking them in the guise of tradition. This strategy has been variously referred to as one of "reinforcing dualism," "incorporative modernization," or according to the slogan of the time, "Western Science, Eastern Ethics." [4] These terms refer to a mixing of the new and the old, a coexistence of tradition with modernity. This dualism was a conscious strategy in that the Meiji oligarchs exploited traditional symbols and cultural norms to minimize unrest while liberating

---

[3] Kazushi Ohkawa and Henry Rosovsky, "A Century of Japanese Economic Growth," in William W. Lockwood, ed., *The State and Economic Enterprise in Japan* (Princeton: Princeton University Press, 1965).

[4] Robert E. Ward, "Political Modernization and Political Culture in Japan," in Claude E. Welch, Jr., ed., *Political Modernization* (Belmont, Ca.: Wadsworth Publishing Co., 1967); Nobutaka Ike, *Japanese Politics* (New York: Knopf, 1972), pp. 3–11.

and focusing mass energies on the task of industrial development. The strategy rested on stressing the august station and mythical divine origins of the emperor, propagating traditional Japanese virtues and nationalistic themes in the schools and media, and keeping the countryside untouched as much as possible by the dramatic socioeconomic changes and foreign influences that were centered in urban areas. Through this dualistic approach to modernization, the Meiji elites sought to retain the purity of the submissive, frugal, hard-working peasantry. The strategy enabled them to foster rapid industrialization through taxes squeezed from the agricultural sector and at the same time maintain a larger reservoir of loyal subjects in the countryside that could be drawn on as needed to supply dedicated soldiers for the army and industrious workers for the urban factories.

Perhaps most of all the Meiji elites wanted to prolong the lag between social mobilization and political mobilization.[5] Social mobilization was necessary for economic development but also carried with it the danger of increased demands for political participation by wider segments of the population. The Japanese elites sought to arrest the development of modern participant orientations, and thereby protect the imperial institution, the aristocratic order, and the privileges of social status and wealth from attack from the republican, egalitarian, and socialistic ideologies of the West. Thus the leadership enacted a series of regulations during the 1870s and 1880s designed to control and suppress a burgeoning party movement, known as the Movement for Freedom and Popular Rights, which aimed at establishing parliamentary rule. By mixing socialization campaigns that preached reverence for the emperor with heavy-handed measures to suppress dissent and co-opt or otherwise tame opposition leaders, a truly mass popular movement capable of mobilizing broad political participation was forestalled. In short, the Meiji leaders fostered "dualism" as a means of achieving rapid, government-

[5] *Social mobilization* refers to a cluster of interrelated socioeconomic changes associated with the transformation from an agrarian to an industrial society, including urbanization, occupational mobility, and rising levels of literacy, education, communications, and transportation. *Political mobilization* refers to the mobilization of broad strata into the political process as a result of rising expectations, an enhanced political consciousness, and involvement in politicized organizations, such as unions and mass political parties.

sponsored development while defusing the threat modernization posed to conservative elites.

This kind of dualistic modernization strategy clearly imposed very real barriers for the democratization of Japan. The mixing of new institutions and tasks with old values and practices also created problems for the coordination and control of the new political structure. In the remainder of this chapter, we will focus on the development of the authority and accountability structures from the Meiji Restoration up until the Second World War. The authority structure refers to the institutions and processes of authoritative decision making within the government. The accountability structure refers to those democratic institutions and processes whereby citizens hold their government accountable for its actions and responsive to their demands.

THE WEAK INTEGRATION OF JAPAN'S PREWAR AUTHORITY STRUCTURE

There has been a considerable amount of scholarly debate as to whether Japan's prewar political system would have evolved into a parliamentary democracy if the Second World War and the events surrounding it had not intervened. Evidently the American occupation authorities concluded from their reading of Japan's prewar political history that the Meiji Constitution did not provide a sound basis for the establishment of a effective democratic government. As a result they summarily dismissed the Japanese-authored constitutional drafts which conformed to the original outlines of the Meiji Constitution and drafted an American-made constitution based on a blend of British and American constitutional principles.

The reasons behind the Occupation authorities' insistence on a completely fresh approach to shaping the legal foundations of the Japanese political system emerge from an analysis of the prewar authority structure. There were at least three fatal flaws in the Meiji Constitution that posed major and perhaps insurmountable obstacles for the development of parliamentary democracy. These were (1) the location of sovereignty in the person of the emperor rather than the people; (2) the failure of the Meiji political structure to subordinate clearly the military to the civilian authorities; and (3) the failure of the prewar constitution to integrate the political structure and decision-making processes or establish clear lines of authority and responsibility. In the following chapter we will see how the occupation authorities sought to overcome these deficiencies in the new political structure they designed for Japan. Here we will survey the historical origins of the weaknesses in Japan's prewar authority structure.

In the 1870s, a small oligarchy led Japan rapidly out of feudalism and into a new socioeconomic order. The last two decades of the nineteenth century saw this leadership move just as quickly from revolution to conservatism in an effort to institutionalize its newly acquired power. By the end of 1881, the Meiji oligarchy had purged itself of dissidents, consolidated its position, and stood at the height of its power. Its efforts to stabilize the political order, however, were to be challenged by its prior commitment to increase the tempo of economic development and social mobilization. Ironically the Meiji leadership's development programs were fundamentally altering the context of political competition and the contenders for power, and undermining the oligarchy's own resource base. As a result, the central and persisting problem which it was to face during the next two decades was how to share power safely with the articulate organized groups outside the oligarchy that were beginning to emerge in the form of political parties.

The weakness of the nascent party opposition in the early years following the Restoration allowed the oligarchs carte blanche in designing the political structure. Yet the oligarchs were committed from an early date to the idea of a Western constitution providing for some kind of representative assembly. They had concluded from their reading of Western history that a constitution was an indispensable prerequisite for modernization and industrialization. It also represented an essential element in their campaign for Western acceptance and revision of the unequal treaties. Finally, after almost annual revisions and modifications of their fledgling political structure, they recognized the need to give it a lasting authoritative expression. While they were willing to accept the existence of the organized "loyal" opposition, they were at the same time determined to keep it isolated from the centers of power. To this end, the framers of the constitution leaned heavily on the Prussian model of controlled participation.[6]

[6] George Akita, *Foundations of Constitutional Government in Modern Japan 1868–1900* (Cambridge: Harvard University Press, 1967), pp. 1–30; Ward, op. cit., p. 101.

In order to legitimize a political structure which permitted only limited participation, the oligarchy relied on the myth of imperial sovereignty. The Meiji Constitution was presented in 1889 as the emperor's personal gift to his people, which was to be esteemed as reverently as the emperor himself. The constitution was protected from possible revision by providing that amendments could be initiated only by the emperor; and, in fact, it was never amended until the sweeping Occupation-sponsored revision of 1946. Questions of authority and responsibility were handled in theory by making all state organs — the state ministries, the military, the Imperial Household Ministry, the Privy Council, and the Diet — responsible to the emperor alone. Since the emperor played only a passive role in decision making, the constitution in effect delegated all authority to his trusted advisors — the oligarchs.

By substituting "oligarchs" for "emperor," we can see how strongly the political structure weighted the scales in favor of the "ins" over the "outs." The Diet was to be open only two months out of the year. The popularly elected House of Representatives (lower house) shared its powers equally with a highly conservative House of Peers (upper house). Even if the lower house succeeded in securing the Peers' approval, the emperor enjoyed an absolute veto; also, he could prorogue the Diet or dissolve the lower house at will. Moreover, the emperor's ordinance power was greater even than that exercised in Bismarck's Germany. In addition to extensive general (administrative, war, and treaty) and police ordinance powers, the emperor could exercise virtually unlimited legislative power in the form of emergency ordinances when the Diet was not in session. When the Diet reconvened, these emergency ordinances required its approval to continue in force, but withdrawal of an ordinance had no retroactive effect. Finally, if the Diet failed to approve the government's budget, the previous year's budget automatically went into effect.[7]

The constitution was applauded at home and abroad at the time of its promulgation, and the oligarchs seemed well-satisfied

---

[7] Harold S. Quigley, *Japanese Government and Politics* (New York: The Century Co., 1932); Robert K. Reischauer, *Japan: Government — Politics* (New York: Thomas Nelson and Sons, 1939); Yale C. Maxon, *Control of Japanese Foreign Policy* (Berkeley: University of California Press, 1957).

with the fruit of nearly a decade of research and drafting. The
constitution soon, however, proved to have two unintended consequences. First, despite the drafters' intentions, it failed to act
as an effective barrier against the growth of party power. The
opening of the first Diet in 1890 actually bolstered the opposition's resources; for the first time it enjoyed a legitimate place in
the machinery of government. The need for a constantly expanding budget, coupled with the oligarchs' desire to prove to the
world that constitutional government could work in Japan, gave
the parties the leverage needed to gain a gradual increase in
power.[8]

Far from providing a barrier against the growth of party power,
the constitution provided the parties with an opening wedge.
Moreover, the parties were quick to realize that much of the
Meiji political structure was based on statutes or customs accumulated from 1881–1900 and presumably were subject to revision
and modification. Thus through omission and interpretation the
constitution proved to be a rather flexible document despite the
difficulty in amending it. This unintended flexibility was one of
the constitution's principal strengths because it permitted marginal adjustments in the locus of decision-making authority in
response to a shifting distribution of resources among the contenders for power. Thus the constitution was able to accommodate dramatic political changes from 1900–45 as Japan moved at
first in the direction of liberal democracy and then abruptly
changed course and headed in the direction of a repressive, mili-
taristic state.

In contrast, the constitution's second unintended consequence
proved to be its greatest weakness. In order to enhance the legitimacy of the oligarchs' exercise of power, the constitution stressed
the centralization of all authority symbolically in the person of
the emperor. Carrying the myth of imperial authority into the
very heart of the political structure crippled the development of
a rationalized decision-making process. The emperor was not allowed to assume responsibility for arbitrating conflicts among his
chief ministers. The purpose of translating the emperor's theoretical absolutism into a practical impotence was to protect the imperial institution from any political controversy which might dim

[8] Akita, op. cit., pp. 75–89.

its prestige and weaken its effectiveness as a symbol of unity. By emphasizing the theoretical absolutism of the emperor, the constitution failed to provide for a central, coordinating locus of real authority. The result was an authority structure which in time came to resemble a system of concurrent majorities with multiple independent decision sites, each of which was directly responsible only to a passive, symbolic seat of authority.

One potential surrogate locus of authority, the prime minister, usually found his powers insufficient for the task of coordinating the decision process. While he could exercise some control over the Lower House through the dissolution power, the House of Peers and the Privy Council were much more insulated from his influence. The Privy Council, composed of twenty-six venerable senior statesmen, was designed to exercise a supervisory role over the constitution and the state; it was necessary to secure its approval for government ordinances related to civil service regulations and the organization and power of the executive departments, ordinances having penal provision, all emergency ordinances, international treaties and agreements, and any matter deemed to be of great significance to the state. Either the Upper House or the Privy Council, therefore, could block government measures.[9]

The greatest threat to the coherence and rationality of the decision process, however, stemmed from the military prerogative of direct access to the throne; that is, the General Staff could make their representations to the throne and through this formality gain the imperial seal of approval. As a result, the military exercised virtually complete autonomy within its own sphere — military planning, administration, and combat operations. Moreover, the military could intervene in civil governmental and political affairs by withdrawing the army and/or navy ministers from the Cabinet and refusing to supply a replacement unless its demands were met. In 1900, the customary practice of selecting army and navy ministers only from the two highest ranks of officers on the active list was made mandatory, thus guaranteeing that the military would continue to exercise the power, as first demonstrated in 1892, to topple cabinets.[10]

9 Quigley, op. cit., pp. 89–128, 160–200; Reischauer, op. cit., pp. 80–106.
10 Maxon, op. cit., p. 13; Akita, op. cit., pp. 102–105.

The constitution was not totally lacking in means for the development of a rationalized authority structure. Both the Prime Ministership and the Privy Council might have evolved the necessary powers for effective coordination. But the oligarchs throughout the first decade of constitutional government seemed intent on reinforcing the diffusion of authority. Why? Part of the answer lies in Japan's historical experience. During the Tokugawa period there was one chief minister, the Shogun. Perhaps it was the attempt to prevent the reemergence of a mighty shogun which led the oligarchs to diffuse direct access to the emperor among a number of independent decision sites, thus preventing the accumulation of power by any one of their number through a monopolization of the authority of the emperor. Moreover, during the 1890s the parties emerged as a real threat to the oligarchy. Obsessed with the problems of preserving "transcendental" government, the oligarchs moved at that time to increase the power and independence of the Privy Council, the military, and the bureaucracy vis-à-vis the Prime Ministership, which appeared to be in some future danger of falling under the control of the parties.

The political structure was also a product of the oligarchs' style of leadership. The twenty-six councillors who formed the Supreme Council of State directly after the Meiji Restoration in 1869 were all men of strong personality and abundant talent. It was clear from the beginning that the greatest threat to this oligarchy stemmed from internal division. Through death, assassination, defection, and purge, the oligarchy was reduced to seven of the original twenty-six councillors by the time it switched from the council to the cabinet system in 1885.

The efforts to stabilize this collective leadership and maintain its preeminent position in the government led to the development of informal structures of coordination. The most prominent example of such an informal structure is the *genro* (elder statesmen) council, which evolved in the early 1880s and was composed of the seven oligarchs. Although eventually the *genro* council's principal public function became the selection of a new prime minister upon the fall of a cabinet, in the beginning it represented an informal, sporadic approach to the coordination of the decision process that the oligarchs found most congenial. As Roger Hackett points out, the practice of calling together this council of elder statemen nurtured a political tradition "in which the most important decisions of state were made outside the formal channels of government, through an arbitrary and even irrational process." [11]

The oligarchs' preference for this informal style of decision making had two important effects on the development of decision-making structures and processes: the proliferation of coequal offices on the highest levels, and the extensive reliance on ad hoc, extraconstitutional decision sites. Rather than subordinating one arm of the government to another or integrating top level offices under a chief executive, there was a tendency to assign to numerous branches and offices essentially coequal and independent power. The constitution rejected the principle of joint responsibility for the Cabinet and instead made each minister responsible to the emperor directly and individually. The prime minister was simply *primus inter pares* — first among equals — and each minister could on occasion exercise the right of independent access to the throne. The military derived its very special position from the fact that the emperor was designated as Commander-in-Chief, in direct command of the armed forces. On the basis of this "imperial prerogative of supreme command" the military claimed independence from any civilian authority. Just as there was no provision for the subordination of military to civilian authorities, there was no one official who exercised control over both the military services; moreover, within the respective branches, powers were divided among the army's Big Three and between the navy's Big Two. Commanders of overseas armies were also not clearly subordinated to any central military authority but were rather in direct chain-of-command line to the throne. The general staff, therefore, had to petition the throne in each case to exercise control over field armies.[12]

Clearly, the chain of hierarchic subordination stopped short of the top. The political structure failed to rationalize the authority structure and assign ultimate responsibility for the administration of both civil and military affairs to a single office. To achieve coordination in the formation of government policy, a top level,

[11] Roger F. Hackett, "Political Modernization and the Meiji Genro," in Robert E. Ward, ed., *Political Development in Modern Japan* (Princeton: Princeton University Press, 1968), pp. 68–69, 97.

[12] Alvin D. Coox, *Year of the Tiger* (Tokyo: Orient/West Inc., 1964), p. 47.

behind-the-scenes, ad hoc decision body had to be convened whenever conflicts developed that required a negotiated settlement between the various leaders or branches of the government or whenever there arose vital decisions involving important policy or leadership changes. Frequently, not even a group meeting was held; instead, messengers informally circulated among the recognized members of the decision group to determine the "collective will." [13]

As long as the oligarchs ran the government, the diffuse political structure they had created in general operated smoothly. They possessed the necessary power, prestige, personal followings, group intimacy, and shared values and goals to coordinate and control effectively this loosely integrated, multiheaded structure of government. By 1901, however, it was already becoming clear that power would soon pass from the hands of the oligarchs. In that year, the last of their number retired from active politics and thereafter directed the government from behind the scenes only in their role as *genro* (elder statemen). During the next twelve years the Prime Ministership alternated between Taro Katsura and Kimmochi Saionji, the respective proteges of the two leading oligarchs, Aritomo Yamagata and Hirobumi Ito. The oligarchs, however, were unable to pass on to others their mantle of power and prestige with the result that death continued to thin their ranks. By 1916, only Yamagata, Matsukata, and Saionji, aged seventy-eight, eighty-one, and sixty-seven respectively, were left; and after 1924, Saionji alone remained to carry on the traditional *genro* functions until his death in 1940.

In place of a single coordinating oligarchy, there emerged after World War I a much larger and more diverse plural elite composed of the court, the aristocracy, the bureaucracy, the military, and the parties. These groups increasingly diverged in their policy preferences and competed for control of the authority structure. At first it appeared that Japan might evolve gradually into a parliamentary democracy, as the parties slowly expanded their dominance of the Diet and the cabinet. Indeed, the years 1924 through 1932 marked an era of party-led governments, when

[13] David A. Titus, *Palace and Politics in Pre-War Japan* (New York: Columbia University Press, 1974).

the parties not only controlled the Prime Ministership and the majority of the other cabinet positions, but also won important allies in the bureaucracy, the House of Peers, and the Court.

The parties, however, were never able to enact the basic institutional reforms necessary to transform the Japanese political system into a true representative democracy. Thus, even at the high point of party dominance, the *genro* council and other imperial court advisors rather than the Diet still selected the prime minister; the Army and Navy were able to control their respective cabinet ministers; and the House of Peers and especially the Privy Council exercised important powers that the elected representatives of the people could neither bypass nor override. Indeed, the parties' gradual rise to dominance was dependent on the existence of a congenial national mood and international environment, as well as on the skills of compromise, maneuver, and coalition-formation in a context of overlapping jurisdictions, numerous competing offices and institutions, and ambiguous lines of authority.

Because the parties failed to integrate the diffuse authority structure they inherited from the oligarchs, their predominance was easily challenged when the Japanese political system was beset by a series of domestic and international crises in the early 1930s, resulting from Japan's economic depression and growing international isolation. When the predominance of the parties was openly challenged by the military, the phenomenon of dual government emerged, with the military moving in one direction while at the same time the civilian government proclaimed sharply divergent policy objectives. By the support of a strategy of nationalistic propaganda campaigns, by the intimidation and assassination of leading opponents, and by the use of a popular and successful program of foreign expansion, the military was able to displace the parties completely and seize the dominant position in the governing coalition during the years 1936–45. The ambiguities in the Meiji political structure permitted the dramatic relocation of decision-making authority from the oligarchs to the parties and then to the military without any constitutional amendments or major structural reforms.

Edwin Reischaeur has characterized these transitions from the period of oligarchic to party to military ascendancy simply as shifts in the balance of Japan's plural elites.[14] Indeed, the decisiveness of these transformations in the ruling coalition was blurred by a consensual, incremental pattern of decision making and a web of interelite and cross-institutional personal alliances. What is clear, however, is that the movement towards the gradual democratization of the Meiji political structure, which began with the opening of the Diet in 1890 and briefly flowered in the 1920s, withered and died in the 1930s in the wake of the military's total mobilization for war. The complete eclipse of the parties occurred in 1940 when they all voluntarily disbanded and were merged into the Imperial Rule Assistance Association.

In this section, we have drawn the outlines of the Meiji Constitution's weakly integrated authority structure and shown how it imposed severe and perhaps insurmountable obstacles to the development of a democratic form of government in Japan. These flaws in the authority structure were successfully exploited by the military to move Japan abruptly in the direction of a fascist model of government in the 1930s.[15] This prewar experience convinced the occupation reformers that the Meiji Constitution, however it was amended, could not provide a sound basis for parliamentary democracy.

THE WEAK DEVELOPMENT OF JAPAN'S PREWAR
ACCOUNTABILITY STRUCTURE

Two of the recurring themes in studies of contemporary Japanese politics are the elitist nature of policy-making and the ineffectiveness of the political opposition. Many writers have pointed out that a triple alliance of the Liberal Democratic Party, big business, and the bureaucracy have dominated decision-making processes in Japan throughout the postwar period. Haruhiro Fukui, for example, has written that the policy process in Japan appears "to operate often like an autonomous and self-contained system impervious to its environment" and he refers to the "marginality of the role played by the opposition groups" and the

[14] John Fairbank, Edwin Reishauer, and Albert Craig, *East Asia: The Modern Transformation* (Boston: Houghton Mifflin Co., 1965), pp. 490–493.

[15] These same flaws, however, also prevented the military from consolidating its authority and reshaping the Japanese political system into the kind of monolithic power structures found in fascist Germany and Italy.

"predominant, almost exclusive, role of the tripartite coalition." [16]

In a recent analysis of democracy and accountability in Japan, James White states that there are three sources of accountability in modern democratic societies, which he labels structural, cultural, and popular; and that structural and cultural accountability are quite weak in Japan, placing an extraordinarily heavy responsibility on popular accountability. Structural accountability refers to institutional forces within the government and constitutional structures that may limit the abuses of power by political leaders, and include the courts, regulatory agencies, and various other checks and balances; but most importantly, structural accountability depends on the "opposition political parties and the threat they pose to the government of the day." [17] Cultural accountability refers to deeply ingrained elements of a nation's political culture which limit the exercise of political power. An example would be the so-called British constitution, those widespread cultural norms and democratic principles that limit what a cabinet can do, despite the absence of any legal written document or judicial review. Popular accountability refers to direct pressure from interest groups and popular movements acting outside the political parties to force national and local government leaders to be responsive to specific demands.

The present weaknesses in structural and cultural accountability in Japan can be traced to the manner in which democratic institutions developed in Japan. In this section we will look historically at the causes of the weak development of political opposition in Japan. In Chapter 5, we will review those factors that have inhibited the diffusion of democratic norms in pre- and postwar Japan and have contributed to the weak development of cultural accountability.

One of the most basic concepts in democratic theory is that of the "loyal opposition." Clearly, without an opposition there is no democracy. The opposition provides one or more "shadow cabinets" that articulate alternative policy programs with the expectation that today's minority may very well become tomorrow's

[16] Haruhiro Fukui, "Economic Planning in Postwar Japan: A Case Study in Policy Making," *Asian Survey* 14 (April 1974), pp. 327–348.

[17] James W. White, "Accountability and Democracy in Japan," in George W. Waldner, ed., *Japan in the 1980s*, Papers on International Studies, No. 3, (Atlanta: Southern Center for International Studies, 1982), pp. 58–72.

majority. The legitimacy of political opposition is clearly tied to the principles of minority rights and majority rule. Historically, however, the acceptance of political opposition has not been an easy lesson to learn. In most traditional absolutist systems, prolonged opposition was neither recognized as legitimate nor tolerated. The right of dissident groups to have a legally sanctioned voice in decision-making forums generally grew out of protracted and inconclusive struggles. Many European societies were marked by deep divisions of region, religion, ethnicity, and class. Where one side of a politically salient cleavage could not obliterate the other, they were eventually forced to come to terms and recognize each other's legitimate interests. Out of such disputes democratic institutions were born, which not only legitimated political opposition but also institutionalized the rotation of power from government to opposition whenever the government of the day lost the support of a majority of the electorate.[18]

Japan, however, was historically a far more homogeneous society, having little in common with the intense ethnic, regional, and religious cleavages found in Europe; therefore, there were few competing and independent interests capable of opposing the centripetal pressures accompanying modernization. Thomas Smith has aptly characterized the Meiji Restoration as an aristocratic revolution.[19] It was aristocratic in leadership and revolutionary in implementing socioeconomic transformations which opened the way for modernization and industrialization. Because Japan's industrial revolution was sponsored by the aristocracy, the classical bourgeois or democratic revolution never materialized. As a result, the initiation and execution of economic and political development was essentially uncontested, which proved to be a plus from the point of view of economic development, but a minus from the point of view of democratic development.

The warrior class, Japan's "aristocracy," did not play a defensive, reactionary role but took the lead as the reforming and innovating class. As a result, there was no sustained conflict between classes or special interests, which undoubtedly contributed to the fact that the principle of the right and legitimacy of the repre-

[18] Dankwart Rustow, "Transitions to Democracy: Toward A Dynamic Model," *Comparative Politics* Vol. 2. (April 1970), pp. 337–363.

[19] Thomas C. Smith, "Japan's Aristocratic Revolution," *Yale Review* 50 (Spring 1961), pp. 370–383.

sentation of diverse and antagonistic interests was never established. During the early years of the Meiji regime, articulate public opinion was mainly limited to the old feudal aristocracy. As an opposition began to take form in the 1870s and 1880s, it not only represented the same class interests as the oligarchs, but, perhaps as a consequence of the international threat, was in close agreement with them on national goals and developmental policies. Moreover, the opposition formed around former powerful figures within the oligarchy who had been forced to withdraw from the government. There was really no other source of strength around which an opposition could rally. Business and agrarian interest groups were still virtually nonexistent; and when they did emerge at the turn of the century, they tended to be closely guided and directed by the government.

In Japan, therefore, the power structure became not only increasingly centralized with modernization as had occurred in Europe, but also increasingly monocentric. It may seem inconsistent to refer to the prewar Japanese system as monocentric after having discussed shifts of power among Japan's plural elites in the previous section. Yet although competition flourished on the elite level, it was conducted in a subtle, behind-the-scenes, invisible mode; moreover, competition and conflict at the mass level were considered inappropriate and illegitimate. In normative terms, Japan's elites adhered to an organic notion of society as a one-family nation with one body and one head, in which all elements of society were hierarchically ordered and valued. Each element was essential, but the lower strata were expected to seek fulfillment in the proper execution of their own functions, which did not include guiding the state. In pragmatic terms, the various economic sectors and social classes by and large failed to develop independent power bases that could effectively challenge the center; according to Junnosuke Masumi, there was a tendency for political opposition to dissolve into the center.[20] The only way that the outs were able to improve their position was to align themselves with the ins in a subordinate position. There was only one source of authority, the emperor, and all roads to power

[20] Junnosuke Masumi, "The Present Condition of Japanese Political Studies." Report prepared for the Joint Committee on Japanese Studies, Social Sciences Research Council, New York, 1968, pp. 10–12.

led to the elite-controlled offices and institutions that guarded the access to the imperial seal.

The monocentric character of Japanese political power can be more clearly seen by examining the extent to which the salient socioeconomic cleavages dividing Japanese society failed to be reflected in the party system throughout the period from the opening of the Imperial Diet in 1890 to the dissolution of the parties in 1940. Prewar Japanese society was crosscut by three major kinds of cleavages: (1) urban-rural and center-periphery cleavages, (2) economic-functional or class cleavages, and (3) cultural and ideological cleavages. Any one of these cleavages could have potentially polarized Japanese society politically and formed a basis around which political opposition could effectively mobilize and gain legitimacy.

The first of the three cleavages, the urban-rural cleavage, was the dominant political cleavage during the years 1880 to 1912. Potentially this cleavage bound the peasantry in common cause with the rural elites against various forces identified with the cities and the central government in Tokyo. Parochial sensitivities were naturally antagonized by the invasion of central government bureaucrats into the provinces with their programs of taxation and conscription. More important was the fact that the government was pushing its industrialization program at the expense of agrarian interests. The land tax remained a highly salient issue up through the Taisho crisis of 1912–13. Government tariff and subsidization policies also clearly favored urban business interests over agrarian interests.

Added to the growing economic gap between the city and the countryside was a widening social and cultural gap that was caused largely by the speed and unevenness of the urbanization process. The government's program of industrialization, which was artificially stimulating this process, was introducing profound and rapid changes into the urban environment. At the same time, the government seemed intent on holding the countryside constant, keeping it untouched by and aloof from the forces of modernization which were agitating the cities. Economic forces also contributed to the stabilization of the agricultural way of life. Population growth cancelled the gains of land reclamation and the demand for industrial labor, so that throughout the period 1880–1940, the size of the average holding per family remained fixed at around one *cho* (2.45 acres). Moreover, experiments in large-scale farming failed to take hold with the result that there was no movement towards the amalgamation of farms. Thus the communal character of village life based on paternalistic landlord-tenant relationships remained almost unchanged.[21]

After the collapse of rural peasant uprisings in 1884–85, which contained some elements of a final feudal counterattack on the encroachments of the national government, mobilization along the center-periphery, urban-rural cleavage was limited to an economic competition between urban and rural elites. The controversy centered around the relative taxation and tariff protection of the industrial and agrarian sectors. From 1890 until 1902, the landlord class dominated the membership of the elected lower house of the Diet. As shown in Table 1.1, in the first six elections to the Diet during these years, an average of 54 percent of the elected Dietmen were classified as having agricultural occupations. In contrast, an average of only 14 percent of the Dietmen had some kind of business background in commerce, industry, or banking. With the ruling oligarchy and the civil bureaucracy committed to a policy of fostering industrialization as their number one economic priority, the urban business versus rural agrarian competition took the form of a Diet-bureaucracy confrontation. Moreover, the contest was not completely one-sided, since, with a majority control of the Diet, the landlord class was able to force the government to modify its probusiness policies and make concessions on a number of antiagrarian measures.[22]

This contest marked a crucial turning point for Japanese democracy, for it was during this same period that the urban and rural middle classes were initially incorporated into the political process. If the forces on both sides of this cleavage could have been effectively mobilized over a long period, the resultant political polarization might likely have forced a recognition of the legitimacy of political opposition.

---

21 R. P. Dore, *Land Reform in Japan* (London: Oxford University Press, 1959), pp. 18, 57–61.

22 The data reported in Table 1 were computed from data presented in Kyoto Daigaku Bungakubu Kokushi Kenkyushitsu. *Nihon Kindai-shi Jiten* (Tokyo: Toyo Keizai Shimposha, 1958), pp. 766–767; Takeshi Ishida, "The Development of Interest Groups and the Pattern of Political Modernization in Japan," in Ward, ed., op. cit., pp. 293–336.

TABLE 1.1. *Changes in the Occupation Classification of Dietmen Accompanying the Growth in the Size of the Electorate*

Years of Elections	1890–98	1902–04	1908–17	1920–24	1928–42	Total Ratio Increase
Number of Elections	6	3	4	2	6	×30
Size of Electorate	460,000	900,000	1,500,000	3,200,000	14,000,000	
Ratio Increase in Electorate Size		×2.0	×1.7	×2.1	×4.3	
Occupational Classification of Dietmen						
Agriculture	54.2	33.4	22.6	19.0	16.6	
Business	14.4	20.7	24.9	33.6	21.9	
Professions	13.8	18.7	24.6	24.2	31.8	
Bureaucracy	5.8	0.7	1.1	4.5	6.3	
Military	0.0	0.7	0.1	0.3	0.3	
None, Other	11.8	25.8	26.7	18.4	23.1	
TOTAL	100.0	100.0	100.0	100.0	100.0	

Source: See footnote 22.

21

The contest proved to be short-lived, however, as the political mobilization of agricultural interests quickly collapsed. Two factors undermined effective mobilization along the agrarian side of the cleavage, hence dimming the political prominence of that cleavage even before new ones arose to crowd it off the political stage. First, the landlord class lost control of the Diet as a result of changes both in the electorate and in the electoral system. In 1890, all but seventeen of the three hundred electoral districts were rural. This balance began to shift as the process of urbanization was reflected in the electoral reforms of 1900, 1919, and 1925. An even more primary cause of the landowning class's waning influence, however, lay in the transformation of vote mobilization operations which these electoral revisions brought about. Table 1.1 shows that with each expansion in the size of the electorate, there was a decrease in the percentage of Dietmen listing their occupation as agricultural. The bulk of this shift actually came rather early. In the first election following the 1900 revision, not only had the size of the electorate doubled, but also the number of electoral districts had been reduced by a factor of 2.45, meaning that there were now five times as many voters in each electoral district. The economic boom following the Russo-Japanese War again nearly doubled the size of the electorate by greatly enlarging the number of taxpayers meeting the 1900 qualification to vote. As a result, the average number of voters per district increased almost nine times between the 1898 and 1908 elections.

In the earliest elections the two most important factors in a candidate's victory were regionalism (being closely identified with one's constituency) and reputation. Both factors contributed to the domination of the elections by local notables through informal, private discussions. Since the electorate was restricted to the top one percent of the population economically, prior to 1900, four hundred to six hundred votes were generally enough to ensure election. As the size of the electorate expanded, so did the expenses necessary to run a successful campaign, which were estimated to have risen by a factor of fifty times between 1890 and 1924.[23]

23 R.H.P. Mason, *Japan's First General Election* (London: Cambridge University Press, 1969), pp. 27–32, 130–184; Yusake Tsurumi, "Universal Suffrage Seen as the Antidote to Big Money Elections." In George O. Totten, ed., *Democracy in Prewar Japan* (Lexington, Mass.: D. C. Heath & Co., 1965), p. 60.

The expansion of the electorate and election expenses had two important effects. First, an expanded electorate increased the candidate's distance from the voters and his dependence on intermediaries to maintain personalistic voter-candidate linkages, a situation which led to the development of a class of local bosses and vote brokers who would often simply line up their blocks of votes behind the highest bidder. Second, the greater demand for campaign funds favored candidates with strong connections with the business community. Beginning around 1908, the business community began to press for a more active role in politics and to work actively for the election of probusiness candidates. As a result, the business-agrarian balance in the Diet had been completely turned around by 1912, with 26 percent of the Dietmen elected that year listing a business occupation compared to only 21 percent listing agricultural occupations.

The second factor which undercut the mobilization of an effective agrarian opposition was the disintegration of the economic basis of agrarian power. The rate of growth of the industrial sector advanced much more rapidly than that of the agricultural sector, with the result that particularly after World War I, agriculture increasingly began to assume the character of a depressed and backward economic sector.

The weakening economic power of rural interests was compounded by the tendency noted above of political opposition to dissolve into the center. Historically there was a propensity for rural elites to be drawn to the center. During Japan's feudal era, the warrior aristocracy had been urbanized at an early period; thus, social status was not achieved by remaining on the land, as in China, but by moving to the cities. Prior to the Meiji Restoration, there was already a tendency for rural elites to move into small-scale entrepreneurial pursuits. With the growing investment opportunities in business following the Russo-Japanese War, large-scale landowners began moving off the land and engaging in entrepreneurial roles in the prefectural centers. Actually, many of the Dietmen elected in the 1890 election who listed their occupations as agricultural were not only landowners but also local entrepreneurs in sake brewing, sericulture, timber, local transport, and banking. An accounting of Dietmen's extraparliamentary careers, which allows for multiple inclusions, reveals that at some time during their careers, 31 percent of the Dietmen elected in the six elections prior to 1900 served as executives of business firms. Moreover, this figure had reached 50 percent by the 1912 election.[24] These figures reveal starkly the transformation of the Diet from an agrarian to a business dominated body. At the same time, the increased absenteeism and displacement of the landed gentry lowered the local base of political power to the economically weaker landed farmers and small-scale landowners. Thus there was a marked tendency (a) for rural elites to be attracted to the urban centers, (b) for the cleavage between agricultural and business interests to be blurred by the movement of agrarian households or some members thereof into commercial ventures, and (c) for the economic power of rural interests to decline relative to urban interests.

The tendency for opposition to dissolve into the center was also stimulated by the weakness of all economic interests vis-à-vis the center. Interest organizations found it difficult to oppose Tokyo when they were so heavily dependent on the central government for legal status, subsidization, leadership, and growth. Both agrarian and business organizations were late in developing; when they did appear, they were organized either on the initiative of the government or with government approval and staffed by former bureaucrats or men with close bureaucratic connections. With this kind of semiofficial coloring, these organizations functioned more as information-gathering and disseminating arms of the government rather than as pressure groups. What signs of independent political initiatives that did appear within interest groups were generally limited to the business community, which, during this period, usually found itself already in close accord with the government's economic policies.

Thus possessing neither economic power nor a strong voice in the Diet, the agrarian interests increasingly came under the influence of the government's centripetal pull. With the government controlling a monopoly of the social and economic rewards in rural Japan, the agrarian interests fell in line to support whoever had connection with the center and could dispense these benefits, be he a party politician, a bureaucrat, or one of the pseudo-bureaucrats who staffed the government-sponsored agricultural cooperatives. The center-periphery, urban-rural cleavage, therefore, moved into political dormancy by 1912 even though rural

[24] Mason, ibid., p. 132; Ishida, op. cit., 1968, pp. 301–309.

resentments continued to mount as a result of the growing cultural and economic disparities between Japan's countryside and its urban centers.

A second major type of social division, which might have polarized political competition and contributed to the development of a viable political opposition, arose from cross-territorial, economic-functional cleavages. These cleavages emerged from conflicts of interest between and within the civil and military bureaucracies, and between the middle and upper economic strata, in both the urban and rural environments. The most explosive of these, however, were the class cleavages which developed out of the growing inequalities between landlord and tenant, entrepreneur and laborer.

The lure of commercial and industrial investment opportunities created an increased desire for capital accumulation, which led some landlords and entrepreneurs to engage in blatantly exploitative practices. The land tax fell sharply during the early Meiji period, but tenant rents remained at the same high 50 percent level. The miniscule scale of farming also kept urban wages low as employers sent recruiters deep into the backward rural areas to search out cheap labor. The growing psychological and economic distance between upper and lower strata further fueled class resentments. Landlords gave up tilling even a part of their own land in favor of more lucrative economic pursuits, sometimes even moving out of the area to become absentee landlords. Employers moved out of the shop and into the office as factories increased in scale; and, at least in the early years of industrialization, many engaged in patently nonpaternalistic practices.[25]

Thus there arose class divisions that became the most politically salient social cleavages in Japan during the years 1918 to 1930. The rapid expansion of the industrial labor force during World War I, the rice riots of 1918, and stories of the Russian Revolution all combined to stimulate greatly the growth of tenant and labor unions during the early 1920s. Politically, these class divisions translated into a rift between progressive forces seeking socioeconomic and political reforms, and reactionary

[25] Fairbank, Reischauer, and Craig, op. cit., p. 517; Koji Taira, *Economic Development and the Labor Market in Japan* (New York: Columbia University Press, 1970) pp. 126–127.

forces trying to preserve the privileges and prerogatives of power that they had enjoyed during the golden era of Meiji (1868–1912).

From the perspective of Japan's democratic development, the mobilization of workers and peasants was both too weak and too strong. Proletarian mobilization by itself was too weak to force democratic reforms. The pre-World War II organization of workers and tenants progressed slowly and met with many obstacles prior to its collapse. Tenant unions achieved their peak membership and peak level of organization in 1927, with 365 thousand members representing only 3.7 percent of the tenants. Labor unions achieved their highest prewar level of organization in 1931 with only 7.9 percent of the industrial labor force organized that year. These movements spawned a number of proletarian political parties, which, however, remained weak and ineffectual and were never able to attract a combined vote of more than 10 percent.

Proletarian mobilization was too strong in the sense that it induced the bourgeois class to overreact and side with the exponents of aristocratic privilege and transcendental government (the court, the peerage, and the military) against its own interests. For the members of the rising middle strata, their experience with democracy as of the 1920s was too new and inconclusive. Because there was little which they could identify that they had gained from Japan's fledgling democratic institutions, their commitment to them was rather weak. Amid the clamor of street demonstrations and protest activities, it became clear that the middle strata were not prepared to accept the full political participation of workers and tenants. Hence, in collaboration with the champions of the prerogatives of station, they first responded with repression in the 1920s and ultimately a retreat from democratic rules in the 1930s. In other words, the net effect of the emergence of class cleavages in Japan in the 1920s was to reinforce the traditional view that political opposition was inherently subversive.

The third major class of prewar social cleavages, that might have polarized political competition and thereby induced a recognition of the legitimate function of opposition, was cultural and ideological cleavages. The pace of modernization and change had a very unsettling psychological and cultural impact. Sweeping innovations were undermining the Japanese citizen's sense of identity. He was being pulled by two opposing poles — one representing traditional Japan, and the other the modern West. There were a number of different strands which made the pattern of cultural and ideological cleavages rather complex. On the cultural side there were conflicts between traditional and modern values, Japanese and Western cultures, parochial and cosmopolitan mores and morals, and the spiritualism of the warrior code and materialism. On the ideological side, confrontation developed between the principles of hierarchy versus egalitarianism, mythology versus secularism, aristocratic privilege versus achievement norms, and authoritarianism versus liberalism. This cultural and ideological cleavage tended to cumulate on the "traditional Japan" side in a generalized expression of antiforeignism, since the new and disturbing cultural and ideological influences were traceable to foreign sources.

During the 1920s the cities became increasingly identified not only with conflictual, interest politics and radical ideologies such as socialism and anarchism, but also with corruption and moral decay, thus creating a tendency for these cleavages to merge in the minds of rural inhabitants with the urban-rural, center-periphery cleavages. Although the cultural cleavages did not address the same economic and social issues which disadvantaged the rural areas, they provided an outlet for some of the frustrations stemming from those inequalities and deprivations. Many of the rural inhabitants' antiforeign, Japanese attitudes were shared by Japan's economic and political elites, the latter having become deeply disturbed by the effects of the urbanization process because of their inability to duplicate in the cities the rural mechanisms of social control. They became convinced that Japan's fundamental social and political order was based on traditional values and the harmonious communal order of the countryside. As a means of countering foreign ideologies that were encouraging deviant and disruptive behavior, Japan's elites promoted a resurgence of Japanese culture and traditional "rural" values and a campaign against "dangerous thoughts."

In the 1930s cultural cleavages came to dominate political debate in an atmosphere of mounting internal disorder and external threat. In this environment of crisis, the hard-liners successfully recast the traditional-modern, East-West value issues into a choice between good and evil values. By exploiting patriotic and nationalistic sentiments, conservative and ultranational forces discredited the reputable exponents of defeudalization, democratization, and liberalism. In this atmosphere, political opposition was synonymous with treason. As previously noted, these changes were reflected institutionally in the exclusion of party politicians from the cabinet and finally in the dissolution of all political parties.

This review of the historical development of the urban-rural and class cleavages shows that these divisions failed to be reflected in any lasting and meaningful form in the party system. When the parties first appeared, they represented the dissident, ex-oligarchs against their former comrades in arms; later, briefly, they represented the landed interests against the government and the business interests. When the agrarian interests lost their domination of the Lower House, neither the urban-rural nor the class cleavages moved into the House in any clearly articulated manner. Antagonistic class or interest support bases neither differentiated nor divided the major parties. The party system largely failed to perform the functions of cleavage definition and interest representation in the case of the first two kinds of important cleavages. Moreover, it was the groups that were totally excluded from the parties (i.e., the young officers' movement) that were in the vanguard of the ultranationalist movement which promoted the salience of the third set of cleavages. Throughout the prewar period, therefore, the kind of prolonged and inconclusive political struggle that might have resulted in a legitimation of the right of dissent and the development of a strong parliamentary opposition failed to materialize. Instead, political developments in the twenties and thirties only served to increase official intolerance of opposition.

This chapter has focused on two problems in the political development of Japan following the Meiji Restoration — the weak integration of the authority structure and the weak development of the accountability structure. This historical experience shaped Japan's political development in the postwar period. The next two chapters will analyze the effects of this prewar experience on the development of the political structure and political competition in Japan following the conclusion of the Pacific War.

CHAPTER 2

The Occupation Reforms
and the Postwar
Political Structure

ON SEPTEMBER 2, 1945, the Japanese government formally surrendered to the Allies aboard the U.S.S. *Missouri*. Thus began a unique experiment in social engineering that lasted slightly over six and one-half years. Japan's brief "American interlude" was nothing short of a massive attempt to transform not only Japan's political institutions but its society as well.[1] The decision to undertake an extensive program of directed political change in Japan was shaped by the American planners who had concluded from their reading of history that the harsh, punitive settlement which the victorious allies had administered to Germany following World War I had ultimately backfired, leaving a residue of bitterness and resentment that fueled the rise of the ultranationalist Nazi movement. In developing the guidelines for the occupation of Japan prior to the surrender, therefore, the American planners adopted a constructive approach which sought to eliminate the Japanese threat by attacking the social and political roots of ultranationalism and militarism that had spawned Japan's aggressive expansionist politics.

An enormous amount of planning for the administration of an American occupation of Japan was undertaken within the State

* Scott C. Flanagan
[1] Kazuo Kawai, *Japan's American Interlude* (Chicago: University of Chicago Press, 1960).

Department and the military services prior to the surrender, dating back at least to the spring of 1942. This planning produced a large number of position papers and approved guidelines that were brought together in a comprehensive statement of America's postsurrender policy towards Japan in August 1945. This policy directive identified the two primary goals of the Occupation as the *demilitarization* and *democratization* of Japan.

The American planners made several other important decisions during the presurrender period that were to have an important effect on the conduct of the Occupation. One was to move rapidly and firmly to ensure that the Occupation of Japan would be essentially an American one. The problems associated with the divided administration of Germany into the occupation zones of the four Allied Powers were already becoming apparent. Despite the fact that the Russians had broken the neutrality pact with Japan and declared war a few days before Japan's unconditional surrender, the United States resisted the Russian effort to establish a Russian general as one of two supreme commanders in Japan. Instead, General Douglas MacArthur was appointed as the sole Supreme Commander of the Allied Powers, and very shortly the initials SCAP came to stand both for MacArthur and the American Occupation authorities in general. The participation of the other allied powers was limited to a strictly advisory role through the Far Eastern Commission, which did not even meet until six months after the surrender. By then, SCAP's basic policies had been formulated and set in motion.[2]

SCAP's authority was further enhanced by the American decision to place the Occupation under a unitary commander, rather than to divide responsibility among different United States government departments and agencies. SCAP was directly responsible only to the Joint Chiefs of Staff in Washington. Moreover, the Joint Chiefs' directives to SCAP made clear that the Occupation's authority over the Japanese emperor and government was absolute and supreme, and should not "entertain any question on the part of the Japanese as to its scope." [3] Finally, the forcible per-

[2] Theodore McNelly, *Politics and Government in Japan* (Boston: Houghton Mifflin Co., 1972), pp. 22–25.

[3] Cited in Robert E. Ward, "Reflections on the Allied Occupation and Planned Political Change in Japan," in Robert Ward (ed.), *Political Development in Modern Japan* (Princeton: Princeton University Press, 1968), p. 489.

sonality and regal disposition of MacArthur further enhanced the authority of SCAP. All these factors combined to provide a small band of American military planners, legal advisors, and social scientists with a unique opportunity to institute a sweeping set of reforms in Japan.

One final important decision was to administer the Occupation indirectly through the Japanese bureaucracry. Originally, the Occupation planners had envisioned a direct military government, at least in an initial period. The suddenness of the total surrender, however, and the magnitude of the job of trying to govern an entire nation as an occupying force, led the American decision-makers to select an indirect administration, with the result that the bureacratic infrastructure of the Japanese government was left intact. Therefore, SCAP's reform directives were implemented by Japanese, not by foreign conquerors; and the fact that the Occupation reforms were carried out through the Japanese government enhanced their legitimacy and popular acceptance and allowed the Japanese authorities to put their own imprint on them. In time, as the reforms proved to be largely popular and successful, the Japanese bureaucracy came to view them as their own. In the one or two areas where the Occupation authorities acted in a dictatorial, heavy-handed manner, denying any significant Japanese input, a lasting atmosphere of resentment surrounded the reforms, leading to delays in their implementation and policy reversals following the Occupation.[4] Thus the Occupation's decision to work through and with the Japanese government contributed greatly to the long-term success of the reforms.

The first goal of demilitarization was by far the easiest to accomplish and was completed rather early in the Occupation. Japan was stripped of its overseas holdings, following the abrupt collapse of the Japanese Empire, and six million military and civilian personnel were repatriated from North and Southeast Asia. All military personnel were disarmed and demobilized, the military services were disbanded, and the armaments industry was destroyed or converted. Finally, the controversial Article 9, the so-called peace clause, was written into Japan's new constitution, declaring that "the Japanese people forever renounce

4 Ward, op. cit., pp. 508–514.

war as a sovereign right of the nation" and that "land, sea and air forces, as well as other war potential, will never be maintained." [5] It is not clear whether the peace clause originated with MacArthur, as a product of a vision of remaking Japan into the Switzerland of Asia, or whether it was actually suggested to MacArthur by Prime Minister Shidehara, in an effort to disassociate the Emperor from militarism and thereby save the imperial institution from the Occupation's reformist ax.[6] In any case, while Article 9 has subsequently been reinterpreted to allow Japan to develop a defensive military capability, the peace clause has been effective in applying significant constraints on the growth and power of the military in postwar Japan.

The second of the Occupation's two major goals, the democratization of Japan, was clearly a much more vaguely defined concept and, because of its sweeping implications, a much more difficult one to achieve. The formal occupation of Japan began on September 2, 1945, and the first step in the democratization effort came on October 4 when SCAP presented the Japanese government with a directive on the "Removal of Restrictions on Political, Civil and Religious Liberties." [7] This memorandum instructed the Japanese government to remove all restrictions on freedom of thought, speech, religion, and assembly, release all political prisoners, and abolish all secret police and government censorship. From this point, the Occupation-directed democratization of Japan proceeded along two lines. The Occupation's first and most pressing concern was to reconstruct fundamentally Japan's political institutions in order to remove the authoritarian aspects of the Meiji Constitution and establish a sound structural framework for democracy. The second and more sweeping aspect of the Occupation's program was to institute a broad set of social reforms designed to transform the socioeconomic structure and political culture of Japan. We will discuss these two aspects of the Occupation's democratization program in turn.

[5] For the full text of the Constitution, see McNelly, op. cit., pp. 261–270.
[6] Theodore McNelly, "The Renunciation of War in the Japanese Constitution," *Political Science Quarterly* 77 (September 1962), pp. 350–378.
[7] SCAP, *Political Reorientation of Japan*, Vol. II (Westport, Conn.: Greenwood Press, 1970) pp. 463–465.

THE POSTWAR POLITICAL STRUCTURE

In October of 1945, MacArthur encouraged Prince Fumimaro Konoye, the Lord Keeper of the Privy Seal, to take the lead in revising the Meiji Constitution along more democratic lines. Subsequently, MacArthur prodded the new Shidehara Cabinet to appoint a committee to produce a draft revision. That neither effort proved acceptable to SCAP is not surprising. It must be remembered that the postwar Japanese government at this time was still operating under the Meiji Constitution and represented the same sociopolitical elites as it had in the prewar period, minus the military. The goal of these men was to preserve the throne and to keep the imperial system untouched. They embarked upon the task of constitutional revision by working from and within the framework of the Meiji Constitution, with the hope that a few minor changes in the original document would make it acceptable to the Occupation. To these Japanese political elites, the essence of Japan and its entire social structure was based on the abstract family-nation concept of the *kokutai* (national polity), which placed ultimate political authority in the unbroken line of emperors who traced their lineage to the Sun Goddess.[8]

In the prewar period, Japan's political elites both staunchly defended and exploited the imperial system in order to command higher levels of loyalty and sacrifice from the people. Partly because of the elites' fear of radical social change in Japan, even efforts aimed at liberalizing the Meiji political system and moving it in a more democratic direction were harshly attacked. For example, in the 1930s Professor Tatsukichi Minobe's theory that the throne was an organ of the state, and thus presumably bound by legal, constitutional authorizations in the exercise of power, was proscribed.[9] In the prewar years, only the communists, anarchists, and other extreme leftists were bold enough to attack the imperial institution and call for its abolition, for which they were vigorously suppressed and jailed.

8 Theodore McNelly, "The Role of Monarchy in the Political Modernization of Japan," *Comparative Politics* 1 (April 1969), pp. 366–381.

9 Frank O. Miller, *Minobe Tatsukichi: Interpreter of Constitutionalism in Japan* (Berkeley: University of California Press, 1965).

This staunch defense of the imperial system did not cease with the defeat. Indeed, some analysts have argued that the atomic bomb had little effect on forcing the abrupt Japanese surrender. Rather it was the entry of the Soviet Union into the war and the fear that a protracted struggle and invasion of Japan would result in the Russian occupation of a considerable portion of the Japanese islands and the almost certain prospect of the abolition of the monarchy. Konoye's advisors were reportedly extremely bitter when they learned that SCAP was insisting on the principle of popular sovereignty. One of the emperor's constitutional advisors, Dr. Cho Shimizu, was so distressed with the Occupation's revised constitution, that on the day it came into effect, he committed suicide, writing, "I have decided to die so that I from the spiritual world may help to protect our national polity [*kokutai*] and wish the safe-being of His Majesty." [10]

When the Matsumoto committee's long-awaited draft revision of the constitution was leaked to the press in early February 1946, the Occupation authorities quickly concluded that the direction of this Japanese effort was totally unacceptable. SCAP was convinced that the imperial system and the national and imperial superiority implied in the myth of divine origins were in part responsible for the rise of fascism and militarism in Japan. The Meiji Constitution, based as it was on the principle of imperial sovereignty, had created a political structure of transcendental authority and transcendental institutions that were above the people and inherently antidemocratic. Minor revisions of the Meiji Constitution, therefore, could not achieve the Occupation's goal of democratizing the Japanese political system.

As a result, MacArthur decided to take matters into his own hands. On October 3, he directed General Courtney Whitney, chief of SCAP's Government Section, to prepare a new constitution for Japan. Within ten days, Whitney's section had prepared a full draft of the new constitution, and Whitney himself presented it to Matsumoto's flabbergasted committee. In the ensuing month of negotiations, some concessions were made, but the basic outlines of the Whitney draft remained unchanged. The

---

[10] Ienaga Saburo, *The Pacific War* (New York: Pantheon Books, 1978), pp. 229–240; McNelly, "The Role of Monarchy," op. cit., p. 372.

Occupation authorities exerted considerable pressure to force the cabinet's endorsement of the new constitution, threatening to go over the government's head to the people or referring the matter to the Far Eastern Commission, in which case the survival of the imperial institution could not be guaranteed. Finally, in an effort to maintain its authority and to forestall its replacement by a more radical leftist government, the cabinet accepted the draft and publicly released its text on March 6, along with an imperial rescript showing the emperor's support for the document.

The fiction of the indigenous authorship of the new constitution thereby was maintained. The acceptance of this new basic law was further enhanced by formally observing the amendment procedures of the Meiji Constitution. Technically, the MacArthur Constitution was simply an amendment to the Meiji Constitution, which at one fell swoop completely replaced all the articles and provisions of the old constitution with a radically new set of provisions. After several months of deliberation over the constitution in the Diet, during which a number of additional minor changes were made, the constitution was approved by nearly unanimous majorities in both Houses. The emperor duly promulgated the new constitution on November 3, 1946, and it went into effect six months later on May 3, 1947.

The MacArthur Constitution, as it came to be known, was so radically different from the Meiji Constitution that its origins did not long remain a secret. In many ways it reflected the New Deal philosophy of the Roosevelt and Truman administrations and was considerably more liberal than the American constitution. It included, for instance, a bill of rights that protected not only life, liberty, the pursuit of happiness, and the usual freedoms of thought, religion, assembly, and petition, but also the right to collective bargaining, full employment, free choice of residence and occupation, academic freedom, sexual equality, and the "right to maintain the minimum standard of wholesome and cultured living." [11]

Given the fact that the new constitution was a dramatic de-

[11] See Chapter III of the Japanese Constitution, full English text reproduced in Robert E. Ward, *Japan's Political System* (Englewood Cliffs, N.J.: Prentice-Hall, 1978).

parture from the Meiji Constitution, it was not received without opposition. Following the conclusion of the Occupation, voices were increasingly raised calling for its revision. These conservative pressures led to the Cabinet's appointment of a Commission on the Constitution in 1957 to study the revision issue. On the other hand, the constitution was not without its staunch supporters. Although it was a more radical document than any that were suggested in 1946 by various Japanese parties and private groups, with the single exception of the Communist Party, many of the basic principles incorporated into the constitution, such as popular sovereignty, were being advanced by liberal Japanese intellectuals.[12]

In 1964, the majority report of the Commission on the Constitution concluded that the Constitution was an "imposed document." However, a sizable minority dissented, arguing that Japanese input had been significant at several stages. By that time, however, the Commission's findings were politically inconsequential, because the requirements for amending the constitution — a two-thirds majority in both Houses of the Diet and ratification by a majority of the people voting in a special referendum — were already beyond the reach of the conservatives. With the rise in the proportion of progressive party seats in the Diet and a growing popular acceptance of the constitution, constitutional revision became a dead issue. Indeed, no formal motion for an amendment to the constitution has ever been introduced into the Diet.[13]

The Emperor. Perhaps the most profound change brought about by the new constitution was the change in the status of the emperor. According to mythology, the Japanese emperors trace their lineage to Emperor Jimmu, who was said to have been a direct descendant of the Sun Goddess, Amaterasu, and to have established the imperial dynasty with his coronation on National Foundation Day, February 11, 660 B.C. According to this accounting, the present emperor, Hirohito, is the 124th monarch

12 McNelly, "The Role of the Monarchy," op. cit., pp. 374–375.

13 Haruhiro Fukui, *Party in Power: The Japanese Liberal Democrats and Policy-Making* (Berkeley: University of California Press, 1970) pp. 198–226.

in a single unbroken dynastic line beginning with Jimmu. Historical records show that the dynasty can be traced back at least to the early sixth century A.D., making it by far the oldest surviving monarchy in existence today. In the beginning, the emperor exercised political and military power, but gradually he lost these powers and came in time to perform mainly religious roles, as the ritual head of the nation and the fountainhead of political legitimacy. Thus during the feudal period, the emperor continued to function as the sacerdotal source of legitimacy, sanctioning the de facto power of a succession of military rulers, the Shogun, which culminated with the rise of the Tokugawa House in the period of high feudalism (1603–1867).

With the Meiji Restoration in 1867, political authority was symbolically returned to the emperor as a means of legitimizing the overthrow of the Tokugawa Shogunate and winning popular support for the modernization program that followed. While the emperor did not actually regain direct political power, the oligarchs heavily emphasized a socialization campaign aimed at firmly establishing the emperor as the source of all legitimacy and the focus of patriotism for the new state. According to the new orthodoxy, the emperor and his ancestors were the fathers of the nation and, as the source of the nation's life and prosperity, were the objects of eternal loyalty and infinite indebtedness. Moreover, as the blood descendant of the Sun Goddess, the emperor held exclusive power to communicate with the gods through the performance of religiomystical rites. Sovereignty was placed in the imperial line rather than the person of the emperor, making the "imperial will" the infallible will of the imperial ancestors. Thus the emperor was neither a free agent nor a partisan political contender; he was the embodiment of the cultural and moral essence of the Japanese nation. This elevated the source of political authority above politics and contention. In practice, the emperor himself rarely exercised discretion in policy-making, but the oligarchs and other political elites derived their authority from their proximity to the throne. Access to the emperor, to his chief ministers, to the chains of command that emanated from these ministers — these were the criteria that differentiated those in authority from the subject masses. In short, the emperor system and the Meiji Constitution were based squarely on the principle of imperial sovereignty; the ultimate source of all authority was the throne.[14]

The Occupation authorities decided to spare the imperial institution, because the emperor had proven to be very cooperative and useful in gaining the compliance of the military and the general populace with the surrender and demobilization orders and the reform programs. However, they determined that while the imperial institution would survive, it would be in a very different form. The Occupation attack on the status of the emperor was two-fold. First the Occupation sought to divest the throne of its divine trappings and separate the emperor from all religious beliefs, rituals, and institutions. At SCAP's request, the emperor renounced his divinity in his 1946 New Year's Message, stating that the ties between the throne and the people were based on mutual trust and affection, not legends and myths, and that such ties "are not predicated on the false conception that the Emperor is divine and that the Japanese people are superior to other races."[15] At the same time the Occupation abolished state Shintoism, which was based on emperor worship. In addition, SCAP prohibited government support of any religion, the teaching of religious beliefs in the schools, and the traditional practice of officials visiting a Shinto shrine upon assumption of office. To ensure that the religious functions of the emperor would never be resurrected, SCAP wrote the principle of the separation of church and state into the new constitution.

The second major change in the status of the emperor was the divestment of sovereignty and political authority. The new constitution states that the emperor is "the symbol of the State and of the unity of the people, deriving his position from the will of the people with whom resides sovereign power." Hence sovereignty was explicitly transferred from the emperor to the people; moreover, the constitution clearly states that the emperor shall have no powers related to government and all acts of the emperor in matters of state require the advice and approval of the

[14] David A. Titus, *Palace and Politics in Pre-War Japan* (New York: Columbia University Press, 1974); Masao Maruyama, *Thought and Behavior in Modern Japanese Politics* (New York: Appleton-Cenutry-Crofts, 1967), pp. 175–176.

[15] Theodore McNelly, ed., *Sources in Modern East Asian History and Politics* (New York: Appleton-Century-Crofts, 1967) pp. 175–176.

Cabinet with whom responsibility resides. Thus while the constitution enumerates a number of roles for the emperor, such as appointing the prime minister and chief judge of the Supreme Court, convoking the Diet, receiving foreign ambassadors and ministers, and awarding honors, all his functions are purely ceremonial and permit no initiative or discretion on his part. Indeed, since the Japanese emperor's legal status is that of the "symbol of state" rather than the "chief of state," his political role is even weaker than that of the British monarch.[16]

Since the emperor under the Meiji Constitution did not personally make national policy, his role did not change as much as that of those around him. In recognition of the fact that the powers of the emperor had been exercised by antidemocratic forces surrounding the throne, the Occupation moved to destroy the bastions of transcendental authority and hereditary privilege — i.e., the court and the nobility. The powerful court offices, such as the Lord Keeper of the Privy Seal and the Grand Chamberlain, were abolished along with the Imperial Household Ministry. In their place a much more modest Imperial Household Agency was established to administer the affairs of the imperial family. The peerage and all titles of nobility were also abolished, with the exception of the immediate imperial family (the emperor's parents, if alive, his siblings, spouse, and children). In addition, all other institutional power bases of the court and nobility ceased to exist, such as the councils of elder statesmen (*genro*) and senior statesmen (*jushin*), whose role had been to select the prime minister. Other such abolished institutions included the powerful Privy Council and the House of Peers. However, while the throne has lost its prewar powers and mystical aura, it still serves as an important unifying symbol for the nation, particularly among older generations. Although there are some signs that the emperor is less meaningful for younger Japanese, there is no movement to abolish the monarchy, and any further change in the Emperor's status is unlikely.

The National Diet. The legislative branch of the Japanese government is composed of the two Houses of the Diet. Under the Meiji Constitution, the emperor and the Cabinet enjoyed exten-

[16] Ward, *Japan's Political System*, op. cit., pp. 147–149.

sive decree powers, thus sharing the law-making role with the Diet. In order to give substance to the principle of popular sovereignty and to ensure that the responsibility for enacting legislation rests squarely with the elected representatives of the people, the new constitution states that the Diet is the "highest organ of state power" and the "sole law-making organ of the state." [17]

The original draft of the MacArthur Constitution provided only for a unicameral legislature. The House of Peers was simply to be abolished, leaving only the popularly elected House of Representatives. The Japanese cabinet, however, argued vigorously for the preservation of a second Upper House, either as an appointive body or as one representing the professions and selected portions of the electorate on a corporatist model. In the compromise that resulted, a popularly elected House of Councillors was established as the Upper House of the Diet.[18] As we shall see, however, its powers are clearly subordinate to those of the Lower House.

At present there are 511 members of the House of Representatives (HR) which are elected from 130 medium-sized electoral districts to a maximum four-year term of office. Following a prewar tradition, the Japanese Diet in drafting the election law selected neither the single-member district system found in the United States and Britain nor the large-district systems found in many European countries. Instead, three to five HR members are elected from each Lower House district, with each voter casting a single nontransferable ballot for only one of the candidates. In practice, HR members rarely complete a full four-year term because the Cabinet can dissolve the Lower House at any time, and the prime minister generally times the dissolution so as to optimize his party's chances of electoral success in the ensuing election. A new election must be held within forty days of a Diet dissolution, and the new Diet must be convened thirty days following the election.[19] In the first thirty-six years following the opening of the first Diet under the new constitution in 1947, there have been fourteen HR elections, or an average interval of 2.6 years between elections.

The 252 members of the House of Councillors (HC) are elected for six-year terms, with half the membership standing for election

---

[17] Constitution, Article 41.
[18] Ward, *Japan's Political System,* op. cit., pp. 151–152.
[19] Constitution, Article 54.

every three years. The HC electoral system is more complex, with seventy-six seats in each contest being elected from forty-seven local constituencies, coterminous with Japan's forty-seven prefectures; and fifty seats from a single nationwide list in a national constituency. Each voter, then, casts two votes in an HC election — one for a local representative running in his prefecture's local constituency race and, until recently, one for one of the one hundred or so candidates competing in the nationwide national constituency race. Because of the enormous costs involved for the national constituency candidates in their having to campaign throughout the entire country, the electoral system for that portion of the HC elections was changed by law in 1982 to a proportional representation system. Beginning with the 1983 HC election, votes in the national constituency race are now cast for a party rather than for an individual candidate, with seats apportioned to each party based on the proportion of the votes the party wins. Prior to the election, each party officially files a list of national constituency candidates, and if a party's percentage of the national constituency vote received entitles it to ten of the fifty contested seats, the first ten candidates on the party's list are elected.

It was originally hoped that the Upper House would bring a less partisan and more reflective and statesmenlike perspective to the policy-making process and that the national constituency would elect men of national eminence. Instead, the national constituency contest has been largely monopolized by large organizations and special interests, such as big business and big labor. Moreover, beginning in the late 1960s, the national constituency race started to attract increasing numbers of so-called "talent" candidates — famous writers or artists and popular TV and sports personalities, who capitalized on their broad name-recognition to gain entry to the Upper House. The adoption of a proportional representation system in the HC national constituency race is too recent to assess its long-term impact. In the short run, it has promoted the appearance of a large number of extremely small parties, some virtually one-man parties (eighteen parties competed in the 1983 HC national constituency race); in the long run, the rules for entry into the national constituency race will make it financially prohibitive for strictly one-man parties to endure.

In a sense, the change from candidate to party voting in the national constituency race marks the final retreat from the original intended role of the House of Councillors. The Upper House has by and large not elected nonpartisan, independent candidates whose objective appraisal of the national interest and freedom from party conflict might have enabled the Upper House to play a distinctive role. Instead, early in the postwar period, the partisan distribution of seats in the Upper House quickly came to mirror that found in the Lower House. As a result, the Upper House has been criticized for adding little to the legislative process except for further time-consuming delays. However, should the ruling Liberal Democratic Party, which has held a majority of the seats in both houses since the party's inception in 1955, lose its control of either one of the Houses of the Diet, the Upper House might begin to play an important independent role.

Another factor that weakens the role of the House of Councillors is its junior partner status in the legislative process. According to the constitution, if the HR and HC pass different versions of a bill, the Lower House version becomes the law of the land if passed a second time in that House by a two-thirds majority. Moreover, the Upper House cannot defeat a Lower House bill simply by refusing to take any action on it. If the House of Councillors fails to act on an HR passed bill within sixty days of receiving the bill, it is considered as rejected by the Upper House, thus opening the way for the House of Representatives to enact the measure by a two-thirds majority. In practice, most disagreements between HR and HC bills are worked out by a joint committee of the two houses, but in these negotiations, the Lower House clearly enjoys the upper hand. In addition, the budget must be submitted to the Lower House first. Finally, in regard to the budget and treaties, if the House of Councillors fails to take any action or the joint committee of both houses fails to reach a compromise, thirty days following the original passage of these measures in the Lower House, the decision of the Lower House becomes the decision of the Diet. In effect, then, the Upper House has no voice in these most important measures.[20]

There is only one situation in which the Upper House may play a commanding role. When the Lower House is dissolved, that body ceases to exist for about seventy days. The Upper House is

[20] Constitution, Articles 59–61.

not dissolved, but it automatically goes into recess. Should a national emergency arise during that period, the Cabinet may call the House of Councillors into emergency session. Measures passed by the Upper House during such an emergency session become law, but only on a provisional basis. That is, all such emergency measures will cease to be in effect unless they are passed by the House of Representatives within ten days of the opening of the new Diet session following the election.[21]

The role and work load of the Diet in the postwar period has greatly expanded over that in the prewar period, when the Diet was typically open only two months out of the year. Presently the Diet is in session the greater part of the year. However, the Diet Law distinguishes between three different types of sessions. The "ordinary" session is convened every year during the final ten days of December, lasts for one hundred fifty days, and may be extended only once. "Extraordinary" sessions may be called at any time by the Cabinet or by a petition of one-fourth the membership of either House. "Special" sessions are those which are constitutionally required to be opened thirty days following an election. The length of such extraordinary and special sessions is determined by the concurrent vote of both houses, and both types of sessions may be extended only twice. The length of the sessions and the limitations on the number of times they may be extended are important, because legislation may not be carried over from one session to the next. Hence, measures that cannot be moved through the entire legislative process before the session ends are effectively killed and must begin the long process anew when the next session begins. In the context of a perpetual conservative majority, the leftist parties, as the permanent opposition, have found the tactic of delay to be one of their most potent weapons.[22]

The Occupation authorities basically modeled the Japanese parliamentary system after the British model and the "fusion of powers" concept, that is, a system in which the executive, legislative, and judicial branches of government are interdependent, with the executive branch dominant. The authorities were, however, clearly influenced at points by the American doctrine of a "separation of powers," in which the major branches of govern-

21 Constitution, Article 54.
22 Hans H. Baerwald, *Japan's Parliament: An Introduction* (London: Cambridge University Press, 1974), pp. 74–102.

ment are more independent and coequal. It is unclear whether they expected the Diet to function as a weak legislature on the British model, where parliament's role is primarily one of the interpellation, or as a strong legislature on the American model, based on the committee system. As a result, the Japanese Diet emerged as a hybrid of the two models. On the one hand, both houses of the Diet have the right of interpellation, that is, the power to require the prime minister and any cabinet ministers to come before the house or its committees to answer questions concerning government policy and draft legislation. This right is a weapon primarily used by the opposition parties to criticize, and on occasion to embarrass, the government and to bring their own views before the people. On the other hand, the members of both houses were organized into sixteen standing committees which parallel the Cabinet ministries — e.g., Foreign Affairs, Finance, Education, Commerce and Industry, Agriculture, and Judicial Affairs. In the United States, the standing committees enable congressmen to specialize in particular substantive areas and gain sufficient expertise so that, with the assistance of supporting staff, they are able to propose counterlegislation or important amendments to government-sponsored bills. As in the United States, most of the important business of the Japanese Diet is conducted within the standing committees. However, given the domination of the Diet by the majority party and the rigidly enforced principle of strict party discipline in Diet voting, the Japanese Diet much more closely approaches the weak parliament and "fusion of powers" model than the American "separation of powers" and "checks and balances" model.

Both Houses of the Diet have similar internal structures and methods for processing legislation. The presiding officers, the speaker and vice-speaker of the Lower House and the president and vice-president of the Upper House, are elected by the members of their respective houses. The speaker and president are formally empowered to make the members' committee assignments, but in practice, these assignments are decided by the leadership of the respective parties, with each party being allocated committee seats in proportion to its parliamentary strength. Committee chairmen are also determined by the party leadership, but in the Upper House the practice has always been to distribute chairmen among the parties generally in proportion to their strength in the

Diet, while in the Lower House, all standing committee chairmen until recently have been drawn from the majority party. Parliamentary bills are first referred to the appropriate standing committee, which may call a cabinet minister to answer questions; hold public hearings; invite expert witnesses; and finally pass, amend, postpone, or reject the bill. Approved bills are then forwarded to the plenary session of the House for final action. As described in Chapter 9, while the Diet does not play the central role in drafting legislation, the above process by which legislation is moved through the Diet does afford the members of parliament with an opportunity to make a significant impact on the policy-making process.[23]

The Prime Minister and the Cabinet. The Cabinet system was adopted in Japan in 1885 and has continued without interruption until the present. The first Cabinet was composed of a prime minister and nine ministers, each responsible for one of the following ministries: Foreign Affairs, Home Affairs, Finance, Army, Navy, Justice, Education, Agriculture and Commerce, and Communications. Over time, new ministries were created and the names of some of the old ministries were changed. Throughout the postwar period, there have been twelve ministries in Japan. As the government has expanded and taken over new functions, the practice has been to add a number of ministers without portfolio to the Cabinet to provide Cabinet representation for several important government agencies without raising those agencies to ministerial status. Thus the Cabinet generally includes the prime minister's appointments to head the Prime Minister's Office, Administrative Management Agency, Defense Agency, Economic Planning Agency, Science and Technology Agency, Environmental Agency, and National Land Agency. The exact number of Cabinet ministers may vary within the legal constraint set by the Cabinet Law that limits postwar Cabinets to twenty members, not including the prime minister. In recent years, the Cabinet has generally been held at this maximum size.

Despite the apparent continuity in the Cabinet system, there have been a number of fundamental changes in the powers, functions, and composition of the Cabinet between the prewar and

23 Ibid., pp. 30–102.

postwar systems. The postwar Cabinet system is based on the British model — that is, the constitution vests supreme executive authority in the Cabinet, with the Cabinet being responsible to the legislature. The prewar Cabinet system was based on the Prussian model — that is, the Cabinet was not responsible to the legislature; and, as noted in Chapter 1, the legislature had no power either to select a prime minister or dissolve the Cabinet. In addition, prewar cabinets shared executive power with a number of other more or less coequal offices and institutions. The more ambiguous role of the Cabinet during the prewar period is indicated by the fact that the Cabinet was not even specifically provided for in the Meiji Constitution of 1889.

The postwar constitution introduced two major kinds of changes in the Cabinet system. First, executive power was vested solely in the prime minister and his Cabinet.[24] Most of the Cabinet's prewar competitors for executive power were abolished — the *genro* and *jushin* councils, the Privy Council, the Lord Keeper of the Privy Seal, and other important court offices; the Army and Navy Chiefs-of-Staff; and the Supreme War Council. And by stripping the emperor of any meaningful executive authority, the Imperial Conference and other ad hoc councils, which had been designed to forge agreement among the competing prewar institutions of executive power, disappeared.

In order to remove the prewar ambiguities in the exercise of authority, the postwar constitution clearly placed the Cabinet and all other executive institutions under the control of the prime minister. The prime minister, no longer simply "the first among equals" within the Cabinet, now enjoys the power to both appoint and remove all Cabinet ministers at will. To hold the military in check, the National Defense Agency has been denied ministerial status and been made a subordinate part of the Prime Minister's Office, thereby ensuring civilian control. As a further guarantee against any military resurgence, the constitution requires that all Cabinet members be civilians.

The prime minister has the authority to control and supervise all the various administrative branches of the government; also, he is empowered to submit bills and reports on national affairs and foreign relations to the Diet. In addition, the constitution specifically authorizes the Cabinet to prepare the budget, ad-

[24] Constitution, Article 65.

minister the civil service, conduct the affairs of state, manage foreign affairs, and, with Diet approval, conclude treaties. In short, the postwar constitution centralizes supreme executive authority in the prime minister and his Cabinet.[25]

In addition to enjoying supreme executive power, the prime minister and his Cabinet have important judicial and legislative powers. In the judicial area, they are empowered to select the chief justice and the other judges of the Supreme Court and to appoint the judges of the inferior courts from a list nominated by the Supreme Court. The Cabinet may also grant pardons and amnesty. In the legislative area, the Cabinet determines the convocation of extraordinary sessions of the Diet, enacts Cabinet orders to execute the provisions of the Constitution and Diet laws, and, of most importance, prepares and submits bills to the Diet.

The second major change in the Cabinet system introduced by the postwar constitution is the clear establishment of Cabinet responsibility to the elected representatives of the people. First, the prime minister is elected by the Diet from among the members of the Diet. In this selection process, as in other Diet duties, the role of the Lower House is dominant. Secondly, not only the prime minister but also a majority of the Cabinet members must be members of the Diet. In practice, nearly all Cabinet members have been drawn from the Diet, and generally all but two or three are members of the Lower House. Thirdly, as noted above, the Diet can command the prime minister and his Cabinet ministers to attend sessions of both houses and their committees to reply to questions on government policy. In addition, either House of the Diet may adopt a resolution of impeachment against any individual Cabinet member. Finally, if the Lower House passes a nonconfidence resolution, rejects a confidence resolution, or fails to support any major Cabinet bill, the Cabinet must either resign en masse within ten days or dissolve the Lower House, call an election, and resign following the opening of the new Diet. In the period following a Cabinet resignation, the old Cabinet continues to function until the Diet has elected a new prime minister and he is officially installed.[26]

It should be pointed out that the Cabinet's dependency on the

---

[25] Constitution, Articles 66, 72–74.
[26] Constitution, Articles 67–71.

continued support of the parliament to stay in office does not necessarily imply a weak and unstable executive. If the parliament is highly fragmented and polarized, as for example in Italy, executive instability will follow; however, where there is a majority party and strict party discipline in parliamentary voting, as in Japan, the executive will be strong and stable.

THE MINISTRIES AND THE BUREAUCRACY

The administrative branch of the national political system plays an important role in the ongoing process of making decisions and setting national goals, as well as in the implementation of policies. Each of the ministers with portfolio in the Cabinet presides over one of the twelve present government ministries — Justice, Foreign Affairs, Finance, International Trade and Industry, Transportation, Post and Telecommunications, Construction, Labor, Agriculture and Forestry, Health and Welfare, Education, and Home Affairs.

Various Cabinet staff offices are directly attached to the Cabinet to assist it in the exercise of its powers. These include the Legislative Bureau, which is responsible for studying and drafting bills, and the Cabinet Secretariat, which provides staff services for the Cabinet. There is, in addition, a National Personnel Authority, which is an independent advisory bureau of the Cabinet that makes recommendations to the Cabinet regarding salaries, working conditions, and the rights and duties of civil servants throughout the entire national bureaucracy, including school teachers. The National Defense Council is also an advisory body directly attached to the Cabinet; in this case, however, the council is more of a subcommittee of the Cabinet composed of those Cabinet members whose areas of competence touch on defense related matters — that is, the prime minister, foreign minister, finance minister, director-general of the Defense Agency, and the heads of MITI, the Economic Planning Agency, the Science and Technology Agency, and the National Public Safety Commission. The role of the National Defense Council, which was originally established as a further safeguard for maintaining civilian control over the military, is to review all defense planning and budgeting for the Cabinet.

The Cabinet also has authority over several interdepartmental committees, including the important Conference of Administrative Vice-Ministers and the Conference of Pariliametary Vice-ministers. Finally, the Prime Minister has at his disposal a large professional and technical staff organized under the Prime Minister's Office that includes a Secretariat which conducts broad policy studies, a Statistics Bureau, and numerous auxiliary advisory councils, agencies and commissions. As noted above, a number of the more important of these offices, such as the Defense Agency, Administrative Management Agency, and Economic Planning Agency are regularly represented in the Cabinet.

New official Cabinets come into being following the selection of a new prime minister, and after each election of the House of Representatives, regardless of whether or not the occupant of the office of prime minister changes. In practice, however, Cabinet posts are reshuffled much more frequently, with virtually annual major reconstructions of the Cabinet in which over half of its personnel are changed. The reasons for this frequent turnover can be traced to the demands of factional politics within the ruling Liberal Democratic Party. The prime minister must reward those intraparty factions that supported him in the LDP presidential race (generally labeled the mainstream factions) by granting them a larger share of the more prestigious Cabinet offices, while at the same time not totally shutting out the members of opposing factions (the antimainstream factions). In turn, each faction leader is under great pressure to secure Cabinet, party, and Diet offices for their own faction members. The need to reward past supporters, gain new adherents, maintain good working relations with factional opponents, and satisfy the incessant demands of Dietmen for prestigious titles and posts, has led to the practice of frequently reshuffling Cabinet positions.[27]

The rapid rotation of Cabinet offices makes it extremely difficult for a Cabinet minister to make a significant policy impact on his ministry or to guide a program to completion. Continuity, however, is maintained by the bureaucracy. In contrast to American practice, there are few offices open to political appointments in the Japanese executive branch. In fact, in each ministry there are only two political appointees, the cabinet minister and the

---

[27] The late Prime Minister Eisaku Sato is reported to have given Cabinet posts to over one hundred Dietmen during his eight years in office. Robert C. Christopher, *The Japanese Mind* (New York: Linden Press, 1983) pp. 220–221.

parliamentary vice-minister, who serves as an assistant to the cabinet minister and in a liaison role between the ministry and the corresponding Diet committee. The ministries and other executive agencies are staffed by career civil service bureaucrats who have generally spent their whole careers within the same ministry, gradually moving up in rank and position through some combination of seniority, personal ability, and internal politics. The second in command in each ministry, the administrative vice-minister, is such a career bureaucrat. The Conference of Administrative Vice-Ministers, therefore, functions as a kind of subcabinet providing continuity, coordination, and direction in the shaping of government policies and programs. This group meets regularly under the chairmanship of the chief cabinet secretary. With the exception of politically controversial issues, most policy matters are decided at this subcabinet level and forwarded to the Cabinet for a fairly routine approval.[28]

The functions of Japan's national administrative bureaucracy include the drafting and implementation of laws and the issuance of ministerial rules, which in some instances are as important as the laws passed by the National Diet. It is the ministries' role in the formulation and drafting of legislative proposals that provides the bureaucracy with an important direct influence on national policy-making. This influence of the bureaucracy on policy flows naturally from its command of technical expertise and its continuity, but there are additional factors that enhance the bureaucracy's power. One factor is the weakness of the Japanese Diet, at least in comparison with the American Congress. Both the comparatively weaker staff resources of Japanese Dietmen and the prolonged dominance of the LDP have caused the most important policy decisions to be made elsewhere. This situation does not mean that the Japanese Diet is denied any effective role; in fact, the Diet has exercised a more active role in amending government-sponsored legislation than it has typically been credited with. However, this is more of a secondary, complementary role than is typically found in the American case, where

[28] The chief cabinet secretary serves as the prime minister's right hand man in the government, and often combines the roles of Diet liaison, trouble shooter within the executive branch and press secretary. Warren M. Tsuneishi, *Japanese Political Style* (New York: Harper and Row, 1966) pp. 62–66.

aggressive confrontation between Congress and the President is often the rule.

Another factor that enhances the influence of the bureaucracy is the fact that career bureaucrats in Japan's higher civil service tend to retire in their late forties and early fifties and move into a second career. Many of these former bureaucrats have gone into politics and have played a dominant role in the ruling Liberal Democratic Party. In recent years, roughly a third of the LDP Dietmen and nearly half of the Cabinet ministers with portfolio have been ex-bureaucrats. Moreover, between 1946 and 1982, the office of prime minister was occupied by a former bureaucrat 75 percent of the time. A further source of the influence of bureaucrats stems from their favorable public image, at least relative to that of politicians. On the whole, the Japanese public views politics as a dirty business, and politicans as corrupt and self-seeking. In contrast, bureaucrats, while not universally loved, enjoy a more positive image as competent, honest, and impartial.

However, there are many voices in Japan, especially on the political Left, that criticize the role the bureaucracy plays in policy-making as inherently undemocratic and reminiscent of the bureaucratic transcendental governments of the prewar period. Throughout the prewar period, the bureaucracy enjoyed high prestige as the social and educational elite in Japan and their attitude towards the common citizen was best described by the old adage *kanson mimpi* — officials esteemed, the people despised. Some have argued that the bureaucracy's transition from the august prewar role as the arms and legs of the imperial will, to the postwar role of public servants, has not been complete, at least in a psychological sense. It has been noted that because of SCAP's need to work through the Japanese administrative infrastructure, the Japanese bureaucracy was the one major participant in the prewar authoritarian regime that was not thoroughly attacked and reformed by the Occupation authorities. While the constitution proclaims that "all public officials are servants of the whole community" and that "the people have the inalienable right to choose their public officials and to dismiss them," old attitudes die hard.[29] In fact, the bureaucracy is well protected from out-

[29] Constitution, Article 15.

side intrusion into matters of promotion, tenure in office, and retirement.

The bureaucracy, however, is far from a cohesive, undifferentiated force in policy-making. Not only are there natural rivalries stemming from conflicts of interest and jurisdictional wars, but also bureaucrats typically spend their entire careers within one ministry, further contributing to the ingrown character of each ministry and a sense of distance from and competition with the other ministries. Moreover, the pluralistic nature of the policy-making process in Japan is enhanced by the fact that the bureaucracy is only one of several important actors in the process. At the same time, the policy-making role of the Japanese bureaucracy is increasingly being mimicked in the older Western democracies, because of the increasing levels of specialized expertise required to draft legislation in advanced industrial societies. In conclusion, then, the Japanese bureaucracy, rather than posing an antidemocratic threat, plays a circumscribed and essential role in the policy-making process.

The ministries, agencies, and commissions, as well as other portions of the national administration, are staffed by the national civil service. Within the civil service there are different ranks; it is the higher civil servants — those administrators who attain the highest three grades in an eight-rank system — who are the most important careerists. Access to these positions is generally limited to those who pass the higher level service examinations. The number of positions in these top three ranks has increased during the postwar period from 3,544 in 1957 to 18,132 in 1976.[30] However, not all of these positions are regarded as important, and the core of the higher civil service, which continues to be limited almost entirely to the male graduates of elite educational institutions, is still a rather small and exclusive group.

The overall size of the Japanese government has also grown in the postwar period. In 1940 there were less than 250 thousand national government employees. By 1955 the total number of national government employees topped one and one-half million, and by 1980 the number had exceeded two million. This figure

---

[30] *Japan Statistical Yearbook*, 1958 and 1977. Changes in the reported categories made it impossible to extend the comparison to years prior to 1957 or after 1976.

naturally includes many different kinds of employees. For example, a little over 280 thousand were employed by the Diet, the Cabinet, the court system, the Board of Audit, the Prime Minister's Office, and the twelve ministries. In addition, nearly 300 thousand employees fall under the national Defense Agency and the military services. Beyond that, over 600 thousand are classified as special accounts employees, this category being composed mostly of postal service, national school, and national hospital employees, as well as several branches of the Agriculture and Forestry Ministry such as the National Forestry Service. Finally, there are an additional 800 thousand workers employed in other government-affiliated agencies of which nearly 99 percent are employed by the Japan National Railways, the Japan Telegraph and Telephone Public Corporation, or the Japan Monopolies Corporation.[31]

When the two million national government employees are added to the over three million local government employees, the result is that nearly one of every ten gainfully employed persons in Japan's labor force is a public employee. The overall size of the Japanese government, therefore, seems very large. In comparative terms, however, the Japanese government is still substantially smaller than that found in most other industrialized nations. For example, in the United States, Germany, and Britain, the public sector is twice as large, employing roughly one of every five gainfully employed persons.[32]

Moreover, since the advent of the first Suzuki Cabinet in 1980, the trend has been towards smaller rather than larger government, and there have been several small annual declines in the numbers of government employees. The expansion of government welfare services in the early 1970s, followed by a prolonged slowdown in the rate of economic growth after the onset of the energy crisis in 1973, combined to produce unprecedented budgetary deficits in the late 1970s and on into the 1980s. The Suzuki Cabinet came into office pledged to a program of administrative reform aimed at balancing the budget without tax increases by cutting down the scale of government. In July 1982, the Cabinet-

---

31 *Japan Statistical Yearbook,* 1981, pp. 660–661.
32 Keizai Koho Center, *Japan 1981: An International Comparison* (Tokyo: Keidanren Keizai Koho Center, 1981) p. 67.

appointed blue-ribbon commission on administrative reform issued its recommendations, which if adopted could dramatically reduce the numbers of public employees. In addition to further small reductions in government employees to be accomplished through combining some departments and scaling down some government services and regulatory activities, the major reduction would come through a proposed transfer of all or major parts of three major public corporations — the Japan National Railway, the Japan Telegraph and Telephone Corporation, and the salt and tobacco monopolies — to private ownership, a move that could affect 800 thousand public employees.[33] Opposition to those reforms is likely to delay or forestall such transfers, but for the time being, at least, the growth of the Japanese bureaucracy has leveled off and even declined slightly.

PUBLIC CORPORATIONS

One of the important features of Japanese government is the presence of a large number of semiautonomous government corporations and agencies which perform very important governmental and economic functions. Altogether there are 113 public corporations, which collectively spend the equivalent of about 50 percent of the national budget. Naturally, the revenues and expenditures of these public corporations are kept distinct from the national budget. Public corporations have their own accounting procedures and are financed by sales or user fees and by deploying the large resources of the postal savings system or other such entities through the Fiscal Investment and Loan Plan.

Like European countries but unlike the United States, Japan has a government-run comprehensive railway system and airline system, although there are also many private local railway, bus, and subway systems, and also some local public transportation systems and some private airlines. In addition to the government salt and tobacco monopolies and the publically owned telephone and telegraph system mentioned in the last section, there are public housing corporations and government banks which promote development and foreign trade. These latter financial institutions supplement the activities of the central bank, the Bank of Japan. In addition, public corporations have been established to de-

[33] *The Japan Times Weekly,* 8/7/82, p. 2; 8/14/82, p. 4; 8/21/82, pp. 2, 4.

velop various parts of Japan's rural sector and to build and run expressways and manage other kinds of major public works projects; they also administer a number of important social programs or perform important public services, such as the NHK national television and radio networks. Specific public corporations are closely affiliated with particular ministries, and depending on their organizational status — there are six categories of public corporations with varying degrees of independence in internal administration and finance — some of these corporations can be seen as more or less branches of the major administrative ministries. The public corporations are also staffed in top echelon positions by retired civil servants from the upper levels of the bureaucracy, which constitutes another important link between the ministries and the public corporations.[34]

LOCAL AND INTERMEDIATE GOVERNMENT

Like most other large countries, Japan has an intermediate level of government between the national and local levels. In Japan these are called prefectures. There are currently forty-seven of these intermediate level administrative units. Because of Japan's small size, some of these prefectures are smaller in territory than counties in the United States. At the same time some of them have very large populations, with Tokyo prefecture currently being the largest with roughly 12 million inhabitants. The prefectures can be compared with states in the United States, provinces in Canada, lander in Germany, and departments in France, in that they are rather large administrative units with important political jurisdictions and responsibilities.

Japan has a unitary or centralized political system. Federal systems, such as those found in the United States, Canada, and West Germany, are characterized by strong intermediate levels of government. In federal systems these intermediate governmental units possess clearly defined spheres of power that are constitutionally protected from encroachment by the central government. In the United States, for instance, powers that are not constitutionally delegated to the national level are considered to be reserved to the states. In contrast, unitary systems are characterized

[34] Chalmers Johnson, *Japan's Public Policy Companies* (Washington: American Enterprise Institute, 1978).

by weak or even largely absent levels of intermediary government. In unitary systems, such as those found in France, England, and Italy, the intermediate and local levels of government are weaker, have fewer powers, and are more subordinated to the control of the central government. For example, in France and Italy, the decisions of local councils are subject to review by a central government official.

Unitary systems, however, are not completely devoid of local autonomy; in Japan today the prefectural and municipal levels of government carry out a number of important functions. For example, the prefectures collect taxes; have an important say in police, educational, and other matters; and pass laws and issue administrative orders which regulate business, control pollution, provide for public and industrial safety, and affect many other aspects of group and individual life. On the other hand, national ministries often send representatives to staff prefectural administrative offices, as well as having their own offices on the local level to collect taxes and carry out other tasks. National ministries also typically submit "model" laws and regulations which are generally adopted in standard form by each prefectural government, thus ensuring national uniformity.

The American Occupation authorities in their democratization program tried in many ways to increase the scope of local autonomy in Japan. Despite the fact that Japan had a tradition of centralized political administration, SCAP felt that the establishment of strong, local self-government was essential for building a robust democracy. With this in mind, the new constitution called for popularly elected governors and mayors respectively for each of Japan's 47 prefectures and 3,257 cities, towns, and villages. Popularly elected unicameral legislatures were also established on the prefectural and municipal levels. In all cases, the term of office for these chief executives and assemblymen on both subnational levels of government was set at four years.

In spite of these and other Occupation reforms aimed at decentralizing political authority, it has commonly been perceived that little real local autonomy has been exercised by the intermediate and local levels of government across the postwar period. The failure of local self-government to flourish has been attributed to Japan's long bureaucratic tradition of centralized administration and the heavy postwar financial and administrative dependency of prefectures and municipalities on the national government. Indeed, the national government enjoys an impressive array of legal weapons that it may employ to ensure local conformity to central directives. First, local governments are legally prohibited from enacting any ordinance that conflicts with a national law. Secondly, much of the business of local governments takes the form of carrying out functions assigned to them by the national government; and in the case of "agency delegated" assigned functions, the local chief executive is legally defined as an agent of the central government under the direct supervision of the concerned ministry. Thirdly, local governments are bombarded with circulars from the central ministries designed to provide so-called administrative guidance. Finally, the central government enjoys pervasive controls over local finances. Local government in postwar Japan has long been characterized as one of "30 percent autonomy," a term that reflects the fact that only about a third of local government revenues has been derived from local taxation. The largest overall source of local revenues comes in the form of national aid. Moreover, local borrowing is so tightly controlled by the national government that some would argue that these revenues should also be considered central funds.[35]

On the other hand, several recent studies have found that the latitude for the exercise of local autonomy in the policy-making process in Japan is much broader than had previously been believed. For instance, it has been found that municipal government policies vary considerably in response to local political conditions and that there is a notable lack of congruence between national and municipal spending priorities. There have been growing signs of a more assertive, innovative role for local administration in the policy-making process. In several instances local governments have rejected national administrative guidance, instituted lawsuits aimed at changing various central-local financial arrangements, and taken the lead in establishing new policies and programs in such areas as pollution control and health care for the elderly. Finally, it has been found that the

35 Kurt Steiner, *Local Government in Japan* (Stanford: Stanford University Press, 1965); Steven Reed, "Local Policy Making in a Unitary State: The Case of Japanese Prefectures," Ph.D. Dissertation, University of Michigan, 1979.

high income, urban prefectures in particular have the capacity to experiment with new programs that are not sponsored by the national government, especially during periods of economic expansion. Particularly during the high growth years from the mid-1960s to early 1970s when leftist and other opposition party administrations were gaining control of an expanding number of prefectural and municipal administrations in urban areas, these intermediate and local governments found themselves with both the motivation and the means to introduce innovative welfare programs in advance of national policy guidelines.[36]

In sum, local autonomy in Japan as exercised by her prefectural and municipal governments is quite limited in comparison with that found in the United States. On the other hand, it is by no means totally lacking and seems to be on the rise. Moreover, the level of autonomy enjoyed by prefectural and municipal governments appears to vary greatly from one unit to another, depending on the issues involved, the partisan setting, and, most especially, on the level of financial dependency on the central government. While 30 percent autonomy may still characterize many prefectural and municipal administrations, the term by no means applies to all. Indeed, the rich, urban prefectures enjoy a far greater degree of financial independence than the poor rural prefectures. For example, in 1979 the poor prefectures of Okinawa and Shimane received 76 and 66 percent respectively of their total revenues from the central government, while the far richer Tokyo prefecture received only 12 percent.[37] Thus, while the level of political uniformity from one prefectural or municipal administration to the next is still extremely high by American standards, there now appears to be more scope for local deviation, innovation, and experimentation than has previously been believed. Recently there has been a worldwide trend among those advanced industrial nations having unitary systems towards a

[36] Steven Reed, "Is Japanese Government Centralized?" Paper presented at the Midwest Japan Seminar, September 1978, Wittenburg College, Springfield, Ohio; Kurt Steiner, Ellis Krauss, and Scott Flanagan, eds., *Political Opposition and Local Politics in Japan* (Princeton: Princeton University Press, 1980), *see* especially the chapters by Kurt Steiner and Ronald Aqua; Scott C. Flanagan and Hae Shik Kim, "National Aid and Local Autonomy in Japan," *Administration and Society* 14 (May 1982) pp. 35–80.

[37] *Japan Statistical Yearbook*, 1982, pp. 520–521.

devolution of power from the center to permit more viable intermediary levels of government. There will likely be a similar trend in Japan in the direction of a somewhat more enhanced exercise of local autonomy.

THE JUDICIAL SYSTEM

Under the Meiji Constitution, the courts lacked any real independence from the executive. The Ministry of Justice was responsible for the administration and supervision of the courts and was empowered to appoint and dismiss judges. The postwar constitution completely transformed the judiciary into an independent, coequal branch of the government. To this end, the constitution declared that "the whole judicial power is vested in a Supreme Court and in such inferior courts as are established by law," and "no extraordinary tribunal shall be established, nor shall any organ or agency of the Executive be given final judicial power." To symbolize further the coequal status of the chief justice of the Supreme Court with the prime minister, the constitution specifies that the chief justice is designated by the Cabinet and appointed by the emperor. The remaining fourteen justices of the supreme court are appointed by the Cabinet. The Supreme Court enjoys sweeping powers to establish the rules of procedure within the judicial branch in matters related to attorneys, prosecutors, the internal discipline of the courts, and the administration of judicial affairs.[38]

By law a system of courts has been established below the Supreme Court which includes eight High Courts, fifty District and fifty Family Courts (one each in each prefecture with four in Hokkaido), and five hundred and seventy-five Summary Courts distributed throughout Japan's municipalities as the initial trial courts of the nation. In addition, there are a number of branch courts at several levels in the hierarchy and a system of civil and family conciliation commissions composed of one judge and two lay mediators to provide for the out-of-court settlement of disputes. The conciliation commissions constitute an interesting adaptation of Western judicial systems to Japanese cultural norms. Typically, Japanese find adversary proceedings distasteful and will resort to going to court only when all the preferred tra-

[38] Constitution, Articles 76–77.

ditional forms of informal mediation and negotiation have failed. Thus we find far fewer lawyers per capita in Japan than in the United States, and it has been reported that only one-tenth to one-twentieth the number of civil suits per capita come to court in Japan compared to the United States, England, and other Western countries.[39]

Despite these cultural inhibitions, the judicial system functions reasonably effectively in Japan, although somewhat slowly and laboriously. Indeed, there have been a few highly visible examples of politically charged cases in which the judicial process has become bogged down in interminable delays. For example, it was not until 1970 that the Tokyo District Court finally issued its decision in a case involving 219 persons implicated in violent disturbances in connection with the May Day rioting in 1952, almost eighteen years after the incident.

The Japanese court system is a unitary one, highly centralized under the Supreme Court. There is, then, no separate system of local or prefectural courts, such as we find with the state court system in the United States. The Supreme Court is the final arbiter in all matters related to the interpretation of the law and the administration of the court system. In an effort to insulate further the judiciary from the executive branch and partisan political controversy, the constitution provides that all judges below the Supreme Court will be appointed by the Cabinet from a list of persons nominated by the Supreme Court. Furthermore, all such judges are appointed for a ten-year term with the privilege of reappointment until retirement age, and can be removed only by being judicially declared mentally or physically incompetent or through impeachment proceedings in which a court of impeachment is set up from among the members of both Houses of the Diet.

The judges of the Supreme Court are in essence appointed for life, but in an unusual move, the drafters of the constitution provided for a popular referendum on their appointment. Thus the appointment of a new judge will be reviewed by the people at the time of the first HR election following his appointment and in each HR election that falls ten years after his previous popular review. If a majority of the voters vote against the justice, he

39 Ward, *Japan's Political System,* op. cit., p. 172.

is removed from office.[40] This measure is somewhat paradoxical in that it seems to violate the principle of the independence of the judiciary and its protection from partisan political controversy. In practice, however, all justices have been approved by overwhelming majorities to date.

The most controversial article in the constitution related to the judiciary has been the specific provision of judicial review in Article 81, whereby the Supreme Court is given the power to rule on the constitutionality of any law, order, regulation, or official act. The notion of judicial review is clearly an American invention based on American experience. The Japanese prewar judicial system was modeled on European practice and allowed no court the power to void the acts of the legislature or the executive. Indeed, in the prewar period, the emperor was in theory above the law and the constitution; hence there was no law or authority that could override an imperial rescript. In practice, the Privy Council, an executive organ, played a kind of judicial review role, in that any bills affecting the constitution were submitted to the Council for approval prior to becoming law.

For the most part, the Japanese Supreme Court has been cautious and conservative in the exercise of judicial review. Indeed, the Court's decisions in the 1950s and 1960s established a number of self-imposed limits on the judicial review power as the Court seemed to shy away from its new constitutionally defined role. For instance, in a series of cases the Court ruled that (1) the Court could not be petitioned to rule on the constitutionality of any law in the abstract, but that questions of constitutionality could be addressed in the courts only "when there exists a concrete legal dispute between specific parties"; (2) the Court in effect could not rule on the constitutionality of treaties; and (3) rulings or acts of state of a highly political nature lay outside the purview of the courts.[41] At the same time, the high court has followed a rather conservative line, reversing on several occasions lower court rulings aimed at voiding, for example, the United States-

40 Constitution, Article 79.

41 John M. Maki, ed., *Court and Constitution in Japan: Selected Supreme Court Decisions, 1948–60* (Seattle: University of Washington Press, 1964), pp. 362–365 and passim; Lawrence W. Beer, *The Constitutional Case Law of Japan: Selected Supreme Court Decisions, 1961–70* (Seattle: University of Washington Press, 1977).

Japan Security Treaty, the Japanese Self-Defense Forces, and ordinances aimed at restricting demonstrations.

This conservative posture on the part of the Japanese Supreme Court is readily understandable when we consider that the power of the United States Supreme Court evolved slowly over many years and is presently defended by the weight of tradition. Nevertheless, despite the United States Supreme Court's great prestige, it has on a number of occasions become embroiled in controversy. Undoubtedly the Japanese Supreme Court has sought to avoid becoming a target of popular criticism, since, compared to the American Court, its defenses against outside attacks are much weaker. First, the Japanese court's new power of judicial review has no support in prewar traditional practices, and secondly, the tenure of its justices can be terminated by popular vote.

Still there are signs from more recent decisions that the Court may gradually come to play a somewhat more assertive and liberal role. For instance, in 1973 the Supreme Court reversed its previous 1950 decision and ruled as unconstitutional an article of the penal code that provided heavier penalties for murder in the case of patricide; and in 1976 it ruled that the existing apportionment of seats among the one hundred and thirty districts for the HR election was unconstitutional.[42] Thus, while the Court has been criticized in the past for being too timid and too reluctant to strike down laws, in time it may evolve into playing a more active role in reviewing the constitutionality of Diet laws and executive ordinances as originally envisaged by the Occupation drafters.

The Japanese hold their constitutions in great esteem and, like the imperial rescripts of yore, view them as documents to be preserved, not evolutionary documents that require periodic change and updating. The Meiji Constitution was never amended, and despite the fact that the postwar constitution has been attacked as an alien document by some and that several factions of the ruling party have long campaigned for the revision of certain portions of it, no amendment has ever been formally introduced into the Diet, and it appears unlikely that any will be in the fore-

---

[42] J.A.A. Stockwin, *Japan: Divided Politics in a Growth Economy* (New York: Norton, 1982) pp. 196–218; Ward, *Japan's Political System*, op. cit., pp. 171–173.

seeable future. However, the Japanese political structure is not completely rigid and static. The constitution, after all, defines only the bare bones of the Japanese political structure. Much of the political practices, processes, and activities of government are established by laws and ordinances which can readily be changed by the Cabinet and/or Diet; in addition, change can occur through reinterpreting the intent of the constitution. Although the Supreme Court has so far played a cautious role on this score, its role has by no means been negligible. For example, in regard to the highly controversial issue of Article 9 of the constitution, which appears on the face of it to outlaw any military force, the Supreme Court has stated that the constitution does not deny the inherent right of self-defense. By deemphasizing the clause "land, sea and air forces . . . will never be maintained" and focusing on the phrase "war potential," the Court has interpreted Article 9 to mean that Japan may establish a defensive military capability but not an aggressive, offensive force.[43]

THE OCCUPATION'S SOCIOECONOMIC REFORMS

Having outlined Japan's postwar political structure, we can now turn to the second aspect of the Occupation's reform program. As noted at the outset of this chapter, SCAP's policy directives were not aimed simply at the Japanese political structure and its institutions of transcendental authority. The Occupation authorities were convinced that democracy could not flourish in Japan unless the structural reforms were accompanied by a thoroughgoing transformation of socioeconomic relations and cultural norms. Thus the Occupation conducted large-scale resocialization campaigns and completely overhauled the curriculum in Japan's educational system to popularize the values of democracy and individualism.

Efforts such as those aimed at transforming Japan's political culture require fundamental changes in political attitudes and values and typically require considerable time, often one or two generations. Thus at the same time, the Occupation sought to involve broad sections of the population in a variety of reform programs in an effort to establish new clientele groups who would defend the constitution and the new rights it guaranteed after the

43 Maki, op. cit., p. 304 and pp. 302–367.

Occupation ended. SCAP planners assumed that the groups that gained new rights and benefits from one or another program would rally to the defense of the new political system as a whole and view an attack on any part of the new order as a potential attack on their own interests.[44] This new support structure was put in place first by weakening or eliminating the antidemocratic forces in Japanese society, as seen in the abolition of the military, the peerage, and a number of powerful court offices. A second complementary thrust was the nurturing of new interests and organizations whose improved position in society was dependent upon the Occupation reforms.

In the economic sphere, the Occupation moved to resolve two potential sources of instability by attacking the problems of workers and tenants. In the prewar period, the workers' and tenants' movements, despite their small size and sharp government repression, constituted disruptive and sometimes violent expressions of political dissent. The Occupation set out not only to improve the working conditions of the industrial labor force but also to establish a strong union movement to represent the economic and political interests of labor. The constitution specifically requires that standards for wages, hours, rest, and other working conditions be set by law and guarantees to workers the right to organize and bargain collectively. While the improvement of working conditions could not be accomplished overnight, particularly in the context of the early postwar period of poverty and destruction, the organization of the work force nearly was. Under the stimulus of the Occupation authorities, the number of organized union members grew from less than four thousand to over four million in the one year period between October 1945 and October 1946. Thus an important new force moved into the political arena in Japan.[45]

In the first three or four decades following the Meiji Restoration, land holdings increasingly became unequally distributed in the countryside with the decline of owner-cultivators and the rise of landlords and tenants. By 1941, 46 percent of the cultivated

---

[44] Steiner et al., op. cit., pp. 444–448; Ward, "Reflections on the Allied Occupation," op. cit., pp. 528–532.

[45] Constitution, Articles 27 and 28; McNelly, *Politics and Government in Japan,* op. cit., p. 31.

land was farmed by tenants, and 70 percent of the farmers rented part or all of the land they tilled. SCAP was convinced that the poverty and discontent in rural Japan in the prewar period had contributed greatly to the rise of militarism. Transforming the countryside into a class of small independent farmers, it was believed, would create a powerful new interest for preserving the Occupation's reforms and a sound socioeconomic context in which democratic institutions could flourish. Through a bold, radical land reform program, the Occupation placed a ceiling on land holdings that averaged about three *cho* or seven and one-half acres (twelve *cho* in Hokkaido), forced owners to sell their holdings in excess of the ceiling to the government, and resold the land to the tenants. Given the extremely high rates of inflation during the early postwar years, this reform program virtually destroyed the economic power of the landlord class and enabled the tenants to buy the land cheaply. While in 1946 only slightly more than 30 percent of the farmers owned the land they tilled, by 1950, 62 percent did; and by 1960, 75 percent owned all and another 18 percent owned over half of their farmland. By all accounts, the land reform program was one of the most successful undertakings of the Occupation.[46]

The Occupation's third major economic reform was aimed at reassessing the balance of influence between big and small business by breaking up the great family-dominated holding companies (the *zaibatsu*) and creating numerous smaller independent and competitive companies. The concentration of vast economic power in a few individuals and families was viewed as inherently antithetical to the kind of pluralistic economic order in which democracy thrives. Indeed, some have argued that the two major prewar parties were simply pawns of the two largest conglomerates, Mitsui and Mitsubishi, and that the influence and money that flowed from these two *zaibatsu* corrupted the parties, turned the people against them, and ultimately led to their demise in the 1930s. Between 1945 and 1948, the large holding companies were dissolved and/or reorganized. The ownership structures of the major companies were reorganized, and securities were sold to the

---

46 Tadashi Fukutake, *Japanese Rural Society* (Ithaca: Cornell University Press, 1967) pp. 16–28; R.P. Dore, *Land Reform in Japan* (New York: Oxford University Press, 1959) pp. 3–198.

public through a stock dispersal program. In addition, the economic elite was infused with new blood as over fifteen hundred top executives were purged. Finally, a number of companies which were viewed as dominating an excessive share of the market were forced to split.[47]

From a political perspective, perhaps the major accomplishment of these antitrust reforms was to break the *zaibatsu's* hold on the political parties. While big business still plays a very influential, and some would say a corrupting, role in party politics, it speaks today with a much more diversified, pluralistic voice. In the prewar period, political activity was concentrated at the top of the business community so that the full economic power of the *zaibatsu* could be felt. Presently, individual large and small companies alike make their own political decisions, including the matter of political contributions.

If workers, tenants, and small-scale businessmen were the beneficiaries of the Occupation's economic reforms, women and youth were the principal beneficiaries of its social reforms. In the prewar period, the Civil Code awarded preeminent status to the family and its titular head, typically the eldest male. The rights of individual members were subordinated to the will of the family, and women and children held a vastly inferior legal status relative to the family head. For instance, a wife had little or no legal competence separate from her husband and had distinctly inferior legal rights in regard to matters of property ownership, inheritance, and the right to divorce. The postwar constitution guarantees equal rights for women in all legal questions related to social, economic, or political relations. Thus, for instance, the prewar rule of primogeniture, whereby the eldest son inherited all family property, was replaced by the principle of equal distribution to all the children regardless of sex or relative age.

Not only was the family system overhauled, but the educational system was as well. The Occupation moved quickly to purge certain courses from school curricula, such as the notorious "ethics" course (*shushin*), which was viewed as pure ultranationalist propaganda. Other practices that instilled emperor worship, such as the daily recitation of the Imperial Rescript on Educa-

---

[47] Eleanor M. Hadley, *Antitrust in Japan* (Princeton: Princeton University Press, 1970).

tion, were squashed. Textbooks were rewritten, reflecting a more democratic, individualistic ideology, and teachers were screened. In addition, a number of measures were taken to democratize the educational system and the educational experience of the pupils. The education system was decentralized by taking control away from the Ministry of Education (Mombusho) and placing it in the hands of popularly elected local Boards of Education. The prewar three-tiered tracking system, that had determined the lifetime career opportunities of students following the completion of the sixth grade, was replaced by a standard educational track modeled on the American system and calling for coeducation at every level. The reforms also extended compulsory education from six to nine years and set in motion a vast postwar expansion of the higher levels of the educational system to accommodate broader public access to educational opportunities. Finally, the atmosphere in the classroom changed as a result of less emphasis on rote learning and deference to the instructor and more emphasis on student participation. In this regard, the organization of the powerful leftist-dominated Japan Teachers' Union (Nikkyoso) helped to carry a new ideology and new attitudes into the classroom.[48]

In addition to these social reforms, there was an important political reform that enhanced the status and influence of women and youth. The voting age was lowered from twenty-five to twenty, and for the first time the franchise was extended to women. All these programs of social, economic, and political reforms benefited a broad array of important groups and social strata that now had a vested interest in preserving the new constitution and associated Occupation reforms. In the political arena, the same approach of creating a clientele with a stake in the new order was applied as SCAP moved quickly in January 1946 to purge numerous central government officials and politicians. The following year a more extensive purge barred many local and prefectural officials from holding public office. These purges, which ultimately removed over 200 thousand individuals both in and outside government, paved the way for the rise of a new class of political leaders, many with little previous experience

[48] Kawai, op. cit., pp. 183–248; Donald Thurston, *Teachers and Politics in Japan* (Princeton: Princeton University Press, 1973).

in politics, including Yoshida Shigeru, who served as prime minister from 1946–1947 and 1948–1954. Again, these new political leaders owed their positions to the Occupation reforms.[49]

On the whole, the Occupation reforms were quite successful. Ironically, however, one reason for their success can be attributed to SCAP's abandonment of a reformist role midway through the Occupation. This change in course was first signaled by MacArthur's ban on a proposed general strike in February 1947, and then became increasingly evident from 1948 on. As the cold war set in, SCAP became apprehensive of the growing influence of the Communist movement in Japan. Thus in 1948 restrictions were imposed on union activities in the public sector, and steps were taken to curb Communist influence, leading to the "red purge" of Communist activists from public life in 1950 and the establishment of a strong non-Communist trade union federation, Sohyo, in the same year. The Americans were also concerned about the prolonged weakness of the Japanese economy and the problems which that weakness posed in terms of its drain on American resources and domestic instability in Japan. Thus the more radical, revolutionary orientation of the early Occupation directives was replaced by an emphasis on consolidation and rebuilding the Japanese economy, which meant that some reform programs that had not been completed by that time, such as the antitrust program and the war crimes trials, were phased out in midcourse.

One result of this change in direction was that many Socialists and other leftist groups felt betrayed by the Occupation. On the plus side, however, was the fact that this change in course coincided with the consolidation of conservative political power in Japan, so that, instead of working at cross-purposes, SCAP and the Japanese government increasingly shared common goals. In time, attitudes of distrust and resistance among Japanese conservative political leaders were replaced by an atmosphere of cooperation and partnership in their dealings with Occupation authorities. During the middle phase of the Occupation, then, roughly from the end of 1947 to the outbreak of the Korean War in June of 1950, the reforms were consolidated, their excesses

[49] Hans Baerwald, *The Purge of Japanese Leaders Under the Occupation* (Berkeley: University of California Press, 1959).

moderated, and the support of the Japanese government was won. Not only had the reforms been implemented through the Japanese governmental framework, but now authority was gradually being passed back to the Japanese leadership, both as a test of the reform's acceptance and durability and as a means of engendering increased support for the new order among influential circles in Japan. In the last two years of the Occupation, up until its termination in April of 1952, SCAP played an increasingly diminished role with a much reduced staff, as the process of returning authority to the Japanese government was virtually completed.

Finally, it is clear that the Occupation reforms, both of the Japanese political structure and in the broader social and economic spheres, would not have long survived the end of the Occupation if they had been totally alien to the Japanese experience. In fact, there were indigenous forces in Japanese society that had been seeking most of the political reforms established by the Occupation. Moreover, the dramatic socioeconomic transformation of Japanese society that accompanied its rapid pace of urbanization and economic development throughout the first half of the twentieth century was already changing the status and influence of women, workers, and other groups. Thus Japan proved to be a congenial environment for most of the Occupation's social, economic, and political reforms.

Those reforms that proved to be the least successful in the long run were those that had no basis in Japanese experience and hence no real indigenous advocates. The clearest examples here are the Occupation's efforts to decentralize power, following the American federalism model rather than the European and Japanese traditions of highly centralized, unitary governments. The Occupation's efforts to decentralize governmental authority, the education system, and the police, and to enhance local autonomy were largely rolled back in the 1950s. It was not until the rise of numerous left-wing local governmental administrations in the more urbanized prefectures and municipalities in the 1960s and early 1970s that new life was breathed into the principle of local autonomy laid down by the Occupation. Most of the Occupation reforms, however, did find strong advocates, both old and new, within Japanese society; and, as a result, these reforms provided the basis of a lasting new social and political order in Japan.

CHAPTER 3

Political Parties
and the Context of
Political Competition

THE WEAK DEVELOPMENT of political opposition in Japan in the prewar period was discussed in Chapter 1. In the last chapter, it was noted that the Occupation authorities sought to remedy that deficiency by actively stimulating the organization and political participation of various groups whose involvement in politics had been repressed in the prewar period. Political prisoners were released from jail, and Communist as well as Socialist activists were permitted to organize freely political parties and mass movements. The intellectual community was protected by new constitutional guarantees of academic freedom, and the prewar restrictions that barred students and faculty from involvement in political activities were abolished. In the early postwar anti-Fascist and reform-oriented environment, the faculties of many universities quickly became dominated by Marxist intellectuals. In the late 1940s, a vigorous student movement, heavily influenced by the Communist Party, emerged on many university campuses and mobilized up to 200 thousand students to participate in strikes opposing tuition increases.[1]

The Occupation authorities also actively encouraged the orga-

---

* Scott C. Flanagan and Bradley M. Richardson
[1] Scott C. Flanagan, "Zengakuren and the Postwar Japanese Student Movement," M.A. Thesis, University of California, Berkeley, 1963.

nization of labor unions, with impressive advances made in a very short period of time. Whereas the prewar labor movement never gained more than 420 thousand members, by the end of 1948 the postwar unions had organized over six and a half million workers. The close identification of these unions with the Socialist and, to a lesser extent, Communist parties rekindled the politically dormant class cleavages and thrust them prominently into the political debate.[2]

By the mid-1950s when the Occupation had ended, Japan's new democratic institutions seemed to have taken root securely in the postwar political environment. Indeed, with the amalgamations of 1955 — the left reintegrating into the Japan Socialist Party (JSP) and the right forming the Liberal Democratic Party (LDP) — Japan appeared headed toward the development of a two-party system. Moreover, as the two parties tended to represent distinct occupational strata and competing economic interests — business and agrarian interests versus working-class interests — the requisite conditions for the growth of an awareness of the legitimacy of a "loyal opposition" and political dissent seemed finally to be present.

The prewar cultural legacy, however, could not be displaced so quickly. The polarization of political competition in postwar Japan inhibited the development of a set of ground rules based on decorum and respect. Instead, suspicion, distrust, and occasional violence marred relations between the progressive and conservative camps from the late 1940s until at least the mid-1970s. The progressives — centering around the Socialist and Communist parties, labor unions, mass movements, students, and intellectuals — viewed the postwar conservative establishment as essentially the same coalition of forces, minus the military, that had led Japan down the prewar ultranationalist path to defeat. Their distrust and hostility were sustained throughout the 1950s by a stream of reactionary proposals and enactments that emanated from the conservative government. The progressives feared that the conservatives' real intention was to return to a political structure more closely approximating the Meiji constitutional order. For their part, the conservatives viewed the prospect of a Socialist

[2] Solomon B. Levine, *Industrial Relations in Postwar Japan* (Urbana: University of Illinois Press, 1958), pp. 66–88.

government as an alarming blend of irresponsible radicalism and administrative incompetence.

These suspicions were sustained in part by the conservatives' perpetual hegemony. The LDP has been able to hold onto the reins of power since its formation in 1955 because of a variety of facilitating conditions discussed below. Certainly one of the most important early causes of their prolonged predominance was the prewar cultural legacy. Particularly prior to the early 1970s, the LDP was able to make effective use of the traditional symbols of power and authority. For instance, the party manipulated its distributive, please-all policies to create a sense of obligation and indebtedness among important segments of the population. The party also tried to project the image that it was the legitimate and permanent ruler of Japan, that no other party or parties were capable either of gaining a majority in the Diet or of effectively governing the nation, and that therefore the only way for a local group or interest to gain any benefits whatsoever from the system was to enlist in a conservative Diet member's support association (*koenkai*).

Thus, especially throughout the 1950s and 1960s, the Liberal Democrats cast themselves as the inheritors of the oligarchic tradition, transforming the roles of government and opposition into those of ruler and ruled, roles which could not be bridged or exchanged. The LDP frequently played this role to the hilt, deigning to tolerate the opposition as subordinate petitioners and pleaders as long as they did not overstep certain boundaries. When those boundaries were overstepped, however, the LDP on occasion displayed an arrogant and high-handed disregard for the opposition and a willingness to circumvent normal parliamentary procedure casually.

Political opposition in Japan, at least on the national level, graduated from a prewar history of suppression and impotence to a postwar history of frustration and ineffectiveness. In turn, their permanent minority status, ineffectiveness in the Diet, and distrust of the ruling party led the opposition parties to engage in irresponsible behavior and factional bickering both inside and outside the Diet. Moreover, the Socialists and Communists displayed an ambivalent posture vis-à-vis Japan's democratic institutions. While there was not any real threat of violent change, both the conservatives and Socialists fostered the image that a turnover of power to a leftist coalition would have revolutionary implications.

Clearly, the weakness of Japan's postwar opposition can be traced to its prewar experience. In Chapter 1 it was argued that historically a prolonged and inconclusive political struggle between competing social groups has generally preceded the recognition of the principle of the legitimacy of opposition and dissent. Because of the failure of such socioeconomic cleavages to emerge and find effective expression in the party system during the years of party contested election, 1890–1937, traditional norms regarding the respective roles of government and opposition persisted, contributing in the postwar period to a (1) distrust between government and opposition that inhibited cooperation in the Diet; (2) self-perpetuating system of power; and (3) generally weak and ineffective role for political opposition in national politics. T. J. Pempel argues that the exclusive and closed nature of the conservative coalition of elites and interests that has dominated Japanese politics throughout the postwar period has consistently denied the Left and the interests it represents any effective participation in the policy-making process.[3] While this statement is somewhat overdrawn, Japan is still the only advanced industrial society in which labor over the last thirty-five years has been completely missing as a constituent member of the coalition of interests supporting the governing regime.

James White even argues that the opposition parties in Japan are not only ineffective but effete, demonstrating a positive fear of taking power. Japanese participants in the political process also have been quoted as saying that if offered power tomorrow, the Socialists would be horrified and would not know what to do.[4] Indeed, there is a widespread perception that the JSP, the largest of the opposition parties, is not a serious contender for power. These public perceptions are important and have undoubtedly played a role in sustaining the political status quo. Public opinion

[3] T.J. Pempel, *Policy and Politics in Japan* (Philadelphia: Temple University Press, 1982), pp. 3–45, 296–300.

[4] James W. White, "Accountability and Democracy in Japan," in George W. Waldner, ed., *Japan in the 1980s*, Papers on International Issues No. 3 (Atlanta: The Southern Center for International Studies, 1982) pp. 58–72; Robert C. Christopher, *The Japanese Mind* (New York: Linden Press, 1983) p. 219.

polls reveal that an overwhelming majority of the Japanese public, including many opposition party supporters, neither want the opposition parties to come to power nor believe that they could effectively govern the nation if they did. Thus White's assessment that Japan is a parliamentary democracy without a loyal opposition does not fall far from the mark. Since there is no credible alternate regime or coalition of parties waiting in the wings, the opposition has had no real leverage with which to hold the ruling party accountable for either real or imagined abuses of power.

THE TRANSFORMATION OF THE JAPANESE PARTY SYSTEM

In the prewar era, two conservative parties dominated the Lower House of the Diet and, during the period of party government (1925–32), rotated power between them. In the early stages of the Occupation, prewar conservative politicians reemerged to form the Liberal and Democratic Parties, whose lineages can be traced directly to the two prewar conservative parties. Now, however, these conservative parties faced stiff competition from the rapidly rising Japan Socialist Party, or JSP. In the 1947 HR election the JSP captured 31 percent of the seats, more than either of the two conservative parties. Thus began a turbulent seventeen month period of coalition government based on an alliance between the Socialists and the conservative Democratic Party. This progressive-conservative coalition experiment constituted the Socialists' one and only taste of power during the postwar period. Because of the severe economic conditions, the Occupation's retreat from further social reforms to a program of economic rehabilitation, the lack of any ideological or policy coherence within the government, and the Socialists' own ineptitude, the experience of a Socialist-led government resulted in a serious setback in the JSP's popularity. In the ensuing 1949 HR election, the Socialists' strength fell to 10 percent of the seats. In the fall of 1948, a coalition of the two conservative parties regained power, and one or both of the conservative parties continued to control the reins of government until their merger into the LDP in 1955; in fact the major reason for the formation of the LDP was to ensure that the Socialists would remain locked out of power.

Despite the LDP's continuous hegemony for almost thirty years since its formation, the Japanese party system has not remained static. In 1955, the party system resembled a one-and-one-half party system, with the LDP commanding roughly two thirds of the votes and seats, and the Socialists the remaining one third. The only other significant party, the Japan Communist Party (JCP), received a bare 2 percent of the vote and less than one half of one percent of the seats. Since 1955, however, two major changes have transformed the Japanese party system from a one-and-one-half to a multiparty system. The first change has been the long-term gradual decline in the conservative vote. In the first post-Occupation HR election in 1952, the two major conservative parties polled 66 percent of the popular vote. When the vote garnered by conservative independent candidates is added in, conservative strength reached 73 percent of the total vote. As shown in Table 3.1, by 1976 the LDP's share of the popular vote in the HR election had fallen to less than 42 percent, and the combined LDP and independent vote to less than 48 percent. LDP support declined to even lower levels in the Upper House contests, with the LDP vote shares in 1977 standing at 39 percent in the local constituency and 36 percent in the national constituency races.

As we will discuss in Chapter 6, this long-term decline has been associated with an erosion of the traditional bases of conservative support in Japan. Rapid economic growth has resulted in a decline in the agricultural sector and the old middle class, an expansion of the blue and white collar wage earning classes, and a growing diversity of interests. Urbanization and increased mobility have created a decline in community solidarity, a change that is weakening the effectiveness of the LDP's traditional areal or community-based mode of vote mobilization and representation. Changing values have reduced voter receptivity to the ruling party's cultural themes and campaign appeals, which for many years were based on traditional values. With the declining numbers of farmers, highly integrated communities, and traditionalistic voters, the LDP has suffered a reduction in the size of its major constituencies.

In the early 1960s analysts were predicting, based on the steady rate of the LDP decline, that a transfer of power to the Left would occur by 1970. Even though the LDP continued to lose support up through the 1976–77 Lower and Upper House elections, the predicted transfer of power did not occur, largely because of an unexpected parallel development — the decline in the support of the major opposition party, the JSP. Thus the second

TABLE 3.1. *Vote by Party in the Postwar Japanese House of Representatives Elections*

Party	1946	1947	1949	1952	1953	1955	1958	1960	1963	1967	1969	1972	1976	1979	1980	1983
RIGHT																
LDP							57.8	57.6	54.7	48.8	47.6	46.9	41.8	44.6	47.9	45.8
Lib. Party	24.4	26.9	43.9	47.9	47.8	26.6										
Dem. Party	18.7	25.0	15.7	18.2	17.9	36.6										
Independent	20.4	5.8	6.6	6.7	4.4	3.3	6.0	2.8	4.8	5.6	5.3	5.0	5.7	4.9	3.5	4.9
CENTER																
NLC	—	—	—	—	—	—	—	—	—	—	—	—	4.2	3.0	3.0	2.4
DSP	—	—	—	—	—	—	—	8.8	7.4	7.4	7.7	7.0	6.3	6.8	6.6	7.3
CGP	—	—	—	—	—	—	—	—	—	5.4	10.9	8.5	11.0	9.8	9.0	10.1
SDF	—	—	—	—	—	—	—	—	—	—	—	—	—	0.7	0.7	0.7
LEFT																
JSP	17.8	26.2	13.5				32.9	27.6	29.0	27.9	21.4	21.9	20.7	19.7	19.3	19.5
Right Soc.				11.6	13.5	13.9										
Left Soc.				9.6	13.1	15.3										
Labor-Farmer			2.0	0.7	1.0	1.0										
JCP	3.8	3.7	9.7	2.6	1.9	2.0	2.6	2.9	4.0	4.8	6.8	10.5	10.4	10.4	9.8	9.3
OTHER	14.9	12.4	8.6	2.7	0.4	1.3	0.7	0.4	0.2	0.2	0.2	0.3	0.8	0.1	0.2	0.1

Sources: Prime Minister's Office *Japan Statistical Yearbook*, various issues, and *The Japan Times Weekly*, 12/24/83, p. 1. *Note:* The pre-LDP conservative parties went through a number of name changes not indicated here. As noted elsewhere, most of the independent vote can be classified as a conservative vote.

important change that has transformed the Japanese party system has been the fragmentation of the opposition party vote. The decline in the vote gained by the Socialists has closely paralleled that of the LDP, so that the LDP has continued to maintain its roughly two-to-one advantage over the JSP. In the 1958 HR election, the JSP garnered 93 percent of the opposition party vote; by the 1980 HR election, its share of the opposition vote had fallen below 40 percent.

This fragmentation of the opposition vote among a growing number of minor parties has enabled the LDP to retain control of a majority of the Diet seats in both Houses and stay in power despite the fact that it has failed to receive a majority of the popular vote in any national election since the 1963 HR election. The HR three-to-five member districts and the HC predominantly one-to-two member districts penalize the small parties in favor of the largest party. In addition, these electoral systems substantially overrepresent rural districts, which remain the bastions of conservative strength. For instance, in the 1979 HR election, there were less than 85 thousand voters per seat in Japan's least populous Lower House constituency and 314 thousand voters per seat in the most populous district.[5] These factors have combined to award the LDP with a substantially higher percentage of the seats in the Diet than their percentage of the popular vote since the early 1960s. For instance, a comparison of Tables 3.1 and 3.2, shows that in the 1980 HR election, the Liberal Democrats won only 48 percent of the votes but 56 percent of the seats. Even if the party should fall slightly below a majority of the seats, as it has in the 1976, 1979 and 1983 HR elections, it can rely on an extra cushion or margin of safety in the form of the vote for independents. Most independents are aspiring LDP Dietmen who have failed to receive official party endorsement; however, should they succeed in winning the election, most of them will be quickly welcomed with open arms into the party. Thus immediately following each of the above cited three elections, eight to ten successful independents joined the party, boosting its strength in the Lower House to a slim majority.

To understand better the causes of the fragmentation of the

[5] Seiji Koho Senta, *Seiji Handobukku: Ichi-gatsu Ban* (Tokyo: Seiji Koho Senta, 1980).

TABLE 3.2.   *The Distribution of Diet Seats by Party in Selected House of Representatives Elections, 1947–83*

	1947	1953	1960	1967	1972	1976	1980	1983
Percent LDP Seats	54	66	63	57	55	49	56	49
Number of Seats:								
RIGHT								
LDP	252	310	296	277	271	249	284	250
Independent	13	11	5	9	14	21	11	16
CENTER								
NLC	—	—	—	—	—	17	12	8
DSP	—	—	17	30	19	29	32	38
CGP	—	—	—	25	29	55	33	58
SDF	—	—	—	—	—	—	3	3
LEFT								
JSP	143	138	145	140	118	123	107	112
JCP	4	1	3	5	38	17	29	26
OTHER	54	6	1	0	2	0	0	0
Total Seats	466	466	467	486	491	511	511	511

Source: Japan Statistical Yearbooks.
Note: Before 1955, LDP refers to the total vote of the conservative parties that united to form the LDP in 1955. The seat total for the JSP for 1953 is the sum of seats won by the two divided wings of the Socialist Party, which were independent parties at that time.

Japanese party system, it is useful to compare the Japanese with the German experience. In the mid-1950s Germany also had an ideologically polarized one-party dominant system, with a ruling conservative party on the right, the CDU, and one major opposition party on the left, the socialist SPD. Both countries experienced very similar kinds of socioeconomic changes — the decline of agriculture and the rise of the new middle class, urbanization and increased residential and occupational mobility, rising levels of education, and value change. These transformations in the composition of the electorate in each country have exerted similar pressures for changes in their respective party systems. Yet in Germany, the CDU and SPD have largely been able to contain those pressures for change, while in Japan, the result has been a growing proliferation of minor parties.[6]

There are at least three factors that explain the marked difference in the performance of the major parties in Japan and Germany. First in the German case, the two major parties broadened their appeals and moved towards the center in response to rising affluence in the 1960s and the declining salience of both industrial and religious cleavages. In Japan, despite growing affluence and the conservative party's adoption of many welfare state types of measures, the ideological polarization between the two major parties remained much higher than in the German case. One source of Japan's prolonged left-right polarization can be found in the fact that in Japan the industrial cleavages merged with a set of deep cultural and value cleavages that reinforced the left-right polarization. Since Japan's feudalistic-authoritarian-militaristic tradition was being challenged by democratic and socialist ideologies derived from Western cultures, Japan's cultural cleavages had an indigenous-foreign as well as a traditional-modern dimension. Many of the Occupation reforms and JSP policy pro posals not only threatened the interests of the economic elites but also were viewed as being culturally alien. In addition, the polarization of the Japanese party system was sustained by the greater continuity in Japan, as compared with Germany, between the prewar and postwar conservative leaderships, a factor that fueled the distrust and suspicion of the Japanese left.

As a result of these sharp left-right divisions, a consensus on the constitution and form of government did not exist in the immediate postwar period and during the so-called "reverse-course" period of the 1950s. With the end of the occupation in 1952, the conservatives moved to roll back a substantial number of the Occupation reforms, especially in the fields of labor legislation, police, and education. From 1952 to 1960 with seemingly increasing frequency, conservative cabinets pushed a number of bills through the Diet over the shrill and sometimes violent opposition of the leftist parties. These measures were aimed at managing strikes and labor unrest, recentralizing control of the police, en-

---

[6] For a discussion of these phenomena in Germany, see Kendall Baker, Russell Dalton, and Kai Hildebrandt, *Germany Transformed* (Cambridge: Harvard University Press, 1981).

hancing police powers for dealing with demonstrations, and recentralizing control of the education system from the content of
textbooks to the performance of teachers in the classroom. These
latter educational measures were designed to counter the leftist
ideological influences of the militant Japan Teachers Union.

Many in the conservative camp also wanted to increase the
political role of the emperor, further centralize state power,
abolish the peace clause of the constitution, reinstate the military,
and generally reform the political system in line with traditional
values. Although the conservatives were largely unsuccessful in
instituting this latter agenda of reactionary measures, the threat
remained throughout the 1950s, and the battle lines were clearly
drawn. The progressive forces in Japan, centering on the Socialists, labor, and students, staunchly defended the Occupation reforms in the Diet and the streets.

In the 1955 election, the Socialists successfully crossed the one-
third barrier (one third of the Diet seats), thereby blocking any
conservative efforts to revise the constitution. Yet in the late
1950s the conservatives intensified the thrust of their reverse-
course policies under the leadership of Prime Minister Kishi, a
former member of the Tojo war cabinet who was purged by the
Occupation and charged with Class A war crimes. Kishi's efforts
to ram a number of measures through the Diet, aimed at weakening the power of the left, further antagonized and mobilized the
progressive forces, and the tempo of street demonstrations and
clashes with the police increased. These clashes culminated in
the violent May-June mass demonstrations of 1960, revolving
around the revision of the United States–Japan Security Treaty
and the arbitrary methods the conservatives employed to secure
its passage. On May 19, Kishi called in the police to remove forc-
ibly the Socialist Dietmen who had been physically obstructing
the speaker of the house from calling a vote on the issue. Late that
night, passage of the treaty was secured with only the LDP Dietmen in attendance. These irregularities sent hundreds of thousands of citizens into the streets and led to the replacement of
the high-handed Nobusuke Kishi with the more conciliatory
Hayato Ikeda as the LDP prime minister.

In the aftermath of these mass demonstrations during the
spring of 1960, the confrontation politics of the reverse course
period largely came to an end, and the political context in Japan

changed markedly. The conservatives shelved sensitive political issues, turned their emphasis more fully to economic growth policies, and increasingly became reconciled to the new constitutional order. This moderation on the right undermined the salience of the cultural issues that defined Japan's polarized party system, with the result that the Socialists lost their *raison d'être* as the defenders of the new constitutional order. Increasing affluence was also weakening the appeal of class rhetoric. In response to these changes, the Socialists should have moderated their revolutionary rhetoric and moved from a Marxist class party to a catchall party. Some moderation did occur, and there were recurring efforts by the right wing of the party to reformulate the party's ideological foundations along the lines of the less revolutionary and more parliamentary structural reform theories of the Western European Communist parties. Ultimately, however, these attempts failed to recast the Socialist Party in the social democratic mold.[7]

The Socialists' ideological rigidity can in part be traced to their organizational dependency on the most radicalized portion of the labor movement. The JSP has often been referred to as a ghost party, with a top-heavy organizational superstructure at the national level but little grass roots organization. As a result, the Socialists have depended largely on their affiliation with Japan's largest national union federation, Sohyo. Sohyo provides the JSP not only with votes but also with campaign organizations and workers, funds, and even candidates. This dependency on Sohyo has fostered a sustained militancy in party rhetoric. Portions of the labor movement became radicalized in the 1950s as a result of the severe rationalization drives in the coal, transportation, steel, and petrochemical industries; these elements remain locked into an ideological "struggle mentality" because of the weak economic clout of Japanese unions. Labor has been enfeebled in the private sector by the lifetime employment system and the organization of unions on an enterprise rather than a craft basis, which combines all blue and white collar workers in a single factory or company in the same union. Labor has remained weak in the public sector because of its failure to gain the right to

---

[7] For example, the JSP continues to call for a "dictatorship of the proletariat." T.J. Pempel, *Policy and Politics in Japan*, op. cit., p. 35.

strike or the right to binding arbitration. As a result, the Sohyo leadership has continued to view its problems as political rather than economic and as requiring a fundamental restructuring of the system to solve.[8]

The Socialists, then, failed to broaden their appeal enough to attract the nonunionized portion of the new middle class and other rising strata who were benefiting from the growing affluence. The LDP also had difficulty, at least initially, in moving beyond its traditional constituencies — big business, farmers, small retailers, and other old middle-class elements and workers in paternalistic, small enterprise settings. Throughout the 1960s, the LDP failed to respond effectively to an agenda of new concerns being voiced by the rising classes of wage earners in the congested, polluted urban centers. This failure of the two major parties to substantially broaden their appeals and/or moderate their ideological positions and move towards the center led to the successful emergence of a number of center parties. Simply put, the continuing polarization of the Japanese party system impeded the easy transference of voters' support from the right to the left, as had occurred in Germany, and created an opportunity for new political forces to move into the political void between the two major parties.

There were two additional factors that facilitated the emergence of the center parties in the Japanese context. First, Japanese political parties, which are almost like elite clubs composed of a number of loosely aligned factions of Diet members, are highly prone to splintering. Indeed, three of the four leading center parties have emerged as factional defections from the major parties, with the Democratic Socialist Party (DSP) and later the Social Democratic Federation (SDF) breaking off from the JSP, and the New Liberal Club (NLC) pulling out of the LDP. But these defections could have disappeared into oblivion had they

---

[8] Ibid., pp. 90–131, 296–300; Robert A. Scalapino and Junnosuke Masumi, *Parties and Politics in Contemporary Japan* (Berkeley: University of California Press, 1962) pp. 95–98; Hisashi Kawada, "Workers and Their Organizations," in K. Okochi, B. Karsh, and S. Levine, eds., *Workers and Employers in Japan* (Tokyo: University of Tokyo Press, 1973) pp. 217–267. While the enormous economic gains of Japanese workers across the postwar period belie the characterization of Japanese labor as weak, here the reference is to the large national labor federations and their inability to exercise effective economic or political power.

not attracted a sustaining support base from within the electorate. Thus a second supplemental condition that facilitated the emergence of the center parties was the availability of a pool of voters who were unattached to the two leading parties. This pool of potential recruits was present because a high proportion of the Japanese electorate (30–40 percent) do not identity with any party, and many of the so-called identifiers have only weak to nominal identifications. Much of the Japanese voting research has emphasized the importance of personal ties in mobilizing the vote, of candidate-centered rather than party-centered campaign organizations, and of social networks within both formal organizations and informal associational contexts in providing voting cues.[9] This situation has meant, on the one hand, that factions could pull out of a major party with their candidate-centered electoral organizations largely intact. On the other hand, rising urbanization, mobility, and occupational diversity have increased the pool of voters who are organizationally unattached either to the established LDP or to the Socialist networks. There are growing numbers of urban voters who lie outside the politicized social networks of the right and left establishments; in many instances, the new center parties have appealed to these unattached and/or marginal elements.

In sum, the processes of urbanization, occupational diversification, increased affluence, residential mobility, and value change have altered the composition of the Japanese electorate and exerted pressures for a realignment of the Japanese party system. These pressures for change have taken the form of an *ecological realignment*; that is, the relative size of the various social groups and economic strata have changed. For instance, the traditional bases of support of the ruling Liberal Democratic Party have shrunk in size as a result of the declining numbers of farmers, highly integrated communities, and traditionalistic voters. At the same time, the salience of the industrial cleavages and the old cultural issues that had defined Japan's bipolar party system in

9 Scott C. Flanagan and Bradley M. Richardson, *Japanese Electoral Behavior: Social Cleavages, Social Networks and Partisanship,* Contemporary Political Sociology Series No. 06–024 (London: Sage Publications, 1977); Bradley M. Richardson, *The Political Culture of Japan* (Berkeley: University of California Press, 1974); Gerald L. Curtis, *Election Campaigning Japanese Style* (New York: Columbia University Press, 1971).

the 1950s had declined markedly by the early 1970s. There emerged new strata and interests that were not well represented by either the established right or the left; a new agenda of issues arose, especially in the cities, that neither major party effectively addressed.

If the JSP had followed the model of the SPD in Germany, it would have moderated its rhetoric, exchanged its unionist, class party image for a catchall party posture, and broadened its appeal to attract wider support among the middle class, especially the nonunionized portion of the new middle class. Instead, the Socialist Party remained the captive of Marxist intellectuals and the militant Sohyo union federation. Ironically the JSP's ideological rigidity can be traced in part to the factional character of Japanese parties and the ease of retaining candidate-centered electoral support bases despite party label changes. The moderating right-wing of the JSP has successively reacted to the frustration of its efforts to reform the party with defections, which not only have spawned two center parties, but also in each case have shifted the Socialists' center of gravity decidedly to the left. The result has been an ideological rigidity within the JSP that has prevented many nonunion, urban, educated, middle class elements from switching their support to the Socialists, despite their increasing disenchantment with the LDP and its traditionalistic patron-client politics and corrupt practices.

As a result of this expanding pool of voters in Japan that are not well represented by or integrated into the support networks of either of the two major parties, the 1960s and 1970s witnessed a growing fragmentation of the party system with the rise of a host of minor parties. By 1976 in addition to the two major parties, there were four minor parties — the right of center New Liberal Club (NLC), the moderate Democratic Socialist Party (DSP), the Buddhist Clean Government Party (CGP), and, on the left, a larger, more popular version of the Communist Party (JCP). Thus while the minor party vote accounted for only 3 percent of the total in 1958, in the 1976 and 1979 HR elections, these four minor parties polled a combined vote of 30–32 percent.

The late 1970s also saw the appearance of several other parties including urban flash parties, such as the short-lived United Progressive Liberals and the Japan Women's Party. The House of Representatives' three-to-five member election district system discourages the further proliferation of parties as 10–20 percent of the vote in any one district is needed for victory. So far, this newest group of minor parties has not been able to garner even one percent of the total national vote in HR elections.

In contrast, the national constituency race in the House of Councillors election facilitates the emergence of new parties as only one percent prior to 1983, and now two percent of the total national vote generally has been sufficient for election. Moreover, the recent shift to a proportional representation system in the national constituency race requiring voting by party has spawned a new set of miniparties, as former independent incumbents have formed parties in an effort to hold on to their Upper House seats. Indeed, twelve new miniparties entered the 1983 HC national constituency race. Some of these were only collections of independent incumbents with no clear policy orientation, such as the Non-Partisan Citizen's Federation and the Dai-Niin Club. But many of these new miniparties assumed the form of single-issue parties in an effort to gain election by appealing to a specific narrow constituency or interest. Thus there was the Salaried Worker's Party, which claimed that the tax system was unfair to salaried workers and called for tax cuts, and the Welfare Party that attacked recent government cuts in welfare spending. There were also an antinuclear peace party, an education reform party, an anti-Communist party, and a gay lib party.

Most of these parties had no success at all and are likely to disappear quickly. But three of the miniparties had some success, with the Salaried Workers' Party winning two national constituency seats, and the Welfare and Dai-Niin Club one each. The HC National constituency race, then, may continue to present an opportunity for narrow, single-issue parties that cannot successfully compete in HR elections to gain some representation in the Diet. While these miniparties may become a permanent fixture in HC elections, emerging and disappearing one after the other, their political influence will remain negligible outside of the publicity factor of advertising their cause.

Prior to this artificial miniparty boom in the 1983 HC election, as the independent vote was in essence converted into a party vote, the national constituency race provided the best estimate of the true strength and nationwide support of the minor parties, since in the HC local constituency and HR elections many of the minor parties contest only the races that are in urban districts where they have the best chance of winning. Only in the HC national constituency election do voters outside the metropolitan centers have an opportunity to choose among the full spectrum of parties. For example, in the 1977 HC election the combined vote of all the minor parties fell below 30 percent in the local constituency race but was only a half percent shy of the 40 percent mark in the national constituency.

There are several factors which suggest that both of the developments discussed above that have transformed the Japanese party system from a one-and-one-half to a multiparty system — the long-term decline in the LDP vote and the fragmentation of the opposition — have nearly run their course. These factors will be addressed in Chapter 6. Suffice it to say here that the present HR electoral system cannot easily accommodate more than the six parties that had emerged by 1976. The most enduring of the post-1976 parties, the Social Democratic Federation (SDF), first appeared in the 1977 HC election as the Socialist Citizens' League. The SDF has had some success in HR elections, gaining two seats in 1979 and three in 1980 and 1983. However, such small parties are not viable representational units in the Diet, and thus in 1983 the SDF experimented with Diet and electoral coalitions with the NLC. It is too early to tell whether any of the minor parties will actually combine in the future, but the recurring discussions in recent years on moves to bring two or more of the center parties into some kind of alliance suggests that the fragmentation of the party system in the Lower House may have already reached its limit. While important realignments, mergers, and defections among the parties in the Lower House may occur, the number of significant political parties competing at any one time is not likely to rise above five or six.

While the precise number of parties that will survive the realignment processes of the last two decades is still in question, it is now clear that Japan no longer has a sharply divided bipolar party system. Thus the traditional conservative-progressive distinction is an increasingly inadequate description of Japanese politics. It is no longer clear, for instance, whether the term "progressive parties" refers only to the left or to all the opposition parties including the NLC. Increasingly, the conservative-progressive terminology is being replaced by right-center-left labels.

Moreover, the rise of the center parties has profoundly affected the conduct of politics. The movement of the center parties into the Diet has greatly reduced the ideological distance between government and opposition, and as a result, attitudes and behavior on both sides of the aisle have increasingly shifted from a posture of confrontation to one of cooperation. In addition, the center parties have introduced a new dynamic into local politics, especially the chief executive races, by enlarging the coalition opportunities. Center-right coalitions are now possible as well as center-left coalitions.

In the remaining sections of this chapter the organization and policy stands of the parties will be discussed. For this purpose, the newer, smaller parties that emerged in the 1970s will be dropped from the analysis, with the focus being on the two major parties, the LDP and JSP, and the three oldest and largest minor parties. The Communist Party, which is the oldest of these minor parties, became important only when it changed its image from an internationalist, revolutionary party to a national, parliamentary party, and when its new grass roots organizational efforts began to pay off in the late 1960s. As shown in Table 3.1, the JCP was attracting only 2–3 percent of the vote in the 1950s but garnered a steady 10 percent of the vote in the 1970s. The Democratic Socialists broke away from the JSP in 1959, but since gaining 8.8 percent of the national vote in the 1960 HR election, the party has gradually declined somewhat to 7.3 percent of the vote in the 1983 HR election. This decline, however, is more a function of the party's shift in electoral strategy, putting up candidates in fewer electoral districts where they had a better chance of winning. Thus the party backed one hundred five candidates in the 1960 election and won only seventeen seats, whereas it backed only fifty-four candidates in the 1983 election and won thirty-eight seats. A comparison of the voting percentages across the Upper House national constituency races reveals that the DSP's national popularity has remained rather stable since the party's inception. The Clean Government Party emerged in the mid-1960s as the political arm of Japan's largest and fastest growing new religion, the Soka Gakkai, a lay movement of a sect of Nichiren Buddhism. The CGP grew to become the largest of the minor parties in the Lower House in 1976, and thereafter has continued to claim that distinction through the 1983 election. However, the rapid rise in the party's popular vote leveled off in the 1970s, suggesting that the growth of the CGP may have peaked.

POLITICAL PARTIES: FORMAL ORGANIZATION

Japanese political parties developed largely as elite, cadre parties; that is, the parties emerged first as parliamentary parties, alliances of politicians and incumbent Dietmen who had to rely on their own personal election machines and their linkages to local nonparty organizations to secure election to the Diet. As a result, the strongest expression of party organization has always been at the national level among the top party elite. Most of the parties have moved only gradually and weakly to establish organizations on the local, grass-roots level. Even the Socialist parties, the JSP and DSP, have not succeeded in modeling themselves on the mass membership parties of Western Europe. Rather, like most Japanese parties, they have tended to be elite, limited membership parties.

The formal structures of the Japanese parties differ at points because of their different histories or ideologies, but there is also considerable similarity between the parties with regard to formal organization, at least at the national level. Each party has an executive. In the Liberal Democratic Party, the executive is the president, supplemented by an executive "top leaders" group and a formal executive committee. The Socialist, Communist, Clean Government, and Democratic Socialist parties each have a chairperson plus collective executives, i.e., central executive committees. Each party also has a "representative" institution, typically a national conference or convention that meets annually (triannually in the case of the Communist Party) as well as a cluster of important national committees which perform different intraparty functions such as policy development or selection of election candidates. Each party also has a parliamentary group or caucus.

The formal organization of the Liberal Democratic Party is particularly important, given the fact that this party has dominated Japanese politics for so many years and has so strongly influenced the direction of Japanese policies. The Liberal Democrats' formal executive group includes a president and secretary general, as well as a collective executive council and some other councils that function near the executive level. The procedures for electing the LDP president merit particular attention because, given the Liberal Democrats' continuous majority control of the Diet, their party president has always been selected as prime minister. According to the party constitution, LDP presidents are to be selected by party conventions for a two-year term. However, during periods of transition from one president to another, party leaders or elders often have chosen the new party president through an informal consultation process, with the choice simply being "ratified" by the convention election process. Indeed, of the first eight LDP party presidents who served between 1955 and 1978, only two (Ishibashi and Tanaka) were initially elevated to that office as a result of a contested convention election.[10]

One reason for choosing this negotiated consensus procedure is to avoid the divisive aftereffects of hotly contested party elections. An even more important reason for having the party leaders negotiate a successor is to avert the spectacle of massive amounts of money being passed around to line up votes behind the leading candidates. Since the LDP formed in 1955, there have been three party presidential elections that were notorious for the unusually large amounts of "dirty money" involved — those of December 1956, July 1964, and July 1972. Since in these LDP presidential contests there are only a small number of eligible electors, the LDP Dietmen and one representative from each of the forty-seven prefectural organizations, large bribes can be very effective in gaining the support of electors not bound to one of the candidates out of personal loyalties. For instance, it has been reported that in the 1972 contest between Tanaka and Fukuda, five billion yen changed hands in an attempt to influence the 487 electors in that contest; that figure translates into $70,000 per vote.[11]

In an effort to reform the system and open it up to broader popular participation, outgoing Prime Minister Miki succeeded in introducing a two-stage primary system as the method for selecting the party president. Under this system all party members are eligible to vote in a primary election, and the two candidates receiving the highest vote in the primary face a run-off

[10] See Table 3.3 and also Hiroyuki Kawaguchi, "The Japanese Method of Settling Disputes," *Japan Echo* 10 (Spring 1983), p. 27.

[11] Mamoru Iga and Morton Auerbach, "Political Corruption and Social Structure in Japan," *Asian Survey* 17 (June 1977) pp. 556–564; *The Japan Times Weekly*, 7/15/72, p. 4.

election via the former party convention election process. Shortly after the first presidential race to be contested via a primary election held in 1978, the future of the primary system became clouded, because the primary election system not only failed to reduce the costs of presidential elections but also unintentionally caused an increase in the severity of factional infighting within the party. As a result, in the spring of 1981, the party again revised the rules, now requiring that the first stage primary election be suspended unless more than three candidates are nominated. At the same time nomination procedures were made much more stringent, with candidates now needing the endorsement of fifty LDP Diet members for nomination instead of twenty, as formerly.[12]

Although at the time some were predicting that these rule changes would effectively abolish the primary, the antimainstream factions in the party decided to force a primary following Prime Minister Suzuki's surprise resignation in the fall of 1982. In that situation, the mainstream Suzuki-Tanaka-Nakasone factional alliance had united behind Nakasone's candidacy and controlled a majority of the party convention votes. On the other hand, only the Komoto faction had been aggressively recruiting party members at the grass-roots level over the last two years, and, by then, the supporters of that one antimainstream faction constituted about 35 percent of the party's one million members. Thus it was felt that in a four-man race, Nakasone might come in second or worse. However, the results of the 1982 primary simply mirrored the factional balance among LDP Dietmen, with Nakasone winning handily. At least to date, the primary has not proven to be an effective strategy for a minority factional coalition seeking to seize a victory it could not gain on the floor of the party convention.[13]

The future of the LDP party primary is still in doubt. Table 3.3 suggests that the primary may be replacing the contested convention procedure. It now appears, however, that the party

[12] *The Japan Times Weekly*, 4/10/82, p. 4; 12/2/78, p. 4; Taketsugu Tsurutani, "The LDP in Transition: Mass Membership Participation in Party Leadership Selection," *Asian Survey* 20 (August 1980), pp. 844–859.

[13] Hans Baerwald and Akitra Hashimoto, "Japan in 1982," *Asian Survey* 23 (January 1983) pp. 53–61; *The Japan Times Weekly*, 4/4/81; 10/16/82; 10/23/82; 11/27/82.

TABLE 3.3. *Selection Processes for the LDP Presidency 1960–1980*

President	Selection by Negotiation	Selection by Convention	Selection by Primary
Ikeda (1960–64)	July 1960		
		July 1962	
		July 1964	
Sato (1964–72)	November 1964		
		December 1966	
		November 1968	
		October 1970	
Tanaka (1972–74)		July 1972	
Miki (1974–76)	December 1974		
Fukuda (1976–78)	December 1976		
Ohira (1978–80)			November 1978
Suzuki (1980–82)	July 1980		
Nakasone (1982–)			November 1982

Source: Asahi Shimbunsha, *Asahi Nenkan*, various. Entries indicate the primary or determining means of selection. However, selections by negotiation or primary were generally thereafter "ratified" by party convention. The December 1974 choice of Miki and the December 1976 choice of Fukuda were both ratified by the Liberal Democratic Party's "assembly of members of both Houses of the Diet," which is one more irregularity in this important political recruitment process.

primary will be held only when the preferred procedure of a negotiated agreement among party leaders is impossible and the field of factional candidates is wide open, with no coalition holding a majority of LDP Dietmen.

Once elected, the presidents of the Liberal Democratic Party select their own principal assistant, the party secretary general. The secretary general represents the president in many intraparty decision-making processes, in addition to being concerned with a variety of intraparty organizational matters. At times there has also been a vice-president within the LDP, but this position is not currently filled.

The Liberal Democratic Party has a very large array of national committees, some of whose real status is nearly as high as that of the office of the president of the party, especially in times of crisis when the president is involved in conflicts with various other top party leaders. The two most important committees are the Party Executive Committee, a kind of party cabinet which addresses itself to both organizational and policy matters, and the Policy Affairs Research Council (PARC), the party's main policy-making organ. The PARC is very large, since it has several vice chairmen, an internal deliberation commission, fifteen divisions, and up to fifty internal special "ad hoc" policy committees in areas of special interest. In certain senses, the PARC is a party within a party, as all members of the Diet are members of several PARC special committees, and these committees may at times be very active in particular policy areas. In theory the committees within PARC are subordinate to the overall structure of the main parent committee's decision-making process, and decisions on policies made by lower level special committees are supposed to be deliberated at higher levels before being passed on to the LDP Executive Council for approval. In reality, the special committees of the PARC participate at times as semi-independent policy groups, and their policy demands have sometimes been so influential that top organs play more of a ratifying than a decision-making role. This power exercised by the "middle" echelons of the national party organization reflects the fact that the PARC special committees in some cases speak for very strong interests outside the party.[14]

In addition to the Executive Council and PARC, the Liberal Democratic Party has several other important national committees, which include the National Organization Committee, the Party Discipline Committee, the Election Policy Committee, the Public Relations Committee, the Diet Policy Committee, and the Finance Committee. Each of these groups performs functions in the area indicated by its name. Of particular importance is the large number of active committees at the national level, which is in sharp contrast with the much more decentralized American political parties and indicates greater centralization than in even some European parties. The Liberal Democrats also have a parliamentary group, the "Assembly of Members of Both Houses of the Diet," which serves as a focus for the discussion of legislative issues and the exercise of party discipline within the party's rank-and-file members of the national parliament. In addition, a party secretariat and various publication and training units are housed

[14] See John Campbell, "Compensation for Repatriates" and Bradley Richardson, "Policymaking in Japan," both in T.J. Pempel, ed., *Policymaking in Contemporary Japan* (Ithaca and London: Cornell University Press, 1977), pp. 103–142 and 173–197.

in the party's impressive headquarters located near The National Diet building in Tokyo.

In much the same way, most of the opposition parties are similarly well organized on the national level. In contrast, most Japanese parties are but weakly developed at the grass-roots level. Indeed, a frequent criticism of Japanese parties has been that they appear to function more like private clubs than mass political parties. One reason for the closed nature of these parties and the low level of mass participation in them stems from the prevalence of cultural norms that view politics as a necessary but tainted activity and hence should be avoided by the common citizen. Moreover, the advocacy of partisan preferences is viewed as divisive in many settings and incompatible with norms of community solidarity. It is also more difficult for Japanese than for Americans to become involved with an organization simply because of shared beliefs and goals, if they lack any personal connections with the members of the organization. These attitudes have inhibited the development of popular enthusiasm for and participation in political parties.

A more direct cause of the weak grass-roots organization of Japanese parties is their close association with and dependency upon nonparty organizations and interest groups. For example, on the local level most JSP organizational units (*shibu*) are located in local member unions of the Sohyo federation; moreover, the JSP membership is made up mostly of officials of Sohyo unions. It was not until the late 1960s that the Socialists began seriously to attempt to attract nonunion members and voters, and these efforts have met with only limited success. One cause is that nonunion local residents have shown little interest in joining a party organization dominated by union activists. Another reason is that the size and stability of Sohyo support, combined with the multimember election districts, have enabled the JSP to continue electing candidates without having to appeal to the broader electorate. In a sense, exclusive interest representation is rewarded by the Japanese electoral system by allowing the parties to gain representation through relying on relatively small, stable constituencies.[15]

In like manner, the DSP's reliance on the Domei labor federation and the CGP on the Sokagakkai religion's organizational

[15] James J. Foster, "Ghost-Hunting: Local Party Organization in Japan," *Asian Survey* 22 (September 1982), pp. 843–857.

networks have retarded the development of strong party organizations on the local level. With these nonparty organizations providing most of the staff, financing, and sometimes even office space, there is little incentive to develop strong grass-roots organizations based on attracting members from the general public on an individual basis. By and large, these parties have been content to rely on the campaign organizations of individual candidates to mobilize nonunion or non-Sokagakkai support through personal ties to school, community, clubs, and other local associations and interests.

A similar pattern also holds for the LDP, only in its case, instead of relying on one specific associational group for organizational support, it relies on a broad variety of commercial, farm, and professional associations. Until recently, local party membership was largely drawn from officials of these organizations and other local influentials who had been drawn into the support associations of a district's LDP politicians (Dietmen, governors, mayors, and assemblymen). Another cause for the LDP's weak grass-roots organization is that the multimember election districts generally force two or more LDP candidates to run against each other, which has encouraged candidate rather than party centered campaigns and hence has retarded the development of strong local party organization.

Most Japanese parties, then, have close, exclusive ties with one or more large interest groups. These interest groups carry out many typical party functions for the party, such as socializing members into an ideology, communicating party policy positions, collecting political funds, and mobilizing support for party candidates, thereby reducing the need for extensive local party organization. The major exception to this pattern is the Communist Party, which does not enjoy the support of any large interest group. Because of this fact, the JCP has had to create a large party infrastructure on the local level along with an associated network of front organizations staffed by party members, such as the Democratic Student Association, the New Japan Women's Association, and the Democratic Merchants and Manufacturers Association. As a result, the Communists have the most developed organizations on the prefectural and local levels, with the largest numbers of organizational units and the biggest full-time staffs.[16]

16 Ibid., pp. 844, 847–854.

Japanese parties have often been criticized for representing large, exclusive organized interests rather than the interests of the common man or the nation as a whole. On the other hand, it has yet to be demonstrated that there is a viable alternative to this approach. Thus the JCP has had to create mass front organizations out of whole cloth to achieve any electoral success. Moreover, the newer parties like the NLC, which have tried to build open parties founded on individual memberships that are not group based, have had very limited success to date. As a result, the memberships of Japanese parties generally have remained very small. There is really very little to be gained by the parties from having large memberships. Only in the case of the Communist Party do membership dues constitute a substantial source of party revenues. Moreover, the highly centralized organizational structures and elite control of decision making within most Japanese parties allow little role for the political amateur. While Japanese parties do not discourage average citizens from joining their organizations, unless new members control important resources otherwise unavailable to the party, they will have little influence over party decisions. There is simply no easy way for local citizens to move into a party and have an effect on its policies or candidates. Rather than join a party, ordinary citizens seeking some involvement in politics are likely to join the support association of a particular candidate.

Table 3.4 documents the low membership levels and exclusive nature of most Japanese parties. It is interesting that the most extreme example here is the Socialist Party, which received 11.4 million votes in the 1980 HR election while having a formal membership of only 50 thousand, or one member for every 228 party voters. The DSP also has a very small membership, fluctuating between 20 to 50 thousand over the last decade. The Clean Government and Communist parties, while much smaller than the JSP in terms of electoral strength, are actually three to eight times larger respectively than the Socialists in terms of party membership, a size that reflects the greater efforts these parties have devoted to enrolling rank-and-file supporters. Even in these cases, however, their membership levels fall far short of the mass party model.

Only the LDP appears ever to have attained impressive memberships levels. Japanese journalists, however, have revealed that these figures are more illusory than real. In an effort to dispel its

TABLE 3.4.   *Claimed Party Memberships in Major Japanese Parties, 1970–80*

	LDP	DSP	CGP	JSP	JCP
1970	744,914	50,000	106,000	50,000	300,000
1972	968,271	50,000	160,000	37,000	300,000
1974	1,157,811	20,000	160,000	50,000	300,000
1976	437,862	40,000	120,000	50,000	380,000
1978	1,405,995	40,000	142,000	50,000	400,000
1979	3,210,000	46,000	167,000	50,000	420,000
1980	1,423,045	48,871	167,000	50,000	400,000

Source: Asahi Shimbunsha, *Asahi Nenkan*, various years. The rounded numbers were typically cited as estimates, reflecting the fact that national party headquarters were not fully certain of the state of local membership.

image as an unresponsive, elitist party, the LDP has conducted repeated campaigns on and off almost since its formation, pressuring its Dietmen to enroll more members. They have responded frequently by simply enrolling their personal support organizations (*koenkai*) en masse. Many of these "new members," however, had their annual dues paid for them, and some did not even know that they had become members. Some estimates have placed the "real" LDP membership as low as 50 thousand and, at least prior to the advent of the party primary, it is doubtful that the active, dues-paying membership exceeded 150 thousand.[17]

After the primary system was adopted, a new motivation for enlisting party members emerged, namely, influencing the outcome of the primary election. Potential candidates and the Diet members in their factions competed in enrolling new members, and in 1978 party rolls swelled to an all-time high of 1.4 million. Following the 1978 primary, it became clear that primary elections could carry a moral force that would make it difficult for the party convention to select the runner-up over the top vote-getter, if the margin of victory was large. Thereafter, the competition for new members became extremely intense and extended the bitter competition among national party factions down to the local level, ballooning party rolls further to 3.2 million in 1979. When it appeared, however, that the party leadership was going

[17] Haruhiro Fuki, *Party in Power: The Japanese Liberal Democrats and Policy-Making* (Berkeley: University of California Press, 1970) p. 57.

to deemphasize or abolish the primary system, party rolls once again began to shrink in the face of the great expense of maintaining (i.e., paying the dues of) these new "members." By the time of the sudden, unanticipated primary in 1982, party rolls were down to one million members. In light of these facts and the doubts concerning the future of the primary system, the LDP is clearly as exclusivistic as any Japanese party.

Centralization of power at the national level and exclusivism go hand-in-hand with weak grass roots organization. One symptom of the weak organization of parties on the local level can be observed from a comparison of party vote totals across different levels of election. Again, as shown in Figure 3.1, the phenomenon of weak support on the local level is most pronounced in the case of the JSP. In the early 1960s, Robert Scalapino and Masumi Junnosuke referred to this pattern of declining strength with successively lower levels of election as the Socialists' *inverted pyramid*.[18] This pattern applies to the DSP as well. As noted, both the JSP and DSP depend heavily on unions for organizational strength, and while unions are very active in national and prefectural level politics, they are less so in municipal politics, at least outside the large metropolitan areas. Figure 3.1 shows that the Socialists' inverted pyramid evened out somewhat between the mid-50s and mid-70s. This change, however, was largely the result of declining national support rather than growing local support, and the JSP is still attracting roughly twice as many votes in national elections as it receives in municipal elections.

The LDP exhibits a somewhat similar phenomenon, only in its case, the party draws increasing strength, as the election level becomes more local, from the expanding pool of independent candidates. These independents are generally tied into conservative networks, although frequently on a personalistic rather than a party-oriented basis. Thus local politics in Japan has often been referred to as a "conservative paradise" because, outside of urban pockets of progressive strength, it is much more heavily dominated by conservative forces than national level politics.[19]

[18] Scalapino and Musumi, op. cit., pp. 95–97.
[19] See the chapters by Terry MacDougall, Gary Allinson, and Scott Flanagan in Kurt Steiner, Ellis Krauss, and Scott Flanagan, eds., *Political Opposition and Local Politics in Japan* (Princeton: Princeton University Press, 1980).

FIGURE 3.1. *Percentage of Popular Vote Received by Conservative and Progressive Parties by Type of Election for the Mid-1950s, 1960s, and 1970s*

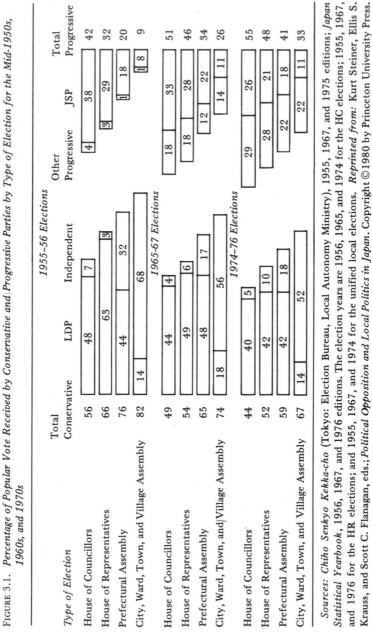

Type of Election	Total Conservative	LDP	Independent	Other Progressive	JSP	Total Progressive
1955–56 Elections						
House of Councillors	56	48	7	4	38	42
House of Representatives	66	63	3	3	29	32
Prefectural Assembly	76	44	32		18	20
City, Ward, Town, and Village Assembly	82	14	68	1	8	9
1965–67 Elections						
House of Councillors	49	44	4	18	33	51
House of Representatives	54	49	6	18	28	46
Prefectural Assembly	65	48	17	12	22	34
City, Ward, Town, and/Village Assembly	74	18	56	11	14	26
1974–76 Elections						
House of Councillors	44	40	5	29	26	55
House of Representatives	52	42	10	28	21	48
Prefectural Assembly	59	42	18	22	18	41
City, Ward, Town, and Village Assembly	67	14	52	22	11	33

Sources: Chiho Senkyo Kekka-cho (Tokyo: Election Bureau, Local Autonomy Ministry), 1955, 1967, and 1976 editions; *Japan Statistical Yearbook*, 1956, 1967, and 1976 editions. The election years are 1956, 1965, and 1974 for the HC elections; 1955, 1967, and 1976 for the HR elections; and 1955, 1967, and 1974 for the unified local elections. *Reprinted from:* Kurt Steiner, Ellis S. Krauss, and Scott C. Flanagan, eds.; *Political Opposition and Local Politics in Japan.* Copyright © 1980 by Princeton University Press. Reprinted by permission of Princeton University Press.

This is not to say that the LDP, JSP, and DSP are totally lacking in local party organization. On the municipal level in the less urbanized areas, however, the party headquarters is often a one-man operation located in the home of a prominent local politician and performs few activities distinguishable from that politician's own personal support organization. Party organization is much better developed on the prefectural level. For instance, the LDP maintains a branch headquarters in every prefecture, and the branch leadership plays an important role in party nominations for the prefectural assembly elections and the selection of delegates to the national party conventions. However, the prefectural branches are often dominated by the incumbent governors and during election campaigns tend to function as their election committees. At times in some areas, ordinary party members have been organized into municipal level branches, following the pattern of the local units of European mass parties. If party organization is weak on the prefectural level, however, on the municipal level inactivity and dormancy are the norm.

The major exceptions to these patterns are the JCP and CGP. In Chapter 6 it will be shown that the Communists have made great efforts to develop dense organizational infrastructures on the local level to provide a number of different services for local citizens and thereby involve those citizens in party support networks. The CGP has also stressed local service and self-help activities directed at ordinary citizens. These grass-roots organizational efforts are reflected in the more uniform support distributions of the "other progressive parties" category reported in Figure 3.1, which includes the combined JCP, CGP, and DSP vote. Indeed, if the DSP is excluded, the other two minor parties display rather even levels of support across national and local levels.

On the whole, therefore, Japanese parties are highly centralized, exclusive, and lack grass-roots organization. In the case of the LDP, for instance, policy decisions tend to involve mainly the national party elites — the party president and secretary general along with the executive committee and possibly the top levels of the PARC. As noted, in some cases policy decisions may include more rank-and-file Diet member participation. There are few ways, however, in which local citizens can participate in the formation of party policy. While Japanese parties may respond to changing currents of public opinion, there is little opportunity for citizens to exercise a direct voice in party affairs.

POLITICAL PARTIES: INFORMAL ORGANIZATION

All parties throughout the world have informal as well as formal organizations. Informal organization refers to interpersonal networks of friendship and mutual ideological agreement and other relationships or groups which come to exist within parties and which are not called for by the party's formal organizational plans. In Japan, informal relationships and groups are so important in party organizations that it is at times possible to see them as more important than the parties' formal structures. Or it may be necessary to view parties as overlapping dualistic structures with informal groups and ties forming important networks that at times dominate decision making and other aspects of formal organizational processes.

The most important informal elements of Japanese political parties are the leader-follower factions which are found in all parties as recognized, permanent fixtures, with the exception of the Communist and Clean Government parties.[20] These factions are especially important within the Liberal Democratic Party, since they play a major role in the selection of the party president/prime minister. While factions may stem from many sources, such as graduation from common elite schools or espousal of a common ideology or interest, the primary basis for the organization of Liberal Democratic factions is a personalistic affiliation of rank-and-file members of parliament with one or another of the party's strongest politicians.

At any time since the LDP's formation in 1955, there have been five or more important leader-follower groups active in the party, particularly in matters related to choices of party leaders or other personnel decisions. Some of the factions have been very large, with memberships as great as one hundred, while others have been very small, dwindling at times to as few as three or

[20] Our treatment of Japanese party factionalism depends heavily on the following: Fukui, op. cit., pp. 107–143; Haruhiro Fukui, "Japan: Factionalism in a Dominant Party System," in Frank P. Belloni and Dennis C. Beller, eds., *Political Parties and Factionalism in Comparative Perspective* (Santa Barbara: ABC-Clio, 1978), pp. 43–72; Scalapino and Masumi, op. cit., pp. 54–81; and Nathaniel Thayer, *How the Conservatives Rule Japan* (Princeton: Princeton University Press, 1969), pp. 15–57.

FIGURE 3.2. *Liberal Democratic Party Factional Continuity, 1959–1982*

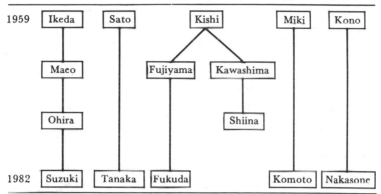

Source: *Asahi Nenkan*, 1972; and *Seiji Handobukku*, various years.

Note: A number of smaller factions have been omitted from the figure. Also the Shiina faction was quite small, and following his death in 1979, virtually disappeared.

four members.[21] Also, some of the factions have had remarkable continuity, in the sense that the groupings around particular leaders have generally been very stable and at least parts of the faction remained an integrated whole even after that politician's death or retirement from politics. In fact, the high level of institutionalization of Japanese factionalism, as well as the importance of the basic personal ties which bind faction members to their leaders, is distinctive of Liberal Democratic factions in particular and to some degree of Japanese factions in general in comparison with those in some other countries. Factions within the LDP, JSP, and DSP are the semipermanent building blocks of party organization. This fact has led some observers to view the Japanese parties, and especially the LDP, as "coalitions" or "confederations" of factions more than as integrated party organizations.

As depicted in Figure 3.2, there has been a strong continuity in factional "families" across time, despite occasional major intrafractional splits (shown) and minor defections (not shown) that have occurred at the death or retirement of a faction leader. Only the five most important factional families have been included, although there have been a number of other significant

---

[21] Seiji Koho Senta, *Seiji Handobukku: 9 Satsu Ban* (Tokyo: 1980), p. 193.

party factions from time to time. The figure also makes no effort to indicate precisely when the transfers of power took place, only the faction leaders at the helm in 1959 and 1982 and the succession of leaders in between. By the end of 1982, the five largest LDP factions in order of size were the Tanaka faction, 108 members; the Suzuki faction, 87 members; Fukuda, 74 members; Nakasone, 50 members; and Komoto, 42.[22]

Many observers of Japanese politics have provided explanations for the existence and continuity of factions in the LDP and Japanese politics in general. Most explanations mention the importance of leader-follower relationships in Japanese history, and sometimes the factions are seen as an extension into the present of traditional *oyabun-kobun*, or patron-client relationships. Although it is probably true that factionalism of some kind is almost universal in Japanese social organization, few of the contemporary Japanese party factions, including those in the Liberal Democratic Party, follow the classic patron-client format, which, after all, was based on gross unbridgeable inequalities in resources and status. In the 1950s and 1960s the factions of Ichiro Kono and Bamboku Ono were both traditional in their emphasis on hierarchy and use of traditional patron-client language. In contrast, most factions these days, and especially those led by former high-ranking bureaucrats, place much less emphasis on the language and protocol of clientelism, and have more the appearance of political clubs united around a core group of leaders, not unlike a board of directors. To be sure, there is a distinct element of hierarchy and deference, and factional leadership is important; indeed, the power of the faction leader has recently been made apparent by the ability of Tanaka and Fukuda, who are no longer viable candidates for the prime ministership, to resist for several years strong pressures within their factions for them to step down in favor of successors. Still, contemporary party factions cannot be equated with purely traditional patron-client formations.

Whatever the internal social organization of Liberal Democratic factions, they do perform very important functions for their members, and their existence undoubtedly owes as much to this as it does to Japanese traditional social organization. First

---

[22] Baerwald and Hashimoto, op. cit., p. 60.

and foremost, LDP factions and their counterparts in the other parties are ladders to top party positions; and in the case of the Liberal Democrats, the factions are the channel for recruitment to top government positions as well. In a process described in Chapter 7, members of an LDP faction can be expected to be sponsored for parliamentary vice ministerships after several terms in the House of Representatives and ministerships after six or seven terms. Likewise, offices in the party and Diet are distributed on the basis of factional membership and seniority. Of course to have any chance of becoming prime minister, one must first become the leader of a faction, preferably a very large one. In effect, the factions are the recruitment machines and launching bases for top party and government positions, and the actual assignments to these positions are negotiated in coalition-building processes involving all of the major faction leaders and at times the minor faction leaders as well.

The second major function of LDP factions, and again a function which is mirrored at times in the factional politics of other parties, is the sponsorship and financial support of members' election campaigns. Some candidates for the Diet run fairly independent campaigns, but the majority of LDP nominees in any given election are either new or old candidates sponsored by and affiliated with the party's informal factions. In the nomination process and in electoral campaigning, the factions function much like miniparties, in the sense that they back their own sponsored members in the negotiations for party endorsements, and faction leaders appear in local election districts to speak on behalf of their faction members during the campaigns.

In addition to sponsoring candidates for elections, the Liberal Democratic factions provide money solicited from corporations and business associations for their members' campaign coffers. Most candidates have other sources of financial support (including some party funding), but they still depend heavily on their faction leaders' contributions to pay the enormous expenses entailed in national election campaigns. Moreover, most factions reportedly provide regular allowances for their members' entertainment of constituents and other costs associated with maintaining support associations on a day-to-day basis to ensure a stable following in future elections. While no one but the participants knows the true scale of factional financial support of individual members, the Japanese press and other sources end-lessly report examples of these financial ties and their impor-tance to factional solidarity and individual politicians' financial viability.[23]

Finally, several authors have discussed the psychological bene-fits that Dietmen derive from belonging to a faction — the se-curity of being attached to a powerful benefactor, the sense of identity and camaraderie derived from belonging to a smaller, more intimate group than simply the entire party Diet delega-tion, and the self-importance that comes from participation as an insider in one of the theaters of party intrigue.[24] The per-vasiveness of leader-follower forms of organization throughout Japanese society suggests that factional groupings must satisfy certain cultural norms. However, the existence of factions within the LDP can be explained purely on the basis of their more tangible functions discussed above.

The Liberal Democratic Party factions hold many policy meet-ings and seminars and social meetings. Some factions regularly meet in plush resort areas, such as Hakone or Karuizawa, to hold seminars on current political problems. Factions also meet reg-ularly in Tokyo to discuss ongoing political problems and issues, as well as to socialize. Most factions also produce some kind of internal policy-oriented journal with high sounding names like the "Journal of Political and Economic Problems." Yet, despite this considerable amount of emphasis on discussions of policy matters, the factions actually don't regularly participate in LDP policy-making processes in a visible way. Nor do the individual factions seem to have a common ideology, even though some factions are noted for conservative or liberal tendencies because of the political ideas visibly favored by the faction's leader and other senior members.

Factionalism in its many forms has clearly been a dominant feature of Japanese party politics. Yet it has at many points throughout the postwar era been a major destabilizing influence. Prior to the formation of the LDP in 1955, the conservative par-ties formed and reformed many times, partly on the basis of factional maneuvers and shifts in interfactional alliances. Since

[23] Katsuyo Sasaga, *Seiji Shikin* (Tokyo: Kyoikusha, 1978), pp. 65, 80–83.
[24] Thayer, op. cit., pp. 39–42.

1955, the Liberal Democrats have been brought to the brink of dissolution at several points because of sharp conflicts among the major factions. The parties of the Left have also suffered from factional conflicts, and often these have been much more intense and disruptive, because in the Socialist and Communist parties, the personalistic type of factionalism found in the LDP has been overlaid by bitter ideological disputes concerning basic party doctrine. As a result, factional conflict within the leftist parties has frequently led to purges of portions of the leadership or party splits.

Beyond these disruptive effects on the stability and coherence of Japanese political parties, the highly visible activities of party factions, especially within the LDP, have transformed politics in the public eye into an elitist power game, devoid of policy consequences, played by and for the personal gain of a few self-seeking politicians. New LDP prime ministers have repeatedly sought to reform the party's image by leading movements to disband the factions, efforts that are related to the fact that factions provide the basis of intraparty opposition to incumbent prime ministers. Occasionally, the LDP factions have been formally dissolved, but they always come creeping back because there are no other agencies within the party that have as yet developed the capacity to perform the essential functions discussed above.

Recent reforms in the election law have limited the size of corporate contributions and the amount of money they may give to any one organization. These changes have had the effect of decentralizing the fund-raising process, so that individual LDP Dietmen are now more responsible for securing their own support than in the past. This change, by reducing the members' dependence on their faction leaders, could potentially weaken the power and coherence of the factions. In addition, a generational changing of the guard is now in progress, with the death of faction leaders Ohira and Shiina, the retirement of Miki, and the expected retirement of Tanaka and Fukuda. Some scholars have argued that in their place a much larger group of faction leaders with lower status, fewer financial resources, and smaller and more fluid followings will emerge, because the three largest factions — the Tanaka, Ohira-Suzuki, and Fukuda factions — have all had a number of capable, ambitious subleaders vying to gain the top spot, and it was thought that the succession struggles would split these factions.[25] However, by the summer of 1983, it was clear that Shintaro Abe (Kiski's son-in-law) was the heir apparent of the Fukuda faction and that Kiichi Miyazawa would take over the Suzuki faction. While the succession issue was still clouded regarding the Tanaka faction, it appeared that Noboru Takeshita might eventually inherit that faction largely intact.

The reasons for the survival of large factions is clear; large factions dominate access to the prime ministership. Since faction leaders are traditionally expected to step down once their tenure as prime minister is over, the ambitions of rising junior faction members may better be served by remaining in a large faction that has a high success rate in placing its leader in the prime ministership and thus a high rate of turnover in the leadership of the faction. We may conclude that while the LDP factions are continuing to evolve in terms of functions and internal power distributions, they will continue to play a central role within the party for many years to come.

In addition to the presence of several major and minor leader-follower factions, the LDP has a considerable number of informal policy groups within its national party framework. The policy groups, which are not as institutionalized as the factions, are less organized and have not usually been as durable as the factional families. Still, the policy groups are an important part of the LDP internal landscape. Recent sources list a total of twenty-five such groups ranging from the right-wing Asian Problems Study Association and Group 21 to the more moderate or even "liberal" Afro-Asian Problems Study Association, Hirakawakai, and Chiyodakai. Until recently the extreme right wing of the party was represented by the Seirankai, but this group has now been disbanded. Although the various policy groups differ considerably in their levels of visibility and degree of participation in the policy process, their presence within the conservative party movement calls attention to the often overlooked heterogeneity of the dominant party.[26]

---

[25] Gerald Curtis, "Social Patterns in the Political Arena," presented at *Japan in the 1980s, II,* a conference sponsored by the Southern Center of International Studies, Atlanta, Georgia, April 23, 1982.

[26] Seiji Koho Senta, op. cit., pp. 196–207.

PARTY ISSUE AND IDEOLOGY CLEAVAGES

Political parties in most political systems differ from each other over basic issues or ideologies, sometimes referred to as ideological cleavages. In Western experience, and most prominently in Europe, differences over religion have long divided political parties; religious issues are the origin of some of the most fundamental cleavages today in a number of Western European systems even in the face of recent declines in the importance of religion to many people. Similarly, differences over social class issues have been prominent dividing lines in most industrialized countries since the writings of Marx and Engels in the middle and late nineteenth century and are in certain senses still important today. Differences over language and regional or ethnic interests have also been the source of sustained, intense party differences in some countries. For instance, contemporary Spain and Yugoslavia are examples of deep regional cleavages, just as Northern Ireland serves as a paramount case of religious conflict which includes interparty cleavages over religious issues.

Not all issues are the basis for cleavages between parties. Some issues in politics are transitory, and only weakly related to long-term party commitments. Some strongly contested issues which divide parties sharply at a particular time also reflect commitments to interest groups. As such, they are different from the issues which will be discussed here in that they are not elements of fundamental party ideology and therefore not components of long-term cleavages between political parties.

Students of American political behavior have also made an important distinction between different *kinds* of interpartisan issues, which is extremely useful to keep in mind in the discussion of issues and ideologies in Japan. At times political parties take positions on issues which are almost indistinguishable from each other and often vary only in regard to where the blame for nonperformance is placed. Issues on which parties take similar positions and mainly try to prove that they have greater capabilities to do a better job in some political arena are called *valence* issues. The best examples of valence issues are conflicts over policies regarding inflation, recession, and peace or war. Even if there are interparty differences on economic theories or security strategies, basic partisan differences on ideological commitments are not generally involved in parties' claims to the electorate that they will end inflation, promote prosperity, fight crime, and ensure peace. Ideologically based issue differences, or issue differences where parties take clearly different points of view, are called *position* issues. It is these position issues and the long-term commitments or ideological foundations underlying the respective positions that will be discussed here.

There have been four basic long-term cleavages in postwar Japanese politics. The first basic divide has been over the preferred form of government, and has focused on the issue of constitutional reform. The second major divide in Japanese party politics is based on class ideology. The Socialist and Communist parties, as well as some of the center parties, have at times espoused the interests of the working or lower classes against their perceived enemies, Japanese capitalists, whom they see as being represented by the Liberal Democratic Party. The other two major long-term interpartisan cleavages have dealt with foreign affairs, specifically security policy and security relationships with the United States and relations with the nations of the Socialist or Communist bloc.

The constitutional issues which divided the left and the right — e.g., the status of the emperor, the role of the Upper House, the peace clause of the constitution, and the newly won rights of labor — lasted from the 1950s into the early 1960s. No fundamental changes in the postwar political structure were ever legislated, because after 1955 the conservatives could not muster enough seats in the Diet to pass a constitutional amendment. But the constitutional issues provide an excellent example of the cleavage between traditionalists and antitraditionalists in postwar Japanese politics. Indeed, the leftist opposition parties were termed the "progressive" or "reformist" camp during most of the postwar era. Some conservative leaders and politicians, for example, wanted a return to a prewar-type system of ethics education, which would teach traditional neo-Confucian values and patriotism to school students, instead of the heavy emphasis on democracy, individual rights, and social problems imposed in the Occupation-led curricular reforms. Eventually, some moderate changes to a more traditional curriculum were adopted in this area, although there has been no full-scale return to the prewar emphasis on education in traditional morality and political loyalties.

The traditional-antitraditional value cleavage was relatively latent in the 1960s, but has emerged again in the 1970s with the appearance of new issues which are related to this fundamental dimension. Some elements in the LDP recently proposed a bill aimed at the preservation of the traditional Imperial Era system of counting time, by which years in Japan are identified by a reigning name selected by each emperor at his coronation and the year of the emperor's rule. For example, 1980 was Showa 55, the 55th year of the Showa era, the period during which Hirohito has been Emperor of Japan. Eventually a bill continuing use of this system for official calendars passed the Diet with the backing of the LDP and traditional religious groups, and opposition from the center and leftist parties. Although the intensity of feeling on this issue was not as great as that on the central constitutional issues at an earlier time, the Era Names Bill brought out once again the existence of a fundamental cleavage over values between some elements of Japan's major political camps.

There clearly is evidence that Japan does not have social classes and class feelings of the kind found in some other countries. While Japan has social stratification, there have been moderating events and forces which have kept the gulf between the upper echelons of society and lower social groupings from being as wide and intensely felt as has been the case in countries like Britain and Germany. Likewise, strong class feelings and self-identifications do not seem present among most contemporary Japanese.[27] Still, there are class parties in Japan, and the rhetoric of class interests has been used repeatedly where these parties have defended the interests of their class clientele. In the early 1950s, for example, the Socialist and Communist parties almost continuously fired verbal salvos at the ruling conservatives, which were laden with Marxist and Leninist vocabulary accusing the conservatives of representing the "evil" forces of monopolistic capitalism and world imperialism.

The theme of advocating class interests runs through the op-

[27] Flanagan and Richardson, op. cit., pp. 22–32.

TABLE 3.5. *Working and Lower Class Defense as an Ideological Basis of Partisan Issue Positions*

		1960	1963	1967	1972	1979
D			Tax wealthy and corporations			
i			Lower taxes for lower income groups			
m				End political contributions of big business to LDP		
e						
n						
s				End pollution by big companies		
i				Provide more public housing		
o						
n						
s						
P	LDP	0	0	0	0	0
o						
s	DSP	+/−	+	+	+	+
i						
t	CGP	na	na	+	+	+/−
i						
o	JSP	++	++	++	++	++
n						
s	JCP	++	++	++	++	++

Note: Based on election statements by the respective parties in the House of Representatives elections.
++ = strong support for issue positions
+ = support for issue positions
+/− = contradictory statements in issue area
0 = no applicable statement on issue
na = not applicable as party did not exist

position parties' issue positions throughout the postwar era as Table 3.5 clearly shows.[28] Across the entire period from 1960–1979, the leftist parties in their campaign statements consistently attacked the conservative Liberal Democrats for their alleged tax concessions to big businesses. The left has also regularly called for heavier taxes for upper income categories and corporations

[28] All election campaign statements reported in the Japanese vernacular press were chronologically evaluated. We began with 1960 because the task was too big to include earlier years and because the contemporary patterns of party system cleavage took form between 1955 and 1960.

and, in most elections, has also favored lowering taxes for their working class constituents or for persons in lower income groups in general. The left and center parties have also attacked the financial ties between big business and the Liberal Democrats, which have been exposed in periodic national scandals. The rhetoric of class conflict has been used to criticize the business-government ties as it has on so many other issues, and there is consequently a basic cleavage dimension to these accusations as well as more practical motivations.

The same merging of specific political pragmatism and ideology has occurred in other expressions of the basic class cleavage, such as in leftist demands that big business stop polluting the country and advocating more public housing for Japan's working classes and lower income groups. In a similar vein, opposition parties have attacked the government's economic growth policies, and other policies as well, for their alleged favoring of the capitalist classes at the expense of workers and the public. While the intensity of debate has diminished in recent years and the use of pure Marxist terminology has abated somewhat, the inter-party cleavage based on defense of lower class interests by the opposition parties continues.[29]

The third, and perhaps the most intense and enduring political cleavage in postwar Japan has been concerned with security issues. Japan entered the "cold war" in the 1950s on the side of the West because of both the influence of the American occupation forces and the strong anti-Communist feelings of Japan's leaders of that time. After the outbreak of the Korean War and at the nudging of SCAP, Japan in 1950 established a paramilitary National Police Reserve which was the forerunner of the contemporary Self-Defense Forces. Then, in 1951, Japan signed a mutual security treaty which became the cornerstone of a defense alliance with the United States which has lasted over the past three decades.

Throughout the 1950s, 1960s, and even 1970s, security has been a paramount issue in Japanese party politics. The conservative forces have opted for a modest defense establishment con-

---

[29] As noted in Table 3.5 the Democratic Socialists and even the Clean Government party, which does not have Marxist origins, took similar positions to the JSP and JCP, although with less intensity or with more moderate proposals.

sisting of a military force of 300 thousand men, costing usually one percent of the GNP or less. This security policy was formulated on the assumption that Japan (a) has a security problem and is threatened by Soviet and Socialist bloc power and (b) needs some kind of security system in the face of such a perceived threat. The Socialists and Communists initially saw things much differently and argued that Japan's security was actually endangered by a one-sided alliance with the United States. Their strongly articulated security policy throughout the 1950s and the 1960s consisted of rejection of the U.S.-Japan Mutual Security Treaty and suggestions for disbanding the Self-Defense Forces and turning them into either a domestic conservation corps or a United Nations peace force contingent. The leftist parties also called for an international treaty between the United States, the Soviet Union, The People's Republic of China, and Japan, guaranteeing the neutrality of Japan in cold war confrontations.

The intercamp confrontation over the Self-Defense Forces and the security relationship with the United States was especially intense in the 1950s. As noted above, the security treaty revision issue produced the largest mass movement in postwar Japanese history in May and June of 1960 when hundreds of thousands of students and union members marched on the Diet. Later in the 1960s, while opposition rhetoric continued to emphasize opposition to the security treaty and the Self-Defense Forces, the emotional intensity of the debate lessened somewhat as new domestic environmental and quality of life issues came to the fore. Moreover, while opposition on security issues continued to erupt in leftist party rhetoric through much of the 1970s, by the end of the 1970s the center Democratic Socialists had come to accept most of the Liberal Democrats' security policy views, and even the Socialists and Communists had come to accept the necessity of some kind of defensive military establishment and some kind of external security relationship with the United States. Still, when the United States began to push Japan toward heavier outlays on defense — a series of moves which began early in the 1970s, but which became particularly conspicuous in the early 1980s — the opposition again took up the theme of resistance, this time emphasizing the need for Japan to hold its defense outlays to one percent of the GNP. Table 3.6, which is based on the parties' stands in different general elections, illus-

TABLE 3.6.   *Defense and Security as Partisan Issues, 1960–79*

		1960	1963	1967	1972	1979
D i m e n s i o n s		Maintain the U.S.-Japan Mutual Security Treaty				
		Maintain and Improve Japan's Self-Defense Forces				
P o s i t i o n s	LDP	++	++	++	++	++
	DSP	−/+	−/+	+	+	0
	CGP	na	na	−	−	0
	JSP	− −	− −	− −	− −	+/−
	JCP	− −	− −	− −	− −	+/−

Note: Based on election statements by respective parties.
++ = strong support for issue positions
+ = support for issue positions
+/− = contradictory statements in issue area
− = opposition to issue positions
− − = strong opposition to issue positions
0 = no applicable statement on issue
na = not applicable as party did not exist

trates the security policy cleavage over time and delineates the moves by different parties on these issues.

The fourth and final cleavage to be discussed concerns Japan's relationships with the Socialist bloc countries in general and, most importantly, with the People's Republic of China. The China issue provoked a heated partisan debate from the 1950s until 1972. To start with, there were two Chinas with which Japan could potentially have relations, the Communist government on the mainland and the rump Nationalist movement on Taiwan, where the Republic of China continued to exist as a state after the banishment of the Nationalist forces from the mainland in 1949. Moreover, certain prominent conservative camp leaders, including Prime Minister Yoshida (1946–47 and 1948–54), had close ties with the Nationalist government as well as being determinedly anti-Communist. This situation produced early opposition to political relationships with the People's Republic, a policy which lasted until the early 1970s, buttressed in part by the United States's own opposition to the mainland government and Japanese appreciation of the importance of economic and security ties between Japan and America. Although some conservative prime ministers actively promoted closer economic ties with China, the conservative camp did not make overt moves toward resumption of political relationships with the People's Republic until the prime-ministership of Kakuei Tanaka in 1972, after the United States's recognition of the Peking government.[30]

Meanwhile, as part of their overall preference for better relationships between the Socialist countries and a neutral Japan, the Socialists, and at times the Communists, strongly advocated political relationships with Peking in the 1950s and 1960s. And, as part of their policy of opposition and promotion of closer ties with the mainland government, leftist party delegations repeatedly visited Peking and joined Chinese leaders in pronouncements favoring Japanese-Chinese solidarity and expressing opposition to the conservative policy of alliance with the United States. Once formal political ties were established with the People's Republic by the Tanaka government with the help of the opposition parties, this dimension of the interparty foreign policy cleavage became a dead issue.

CONCLUSION

This chapter has shown that Japan's prewar political history bequeathed a legacy of weak and ineffective oppositions. This historical experience has been an important contributor to the prolonged dominance of the LDP throughout the postwar era. Also discussed were the important ways in which the Japanese electorate has been changing and the effects this change has had on the Japanese party system. With the decline in the relative size of the LPD's traditional constituencies and the failure of the

[30] Fukui, *Party in Power,* op. cit., pp. 227–262; Haruhiro Fukui, "Tanaka Goes to Peking," in Pempel, op. cit., pp. 60–112.

Socialists to broaden their appeal, the Japanese party system has undergone a long-term transition from a one-and-one-half-party to a multiparty system. An examination of the Japanese parties has shown that they are highly centralized, exclusive, and generally lacking in grass-roots organization. Moreover, their factionalized nature has condemned them to a history of internal conflict and instability. Finally, four ideological issue dimensions have been identified that have defined the basic left-right party system cleavage throughout the postwar era.

A brief outline of the five major periods that describe the changing context of political competition in postwar Japan will conclude this discussion. The Occupation reforms and postwar political and economic reconstruction constituted the first major separate period of Japanese politics. Following the end of the Occupation, there was a second period of eight years (1952–60) in which the party system was consolidated and some of the Occupation reforms were tested in the heat of debates over "reverse-course" policies. As described in the sections above, the result was a partial return to earlier Japanese administrative practices in some instances, amid preservation of most of the postwar institutional reforms including the Constitution itself. A third period covering most of the 1960s was Japan's era of LDP-led high-growth economic development. The doubling of national incomes was the slogan of the day, and while some reverse-course issues lingered, most political debate was focused on measures related to economic growth policies or lingering problems of Japan's security and relations with the West and the East in the cold war.

The late 1960s brought a new period in Japanese politics. There were important shifts in the configuration of the political system as high growth produced major pollution, housing, transportation, and other problems in Japan's already overcrowded cities as well as in a number of rapidly industrializing regional districts. Quality of life concerns came to dominate both local and national politics, particularly with the rise of opposition-party-led local prefectural and municipal administrations in many of Japan's metropolitan areas. These issues remain important themes in Japanese political life today.

The fifth and final period emerged as a result of the partial and perhaps temporary eclipse of these quality of life issues by a new set of economic problems. This last period was ushered in by the Arab oil boycott in the fall of 1973. As a result, energy problems, a "structural recession," and growing overseas economic competition and resistance to Japanese exports have commanded increasing attention along with the crumbling of the old cold war international alliances and new security problems. This shift in the issue agenda has been associated with a small and uneven LDP resurgence at the polls in the late 1970s and early 1980s, bringing the party's long-term erosion of popular support at least temporarily to an end.

CHAPTER 4

Culture and
Society

AMERICAN TEXTBOOKS ON POLITICS in other Western democracies, such as England, France, or Germany, rarely introduce cultural themes to explain political phenomena. Because the Western nations all share a common cultural heritage, the cultural context of politics in these nations is an assumed constant, and cultural differences are minor enough that their impact on political behavior rarely warrants detailed attention. These assumptions cannot be made in the Japanese case. Japan's cultural heritage and traditional values and beliefs, which are strikingly different from the Western experience in many important ways, have a great impact on Japanese political behavior. Consequently, a knowledge of some of the major outlines of Japan's traditional culture and contemporary patterns of social relations is important to our understanding of Japanese politics.

The discussion of Japanese culture and society will begin by discussing two major dimensions of Japan's traditional culture that differentiate it from the Western experience — *personalism* and *holism*. Contrasting the more personalistic and holistic cultural tradition in Japan with the more legalistic and individualistic Western tradition does not imply that the differences on these dimensions are absolute or represent black and white opposites. These dimensions represent cultural continua, not dichot-

* Scott C. Flanagan

omies, and the differences are in degree, not in kind. Moreover, culture is not static but is continually evolving as the conditions of society change. By describing Japanese culture as personalistic and holistic is to affirm that, relative to Western culture, Japanese culture has always placed, and continues to place, greater emphasis on these values as opposed to legalistic and individualistic values.

While the cross-national differences on either dimension are not absolute, they are still substantial. Moreover, the configuration of traditional attitudes and beliefs found in feudal Japanese society present a composite cultural tradition that is not only very different from that found in the West, but in many ways is unique in the world. Indeed, because of this unique cultural mix, Americans who first began visiting Japan in the latter half of the nineteenth century often found themselves confused and adrift in an alien world with few familiar guideposts to help them understand Japanese behavior. The Japanese people soon acquired a reputation in the Western mind as being enigmatic and inscrutable, and writings about Japan focused on her exotic customs, art forms, and ascetic disciplines. When cultural anthropologist Ruth Benedict wrote her pathfinding study of Japanese culture in 1946, she noted that Japan was depicted in Western writings as a society of contradictions and that no other society in the world had been described by such a fantastic series of "but also's." The Japanese were said to be unprecedentedly polite *but also* insolent and overbearing, incomparably rigid in behavior *but also* readily adapting themselves to extreme innovations, submissive *but also* not easily amenable to control from above, loyal and generous *but also* treacherous and spiteful.[1] Indeed, the typical tourist-oriented books of that period delighted in informing the reader that the Japanese did everything backwards, from the way they read books, to men preceding women through doors, to smiling when insulted, to appearing to say yes when they really mean no.

Fortunately, a growing body of excellent scholarship by anthropologists, sociologists, psychologists, and other observers is

[1] Ruth Benedict, *The Chrysanthemum and the Sword* (Boston: Houghton Mifflin Co., 1946), pp. 1–2.

now available to help us pierce the veil of mystery that has shrouded Japan's traditional culture. In addition, the rapid pace of economic development in Japan over the last one hundred years has been a profound force for cultural change as has the increased tempo of cross-cultural exchanges and borrowings. In contrast with Commodore Perry's landing party in 1853, a contemporary American visitor to Japan would find much that is very familiar in Japan's large metropolitan centers, including McDonald's hamburgers and Baskin Robbins ice-cream parlors. Moreover, studies have shown that as the material technological environment and conditions of life have changed in Japan, so have Japanese values, and often the direction of change is the same as that found in the advanced industrial societies of the West. Nevertheless, the Japanese have not become just like Westerners, and cultural misunderstandings continue to complicate relations among Japanese and Americans at the social, business, and even governmental levels.

Indeed, Americans visiting Japan today are still confronted with a baffling array of seemingly contradictory images. A society which has achieved the greatest equalization in income distribution among the advanced industrial democracies at the same time places a strong emphasis on hierarchy and social deference. In a country in which the interests of the group are said to come first, often requiring the suppression of individual feelings and desires, interpersonal dealings are characterized by an unusual degree of pragmatic, even calculated, self-interest. A "Japan Incorporated" economy, which is thought to be harmoniously orchestrated through government-coordinated planning and cooperative agreements among companies, displays some of the most ruthless examples of cutthroat competition, as companies cut profits to the bone in an almost irrational drive for a larger market share. One of the world's most conservative and stable societies produces some of the most violent and fanatical radical groups. A nation which extols the virtues of nature has created some of the most horrendous examples of environmental pollution. A Zen heritage of contemplation and ascetic disciplines of self-denial coexists with a burgeoning pursuit of materialistic consumption and hedonistic pleasures. A nation that jealously guards its insularity and exclusiveness and finds intimate contact with or exposure by foreigners disturbing, at the same time displays an excessive fear of isolation from the world community.[2]

These seeming paradoxes arise from the difficulty of understanding behavior in one society through the cultural lens of another. Culture is an interpretive code which enables those who share a particular historical tradition to grasp large meanings from small gestures and to know what behaviors are associated with what attitudes. Without this knowledge, an observer may find himself off-balance, misinterpreting the meaning of a familiar behavior or expecting attitudes and behaviors to fit together that do not. Thus while Japan is experiencing many of the same problems and pressures for change as other advanced industrial societies, the distinctiveness of her cultural heritage requires that a study of Japanese political behavior be prefaced with an analysis of her cultural foundations.

This analysis is all the more important because contemporary Japanese society is chronologically much closer to its feudal origins than are Western societies. While from an economic perspective Japan has been transformed from an agrarian to an advanced industrial society in just over one hundred years, culture changes much more slowly, so that remnants of a cultural value system born in a feudal, peasant society can still be found in Japan today. To understand present-day Japanese society, therefore, we must first investigate several aspects of Japan's cultural origins and feudal tradition that distinguish it from the Western cultural tradition. Here we will focus on the dimensions of personalism and holism and several subdimensions that are associated with these two major axes of cultural differentiation.

PERSONALISM

Personalism is a label applied to identify a cluster of cultural norms including particularistic-diffuse authority relations and social relativism. The personalism-legalism value dimension contrasts the more personalistic and interactive authority relations in traditional Japanese society with the more legalistic and unilateral authority relations found in the West. Traditional, feudal

---

[2] Y. Sugimoto and R. E. Mouer, *Japanese Society: Stereotypes and Realities* (Melbourne: Japanese Studies Center, Melbourne University, 1982) p. 6; *Time*, Special Issue — Japan: A Nation in Search of Itself, 8/1/83, p. 19.

polities have generally been based on some organic concept of society. In this view human society is founded on a natural organic unity of hierarchically ordered roles. While some roles are more highly valued than others, all are indispensable and interdependent, and all contribute to the common good. Harmonious social relations, therefore, depend primarily on proper role fulfillment. Hence such societies assign high values to the strict observance of prerogatives and obligations. These prerogatives and obligations are situationally defined, both by an individual's position in society and by the matrix of personal interactions and exchanges that surrounds him at a particular location in time and space.

These organic notions of social organization were present in Western feudal societies as well, but were tempered by the presence of legalistic principles. Moreover, during the hundreds of years following the Middle Ages, with the development of urban market cultures and then the occurrence of the industrial revolution, organic concepts ultimately were mainly replaced by legalistic modes of thought and the concept of the social contract. *Legalism* as here defined lays stress on impersonal, contractual relations which limit the scope and magnitude of authority but also clearly define the lines and direction of authority and responsibility. In contrast, *personalism* attaches primary importance to face-to-face relations in the exercise of authority. While authority and obligations are in principle unlimited, duties and responsibilities are only vaguely defined and may vary markedly from situation to situation. In Parsonian terms, authority relations are particularistic and diffuse rather than universalistic and specific.[3] Personalism, then, is characterized by a rigid, hierarchical ordering of roles combined with rather relativistic and situationally defined authority relations.

In Japan, the emphasis on personalism in the traditional culture was unusually strong precisely because of the near-absence of legalistic modes of thought. Japanese culture has been uniquely devoid of absolutes of either a transcendental or legalistic nature. There was no Bible, no Koran, no set of commandments, in short, no law that set down what people should and should not do in clear and unambiguous terms. Instead, Japanese thought stressed

[3] *See* Talcott Parsons, *The Social System* (New York: Free Press, 1951).

the impermanency and mutability of the human condition; therefore, what is true today may not be true tomorrow and nothing could be absolutely certain. The Japanese have been staunch relativists, feeling that it would be inhuman and unjust to attempt to regulate the affairs of people through the application of inflexible, abstract laws. Right and wrong behavior could be determined only by the circumstances. Rules were to be broken if they failed to meet human needs in a particular situation.[4]

Herein lies the basis of Japanese humanism and the peculiarly strong strain of personalism in Japanese culture. Since there were no universal truths, society could not be organized on the basis of abstract principles and inflexible laws. Instead, Japanese society was structured on human relations. The only inviolable rules were *on* (indebtedness), *chu* (loyalty), and *giri* (social obligation). These rules ensured that all debts and favors would remain in force — registered on some mental balance sheet, guaranteed by one's family, and regularly audited by one's neighbors — until they were eventually repaid. The passage of time, rather than dissipating a sense of obligation for a past favor, would only increase the sense of burden and debt, as if the favor were a commercial loan accumulating interest.

Thus Japanese society was built on personal exchange agreements incurred on a face-to-face basis. It was in these exchange agreements that the individual sought and found security, not in any legal code or set of statutes. In the feudal context these relationships tended to be between persons of unequal status, to be diffuse in scope and to involve the exchange of noncomparable goods. The strength of any dyad relationship depended on the amount of face-to-face contact, the degree of intimacy, and the amount of benefits and services exchanged. To ensure one's security, an individual required a permanent, primary relationship to a paternalistic patron or benefactor; this system of personalistic attachments was institutionalized in the Japanese feudal system. To a unique degree, then, personalism provided the philosophical basis for ordering human society in premodern Japan.

---

[4] Hajime Nakamura, *Ways of Thinking of Eastern Peoples* (Honolulu: University Press of Hawaii, 1964) pp. 350–372; Isaiah Ben-Dasan, *The Japanese and the Jews* (New York: Weatherhill, 1972) pp. 71–104.

The Ambiguities in Authority Relations. In comparison with the West, authority relations in Japan have traditionally been more situationally defined rather than governed by universal rules; that is, they have been more particularistic. Authority relations have also been more diffuse, in that the superior-subordinate relationship has been viewed as essentially boundless, extending into every area of life rather than being limited by contract to a specific set of duties and obligations. The peasant's obligations to his landlord or the samurai's to his lord were not limited to certain hours in the day or to certain specified responsibilities. In turn, the superior was responsible for the total physical and psychological well-being of his subordinates, not simply their working conditions. This diffuse nature of Japanese authority relations has blurred the distinction between one's public and private life.

The strong strain of social relativism in Japanese personalism introduced other kinds of ambiguities into authority relations. For instance, in conflict situations, there has been a tendency to avoid perceiving the participants in dichotomous good-bad, right-wrong terms. As the Japanese saying goes, "even a thief may be 30 percent right." The Japanese tend to hold everyone involved in a conflict as responsible and to resolve such conflicts through mutual compromises and apologies.[5] Right and wrong, then, are relative, and the special circumstances on each side that provoked a dispute must be taken into account in assessing responsibility.

Traditional Japanese philosophies and religious beliefs have also rejected clear lines of clausal influence. The Japanese did not see the world as being controlled and acted upon by a prime mover or prime creator. In fact, the Japanese did not clearly distinguish between God and man, but rather brought the supernatural down to the level of man. Shintoism, for instance, rejects the notion of a single, supreme creator, but rather views the spiritual world as inhabited by a myriad of spirits, souls, ghosts, and other spiritual forces. The spirit world was defined in particularistic terms, with each village having its own exclusive deity and protector. Spirits could be both good and bad, depending on

[5] Takie Lebra, *Japanese Patterns of Behavior* (Honolulu: University Press of Hawaii, 1976) pp. 11–14.

their moods, and tended to have no clear physiognomies, residing sometimes in a mountain, tree, or manmade abode and sometimes moving into an animal or taking possession of a living person. In fact, there was no clear demarcation between the natural world and the world of the spirit. All living things, including plants and animals, as well as some material things like waterfalls and large rocks, were believed to have spirits.[6]

We can find in these religious notions one source of the Japanese variant of fatalism. The failure to identify authorship or responsibility for creation with one supreme being or to clearly distinguish between man and God was manifested more broadly in a cultural reluctance to differentiate between the actor and that being acted upon. If one could not conceive of God as doer or maker, then neither was man. Rather, man was seen as being surrounded by forces beyond his control that could profoundly affect his life for good or for ill. To survive in that kind of world, one had to learn to be flexible and adaptable and to adjust quickly to whatever new situation might arise. In other words, a person is viewed as being controlled by events over which neither that person nor anyone else has much control. Things just happen, and what is required of one is to be able to test the winds skillfully and bring oneself into accord with the flow of events and the force of circumstances.[7]

A final ambiguity in authority relations stems from the mutual interdependence of superiors and subordinates and the flexible assignment of roles within the group. Although the obligations of subordinates were in principle limitless, the authority and discretion of the leader was by no means absolute. In many respects, the higher an individual's position in Japanese society, the more his or her freedom and authority were limited by social obligations. For example, far from holding a monopoly of power, the emperor actually exercised little or no discretion in most decisions of state, either in the Fujiwara Period (857 to 1160) or after political authority was returned to the emperor with the Meiji Restoration in 1867.

---

[6] Harumi Befu, *Japan: An Anthropological Introduction* (San Francisco: Chandler, 1971) pp. 95–119.

[7] Yuji Aida, "The Anatomy of the Japanese Consciousness," in Hyoe Murakami and Edward Seidensticker, eds., *Guides to Japanese Culture* (Tokyo: Japan Culture Institute, 1977), p. 67.

Indeed, any expression of individual willfulness or self-seeking ambition on the part of a leader has been viewed as illegitimate. The leader and his subordinates are mutually interdependent and mutually subordinate to the interests of the group. While Japanese personalism, on the one hand, lays stress on the principles of hierarchy, status, and rank, it does not imply authoritarianism or dictatorial leadership. Instead, a more collective type of leadership exists in which superiors are as much guided by the opinions of close subordinates as the reverse. In this model of mutual interdependence, there is often a fusion of actor and object such that it is impossible to identify authorship in decisions or clear lines of influence.[8]

HOLISM

The above discussion of the ambiguities in authority relations associated with the personalism dimension of Japanese culture merges at points with the *holism* dimension and so leads into a discussion of this second major dimension. In the holistic view, the whole is greater than the sum of its parts so that the highest value must be attached to the goals and interests of the group, even if that requires a great sacrifice of individual wants and needs. Since the harmony and solidarity of the group must be maintained for the sake of the collective good, great emphasis is placed on the values of conformity, dependency, and conflict avoidance. If holism stands at one end of our second dimension of cultural differentiation, individualism defines the other end. Individualism stresses the principles of equality and self-determination and attaches highest values to the needs, preferences, and self-fulfillment of individuals.

Naturally, neither Japan nor any Western country falls at either extreme on this dimension, and individualism has certainly not been a trait historically associated with Western agrarian societies. However, anti-individualism appears to have been stronger in Japan than in any other major tradition.[9] Undoubtedly Japan's

---

[8] We are not suggesting that Japanese leaders have been timid, without ambition, or always benevolent. Japanese cultural norms, however, have required that personal ambitions remain publicly hidden and that leaders draw their authority more from personal relationships with subordinates than from the impersonal authority of official roles. Lebra, op. cit., pp. 14–16.

[9] Charles A. Moore, *The Japanese Mind* (Tokyo: Tuttle, 1973) pp. 299–300.

holistic or group-centered value orientation grew out of the absorption of successive generations in the communal life of the hamlet and out of the high level of unified and cooperative effort needed for an economy based on rice cultivation. Work schedules had to be closely coordinated to maintain the road and irrigation systems and to exchange labor services for transplanting, harvesting, roof thatching, and other anually shared activities. As many peasants lived on a bare subsistence level, any farmer who went his own way was a burden and a liability for the entire hamlet. The supply of water, firewood, and grass for fertilizer was communally controlled, and heavy economic sanctions could be directed against any recalcitrant individualist. Since ostracism, hunger, and destitution were the price of independence, it is little wonder that individualism did not flourish.

Economic sanctions by themselves would not have produced the highly group-centered orientations we find in Japan; however, they were supplemented by numerous positive, cultural, and psychological factors designed to heighten the sense of solidarity and oneness of purpose. For instance, many practices were adopted that served to reinforce symbolically the sense of unity — tending the community shrine and cemetery, performing cooperative tasks with the community in festivals, weddings, and funerals, and observing the consensual form of decision making in the hamlet councils in which each household was represented.

Group consciousness was further advanced by culturally instilling the values of conformity, submissiveness, dedication, and self-sacrifice. In this regard the family served as the training ground both in teaching the suppression of one's own wishes to the will of the group and encouraging obedience and subservience to patriarchal authority. Kinship terms of address were extended to nonkinship relations between landlord and tenant, and householder and servant, to betoken the sense of connectedness.[10] The popular ethics of the Tokugawa period taught the Confucian concepts of unlimited, unending obligation to one's parents and, by extension, to one's lord. What the individual had received was so much greater than what he could ever return that even if he devoted his entire life to serving his parents and lord, he could never hope to repay more than one ten-thousandth of his debt. The good

[10] Befu, op. cit., pp. 57–62.

peasant, then, should deny self-interest and lose all sense of self-hood by thinking only of his parents, his village, and his lord. Vassals were exhorted to inculcate the spirit of service above self, meaning that they should be ready even to lay down their lives for their lord at a moment's notice.[11] In this cultural milieu, individualism was tantamount to selfishness, ingratitude, and disloyalty.

The philosophical basis for holism is found in Confucianism, which views society as a magnified family, composed of numerous functionally differentiated primary and secondary groups that are hierarchically ordered and vertically integrated, all working in harmony for the common good. In this view, the basic unit of society is the group, not the individual. Goals are defined in group terms, and achievements are credited to the group as a whole rather than singling out individuals for public recognition. Responsibility for the misjudgments and misdeeds of individual members is collectively born.

In many respects the Japanese stem family was the prototype for all traditional Japanese groups. The stem family was based on primogeniture and adoption. Primogeniture required the inheritance of the family house and lands by the eldest male to ensure the family's continued economic strength and viability. If there were no male heir, a daughter's husband was adopted into the household to assume the family name, or a childless couple would adopt a relative's child, often a daughter, who upon reaching marriageable age would be wed to a man who was willing to be adopted by her adoptive family. In this way the family's continued existence could be ensured throughout all generations. Moreover, since the stem family included all those living under the same roof, often incorporating distant kin or nonkin in kinshiplike relationships, it has been viewed as more of an economic organization than a kinship unit. The Japanese stem family was a corporate group organized to perpetuate itself from generation to generation.[12]

Following this basic model of group organization, all groups in Japanese society have been perceived not as artificial creations of

---

[11] Hiroshi Minami, *Psychology of the Japanese People* (Tokyo: University of Tokyo Press, 1971) pp. 11–17.

[12] Befu, op. cit., pp. 38–48.

their members, but as having a life of their own that transcends the current membership. Individual members will eventually die, but the group can endure throughout all generations. Each generation of members is only a vehicle for carrying on the group's mission, a link between past and future generations. The current membership, out of a deep sense of obligation for the great sacrifices and achievements of prior generations of leaders and members, is instilled with a dedication to struggle mightily for the preservation of the group and for those that will follow.

Affectivity. An important corollary of holism is *affectivity,* or emotionality. In the West, emotions have tended to be viewed, at best, as unmanly and more typically as unstable and dangerous, revealing the darker side of man. To escape being ruled by unpredictable passions, the wise man was taught to seek refuge in the path of reason. Hence logic and intellect were highly valued in the West, often at the expense of the affective side of human nature.

Traditional Japanese culture assigned quite contrasting values to rationality and affectivity. First, philosophy and metaphysics were never accorded prominent roles in Japanese society. What is entirely missing from Japanese culture is the peculiar mix of Greek and Christian thought that has been so enduring and influential in the West — namely that there are some eternal truths that man's reason could uncover, that his natural proclivities are evil (original sin), and that he must save himself from the governance of his unruly passions by bringing his life into accordance with these truths. The rules that governed Japanese life were social and given, requiring no application of logic to divine; therefore, reason served no central function and was not highly valued.

Secondly, the central dilemma that has preoccupied generations of Japanese is more social than philosophical — not the war between reason and the emotions but the conflict between duty (*giri*) and human feelings (*ninjo*). While typically the individual is pictured as being torn between two opposing courses of action as a result of this conflict, neither force is viewed as illegitimate, bad, or self-defeating. Since duty is a higher-order social value, the individual's feelings in the end must be sacrificed. Virtue is found in learning to resign oneself to this loss, but in this process of resignation (*akirame*) there is a glorification of purely personal feelings and emotions. In the performance of one's social duties and obligations, therefore, human feelings and emotions are hidden as much as possible from the outside world and privately nurtured, cherished, and indulged. This has created a heightened concern and sensitivity for the affective side of human relations.

Affectivity, then, is here defined as a culturally heightened sensitivity to emotional stimuli and responses, and it is a corollary of holism in the sense that an emphasis on group solidarity leads directly to an emphasis on affective tasks within the group. Chie Nakane goes so far as to say that membership in a Japanese group is emotionally based, and if purely personal and psychological needs are not satisfied, members will begin to neglect their assignments or even resign from the group.[13] As stated in the discussion of personalism, the concept of contractual relations limited to the exchange of specified services for specified benefits has been slow to develop in Japan, having failed to emerge during Japan's feudal period in marked contrast to the European feudal experience. Since the Japanese individual has sought security in personal relationships and has been to an unusual degree psychologically dependent on the group for support and approval, his emotional security has been a prerequisite for effectively engaging in cooperative work. Great care must be taken in arriving at decisions within a group to ensure that the emotional needs and sensitivities of its members are not frustrated or otherwise upset.

The emphasis placed on affective tasks within the Japanese group has often been at the expense of the attention devoted to the cognitive, rational, evaluative side of group activities. A tendency to devalue clear and direct communication and evaluation has been culturally reinforced by a number of factors, but here only its philosophical manifestations will be considered. Traditional Japanese thought displayed a culturally inbred preference for subtlety, indirectness, and meaning by implication. For example, Buddhist thought not only did not aspire to the kind of higher philosophical synthesis esteemed in the West, but even

13 Chie Nakane, *Japanese Society* (Berkeley: University of California Press, 1970) pp. 76–80.

denied its existence. To the Japanese way of thinking, the compulsion with which the Western mind tries to impress order on its world and erect eternal verities produces only artificial fabrications that distort and exclude much of reality. The Japanese mind is at peace with asymmetry and delights in the irregularities it finds in nature.[14]

To the traditional Japanese way of thinking, reality is incompleteness and confusion. Truth is hidden in paradoxes and contradictions, and life is revealed in absurdities and emptiness. Indeed, what was valued in Japanese society could not be grasped by the intellect, being too vague and abstract to make logical sense. Truth, therefore, defied logical reasoning processes and could be absorbed only as a whole with all of its incompleteness and contradictions through intuition and sentiment, a spiritual union with the object or mystery the student was trying to master. As a result, the Japanese developed learning processes that emphasized nonverbal communication and a heightened sensitivity to implication, grasping another's meaning from what was left unsaid. Truth was to be found in what was implied rather than stated.[15]

In Japan, then, words have been employed not so much to persuade or convey a particular meaning as to establish an atmosphere, a "community of emotion."[16] The Japanese speaker is fishing for assurances that his listener is sympathetic and sensitive to his situation. When offered food or drink, a guest will decline, presumably because he does not want to inconvenience his host. At the same time, however, the guest fully expects to be pressed to accept the offer by further entreaties that express a concern for his physical comfort and encourage him to partake of a relaxed, family atmosphere. This and other little rituals are played out daily to reassure the partners of any verbal exchange that they can depend upon the other's benevolence. It is this seeking and granting of special treatment, this indulgence of favors and allowances, that is the lubricant of interpersonal relations in Japanese society.

[14] Kurt Singer, *Mirror, Sword and Jewel* (New York: George Braziller, 1973) pp. 44–61.

[15] Moore, op. cit., pp. 288–293; Ben-Dasan, op. cit., p. 111.

[16] Masao Kunihiro, "Indigenous Barriers to Communication," *The Japan Interpreter* 8 (Winter 1973), pp. 96–108.

What is expressed in words, then, is not what is important in terms of what passes between people. More often than not, language is used to hide one's true feelings while probing for cues that will reveal where the other person stands. Therefore it is necesary to look beyond the spoken words to penetrate the thick cloud of propriety, politeness, deference, and restraint that surrounds most verbal communications. To accomplish this, the Japanese have developed a special sensitivity to nonverbal cues, to moods and unexpressed feelings that reveal the real intent of the heart. The person who is esteemed in Japan, then, is not the elegant debator, but the one who can read another's thoughts by a facial expression, a gesture, a certain turn of phrase. The superior host would sense his guest's need without a word passing between them, and simply produce the food and drink at the appropriate time.

CULTURAL CONTINUITIES

Several aspects of Japan's cultural tradition have now been discussed, providing a sense of where Japan is coming from, and what values and attitudes have molded social and political behavior in the past. The question to be addressed now is to what extent do the two principal cultural dimensions discussed above, personalism and holism, continue to characterize Japanese society.

Any sweeping generalizations in this regard are difficult to substantiate because, as with most large, complex, industrialized nations, there can be observed a wide variety of divergent behavior patterns within contemporary Japanese society. Vivid examples of cultural continuity seem to exist side by side with equally striking signs of cultural change. This juxtaposition of the new with the old is particularly pronounced today because value change in Japanese society has been so recent, so rapid, and so uneven, affecting some segements of society far more than others.

A further complicating factor is that there are two kinds of cultural change occurring. The first is the more dramatic and obvious — the appearance of new behavioral patterns that represent a sharp break from traditional values and seem to be almost un-Japanese. The second is more subtle but perhaps more important. It is the emergence of new behavior patterns that represent adaptations of traditional values to adjust them to the realities of a modern socioeconomic context. Such traditional values as deference to authority and loyalty to the group are still much in evidence in Japan, especially in comparison with American society. However, in speaking of hierarchic or patron-client relations in Japan today, it must be recognized that these modern-day patterns are vastly less hierarchic than those found in fuedal times when superiors held the power of life and death over subordinates. From that perspective, contemporary vertical relationships appear to be not only different in degree, but different in kind from traditional models. Nevertheless, in comparison with the United States, there still appears to be a marked emphasis on hierarchy and formal deference in Japanese social relationships. In an American group of executives, it is often difficult for an outside observer to tell who is the senior official, particularly in public situations or at social gatherings. But in the Japanese group, the bow, the deferential forms of speech, the focus of attention, and many other signs leave no doubt as to who is the head man.

Similarly, there is still great emphasis on loyalty to the group. As in the case of hierarchy, however, the degree and intensity of that loyalty has waned. For instance, no longer is there a glorification of loyalty unto death as seen in the traditional practice of ritualistic suicide, often to preserve the honor of one's group. While the story of the forty-seven *ronin* who symbolize this traditional virtue is still honored in Japan, the few rare acts of political suicide and assassination that have occurred in the post-war period have been viewed universally as fanatical and misguided. Nevertheless, while the degree of commitment to one's group has been declining, it is still much higher than what is typically found in the United States. Thus, for example, while absenteeism among American workers sometimes reaches as high as 20 percent, it is virtually nil in Japan, and commitment to the work group and the quality of its products have produced levels of reliability unsurpassed throughout the world.

When we speak of cultural continuities, therefore, we are not referring to a static persistence of traditional values in their pure form, but to a subtle process of adaptation in which both the influence of traditional values and the realities of the modern socioeconomic context blend in ways that preserve something of the traditional Japanese character. This chapter will focus on these continuities, reminding the reader at times that they neither perfectly mirror Japan's traditional cultural norms nor characterize all segments of contemporary Japanese society. To achieve a fully balanced view the theme of cultural change will be addressed in Chapter 6.

Situationally Defined Behavior. A great deal of evidence can be marshaled to support the observation that Japan is still in many ways a particularistic society. Rather than applying a set of universal standards to the treatment of others, an individual's behavior in his or her relations with other people depends on the relationship with them. Takie Lebra speaks of three domains of behavior in which completely different standards apply.[17] The intimate domain includes interactions with family, friends, and coworkers in relaxed, informal settings, generally set apart from the work day, such as after hours meetings in bars, coffee houses, and public baths. In these settings, unity and emotional attachments among the participants are stressed, hierarchic distinctions are relaxed, and individuals are able to express their true feelings, free from the restraints, inhibitions, and formalities that characterize the work-a-day world. Drinking frequently plays an important role here in establishing an atmosphere of camaraderie and lowering inhibitions.

The ritual domain covers interactions with acquaintances, superiors, and other known individuals. Generally these acquaintances lie outside a person's intimate circle of family, friends, and coworkers, but there are also formal social situations that call for ritual behavior in the presence of intimate friends. Ritual behavior is based on elaborate rules of social interaction, designed to save face and avoid embarrasing either oneself or others in the eyes of the world. Ritual behavior, then, is a kind of social mask that enables the individual to hide his or her true feelings behind a facade of formality, politeness, restraint, and physical distance. While this meticulously controlled ritual behavior appears tense, stilted and disingenuous to Western observers, it nevertheless enables the participants in these interactions to maintain proper relations, fulfill their social obligations, and demonstrate respect and humility while still preserving their dignity.

The anomic domain covers interactions with strangers that have

17 The following discussion of the three situationally defined domains of behavior is based on Lebra, op. cit., pp. 110–136.

no influence over an individual's life, and situations, as in a crowd, where one can expect to remain anonymous. These are normless situations in which neither the empathy of intimate interactions or the politeness of ritual interactions are exhibited. When the Japanese encounter strangers or novel situations, as in traveling abroad for the first time, the rigid constraints on their behavior no longer apply, and they are not bound by considerations of face. Hence they may either be at a loss as to how to behave or may feel free to be arrogant, unfeeling, or offensive.

The marked differences in behavior from one situational domian to another often seem incongruous to foreigners. Thus, for instance, the traditional reserve and politeness of Japanese can be totally forgotten at the subway platform where passengers push and shove each other with abandon on entering and exiting the trains. Also the compulsive cleanliness and neatness that marks residential neighborhoods is replaced by a careless, slovenly propensity for littering in public places such as parks and public transportation vehicles. Foreigners are also amazed by the speed with which an individual may shift from one mode of behavior to another as the situation changes. Hence, a woman may fight her way out of a subway car with a few well-placed elbow jabs and then bow deeply to an acquaintance she meets on the train platform. Or a man may act rudely and arrogantly to a stranger he has just met until learning that he is a relative of his former high school teacher, at which point, with embarrassment and sincere apologies, he switches to the respectful ritual mode of behavior.

Localism. How an individual behaves, therefore, depends heavily on the nature of his relationship with the person he is interacting with. This particularistic conception of society is closely associated with the more parochial, localistic outlook that is found in Japanese society. The parochial view pictures society as a series of concentric circles emanating outward from the individual at the center and representing diminished levels of intimacy with increasing distance. Respect, obligation, and trust fall off rapidly when we move beyond the spheres of intimate associates and meaningful acquaintances. As a result, outsiders and strangers are frequently viewed with a coolness and suspicion, if not outright hostility and distrust. There is, then, a built-in preference for what is proximate, intimate, and known, and an unwillingness to embrace individuals or groups that are viewed as outsiders, unconnected with one's own intimate circles.

Vertical Ties. If the cultural dimension of personalism implies a higher emphasis on particularistic and parochial attitudes than are typically found in the West, it also implies a greater stress on face-to-face relationships. Because to an unusual degree Japanese do things through known people, chains of connections play an extremely important role in the average citizen's daily life. In the effort to establish and maintain these extensive networks of personal relationships, great emphasis is placed on both vertical and horizontal ties.

Chie Nakane's classic analysis of Japanese society stresses the vertical dimension of personalistic ties.[18] Indeed she considers Japan a vertical society pointing to the emphasis on hierarchy, rank, and social deference to superiors. As Nakane notes, Japanese cannot speak, sit, or eat without an awareness of relative rank. The Japanese language itself reflects a cultural emphasis on rank by the use of completely different words for common pronouns such as *I* or *you*, depending on the relative rank of the individuals being addressed. In many other ways, speech patterns, honorifics, prefixes, and endings sharply differentiate the mode of address of superiors and inferiors. Thus Japanese generally exchange name cards when they first meet so that they can gauge the relative status of a new acquaintance and then adapt their behavior and mode of speech accordingly. Other customs, such as seating arrangements and serving orders at meals, also emphasize hierarchic distinctions.

Nakane claims that Japanese seek out and form special relationships with one or more persons of superior status or position who play a benefactor or advisor role. This role encompasses nurturing a disciple's career aspirations and involving oneself in his or her important life decisions and personal crises, in return for loyalty and service. Moreover, she says, it is these vertical chains of connections that are most effective, as seen in the emphasis placed on securing letters of introduction. When someone has to conduct business or seek a favor from a person who is a stranger, say a

18 Nakane, op. cit., pp. 23–103.

Mr. A, a letter of introduction from a Mr. B who is connected with, but stands superior to Mr. A, will ensure special treatment.

These vertical ties are reinforced by the Japanese cultural preference for diffuse authority relations. As noted before, traditional authority relations in Japan were not viewed in the same contractually bounded sense as they have been in the West. The landlord's obligations to his tenant were not limited to providing land, but extended to helping the tenant find a suitable wife and providing aid in case of natural disasters or injury. Today Japanese employers are fond of saying that they employ the whole person. In other words, they are concerned not only with their employees' productivity on the job, but also with their personal and psychological well-being. Accordingly, Japanese companies provide many more fringe benefits, leisure activities, and counseling services for their employees than do American or European companies.

While many values have been changing in Japan, the preference for diffuse vertical relationships has not. For instance, across six National Character Surveys (NCS) conducted every five years between 1953 and 1978, overwhelming majorities of the respondents have consistently said they would prefer a demanding boss who looks after them personally in matters not connected with work, to an undemanding boss who does not involve himself in their personal matters.[19] On another NCS item, 72 percent of the respondents felt it best to have social contacts with their superiors outside of work. These attitudes contrast sharply with American preferences for separating their personal lives from their working relationships with superiors. For instance, in a comparative survey of Japanese and American workers, 60 percent of the Americans felt that a superior should *not* involve himself in such personal matters as an employee's decision regarding marriage, compared to only five percent of the Japanese.[20]

Superiors in Japan, then, are still expected to play a paternalistic, father-figure role and to look after the concerns and feelings

[19] Research Committee on the Study of Japanese National Character, *Nipponjin no Kokuminsei*, Vol. I, II, and III (Tokyo: Shiseido, 1961, 1970, 1975); Research Committee, *Kokuminsei no Kenkyu: Dai 6-kai Zenkoku Chosa*, Research Report No. 46 (Tokyo: Institute of Statistical Mathematics, 1979).

[20] Arthur Whitehill and Shinichi Takezawa, *The Other Worker* (Honolulu: East-West Center Press, 1968) pp. 170–174.

of their subordinates, even in matters totally unrelated to the work place. These vertical relationships are strengthened by the amount of face-to-face contact and the frequency and magnitude of exchanged favors. In this hierarchic context, the exchanges are naturally different in kind. For example, subordinates exchange loyal service beyond the letter of the contract and even outside the work place for special benefits and promotion of their interests. Thus Nakane, Nobutaka Ike, and other scholars have described Japan as a patron-client society, in which the basic unit of social organization is the vertical dyadic relationship of superior and subordinate.[21] This dyadic relationship is multiplied throughout organizations and society in general, with men forging vertical ties both upward and downward by attaching themselves to a leader of higher status and drawing to them a number of promising followers of lower rank. According to this view, social organization in Japan may be schematically depicted as a series of interlocking patron-client pyramids.

The continuing emphasis on vertical ties is reflected in the large number of terms used to describe these relationships in Japanese and their frequency of use — terms such as senior-junior (*sempai-kohai*), teacher-disciple (*sensei-deshi*), and parent role-child role (*oyabun-kobun*) relationships. These relationships are marked by a degree of formal deference not found in the West. For instance, a recent investigation by a leading Japanese magazine found that while the Japanese do not now bow as frequently as in the prewar period, they still bow a great deal. As an example, on a given day it was found that a typical assistant section chief in a large corporation bowed over 180 times. Moreover, a subordinate is not likely to disagree openly with a superior in public. Instead, superior-subordinate conversations tend to be "one-sided sermons" with the senior member of a group carrying the conversation and his subordinates politely agreeing at the appropriate moments with whatever he is saying. Comparative evidence of this deferential behavior comes from the survey of American and Japanese workers cited above; 63 percent of the American workers would neither offer their superior their

---

21 Nobutaka Ike, *Japanese Politics: Patron-Client Democracy* (New York: Alfred Knopf, 1972); Ike, *A Theory of Japanese Democracy* (Boulder, Col.: Westview Press, 1978); Nakane, op. cit., pp. 40–63.

seat nor hold the superior's package on a crowded bus, compared to only 5 percent of the Japanese.[22]

It should be noted that these vertical relationships ought not be confused with the type of patron-client relationships typically found in traditional or late-developing societies. In contemporary Japanese society, the magnitude of authority that a superior can exercise over an inferior is limited, and these relationships are largely benevolent and mutually beneficial rather than being extractive or exploitative. Moreover, there is considerable evidence demonstrating the decline in hierarchic authority throughout the postwar period and the infusion of society with egalitarian norms.[23] Some observers contend that the Japan of today is a vertical society more in forms and formalities than in substance. As the traditional hierarchic distinctions of status have declined in importance during the postwar period, the character of Japanese personalism has been undergoing a subtle change toward a personalism based more on instrumentalism, reciprocity, and other more enduring elements drawn from Japan's rich cultural tradition.

Horizontal Ties. An exclusive emphasis on vertical relationships, therefore, distorts the true picture of Japanese social interactions. In fact, Japanese cultivate horizontal ties, that is, relationships with those of a more or less equal status, as intensely as they do vertical ties. It may not be too much of an exaggeration to say that Japanese society is based on the exchange of favors. Even when conducting business, Japanese prefer to work through known friends and acquaintances, because they feel that they will receive better treatment in that way. Thus it is important to cultivate all kinds of personal ties, both horizontal and vertical. Any kind of connection, based on common birthplace, common school or any shared experience, can be exploited to gain a favor.

Japanese are able to ask their friends and acquaintances for

[22] *The Japan Times Weekly*, 8/6/83, p. 5; Nakane, op. cit., pp. 34–35; Whitehill and Takezawa, op. cit., pp. 174–178.

[23] Ronald Dore, *City Life in Japan* (Berkeley: University of California Press, 1967 ed.) pp. 269–287; Dore, *Shinohata: A Portrait of a Japanese Village* (New York: Pantheon Books, 1978) pp. 282–311; Robert E. Cole, *Japanese Blue Collar* (Berkeley: University of California Press, 1971) pp. 141–142.

favors that Americans would consider a gross imposition because of the expectation of reciprocity. An unrepaid debt induces guilt and social criticism. One must be very careful to repay all favors to protect one's reputation and ensure that one can continue to receive more favors as needed in the future. Indeed, Japanese feel uncomfortable being heavily in another's debt, and often regard favors received as burdens to be discharged as quickly as possible by returning a favor of more or less equal value.

At the same time, relationships are strengthened by the frequency of such exchanges. As a result, gift-giving has become a highly cultivated custom in Japan, and a great variety of occasions have become culturally defined as requiring gifts. For instance, birth, deaths, marriages, and special occasions such as passing school entrance examinations, graduation, getting a job, promotions, buying a house, opening a store, or becoming a victim of an illness, fire or robbery all require gifts. In addition, there are annual midsummer and year-end gift exchanges. Moreover, when someone goes off on a trip, gifts are presented to him or her at a going-away party, and upon return he or she reciprocates by bringing presents back from the places visited. Finally, whenever one visits another's home, whether for business or pleasure, one must bring a small gift, and the host reciprocates by providing food and tea.[24]

Evidence of the continuing importance of personal ties and connections in all walks of Japanese life is found in the responses to public opinion surveys.[25] In Table 4.1, we find that the overwhelming majority of Japanese place great stress on the cultivation of personal relationships. Moreover, very few discount the importance of connections and intermediaries in conducting business or even visiting a government office. Obviously, when the practice of exchanging favors and gifts is carried over into public relations with government officials, it smacks of bribery. Even here, however, the cultural practice of gift-giving is so ingrained that only a minority of the respondents, 43 percent, felt that such practices were clearly wrong.

---

[24] Lebra, op. cit., pp. 90–96.

[25] The data reported in Table 4.1 are taken from the JABISS Japanese Election Study, a 1976 nationwide panel survey conducted by J. Watanuki, B. Richardson, I. Miyake, S. Kohei, and S. Flanagan. Here as elsewhere in this chapter the percentages reported are based on the exclusion of missing data.

TABLE 4.1.   *The Importance of Personal Ties and Connections*

	Agree	*Depends*	*Disagree*
Whether at one's place of work or the place one lives, one must take great care of personal relationships.	87	12	1
When one lacks personal connections, one is greatly handicapped, whether in finding a job or doing business.	58	29	13
When one goes to request something from a national or local government office, if a representative (Dietman or Assemblyman) serves as an intermediary, things go well.	51	32	17
When you receive assistance from a government office, there is nothing in the least bit wrong with giving a suitable year-end or midyear gift to the official that principally took care of you.	28	29	43

Source: 1976 JABISS Japanese Election Study.

Personalistic Contracts. Evidence that personalistic norms continue to be emphasized over legalistic ones can be found in the comparatively low emphasis placed on the law and contracts in Japan even today. Presently there is one practicing attorney in the United States for every four hundred Americans, but only one for every ten thousand citizens in Japan. Most Japanese companies still frown on the practice of using lawyers to draw up contracts, and many do not even bother to employ formal, written contracts with either their suppliers or customers. Where contracts are used, it is said that what the contract establishes first and foremost is a human relationship. For example, Japanese contracts do not set down detailed provisions for various possible future contingencies as do American contracts. Instead, they include what is known as the "sincerity clause" which states that "when a dispute arises concerning this contract, the two parties will talk it over with sincerity." When such disputes occur, it is felt that the most important thing is not honoring the letter of the contract, but rather maintaining amicable relations and saving the face of both parties. If both parties are sincere in this desire, a mutually agreeable solution can always be reached, irrespective of what is stipulated in the contract. Thus if market conditions change suddenly, making it difficult for a supplier to produce his product at the agreed-upon cost without suffering grave losses, the buyer is likely to volunteer to pay more. The execution of contractual relations in Japan, therefore, depends to an unusual degree on the maintenance of good human relations.[26]

Another example of the comparatively low emphasis placed on legalistic norms can be found in the low proportion of civil disputes that end up in court. First, the rewards of going to court are likely to be meager. Not only is the process time-consuming, but settlements tend to be low. Second, going public with a conflict and taking it to court violates the norm of community solidarity. Many Japanese still feel that it is preferable to settle disputes informally, through a go-between, rather than have the disputants confront and accuse each other in public, thereby irrevocably damaging the sense of community harmony. In fact, there have been cases in which Japanese who have taken their neighbors to court and won have become the targets of intense public criticism. Even when civil disputes are brought to court, the majority of them are resolved either through an out-of-court settlement or an in-court compromise, the latter being a protocol recorded by the court that avoids the assessment of blame and loss of face associated with a judgment.[27]

Still signs of change are present on this aspect of the personalism-legalism dimension as well. It has been noted that there has been a marked increase in recent years in the number of suits against physicians and teachers, something that would have been unheard of in the past. It has also been observed that younger workers are developing more contractual orientations.[28] Legalistic norms, then, are making an advance, at least in some sections of Japanese society, in response either to a weakening of the norm of community solidarity or to a change in the definition of which individuals are within the group as members of the same community and which are outsiders to whom the warm, empathetic bonds of Japanese personalism do not extend.

26 *Time*, 8/1/83, pp. 64–65; *Japan Times Weekly*, 4/9/83, pp. 4–5.
27 Tomoyuki Ohta and Tadao Hozumi, "Compromise in the Course of Litigation," *Law In Japan* 6 (1973) pp. 97–110.
28 Rodney Clark, *The Japanese Company* (New Haven: Yale University Press, 1979).

A cluster of orientations that exemplify the continuing influence of a personalistic cultural tradition in contemporary Japanese society has been identified. The dimensional label that has been employed, personalism, is simply a convenient shorthand term used to designate this cluster of social norms — particularism, social relativism, localism, diffuse relationships, an emphasis on hierarchy and ranking, social deference, the nurturing of vertical and horizontal ties, the reciprocal exchange of gifts and favors, and the role of go-betweens and intermediaries. As noted, some of these norms, such as hierarchy, are declining in importance faster than others, and probably none of them are as widely and intensely adhered to today as they were one hundred years ago. Nevertheless, this personalistic set of traditional norms, in whatever modified form, continues to shape interpersonal relations in Japan sufficiently to differentiate behavior patterns in that society markedly from those found in America.

Group Centered Life. In a similar vein, Japan's holistic cultural tradition has strongly shaped contemporary Japanese society. Because holistic concepts remained largely unchallenged during the prolonged feudal period in Japan, they were carried over into the new industrial, urban culture that grew up rapidly in the late nineteenth and early twentieth centuries. For this reason, Japan may still be characterized as a society built on small, cohesive groups. The small group consciousness that constituted the spiritual backbone of the rural farming hamlet has, to a surprising degree, been transferred to the modern industrial work team.

Nakane states that the close identification of the Japanese with his or her group can be traced to the unique basis of group organization in Japan.[29] In most cultures groups are organized on the basis of some shared common attribute — a trade, skill, or profession. In Japan, groups are organized on the basis of what she calls the *ba* — the frame, location, or place. For example, a male employee is identified not so much by his attributes, personal achievements, skills, or function as by the hometown he comes from, the school he graduated from, and the company he works for. Thus, when that employee introduces himself, he is

[29] Nakane, op. cit., pp. 1–8.

more likely to identify himself by whom he works for rather than what he does. The more powerful and prestigious the group he belongs to, the greater his self-esteem. Thus it is often said that Japanese would prefer to be employed at the middle level of a large, prestigious company than as a top executive in a small organization, even at a higher salary.

To say that Japanese groups are organized on the basis of the *ba,* or frame, means that groups are organized around a shared location — the hamlet company or factory. These groups, therefore, necessarily contain individuals of markedly different attributes in terms of their skills, statuses, and functions. A good example of the distinction Nakane is making can be found in labor organizations. In the West and most other societies, unions are organized on the basis of the worker's craft or function. Regardless of whom they work for, each skill position — the electricians, the machinists, the truck drivers, and the clerical workers — have their own unions. In Japan, unions are organized on the basis of the enterprise, not the craft. Everyone working for the same company or in the same factory are members of the same union, regardless of their function and regardless of whether they are blue or white collar workers. Indeed, from a Western perspective the relationship between management and labor in Japan at times may appear to be almost incestuous. For example, a 1981 study of executives in 313 corporations found that one of every six was a former leader of an employees' union.[30]

One reason for the high level of group consciousness found in Japan, therefore, is that society identifies and evaluates the individual on the basis of the group he belongs to. Another reason is that groups in Japan are viewed as natural phenomena, not artificial human creations that an individual may or may not choose to associate with. Membership in Japanese groups tends to be automatic and compulsory, being defined by one's location. If you live in a rural hamlet, you are a member of the hamlet association. If you work for a company, you are a member of the company union. Moreover, while Japanese may frequently belong to more than one group, they are socially defined in terms of one primary membership, usually revolving around their place of employment. It is expected that an individual's company or

---

30 *The Japan Times Weekly,* 2/27/82, p. 3.

work group should be able to lay claim to his undivided loyalty. Other memberships tend to be either associated with or subordinate to that primary membership.

Even today, amid growing signs of individualism and self-indulgence, the mutual commitment of worker to company and company to worker contrasts sharply with that found in the West. The bonds between the company and its workers are nurtured by a host of symbolic and paternalistic practices — calisthenics en masse before work, the daily singing of the company song, wearing company uniforms, caps, and lapel pins, living in company-owned dormitories, marrying in a company chapel at a greatly reduced cost, receiving company-subsidized mortgages for employees purchasing a home, and vacationing in company-owned retreats at nominal cost. The company's commitment to the worker is further symbolized by the lifetime employment system, and while many Japanese workers are not covered by the system, there are also many examples of companies that retain redundant workers rather than laying them off or else retrain them for new jobs. For example, when Nippon Steel closed one of its furnaces because of declining sales, it opened up an agricultural subsidiary in the same area and set its displaced workers busy raising cattle.[31]

While a decline in worker loyalty to the company has been noted in recent years, especially among younger workers, survey evidence reveals that Japanese workers continue to feel a much stronger commitment to their companies than American workers. For example, 66 percent of Japanese workers reported that their company was a central concern in their life, as important or more important to them than their personal life, compared to only 23 percent of American workers. Even among the younger generation, cultural differences are still striking; 45 percent of Japanese youth reported that they preferred a father who put his job before his home and family, compared to only 8 percent of American youth. A recent poll of Japanese college graduates found that 51 percent reported that they would follow their company "even if it involved doing something unfair or violat-

[31] Robert C. Christopher, *The Japanese Mind: The Goliath Explained* (New York: Linden Press, 1983) p. 245.

ing social justice." [32] This "my group right or wrong" attitude is evidently still quite prevalent in Japanese society. Undoubtedly the seventeen Hitachi and Mitsubishi executives, who were arrested or indicted in absentia in California in the summer of 1982 in an FBI sting operation for buying IBM computer secrets, were not professional industrial spies and did not think they were doing anything morally wrong.

According to traditional Japanese norms, ideally the individual should be totally committed and loyal to one's group, and in turn the group should take care of all the needs of its members. By identifying with the collective goals of one's group, the individual sacrifices much autonomy, but at the same time is also relieved of the burden of responsibility. The norm of collective responsibility is so pervasive in Japanese society that individuals often will not make even trivial choices without consulting other members of their group. Thus a customer's simple question in a department store is likely to set off a miniconference among the sales people. Westerners are even more startled when they observe that if a child is directly asked a question in a classroom situation, he or she will typically consult with a neighbor before answering. Even so personal a decision as choice of a marriage partner was traditionally viewed as a group decision. While the Western model of a "love marriage" has been increasingly idealized among the young, recent surveys report that 40 percent of all Japanese marriages are still arranged by go-betweens.[33] For many Japanese, then, marriage remains at least symbolically a group responsibilty.

The intensity of the individual's involvement in group life in Japan may strike Americans as an unwanted invasion of privacy and loss of autonomy. In Nakane's words, "Just how much a Japanese depends on, and expects from, his friends may be incomprehensible to the outsider." [34] It has been found that even native Japanese, who have lived abroad for several years, have had difficulty upon returning to Japan in readapting to the de-

---

[32] Whitehill and Takezawa, op. cit., pp. 110–113; Youth Bureau, *The Youth of the World and Japan* (Tokyo: Prime Minister's Office, 1978) pp. 6, 38–39; *The Japan Times Weekly*, 5/21/83, p. 5.

[33] Christopher, op. cit., p. 63.

[34] Nakane, op. cit., p. 121.

mands of group life. Especially the children of overseas businessmen and diplomats have experienced problems in fitting in and
have been frequently criticized as being selfish for not going along
with the group. It has been said that Japanese feel really alive
only when in a group and that they thrive on intensive interactions among group members that reinforce a sense of mutual
solidarity. It has also been observed that Japanese are very sensitive to isolation and loneliness and have an inordinate anxiety
about being left out or left behind. This fear of exclusion gives
rise to the phenomenon of faddism, in which the whole country
seems to be reading about, discussing, or doing the same thing
at the same time.[35]

One thing that binds the Japanese group together is a socialization process that breeds a great sense of sameness. The Japanese
education system, for instance, instills an expectation of homogeneity and equality within the group. Thus there is no tracking
by ability within elementary and secondary schools. While there
is some tracking by schools, especially at the higher educational
levels with the better students going to the better schools, no
such distinctions are made within an institution. Rather, great
emphasis is placed on avoiding anything that would suggest that
one student is in any way different from the rest. As a rule, no
child skips a grade and no child is held back, regardless of performance. The goal of this socialization process is to enhance
the sense of homogeneity and group harmony. The message is
that it is bad to be different, a message that is aptly illustrated
by such Japanese proverbs as "The nail that sticks up gets hit"
and "The pheasant that flies gets shot."

Another cement holding the Japanese group together is the
great attention placed on human relations within the group.
As noted in our previous discussion of affectivity, Japanese in-
vest a great amount of energy in preserving rapport and cohesiveness within the group. Indeed in many situations, affective
tasks continue to take precedence over instrumental tasks. For
instance, in a series of recent surveys, it was found by overwhelming majorities (roughly three to one) that Japanese preferred a company with a familylike atmosphere over one with
high wages, and congenial coworkers over capable ones. It has

[35] *The Japan Times Weekly,* 4/2/83, p. 4; Lebra, op. cit., pp. 22–29.

also been observed that when Japanese interact on matters of business and mutual interest, it is first necessary to establish a sense of intimacy and rapport before they can effectively work together or reach a common agreement.[36] This is the reason why so much of Japanese business and politics is conducted in after hours meetings in bars, night clubs, and geisha houses.

It may be that one of the reasons that such great care and attention is given to intragroup relations is that Japanese groups, organized as they are on the basis of a common frame or location, are by nature heterogeneous in terms of member attributes and statuses. In order to overcome these internal differences so that the group can function at all, great efforts must be made to deemphasize hierarchy, competition, and rivalry and to build a sense of group solidarity. One way this is done is to emphasize seniority rather than merit as the basis of advancement within the group. For example, it is common for a worker in his twenties to receive only a third the salary of a worker in his forties for doing essentially the same work. Survey evidence demonstrates that Japanese still strongly resist the idea of any kind of comparative performance evaluations. Moreover, even among Japanese youth, 59 percent prefer seniority over performance as the basis of promotion compared to only 17 percent of American youth.[37]

Many steps are taken to minimize distinctions and hierarchical distances within the group. Section chiefs work in the same room with their subordinates, rather than being walled off in separate offices. White collar workers begin their careers in menial jobs on the plant floor. Plant managers mingle freely and frequently with their employees and make it a point to know all their names and keep track of important events in their lives, such as births, deaths, and marriages. In a recent comparative study of factories in Japan, America, and Britain, it was observed that in the Japa-

36 Research Committee, *Kokuminisei no Kenkyu: Dai 6-kai*, p. 52; Daiji Kazama and Toyoko Akiyama, "Japanese Value Orientations: Persistence and Change II," *Studies of Broadcasting*, No. 16 (Tokyo: Japan Broadcasting Corporation, 1980) p. 7; NHK Public Opinion Research Institute, ed., *Nihonjin to Amerikajin* (Tokyo: Nihon Hoso Shuppan Kyokai, 1982); Kinhide Mushakoji, "The Cultural Premises of Japanese Diplomacy," *The Japan Interpreter* 7 (Summer-Autumn 1972) pp. 287–289.

37 Nakane, op. cit., pp. 8–22; Youth Bureau, op. cit., pp. 52–53; Whitehill and Takezawa, op. cit., pp. 207, 302.

nese plant all employees from janitor to chief executive ate in one common dining room, used the same toilet facilities, and wore the same uniforms. In the American factory, there were two separate eating and washroom facilities for executives and workers, and in the British plant, there were three sets of facilities for executives, clerical employees, and blue collar workers.[38]

The Japanese employee's primary work group makes demands upon not only his loyalty but also his time. Much of the Japanese employee's after-hours socializing takes place within the same group that he works with. For the blue collar worker that may be the quality-control circle, and frequently all the members of such a circle may jog, drink, or even vacation together. For the white collar worker, the office group becomes the focus of after-hours socializing. Japanese offices are not quickly deserted when the five o'clock whistle or musical intercom message signals the end of the day. Rather food and drink will be ordered in and groups here and there will chat and smoke, while others will gather around the *shogi* board (Japanese chess) and watch their colleagues play. Later various groups will drift off to a bar and spend several more hours drinking in a very intimate atmosphere (Japanese bars are small and cozy) to unwind from the pressures of the day and smooth over petty annoyances and conflicts that may have built up within the group. So much time is spent among one's coworkers, that the suburban apartment complexes (*danchi*) where many white collar office workers live are called "bed towns," because these salarymen often do not return home to their families until late at night, just in time for them to go to bed.

Over the last decade or two, as the work week has shortened and values have begun to change, Japanese workers have increased the proportion of the time that they spend with their families or devote to other leisure activities outside the work group. Substantial majorities of Japanese employees, however, continue to feel that after-hours socializing within the group is extremely important, and they continue to value the sports days,

[38] Herbert Passin, "The Sociology of the Japanese: An Historical and Cultural Perspective," presented at the conference on *Japan in the 1980's*, Southern Center for International Studies, Atlanta, Georgia, April 22–23, 1982.

picnics, overnight excursions, and other company activities that promote interactions with colleagues outside the work day.[39] These and other little daily rituals — morning calisthenics on the company roof, the collective recitation of company principles, hitting a volleyball back and forth in a circle during the lunch break — build a sense of group solidarity and oneness of purpose.

The Group and Social Control: Harmony, Competition, and Conflict. To a greater degree than hierarchic authority, the group in Japanese society acts as the primary social control mechanism. Because the pressures for compliance are collective rather than simply hierarchic, they are both more acceptable and more difficult to resist. The group exercises this control because it is the group rather than the individual that is most often the unit of accountability. This lesson is learned early in Japanese society; Japanese students are responsible for cleaning their own classrooms and in the performance of these tasks as well as individual academic assignments and projects, typically all must stay until the last student has finished his or her work.[40]

Even within organizations, competition for rewards is structured in group rather than individual terms. Japanese organizations emphasize that the individual's fortunes rise and fall with that of the group. As the founder of Sony, Akio Morita, is fond of telling his workers, the company is a "fate-sharing vessel." [41] If one person is lazy or fails to perform his or her task adequately, the entire group suffers. In order to avoid a poor group performance record, someone must step in and take up the slack, and thus other members are inconvenienced. Moreover, no one who disgraces the group is tolerated. Many shortcomings and deficiencies may be hidden within the group, but should a dishonorable action be exposed to the outside world, the group's collective shame will be most acutely felt, and the culprit will be severely chastened and perhaps even expelled from the group. Peer group pressure, then, is an extremely strong force that may

39 Whitehill and Takezawa, op. cit., p. 270; Research Committee, *Kokumin-sei no Kenkyu: Dai 6-kai,* p. 52.

40 Christopher, op. cit., p. 83.

41 *Time,* 8/1/83, p. 20; Thomas Rohlen, *For Strength and Harmony* (Berkeley: University of California Press, 1974), pp. 93–120; Lebra, op. cit., pp. 33–37.

be mobilized to pull a recalcitrant member back into line or to monitor and rectify any deviant attitudes and behaviors that threaten the solidarity of the group.

According to Akira Kubota, the pressures for conformity are so great in Japanese society that in some aspects it may appear almost totalitarian to Americans. He notes that all workers in the Toyota family, including small-parts suppliers, may not be able to buy a Datsun, and that employees are not really free to decline participation in the work group's calisthenics.[42] Moreover, the norms of group harmony and conflict avoidance are so strong that dissenters will generally avoid expressing disagreement with whatever appears to be the majority opinion, unless their interests are seriously challenged. In the consensual decision-making process within Japanese groups, decisions are reached when a dissenting minority signals its agreement or acquiescence by falling silent. A decision can then be anounced without a vote, thus preserving the appearance of unanimity. While these procedures may appear to inhibit the expression of true opinions and demand an excessive degree of conformity, Japanese culture relaxes the oppressiveness of group pressures by recognizing that outward consent may not reflect inner agreement. The Japanese distinction between *tatemae,* the face one presents to the world, and *honne,* one's true feelings, provides the individual with an inner autonomy not allowed in group activities.[43]

The internal unity of the Japanese group is further bolstered by cultivating feelings of external threat. Japanese groups tend to overdramatize the competition of outside groups and to see themselves as surrounded by a hostile environment. This sense of rivalry and competition with outside groups is used to spur greater efforts and dedication to group objectives. Americans are often amazed at the Japanese worker's diligence on the job and his enthusiasm for striving to improve his performance. While recent survey evidence points to a decline in commitment to work and company loyalty among the young, dedication to one's company and work group are still very high by Western standards. Thus, not only is absenteeism not a problem in Japan,

---

[42] Akira Kubota, "Japanese Employment System and Japanese Social Structure," *Asian Thought and Society* 8 (March–July 1983), p. 55.
[43] Nakamura, op. cit., pp. 407–413.

but also workers often voluntarily return to their companies
part of their paid annual leave. For example, the Labor Ministry's 1981 report indicated that Japanese workers as a whole used
only 55 percent of their paid vacation leave, choosing to stay on
the job and lend their energies to the performance of their work
groups, even when they were not required to do so.[44]

As in the case of personalism, a second cluster of contemporary
social norms has been identified that can be traced to Japan's
cultural tradition — strong group identification and loyalty, an
emphasis on group harmony and conflict avoidance, a preoccupation with human relations and feelings, self-sacrifice and diligence to achieve group goals, collective rewards and shared responsibility, consensual decision making, conformity, intolerance
of those who deviate from group norms and expectations, and
the outward projection of rivalry and hostility toward competing
outside groups. The term holism has been used as an umbrella
label to represent this set of cultural norms. Holism has been
preferred to the more familiar term collectivism, because the
latter concept has typically been applied to Communist states
where not only are the demands of the group given precedence
over individual goals, but also there is only one power center.
In contrast, Japanese society is pluralistic rather than monistic,
being characterized by a plurality of highly cohesive and often
fiercely competitive groups. Indeed, it could be argued that Japanese holism is based on pluralism, since competition with other
similar kinds of groups (one neighboring village versus another,
Waseda versus Keio Universities, Toyota versus Nissan) is an
essential ingredient in reinforcing a sense of group unity and
mobilizing group energies to achieve group goals.

As in the case of personalism, some elements in this set of
holistic norms have been declining in salience faster than others,
and undoubtedly all of them have experienced some change over
the postwar period. Individualistic norms, which were implanted
by the Occupation authorities in the Japanese education system,
have been spreading throughout Japanese society and are increasingly competing with holistic norms. Growing evidence of
a decline in loyalty to and identification with the group and a

---

[44] Herbert Passin, "Changing Values: Work and Growth in Japan," *Asian
Survey* 15 (October 1975), pp. 821–850; *Parade Magazine*, 10/21/82, p. 10.

decrease in the absorption of time and energies in group activities is being reported, especially among the young. These trends will undoubtedly continue. Still, the role played by these holistic norms in Japan even today is much greater than what is typically found in the West.

Moreover, the continuing influence of these holistic norms across the postwar period has had a number of visible impacts on Japanese society. The greater stress on seniority versus merit in promotion up the career ladder has made Japan a gerontocracy. For example, in 1982 the average age of the presidents of Japan's 2,443 largest companies was 63, and the average age of the 16 postwar prime ministers (Shidehara through Nakasone) at the time of their inauguration was 65. At the same time, the emphasis on minimizing distinctions within the group to maximize the sense of unity has led to a more egalitarian distribution of income. The income gap between the highest and lowest one-fifth of the population in Japan is only 60 percent of what it is in the United States.[45]

An aspect of holism particularly paradoxical to someone from a Western country is that a culture which stresses harmony and conflict avoidance and provides group members with a great sense of security could at the same time create such a competitive spirit. For example, Western theories of management suggest that a system based on promotion by seniority and guaranteed lifetime employment would breed worker laziness and inefficiency. But in Japan, it is the importance of the group — gaining admission to the right group and maintaining one's good standing within the group — that stimulates a high need for achievement. One Japanese commentator, writing about his own age cohort of middle-class salarymen who are now in their thirties, observes that his generation is obsessed with a sense of competition in whatever they do.[46] First, there is the intense competition to get into the best schools and ultimately the best universities, labeled aptly as Japan's "examination hell." This academic competition is aimed at securing a position with one of Japan's leading companies or institutions. After employment, there are constant

[45] *The Japan Times Weekly*, 2/19/83, p. 5; Christopher, op. cit., p. 142.
[46] Kato Hitoshi, "Japan's First Postwar Generation," *Japan Echo* 10 (Spring 1983), pp. 80–82.

admonitions and reminders that one's group or organization is competing with some other group or groups and that one must constantly try to improve one's performance simply to keep pace in the race.

This competitive drive is not motivated simply by personal ambition. It is also stimulated by the expectations of one's group — one's family, school, or work group. There is always someone there exhorting the individual to greater efforts. For children it is often the "education mama," the mother that is so concerned about her child's performance that she will attend his classes to take notes for him when he is sick. Extreme cases of mothers stealing exams for their children have even been reported. For the worker, it is often his supervisor or company president. But it is not for an individual that the Japanese performs, but for the honor and glory of the group, for the standing of that group in society is intimately associated with his or her own self-esteem. The results of this keen sense of competition are a matter of record. Japanese students have scored higher than those in any other country on several cross-national measures of academic achievement, and a number of Japanese companies have achieved quality control standards unsurpassed throughout the world. At the same time, competition among companies within the same industry has at time encouraged ruthless, almost self-destructive practices. The drive within each group to become "number one" has led Japanese companies to measure success, not in terms of profits, but in terms of a quest for an ever-increasing market share, sometimes even at the expense of profits.[47]

As this discussion of competition suggests, the emphasis in Japanese culture on group harmony and conflict avoidance does not mean that conflict has been successfully expunged from Japanese society, but only that it takes other forms than typically found in the West. In most face-to-face groups, individualistic competition and conflict are discouraged. But the myth of internal unity is bought at the expense of promoting the myth of external war. The more emphasis placed on preserving harmony within the group, the greater the difficulty in effectively cooperating with outside groups. Small group cohesion can even lead to dysfunctional factionalism within large organizations, such as companies,

47 *Time*, 8/1/83, pp. 38–41, 66; Christopher, op. cit., pp. 79–80.

bureaucracies, and political parties. But as a rule, the larger the groups involved and the higher the level of organization, the more intergroup relations will be removed from the constraints of interpersonal pressures for achieving harmony and consensus. The greater the affective distance between the groups which are engaged in any conflict situation, the greater the likelihood that the conflict will move into the anomic domain where conflict may be unrestrained. It is therefore likely that conflict will be greatest among large interest groups and organizations operating at the national level.[48]

Another byproduct of the holistic norms of group harmony and conflict avoidance is that the greater the emphasis placed on maintaining group unity in normal relations, the more intense an internal conflict will be when it finally does erupt. Such overt disruptions of the group associated with open intragroup conflict tend to be short-lived but are often extremely emotional and occasionally may even break down into irrational violence. Because such overt demonstrations of internal conflict are so costly to all parties concerned and leave deep scars, they are avoided wherever posible. In the Japanese context, a resort to confrontation tactics within the group signals that one has already lost the game and may in fact precipitate one's defection or expulsion from the group.[49] Thus conflict and competition within the group is often disguised and played out in subtle ways hidden to an outside observer.

To the Western mind, Japan's holistic norms may exert too great a price in terms of the sacrifice of individual autonomy and the intolerance of nonconformity. Japanese society provides the individual with great security and acceptance, but only if one is willing and able to fit in. However, while the individual costs may seem high, the social benefits are great. Despite its very rapid pace of urbanization and socioeconomic transformation over the past thirty to forty years, Japan has not experienced some of the negative, destabilizing side effects of advanced industrialism to the same degree as many Western societies have. For example, levels of alienation and social dislocation have

---

[48] Ellis Krauss, "Japan a Land of Harmony — and Hostility," *The Japan Times Weekly*, 7/2/83, p. 4.

[49] Christopher, op. cit., pp. 54, 114.

been low — there are few ghettos of human cast-offs, drifters and the chronically unemployed. The rate of crime and other kinds of antisocial behavior has been far lower than that found in North America and Western Europe. At the same time, Japan's holistic norms are associated with low work absenteeism, high quality control levels, and shorter, less damaging strikes. Finally, the influence of these norms can be seen in the high levels of continuity and stability found in all kinds of groups in Japan from the neighborhood, to the business community, to politics.

Dependency. There are two other important behavioral patterns which do not fall neatly into either the personalism or holism clusters of social norms. These two subsidiary patterns, dependency and fatalism, are associated with both of our major dimensions of cultural differentiation. For example, the first of these, dependency, reinforces both the psychological preference for vertical patron-client relationships and the individual's attachment to his group.

Takeo Doi mantained that Japanese child-rearing practices develop a heightened need for *amae* — the desire to receive love passively and to be indulged and pampered, as when a child snuggles up to his mother or suckles her breast.[50] As the theory goes, the indulgent, nondisciplinary behavior of Japanese mothers towards their children coupled with a great deal of physical contact and proximity develops an intense dependence in the children on their mothers. Japanese mothers avoid physical separation from their infants, lie down with them when they go to sleep, carry them on their backs, and feed them or otherwise attend to them whenever they cry. To a large degree, these children are not forced to handle emotional problems by themselves, and as they mature to adults, the feeling of dependency on others for emotional support is prolonged and diffused. As a result, Japanese tend not to develop "an emotional independence from 'meaningful' others," but rather continue to seek the warmth and security of a parent-child relationship even as adults.[51] In contrast, American mothers allow their children to cry themselves to sleep

[50] Takeo Doi, *The Anatomy of Dependence* (Tokyo: Kodansha International, 1973).
[51] Befu, op. cit., pp. 151–169.

and instead of being solicitous of demanding and disobedient children, approach child rearing as a confrontation of wills in which, inevitably, the child generally loses. The American mother, then, is a source of anxiety and threat as well as security and love. Thus as the American child matures, he develops a strong desire for autonomy and independence.

It is clear to see how the psychological need for *amae* translates into a desire to establish intimate dependency relationships with superiors and other benefactors. The Japanese seem to derive great emotional satisfaction from placing themselves fully in the care of others, whether it be a host, a masseuse, or a former teacher. In these relationships, the Japanese prefer to remain passive participants who are carried along in a comfortable emotional environment without having to do or decide anything by themselves. Whereas Americans are likely to find dependency relationships very distasteful, Japanese are more likely to find them immensely satisfying, as long as the dependency is mixed with warmth and sympathy which make them feel that the superior partner in the relationship has a genuine concern for their well-being.

The *amae* phenomenon also reinforces holistic norms and an individual's attachment to his or her group. Group members not only indulge each other by the often burdensome and time-consuming favors and services they exchange. They also permit a member in intimate group contexts to indulge in childish, vulgar, rude, and other unconventional forms of behavior that would be unacceptable in any other setting. This form of what Lebra calls social nudity reassures the individual that one is accepted and loved regardless of whatever personal shortcomings or inadequacies one may display.[52] Thus the psychological rewards of suppressing personal aspirations and adjusting to group expectations are great in that they ensure one's continued good standing in and ability to rely upon the group.

The Invisible Leader. The style of leadership in Japan is strongly affected by what might be called the Japanese variant of fatalism. In the earlier discussion of personalism, it was noted that there are a number of ambiguities in Japanese authority

---

[52] Lebra, op. cit., pp. 116–117.

relations. Despite the strong emphasis on hierarchy and deferential formalities, decision-making authority is not necessarily lodged at the top of the hierarchy. In fact, unilateral decisions made by a leader without consulting the group are likely to be resisted as illegitimate. For instance, in the survey of Japanese and American workers, 52 percent of the Japanese workers, compared to only 12 percent of the Americans, felt that supervisors in deciding upon promotions should first secure the agreement of all subordinates who would be affected by the decision and/or the agreement of the union.[53] Since broad consultation and consensual agreement are a vital part of the Japanese decision-making process, the ability of Japanese leaders to originate ideas and implement them is severely constrained; in fact, in the Japanese decision-making process, the authorship of decisions is obscured. From a Western perspective, if one cannot locate the originator of an idea or the driving force behind it, the leader remains hidden, invisible.

Holistic cultural norms also contribute to the invisible leader phenomenon by promoting a lack of awareness of the individual's personal role and responsibility in the decision-making process. The dependency on the group, the emphasis on harmony and unity, and the repression of individual opinions and interests in the consensus-building process — all obscure an awareness of individual choice or a sense of responsibility for one's actions and decisions. As a result, even today many Japanese tend to view things as happening to them rather than seeing things as occurring as a result of their own conscious actions. The continuing influence of this fatalistic outlook on life is found even among the young. For instance, in the 1977–78 World Youth Surveys, 44 percent of the Japanese youth compared to only 9 percent of American youth listed "luck or fate" as the first or second most important factor for becoming successful.[54]

Kinhide Mushakoji's distinction between *erabi* cultures (cultures that choose) and *awase* cultures (cultures that adjust) gets to the heart of the cultural distinction addressed here.[55] In America we tend to pose every situation in terms of a choice

[53] Whitehill and Takezawa, op. cit., pp. 304–310.
[54] Youth Bureau, op. cit., pp. 46–47.
[55] Mushakoji, op. cit., pp. 282–292; Doi, op. cit., pp. 12–13.

even when the situation allows no real choice or the choice is a foregone conclusion. Herein we find a decision-making strategy. In America, the advocate of a particular policy option will win if he can successfully present all the alternatives to his preferred course of action in highly unattractive and unacceptable terms, so that there remains, in fact, only the illusion of choice. In Japan we find the opposite tendency, that is a cultural propensity to deny the existence of choice. The control of events is not in the hands of individuals, but rather in larger forces that they must bend and flow with. The advocate of a policy option in Japan, then, is likely to win to the extent that his personal preference remains obscure and he is successful in depicting his desired outcome as emerging inevitably from the natural flow of events.

This disregard of the human actor in Japanese culture is reflected in the language itself. In the Japanese sentence, a subject is rarely included, an omission that is frequently the source of a great deal of confusion to Westerners. The fact that the active, doing subject is only implied, rather than explicitly stated, is a measure of just how important the human agent is felt to be in the train of events that compose history. Indeed, when a doer becomes visible in Japanese society, his very visibility is likely to stir up resentment and opposition. It has been noted, for instance, that in a typical Japanese meeting if one were to report, "(implied I or We) *did* thus and so" (*ko shimashita*), numerous questions would immediately be raised and the meetings would be thrown into confusion or become bogged down in endless discussion. If, however, one were to express the same point in the form, "*Things came about* in thus and such a fashion" (*ko narimashita*), the meeting would proceed smoothly, without dissension or discord.[56] As long as events are perceived as flowing naturally and inevitably of their own accord, there is a feeling that things have been handled properly. But when an actor becomes visible, and particularly when his will becomes visible, his very interjection into the process conveys the distinct impression that something has been done arbitrarily or capriciously.

[56] Shinichiro Nakamura, "The Unending Nightmare," *The Japan Interpreter* 8 (Winter (1974), pp. 525–531.

The effective actor in Japanese society is the selfless arbitrator between conflicting interests and opinions, the messenger and negotiator who, in a flurry of activity, smooths away all disputes, differences, and injured feelings, all the while maintaining a pure detachment and neutrality. It should be noted that, from the Western perspective, he does not really *do* anything. He only adjusts and connects (*awaseru*). He adds no new or dramatic elements that might, for instance, attempt to resolve the issue by changing the power equation. His role is not to find new solutions, but to seek accommodation among old ones, and this privately, behind the scenes so that the dispute can be contained as much as possible. Hence the leader in Japan remains invisible.

CONCLUSION

In this chapter, Japan's cultural tradition has been depicted as differing markedly from that of the West. These differences, combined with the relative recency of Japan's modernization, have produced a contemporary cultural context that is far more personalistic and holistic than that found in most Western countries. A large cluster of social norms and behavioral tendencies directly and indirectly associated with these two major dimensions of cultural differentiation have been identified. This chapter has stressed the continuities in traditional values, while at the same time noting that their contemporary expression does not mirror that found in feudal Japan either in form or in relative emphasis. Thus some norms, such as the degree of commitment to the group, have been declining. In contrast, others, such as a preference for face-to-face, diffuse relationships or consensual forms of decision making aimed at preserving group harmony, exhibit few signs of decay. Moreover, a shift in the relative emphasis given to some traditional norms constitutes an important form of change in itself. Thus the decline in the relative emphasis placed on hierarchy has brought the egalitarian values implict in Japan's traditional holistic norms more strongly to the forefront. Despite this continuing pattern of adaptation and change, Japanese culture today represents a configuration of value and behavior patterns that remain quite distinct from those found in Western societies.

The preceding description of contemporary Japanese society presents the orthodox view of Japanese culture shared by most

Japanese and Western observers. There is an alternate view, however, advocated by many Japanese Marxist and other left-leaning scholars. According to their views, the orthodox interpretation is simply a myth propagated by Japan's economic and political elites for both internal and external consumption purposes. These writers argue that Japanese elites have found it advantageous to push the image of Japan's uniqueness abroad to ward off Western criticism. The more Japan is viewed as different, the less it will have to abide by Western rules of negotiation and fair play. At home, the advantages of selling the view that Japanese society is an integrated, harmonious whole are obvious for a ruling class bent on maintaining its domination.[57]

Whether or not we accept a class conspiracy theory of the origins of the orthodox interpretation of Japanese culture, this revisionist perspective does offer several useful insights. Some advocates of the orthodox perspective have painted a rather extreme view of Japanese society as one that is virtually conflict free and dominated by vertical loyalties to benevolent, warm-hearted elites. Such descriptions are clearly a distortion for which the revisionist emphasis on highlighting both past and present examples of conflict, brutality, and class struggle is an important corrective. As we have pointed out, conflict is not missing from Japanese society, it simply assumes somewhat different expressions than typically found in the West. In addition, the revisionist view emphasizes the distinction between culture as norms and culture as behavior. For example, the norm of group unity and internal harmony may well be an accepted ideal towards which all groups strive, but it is just that, an ideal. As in Western society, some cherished norms are honored more in the breach.

Finally, the revisionist view stresses important subcultural variations. Any set of dominant social norms are likely to be held most strongly by those groups and classes who benefit most from them. For example, it has been estimated that only about a quarter of the Japanese labor force, an elite class of blue and white collar workers, are involved in the lifetime employment system at any one time. For those workers who experience few company fringe benefits, low wages, and little job security, it can be expected that their loyalty to their companies will be corre-

[57] Sugimoto and Mouer, op. cit., pp. 7–29.

spondingly weaker. Indeed, there have always been important subcultural differences in Japan, and traditional values, such as those exemplified by the warrior code (*Bushido*), have consistently been more fully diffused among Japan's middle classes than its lower classes.

CHAPTER 5

Political Culture I:
Continuities in Mass
and Elite Behavior

IT HAS BEEN ESTABLISHED that Japan's cultural foundations differed markedly from those found in the West and that contemporary behavior patterns still reveal the strong imprint of Japan's personalistic and holistic tradition. But how does this discussion enhance our understanding of Japanese politics? Culture shapes not only social behavior but political behavior as well. At points in the above discussion of contemporary behavior patterns, such as the invisible leader phenomenon, the connections between culture and politics are clear. At other points, the linkages may not be immediately obvious to the reader. In this section, we will elaborate in more detail the ways in which personalistic and holistic cultural norms continue to pattern political behavior on both the mass and elite levels.

At the outset, it is best to clarify the linkage between culture and behavior that will be discussed. Many social scientists studying Japan today prefer to exclude cultural explanations from their analyses because culture has been overused and misused in the past as an undifferentiated, residual category to explain nearly everything in Japan that differed from Western practice. In reality, all of behavior is overdetermined in the sense that there are multiple causes, any one of which may appear to explain the phenomenon at hand. By stressing one factor alone,

* Scott C. Flanagan

one is likely to fall into the trap of reductionism, or at least appear to do so. It should be emphasized that the point is *not* that culture causally determines the various behavior patterns and tendencies to be discussed. The point is that culture conditions behavior.

For instance, in Chapter 3 it was noted that there were a number of instrumental functions that party factions perform in Japan. The existence of party factions, then, can be explained without recourse to cultural factors. Moreover, the organizational expression of party factions in Japan in the postwar period, and especially after 1960, cannot be found in the prewar period. Present-day party factions are not mirrored expressions of ancient practices but are in many ways new political expressions adapted to the conditions of Japan's contemporary political context. Finally, cultural explanations cannot account for why alternate forms of informal party organization that were also compatible with Japan's personalistic norms did not develop.

Culture conditions behavior by providing certain resources that may be drawn upon as a new problem emerges and by setting certain limits on what kinds of solutions to the problem will be compatible with social sensibilities and expectations. As the environment changes, new institutions and practices are called forth to meet new needs. Such institutions and practices represent true innovations that do not duplicate traditional practices but rather emerge as an amalgam of traditional elements adjusted to modern structural requirements and situational exigencies. In addition to the party faction, another example of a modern institution that arose as a result of such a creative amalgam is the lifetime employment system. The pattern of permanent employment in large-scale enterprises was not introduced in Japan until the World War I period. This new pattern met a number of pragmatic needs, such as the need for a skilled, stable work force in the context of a tight labor market. The lifetime employment system emerged as one possible solution to these labor market problems. At the same time, the form this particular solution assumed drew heavily upon norms and structures that had been operative in earlier periods.[1]

---

[1] Robert E. Cole, *Work, Mobility and Participation: A Comparative Study of American and Japanese Industry* (Berkeley: University of California Press, 1979), pp. 22–25; Koji Taira, "The Labor Market in Japanese Development," *British Journal of Industrial Relations* 2 (July 1964).

Culture both constrains the range of choice in seeking a solution to a new problem and provides certain societal resources that may be manipulated to fashion the solution. Cultural and structural explanations, therefore, should not be viewed as antagonistic but rather as reinforcing. For example, one can explain the Japanese worker's dependency on and loyalty to one's company in terms of certain structural practices, such as the seniority system and a system of extensive, almost paternalistic, fringe benefits. However, *amae* and other traditional personalistic and holistic cultural norms not only are compatible with such practices but also were drawn upon to gain their acceptance and wide diffusion.[2]

In tracing the linkages between culture and behavior in one cultural tradition as contrasted with another, it is clear that no culture provides optimal solutions to the problems of economic and political behavior in large complex societies. Rather, different cultures provide different answers that simply represent different mixes of strengths and weaknesses. For example, individualism and legalistic, rationalistic modes of thinking, that have been stressed in Western cultures, have contributed to the creation of new concepts and ideas and the discovery of new techniques and procedures. But these same modes of thinking have often impeded the broad acceptance and diffusion of these new discoveries. In the Western dichotomous, Aristotelian logic, things are viewed as being either A or non-A. Thus, if a new idea is not logically compatible with an old one, the old must be rejected before the new can be accepted. Hence the heresy trials and the extended, bitter battles between the church and science that impeded the advance of Western nations out of the dark ages.

In the Japanese case, it has been argued that the emphasis on consensual decision making and conformity to the group has stifled creativity and the discovery of new ideas.[3] On the other hand, the Japanese throughout their history have demonstrated a remarkable talent for importing and assimilating new ideas, in part because of the high tolerance for ambiguity in Japanese modes of thinking. By rejecting Western dichotomous reasoning

[2] Cole, op. cit., pp. 245–249.

[3] Heisuke Hironaka, "Traits That Foster Basic Research," *Japan Echo* 10 (Spring 1983), p. 77; Takemochi Ishii, "Curiosity Nurtured by Seclusion," *Japan Echo* 10 (Summer 1983), pp. 79–84.

and allowing that something may be both A and non-A at the same time, the Japanese mind can accommodate many diverse elements that are seemingly logically incompatible.[4] This capacity has meant that innovations have not challenged cherished traditions in the same way as they have in the West, and so have met with less resistance. Moreover, once the practical advantages of a new idea have been demonstrated, the holistic drive to keep in step with one's group and one step ahead of every other group, has spurred the rapid diffusion of new technologies.

Different cultural traditions, therefore, provide different resources and strengths. Some have argued, however, that the particular set of resources provided by the Japanese cultural tradition is more suited to harnessing economic energies than political energies. Akira Kubota noted that if we use Western societies as a point of reference, Communist states have demonstrated a higher capacity to mobilize political energies and a lower capacity to stimulate economic energies. In comparison, Japanese society has exhibited the opposite pattern of capabilities for harnessing collective energies, higher than the West in the economic realm and lower in the political realm.[5] Other observers have argued that in the international arena, the Japanese have become economic giants, but as yet are political pygmies.[6] However, Kubota's point is not directed at politics and the political system as a whole, but rather at the input side of the system. He is referring to certain residual "feudalistic and paternalistic" practices that inhibit mass involvement in politics. Other observers have focused on a number of other deficiencies in Japan's input institutions and processes including the corrupting role of "money power" in Japanese elec-

[4] Masao Kunihiro compares Western Aristotelian logic with the "oriental tetralemma" which allows four possibilities: (1) something may be A; (2) it is non-A; (3) it is both A and non-A; and (4) it is neither A nor non-A. In Western thinking, if A is good, then non-A is bad, and the something in question must be identified as being one or the other. The Western mind is less comfortable than the Japanese with perceiving something as being both good and bad at once, or as being neither good nor bad. Kunihiro, *Nucleus* 27 (March 1974), pp. 22–28.

[5] Akira Kubota, "Japanese Employment System and Japanese Social Structure," *Asian Thought and Society* 8 (March-July 1983) pp. 68–69.

[6] For more information on this subject, *see* Robert A. Scalapino, "Foreign Policy of Modern Japan," in Roy C. Macridis, ed., *Foreign Policy in World Politics* 5th Edition (Englewood Cliffs, NJ: Prentice Hall, 1976).

tions, the high incidence of election law violations, and the low respect and support for Japan's elected political leaders.

In contrast to the critical evaluations often directed at certain aspects of Japan's input processes, the decision-making and output components of the system have more typically drawn praise in recent years. One reason for these contrasting evaluations of differing aspects of the Japanese political system may be found in the contrasting impact of culture on different parts of the political process. In the areas of policy planning and implementation, Japan's personalistic and holistic norms have clearly served as sources of great strength. While Japanese groups often seem locked in factional bickering and rivalry against out-groups, they also display a unique capacity "to transcend the in-group for the benefit of the 'larger we.' "[7] In the context of an outside threat, Japanese groups seem to be able to transfer the intense loyalty and dedication of purpose displayed within the in-group to ever-broadening group boundaries that build up pyramidally until, if the threat is foreign, the entire nation is combined into one "we Japanese" group. This ability to act as a unified state, if only temporarily, can be seen in the national response to the OPEC "oil shocks," the preparations for the summer and winter Olympics held in Japan, and the unusual success in implementing pollution-control measures once consensus was reached on the issue.[8] These behavioral tendencies provide the Japanese polity with enormous strength and stability which have likely given it a competitive edge in the international marketplace.

The Japanese appear to be unusually adept at targeting a problem, planning for future exigencies, and mobilizing mass energies for a concerted attack on it. In the few short years following the first oil shock in the fall of 1973, the Japanese implemented what has been judged the most coherent and effective energy program in the world. As a result, Japan weathered the second oil shock in 1979 far better than any of the Western industrial democracies. More recently, the Japanese have recognized that with the spread of industry to third world countries where labor costs are lower, in time they will be unable to compete in many of the traditional

[7] Lawrence W. Beer, "Group Rights and Individual Rights in Japan," *Asian Survey* 21 (April 1981), pp. 444–445.

[8] Robert C. Christopher, *The Japanese Mind: The Goliath Explained* (New York: Linden Press, 1983), pp. 236–237.

mainstays of their economy, such as steel and shipbulding. As a consequence, Japanese planners have decided to focus the nation's energies on dominating the high tech field, those knowledge industries in which the educational level of a population is the primary requisite for effective competition. By the early 1980s, the Japanese educational system was graduating in per capita terms roughly 1.7 times as many engineers as the American system, had caught up to the United States in the percentage of its GNP spent on research and development with plans soon to become the world leader in that area, and had launched the most comprehensive program to build the computer of the future, the so-called fifth generation computer.[9]

Many of these kinds of strengths will become evident in later sections of this book, where the policy process, system outputs, and performance are discussed. This chapter will focus on a number of apparent weaknesses in the Japanese system, and particularly those that may appear somewhat unusual or unexpected to the American student because they are, at least in part, associated with Japan's distinct cultural tradition. The purpose of this chapter is not to show that the Japanese political system is somehow more flawed than some other systems, but that the areas of strength and weakness and the sources of those strengths and weaknesses are different.

As noted above, many of the areas of weakness in the Japanese political system are associated with its input processes and those institutions unique to democracies. This should not be surprising as it is the input structures and the institution of competitive parties and parliaments that distinguish democracies from authoritarian systems. While Japan is an old state, it is a relatively new democracy. Thus the newness of Japan's postwar democratic institutions has meant that a political culture formed under an authoritarian tradition has had little time to adapt. Following the Meiji Restoration, the Japanese political structure was transformed from an authoritarian, feudal political structure under the Shoguns, to an oligarchic constitutional monarchy with limited democratic trappings from 1889 to 1945, and finally to a fully democratic political structure in the postwar period. Clearly

[9] *Time,* Special Issue — Japan: A Nation in Search of Itself, 8/1/83, pp. 43, 56–57.

the political attitudes and behaviors that are appropriate for each of these three types of political structures are very different. The role of the citizens in the Tokugawa or Meiji periods did little to prepare them for the role the Occupation reformers expected them to assume under the MacArthur Constitution.

It is not only the newness of Japan's democratic institutions but the manner in which they were introduced that has affected the adjustment and adaptation of the Japanese political culture to those institutions. Many traditional norms associated with Western feudal societies were also undemocratic or even antidemocratic and ill prepared the peasant to assume the role of participant in a democratic society. However, in most Western societies, those undemocratic norms were sharply challenged by new political forces associated with the modernization process, resulting in their eclipse by norms more compatible with democratic principles. In contrast, the major introductions of democratic institutions in Japan in 1889 and 1946 were largely uncontested. The first was the gift of a modernizing oligarchy designed to enhance Japan's image abroad, and the second was a forced conversion by a foreign occupying power. Because the adoption of democratic institutions was not the result of a social revolution that required the mobilization and resocialization of large social strata to achieve success, the development of a democratic form of government in Japan did not entail a conscious rejection of those traditional norms that were incompatible with democratic principles.

The Japanese Constitution of 1889 was not wrested from the Meiji oligarchs by a rising bourgeois class. Rather the urban entrepreneurial interests grew up under the tutelage of the traditional social-political elites. While the business class was still in its infancy, the special privileges of the warrior aristocracy were abolished by its own representatives. Moreover, the oligarchs' ambitious economic development programs and special subsidies and benefits for business greatly reduced the need for the bourgeois class to mobilize to win new rights from the old aristocracy. Indeed, in the context of foreign threats and the extraterritoral treaties, the self-assertion of group or class interests was seen as illegitimate. Because business, professional, and other bourgeois groups had not fought to achieve representation and structural reform, they remained uncommitted and unconvinced democrats. This ambivalence was reinforced during the 1920s when the working class initially began to mobilize. The result was that all serious prewar attempts at reform were shelved except for the Universal Male Suffrage Act of 1925. Even this measure was coupled with an instrument of repression, the Peace Preservation Law, which ensured that the extension of the suffrage did not effectively incorporate any new social group interests.

The second incorporation came with the American-made Mac-Arthur Constitution of 1946 and was even more uncontested than the first. As noted in Chapter 1, worker and tenant organizations remained weak and ineffective throughout the prewar period; hence they were in no way responsible for the postwar reforms. Working class organizations, however, have strongly defended the postwar constitution. Thus there has been a recognition, after the fact, among elements of some lower and middle occupational strata that a number of the postwar gains that they have made are tied to the political rule changes. This is an important plus for Japan's political development, and yet many traditional norms which weaken the accountability of Japan's democratic institutions continued into the postwar period because the democratic reforms had not depended on the conscious rejection of those norms.

The argument here, then, is that the incomplete diffusion in Japan of cultural norms appropriate for democratic structures can be attributed not only to the relative newness of its democratic institutions but also to the manner in which those institutions were introduced. Because the major introductions of democratic rules incorporating broader segments of the populace into the political process were largely uncontested, there were no sharp societal conflicts between in-groups and out-groups, the privileged and the excluded. Without this kind of direct challenge, traditional submissive, conformist, and fatalistic orientations towards politics will not begin to be questioned and modified, and the development of modern, democratic norms will be slowed.[10]

Culture, of course, is not static. Thus we are referring to a temporary phenomenon, not a permanent one. Those residual

[10] Scott C. Flanagan, "The Genesis of Variant Political Cultures: The Origins of Contemporary Citizen Orientations in Japan, America, Britain and Italy," in Sidney Verba and Lucian Pye, eds., *The Citizen and Politics: A Comparative Analysis* (Stamford, Conn.: Greylock, 1978), pp. 129–165.

traditional norms and behavior patterns that are out of phase or inconsistent with Japan's postwar political structure can be expected to be modified and adapted over time. Indeed, there is already much evidence that a considerable amount of attitude change in these areas has taken place during the postwar period. The pattern of change has been uneven, however, in the sense that it has affected some sectors of Japanese society more than others. The next chapter will show that the young, urban, highly educated, and those employed in the more modern sectors of the economy (the new middle class and workers in large factories) are far more likely to evince modern, democratic, participatory attitudes than the old, rural, low in education, and those engaged in the more traditional sectors of the economy (farmers, small retailers, and workers in small enterprises). Moreover, in some areas it is the unevenness of attitude change — the persistence of old values among some elements of the population and the adoption of new kinds of value orientations by other segments — that has intensified the adjustment problem.

The evidence of incompatibilities between Japan's traditional cultural norms and her new democratic institutions was most apparent in the early postwar years. At that time, a number of intellectuals were greatly concerned over the feudalistic attitudes that prevailed and that prolonged undemocratic practices despite Japan's new political structure. One Japanese commentator, for instance, wrote that Japan "is undergoing a democratization process that is unnatural and totally lacking in internal spontaneity," that "popular attitudes and popular ethical norms of behavior and judgment are neither modern nor democratic," and that "a complete reorientation of the people's ethical outlook is the only way by which Japan can achieve the results that 'evolved' in Europe." [11] Japan has now had over thirty-five years to adapt to the democratic institutions put in place by the Occupation. If the adaptations have not always been precisely as envisioned by the American authors of the constitution, they have nevertheless been effective. Clearly when viewed from most perspectives — stability, prosperity, distribution, regulation — the Japanese political system must be given high marks in perfor-

---

[11] Hisao Otsuka, "The Formation of Modern Man: The Popular Base for Democratization," *The Japan Interpreter* 6 (Spring 1970), p. 2.

mance. Yet some nagging weaknesses remain which suggest that while Japan's economic development has soared ahead, her political development, in some respects, has lagged behind.

There are, then, still a few problem areas regarding Japan's political development. In most cases, these problems or the particular form they have assumed in Japan today can be traced to the impact on political behavior of the cultural heritage of personalism and holism. In this chapter, then, the focus is on the persistence of the old, traditional values that remain among substantial portions of the population and the implications that these traditional value orientations have for political behavior. In addition, in tracing the linkages between traditional cultural norms and contemporary political behavior, the negative will be stressed — those areas where cultural norms inhibit appropriate patterns of democratic behavior and performance, at least when judged from an American perspective. As already noted, there is also a very strong plus side of the impact of Japan's cultural heritage on political system performance. Moreover, even in the problem areas that will be touched upon, there are many promising signs of adaptations and change in progress. Finally, it must be kept in mind that the behavior patterns under discussion in this chapter are not characteristic of the entire population. New kinds of attitudes and behaviors that are found among the more modern sectors of Japanese society will be discussed in the next chapter.

PERSONALISM IN POLITICS

In the previous discussion of particularism and social relativism in Japanese culture, it was shown that because traditional Japanese thought was largely devoid of universal truths and inviolable laws, the Japanese have not tended to think in terms of abstract principles or ideologies. Among those segments of the Japanese population for whom personalistic norms continue to take precedence over universalistic norms in shaping their perceptions of national politics, voting is likely to be based more on the individual's relationship to the candidates or his assessment of the candidates' personalities and attributes than on party labels, issues, or ideologies. National opinion surveys held in conjunction with Japan's general elections over the postwar period reveal that until the 1970s even in national elections, more Japanese

TABLE 5.1.   *Voting on the Basis of Party or Personality in Lower House Elections*

Year	Party	Personality	Both	DK	N
1958	32	45	10	13	2157
1960	33	43	19	5	2228
1963	31	51	14	3	2107
1967	37	47	11	4	2163
1972	48	38	12	2	2151
1976	46	40	12	2	2048
1979	41	46	12	1	2003
1980	49	38	11	1	2112

Source: See footnote 12.

voters based their decisions on candidate personalities than on party affiliations (see Table 5.1).[12] Considering that Japan has a parliamentary rather than a presidential system and that strict party discipline is maintained in parliamentary voting, selecting candidates on the basis of personalities rather than parties and platforms makes much less sense in Japan than in the United States. In Japan the issues separating the parties are substantial. In addition, the candidate's individual issue preferences will not affect the way he votes in the Diet. The party will make those decisions for him. In the context of Japan's postwar parliamentary institutions and processes, therefore, a personalistic value orientation serves only to weaken the ability of elections to return to the people the power to determine the general policy directions of the government.

We do note, however, that there has been a trend since the early 1970s towards a heavier emphasis on party as a basis for

[12] The emphasis placed on personality increases with the lower the level of the election and the smaller the size of the election district (see Chapter 6). The findings reported in Table 5.1 are from the reports of the Kommei Senkyo Renmei (reorganized into the Akarui Senkyo Suishin Kyokai in 1976), which has conducted election surveys on national and local elections in Japan and published reports on its findings for each election since the late 1950s. The 1979 election report is published as *Shugiin Giin Sosenkyo no Jittai, Vol. 1, Genshiryo, Vol. 2, Chosa no Gaiyo* (Tokyo: Akarui Senkyo Suishin Kyokai, 1980). Many of these fiindings are cited in Bradley M. Richardson, *The Political Culture of Japan* (Berkeley: University of California Press, 1974).

making one's voting decision. This trend is particularly noteworthy among the supporters of the opposition parties, especially those supporters of the Communist, Clean Government, and Socialist parties. The emphasis on party label is also strong among the young, the highly educated, the urbanized, managerial employees, and males. In contrast, there is still a pronounced orientation towards candidates and personalities among the old, the rural, those with low educational achievement, farmers, and women. This suggests that the orientation of the Japanese electorate towards politics is beginning to change as younger voters with more modern values are gradually replacing older voters with more traditional values. Still, a substantial proportion of the Japanese electorate continues to display a personalistic orientation towards politics.[13]

An identification with individual candidates rather than party labels makes sense only if the voter is more concerned about what a candidate can do for him personally or for his local area than about the major policy issues being decided in the Diet; in fact, this kind of parochialism goes hand in hand with particularism. Public opinion surveys show that a large segment of the Japanese populace, approaching roughly half of the electorate, continue to relate to politics primarily in terms of local issues and local concerns. For instance, in the 1976 JABISS study, 45 percent of the respondents reported that local politics, not prefectural, national,

[13] In a recent analysis, Thomas Rochon has demonstrated that perhaps the most important cause of the emphasis on candidate personality in Japanese voting is the electoral system that pits candidates of the same party against each other in many districts, and virtually forces the voters in those districts to make their choice on the basis of candidate names rather than party labels. Rochon concludes from his analysis that culture plays less of a role in promoting a personalistic vote choice than had been previously believed. Undoubtedly Rochon is right in identifying the important influence of structural factors in encouraging personalistic voting. However, it seems likely that culture has played some role in the adoption and continuation of an electoral system that emphasizes considerations of personality over party. Moreover, Rochon did find some support for the cultural hypothesis, and for methodological reasons too complicated to go into here, it appears that his analysis underestimates the strength of the cultural factor. See Thomas R. Rochon, "Electoral Systems and the Basis of the Vote: The Case of Japan," in John C. Campbell, *Parties, Candidates, and Voters in Japan*, Michigan Papers in Japanese Studies, No. 2 (Ann Arbor: University of Michigan Center for Japanese Studies, 1981), pp. 1–28; on personalism, see also Richardson, op. cit., pp. 102–127, 235.

or international politics, was the level of politics they were most interested in. In addition, by a ratio of over two to one, the respondents agreed that events in one's local area were more important than national events (see Table 5.2).

A parochial orientation describes not only one that highly values proximate and familiar objects, but also one that distrusts or disdains more distant ones. Table 5.2 reveals that length of residence is still an important criteria in the minds of many Japanese for election to local office. Other studies have noted the

TABLE 5.2. *Parochial Attitudes Among Japanese and American Respondents*

	Japan	U.S.
1. What level of politics are you most interested in?		
International politics	5	
National politics	41	—
Prefectural politics	8	
Local politics	45	
2. Events in the area one lives in are more important than national incidents such as the Lockheed scandal.		
Agree	46	
Can't say	33	—
Disagree	21	
3. It is better to give important posts in one's community to people who have lived there a long time rather than to newcomers.		
Agree	49	
Can't say	36	—
Disagree	15	
4. Would you say that most of the time people are helpful or that they are mostly just looking out for themselves?		
Try to be helpful	25	59
Look out for themselves	75	41
5. Do you think that most people would try to take advantage of you if they got the chance, or would they try to be fair?		
Take advantage	71	33
Try to be fair	29	67

Source: Questions 1–3 are taken from the 1976 JABISS study, and questions 4 and 5 from the 1980 NHK Cross-National Survey. The number of non-missing cases for these items ranged from over 1,300 to over 2,300. See note 14.

difficulty newcomers continue to encounter in being accepted by and gaining the confidence of local residents, particularly in rural areas, but also in some established urban residential areas as well. The comparative items reported in the table also demonstrate that the Japanese are much less trusting of people in general (as opposed to intimate friends and neighbors) than Americans.[14]

While the trust of the proximate has strengthened local, community-based organizations in Japan, the distrust of the distant and unfamiliar has impeded the horizontal mobilization of socioeconomic strata and interests. Since, as Nakane argues, the unit of organization in Japanese society is the frame, rather than common attributes, those people who share similar interests but are located in different communities or companies are likely to view each other as rivals rather than allies. The urban Japanese company has been called the "new village" in Japanese society, and this village consciousness has weakened the strength and effectiveness of nationally organized interests and peak associations, such as labor federations, consumer interests, and environmental groups. Only the government stands on top of society and can effectively integrate all groups vertically. The fact that the various strata and interests in Japanese society are personalistically fragmented and fenced off from each other in competing clusters has greatly enhanced state power and weakened reform movements. There may be outbreaks of violence by unions, students, or other radical groups, but these rarely touch the mass of society and often do not even stir to action other groups with similar interests.[15]

Parochialism translates into a local rather than a national political consciousness, an emphasis on special benefits for one's

[14] The JABISS Japanese Election Study is a nationwide panel survey conducted in 11/76–12/76 by J. Watanuki, B. Richardson, I. Miyake, S. Kohei, and S. Flanagan, containing data on 1,920 respondents on over 400 items. The NHK Cross-National Survey was conducted in 11/80–12/80 with 2,544 Japanese respondents and 1,680 American respondents by Shinsaku Kohei, Toyoko Akiyama, and their colleagues at the NHK Public Opinion Research Institute. The findings from this second study are reported in NHK Public Opinion Research Institute, ed., *Nihonjin to Amerikajin* (Tokyo: Nihon Hoso Shuppan Kyokai, 1982).

[15] Nakane, op. cit., pp. 87–103, 149–151; Richardson, op. cit., pp. 151–152, 234–235.

local area (*jimoto rieki*), and an inattention to the language and issues of debate over which national politics are being fought. Surveys have shown that Japanese citizens' level of identification with national political objects is unusually low for an advanced industrial society. It appears that many Japanese simply do not feel that politics lies within the domain of the average citizen. Very few Japanese derive any sense of pride either from their political institutions or from such political outputs as social legislation. Levels of strong party identification are comparatively very low and levels of nonidentifiers are very high. Moreover, images of national parties and party leaders are remarkably thin and, for many, largely nonexistent. While organizational memberships are high, Japanese tend to be less active in their organizations than Americans, and Japanese organizations are less likely to discuss political matters or involve themselves in community issues and problems.[16] Thus for many Japanese, politics, and particularly national politics, is not an activity that they either identify with or see themselves as appropriately participating in.

Politics is not only a somewhat distant, alien activity, but a difficult one as well for many Japanese citizens, among whom deferential attitudes are still quite prevalent. As noted in the last chapter, the volume of authority that a superior can exercise over an inferior has declined dramatically since the feudal period when a samurai could decapitate a commoner at will for the slightest display of disrespect. Still, as Ronald Dore observes, the taxi driver is likely to bow to the policeman. The greater the hierarchic distance in status, the weaker a subordinate is in his dealings with a superior. A lowly manual worker is not likely to

16 The data on pride come from the 1972 Japanese replication of the Civic Culture Study reported in Kikuo Nakamura, ed., *Gendai Nihon no Seiji Bunka* (Kyoto: Minerva Shobo, 1975); on the American Civic Culture from the revised 1974 edition of the ICPR Civic Culture Study codebook; on party identification from Scott C. Flanagan and Michael McDonald, "Party Identification as a Cross-National Concept: A Comparison of Japanese and American Identifiers," presented at the annual meeting of the American Political Science Association, September 1979; on organizational and political involvement from the cross-national Participation Project Study, in Sidney Verba and Norman H. Nie, *Participation in America* (New York: Harper and Row, 1972), and Hajime Ikeuchi, et al., *Shimin Ishiki no Kenkyu* (Tokyo: Tokyo University Press, 1974).

feel that he could openly and individually confront his company president. It is only in the context of collective unity that subordinates can impose their will on superiors. Dore argues that the continuing demand for overt deference to those in positions of authority is one of the reasons for the popularity of the mass demonstrations so characteristic of Japan's postwar annual spring labor struggles. These mass demonstrations, which are an expression of the solidarity of the subordinates, provide them with a rare context in which they can "breathe defiance at their superiors." [17]

As shown in Table 5.3, survey evidence demonstrates that deferential attitudes towards authority figures in the family and at the work place are still much more widespread in Japan than in America. This is significant because the socialization experience in these settings and the attitudes developed towards social and economic superiors strongly conditions one's attitudes towards political authority figures. Other evidence presented in Table 5.3 reflects the continued great emphasis in Japan that is placed on respect for parents, seniors, and all those in positions of authority. The last item in the table discloses that the great majority of Japanese feel that it is quite appropriate to delegate responsibility for politics to elected leaders rather than personally involving themselves in politics in any way.[18]

Since high status has traditionally been associated with the legitimate exercise of power, certain segments of Japanese society continue to take their cues from local notables who, together with the centers of power, are regarded as somewhat analogous to a legitimate ruling class. The persistence of deferential norms among some elements of Japanese society have slowed the widespread acceptance of those democratic norms necessary to enable the people to hold their elected leaders accountable for their actions. As in the case of other traditional norms, these deferential

[17] Ronald P. Dore, *Aspects of Social Change in Modern Japan* (Princeton: Princeton University Press, 1967) pp. 12–13.

[18] See note 14 on the JABISS study and note 16 on Civic Culture Studies. The 1973 NHK Japanese values study findings are reported in NHK Public Opinion Research Institute, ed., *Nihonjin no Ishiki* (Tokyo: Shiseido, 1975); 1978 NHK Japanese values study findings in Daiji Kazama and Toyoko Akiyama, "Japanese Value Orientations: Persistence and Change II," Studies of Broadcasting, NHK, No. 6, 1980, pp. 5–26; see also Richardson, op. cit., pp. 91–101.

TABLE 5.3.　*Attitudes of Deference to Authority*

	Japan	U.S.
1. Percentage who feel free to complain about a decision that they strongly disagree with:		
In family	30	52
On job	38	81
2. The traditional Japanese moral principles of filial piety and respect for one's seniors must be strongly supported.		
Agree	76	
Can't say	19	—
Disagree	5	
3. Since those who have attained positions of leadership over others are outstanding people, it is proper to respect their opinions.		
Agree	40	
Can't say	40	—
Disagree	20	

	Japan 1973	Japan 1978
4. What is the most desirable form of behavior for the general public?		
Select an excellent politician and entrust things to him.	63	61
Make a request to the politician one supports when a problem arises.	12	15
Help organize and work with the party or group one supports to realize one's views.	17	17

Sources: Question 1 is from the Japanese Civic Culture Study replication and the original American portion of the Civic Culture Study. Questions 2 and 3 are from the 1976 JABISS study, and Question 4 is from the NHK 1973 and 1978 studies of Japanese values. See note 18.

attitudes are more pervasive among the older, rural, and less educated elements of the population, among women and those employed in the more traditional sectors of the economy, and among the supporters of the ruling LDP.

A further reason for this passive, deferential orientation towards politics and political leaders is that many Japanese citizens lack confidence in their ability to exercise any influence over

TABLE 5.4. *Attitudes of Efficacy and Political Competence*

	Japan	U.S.
1. People like me don't have any say about what the government does.		
Agree	58	42
Can't say	20	—
Disagree	22	58
2. Percent who say they can do something about an unjust national or local law or regulation.		
National	42	75
Local	58	77
3. Percent who think they would be given equal treatment by a government office or the police.		
Government office	25	83
Police	34	85
4. The need for connections when contacting a government official and the difficulty of finding a connection.		
Could contact an official directly	37	74
Would need a connection, and connection is easily found	28	14
Would need a connection, and connection is difficult or impossible to find	35	12

Sources: Question 1 is from the 1976 JABISS study and the 1976 CPS/SRC United States Election Study, Questions 2 and 3 are from the Civic Culture Studies, and Question 4 is from the Cross-National Participation Project Study. See notes 14 and 16.

political affairs. The low evaluations of one's own political competence in a society with such high levels of educational attainment are strikingly revealed when we compare the Japanese with the American respondents. In Table 5.4, we find that only 22 percent of the Japanese respondents are confident that they have some say about what government does, compared to 58 percent of the Americans. Elsewhere it has been shown that education and efficacy are much more weakly correlated in Japan than in the United States and that it is among Japanese and Americans with the highest levels of education where there is found the biggest differences in the levels of political efficacy.[19] The second item in

[19] Flanagan, op. cit., pp. 157–158.

Table 5.4 reveals that Japanese citizens are also much less confident than Americans about their ability to do anything about unjust laws or regulations, particularly on the national level.

The last two questions in the table provide clues as to why there are substantially lower levels of efficacy and political competence in Japan. Only a quarter to a third of the Japanese compared to over 80 percent of the Americans report that they would expect to receive equal treatment if they had to go to a government office or the police about some problem. The largest proportion of Japanese respondents on both questions (40 and 47 percent) report that the treatment they received would depend on the circumstances. In a particularistic culture, the treatment one expects to receive depends on the nature of one's connections with the officials one is going to see. Thus in the last question in the table, only a little over one third of the Japanese respondents felt they could directly contact an official without an intermediary or connection, compared to three fourths of the Americans.

Even here the figures underestimate the cultural differences. Paradoxically, it is in the modern urban areas, rather than in the traditional rural areas, where the need for traditional, personalistic connections is most strongly felt in Japan. In the rural areas over a half of the respondents felt they could approach an official directly, while among those that needed connections, over half reported that a connection would be easy to find. In the seven largest cities, only 15 percent felt they could contact an official directly; while among the 85 percent needing contacts, two thirds felt a contact would be difficult or impossible to find.[20]

These findings do not mean that personalistic norms are less prevalent in rural areas but only that in smaller environments direct personal connections between the inhabitants and government officials are well established, so that the need for intermediaries is not nearly so strongly felt as in the large, impersonal urban environments. For example, police officers in rural areas are transferred from community to community every two to three years to prevent more deep-seated and corrupting personalistic ties from developing. When a new officer arrives in a community, he is treated to a round of gifts, dinners, and drinking parties by

[20] Ikeuchi, et al., op. cit., pp. 320–332.

the villagers to create a close personal rapport with the officer and ensure that the law is not aggressively or harshly enforced. The relationship between gift-giving and lenient treatment or non-enforcement amounts to a subtle form of bribery in which defer-ence and hospitality are exchanged for noninterference in the life of the community.[21]

As a result of these personalistic practices, rural inhabitants feel closer to their officials and politicians and feel that they are more approachable and responsive than do their urban counter-parts. Because this official-inhabitant intimacy cannot be dupli-cated in large settings, the larger the size of the community and the higher the level of politics, the less confidence the Japanese citizen has in the efficacy of his dealings with government and politics. Low levels of efficacy and the norms of deference and delegation of responsibility to those in positions of authority have weakened the Japanese citizen's ability to participate effectively in politics. In turn, low levels of active citizen participation have meant that politics in Japan, to a greater extent than in many other advanced industrial democracies, has remained an elite rather than a mass activity, operating through a complex network of face-to-face channels of influence.[22]

Since politics in Japan tends to be an elite activity, it is im-portant to investigate the impact of personalistic norms on the elite level in the behavior of politicians. According to some criti-cal observers, high rank is often associated with arrogance towards those in low status positions, with Japanese politicians behaving more like imperial ministers than public servants. However, there has been a trend away from the old style politician who expected deferential treatment towards a newer type of politician who cultivates a friendlier, more approachable image.

Some of the less beneficial side effects of personalistic norms on elite behavior can be seen more readily in the area of informal party organization. The emphasis on vertical ties and personalistic exchanges in Japanese culture is reflected in the leader-follower faction in Japan's political parties. As discussed in Chapter 3, since these factions perform a number of essential functions for

---

21 Richardson, op. cit., pp. 128–188; Walter A. Ames, *Police and Community in Japan* (Berkeley: University of California Press, 1981).
22 For a full discussion of political participation in Japan, see Chapter 6.

their members, they continue to endure despite public criticism. However, other structures and procedures, which did not have the detrimental features of personalistic factions, could have been developed to perform those functions. Clearly the leader-follower faction is congenial with Japan's cultural tradition and personalistic norms. As noted in the discussion of vertical relationships, employees bear a duty and loyalty towards their boss that extends beyond the work relationship, and seniors are expected to look after and take care of juniors even to the extent of involving themselves in their personal lives. These diffuse relationships are maintained through the exchange of gifts, favors, and indulgences. When these values are carried into a political setting, it naturally develops that faction leaders are expected to provide financial support for their followers. But when large sums of money begin changing hands, this practice smacks of bribery and vote buying, especially in the context of party presidential elections.

The leader-follower faction has also meant that personal loyalties predominate over institutional loyalties. The emphasis on factional interests and allegiances over party has led to intra-party feuding and the recurrent threat of major defections and party splinterings. Finally, while in Western democracies, politicians often stake their careers on the popularity of certain issues, in Japan the politician is more likely to tie his career to the rise of a particular faction leader. As noted before, Japanese party factions, especially those in the LDP, are not based on policy issues or ideological differences and therefore serve no representative function. In short, the leader-follower faction has transformed national politics into an exclusive, personalistic power game among elites which further inhibits popular participation in politics and ill serves the public interest.

The most damaging impact of personalistic norms, however, is found in their association with disquieting practices of political corruption. The cultural norms of reciprocity, exchange of favors, and gift-giving seem to legitimate influence peddling and bribery in the minds of many Japanese. Although the media have often highly publicized various corruption scandals, public officials have generally not been repudiated by the public for their malfeasance in office. For example, the great majority of the LDP Dietmen whose names figured in the 1966–67 "black mist" scandals were returned to office, some with an even larger vote than before. There have even been cases of candidates involved in bribery and vote buying conducting successful campaigns from jail.[23]

Despite the growing attention paid to political corruption by the media in the 1970s, many elements of the Japanese electorate remain quite forgiving of such misdeeds by their representatives in the Diet. Apparently they feel that many of the benefits of such bribery schemes have been funneled down to their local areas or that at least in some sense their representative's involvement in corrupt practices was designed to aid them. Kakuei Tanaka, for example, has been involved in long, drawn-out legal proceedings since 1976 for allegedly receiving $2.1 million in bribes from the Lockheed Corporation for promoting the sale of Lockheed's Tristar to the All Japan Airways during his 1972–74 tenure as Prime Minister. In spite of this, he has had no difficulty in being reelected four times by his constituency since then. In the 1976 election, which was viewed by many as a referendum on the Lockheed scandal, Tanaka emerged as the top vote-getter in his district. When interviewed by the press, a local supporter explained that the district was a poor and declining rural area and that Tanaka had brought the people many needed benefits, such as using his influence to build a highway through the district and adding a local train-run through the area at a time when the National Railway was cutting back its service. As the supporter put it, "If the father had not been a thief, we children would have died." [24]

In 1983, while public opinion polls were showing that the great majority of the Japanese people wanted Tanaka to resign his seat in the Diet and retire from politics, Tanaka still commanded overwhelming support in his home district in Niigata prefecture. The source of that support lay in Tanaka's demonstrated power to direct national funds to his district. Indeed it has been reported that government spending per person on public works projects in Japan is highest in Tanaka's district.[25] Niigata's third

23 Scott C. Flanagan, "Voting Behavior in Japan: the Persistence of Traditional Patterns," *Comparative Political Studies* 1 (October 1968), p. 392.

24 Asahi Shimbun, 12/7/76, as quoted in Nobutaka Ike, *A Theory of Japanese Democracy* (Boulder, Colo.: Westview Press, 1978) p. 148.

25 According to figures published by the Home Affairs Ministry for fiscal 1980, if we take the national average as 100, the per-capita public works investment index for Niigata was 255. Second place went to Okinawa with 220. Tokyo and Kyoto placed last with indexes below 40. *The Japan Times Weekly*, 10/8/83, p. 3.

district has been so showered with such projects that many of them seem to be designed more to demonstrate Tanaka's power than to provide judicious, cost-effective allocations of public funds. For example, one village with only three hundred households sports a fine gymnasium accommodating seven hundred persons. Another tiny hamlet of only sixty households was blessed with a tunnel blasted through a mountain to ensure that one access route out of the hamlet would stay open in winter, while a third tiny community acquired an extension of a national highway to their doorstep. As Ronald Dore writes, the typical rural constituent expects politicians to engage in a certain amount of influence peddling, kickbacks, and other irregularities.[26] It simply goes with the territory. The bigger the man, the greater the resources he will need to look after all those that depend upon his largess, hence the greater the latitude and indulgences he should be allowed.

The sustained support Tanaka received despite his indictment and prosecution, however, was not simply a parochial hinterland phenomenon. His central involvement in the scandal had no discernable impact on his influence among Japan's political and economic elites. For appearances, he resigned his membership in the party in 1976, but that disassociation was in name only. Up through the fall of 1983, he continued to control the largest LDP faction and was considered to be the most influential power broker in the ruling party. Dubbed the "Shadow Shogun" by the press, he has been credited as being the kingmaker of the last three cabinets and a sustaining and influential key pillar in both the Suzuki (1980–1982) and Nakasone (1982–present) administrations. Not only did the party stand by him, but apparently so did his financial backers in the business world as well. In the United States, the congressmen implicated in Abscam were censured and forced to resign their seats in the House and Senate for receiving comparatively minor bribes that were further clouded by the issue of entrapment. In marked contrast, Tanaka continued to receive respect and protection from Japan's political and economic elites despite the evidence that he had repeatedly exploited his position to acquire enormous sums of money.

So ingrained are many of these influence-peddling practices in

[26] For more examples of such excessive public works gifts to constituents by other conservative politicians, see Ronald Dore, *Shinohata: A Portrait of a Japanese Village* (New York: Pantheon Books, 1978) pp. 241, 244–245.

Japanese politics that a number of social critics have applied the label "structural corruption." The term implies that corrupt practices are woven so deeply into the fabric of Japanese politics that reform programs are virtually doomed to failure short of a radical purging and restructuring of the entire system. Some observers have pointed to various aspects of Japanese culture to explain the origins of this systemic corruption.[27] For example, personalistic norms have created the practice of bringing small gifts whenever one pays a visit, a gesture that serves to offset partially the inconvenience one's visit has caused the host. It would, then, be impolite for a candidate or campaign worker to visit a voter's home without leaving a gift. The gift, however, is likely to create in the voter a sense of obligation and a need to reciprocate, and so becomes a form of vote-buying.

Traditionally, local influentials served as patrons for their communities, dispensing material benefits in return for loyalty and service. Even today, especially in rural areas, many voters feel that they are entitled to some direct favor or gift from a candidate in return for their support. Thus prospective and incumbent Dietmen are expected to contribute money and other gifts for special community events such as funerals, weddings, conferences, the opening of a new business, the construction of a community project, sports days, festivals, and other special group and community activities. Politicians also feel obliged periodically to treat their supporters to dinners, drinking parties, and even sightseeing tours and excursions to hot-springs resorts. In many rural areas, households are still given cash gifts at election time directly proportional to the number of votes the household can supply. This is not vote-buying in the Western sense, however. Money, often presented in an envelope or wrapped in fine paper, is a common and accepted form of gift-giving for most social occasions, such as weddings or funerals. In the case of a voter, the sum involved is typically small, but it does acknowledge the candidate's debt to the voter, and fulfills traditional reciprocity norms by returning something immediate and tangible for the voter's gift of support.[28]

27 Masakuni Kitazawa, "The Lockheed Incident and Japanese Culture," *The Japan Interpreter* 11 (Autumn 1976), pp. 219–223.

28 Mamoru Iga and Morton Auerbach, "Political Corruption and Social Structure in Japan," *Asian Survey* 17 (June 1977), p. 561; Kanichi Fukuda, "Grassroots Base of Money Politics," *The Japan Interpreter* 9 (Spring 1975), pp. 495–498; Dore, *Shinohata,* op. cit., p. 232.

The new 1975 election law attempted to curtail many of the above activities by explicitly outlawing them, but most politicians have ignored some or all of the new regulations. Moreover, it has been reported that those who attempted to comply have received a cold reception from their constituents. For example, in the 1976 HR election, one Saga Prefecture candidate reported that a rumor was being spread among his supporters that he had suddenly become a miser. An Iwate Prefecture candidate related that his failure to send sake or some other offering to senior citizens' gatherings had led a number of those former supporters to declare their defection openly, while another campaigner who had stopped sending cash gifts to athletic meetings was asked if he had resigned from politics.[29]

In most cases the amounts of money or gifts given to any one constituent are rather small, but in the aggregate, the funds needed to finance these activities are enormous. Moreover, as one moves up the political hierarchy, the amounts of money that exchange hands become larger and larger. Since the number of personal contacts that any one politician can establish among his constituents is limited, national election candidates have to rely on local politicians and vote brokers to gather votes for them through grass-roots activities. It is estimated that in national elections, candidates will donate $1–$5 thousand to a small boss, $5–$20 thousand to a middle-sized boss, and $20–$50 thousand to a big boss. Most of these funds are not pocketed, but are spent on gathering the vote. If these middlemen are successful in delivering a large proportion of the votes from their communities to a particular candidate, the payoff they receive may well come in the form of some cherished public works project and the local prestige that such a demonstration of their political clout brings.[30] While these sorts of activities peak at election time, they continue throughout the year. Even in nonelection years, then, the day-to-day expenses of nurturing one's constituency are enormous. No

---

29 *The Japan Times Weekly*, 6/1/76, p. 10.

30 Dore gives an example of a case in which the local influential succeeded in delivering nearly 300 votes and in exchange secured the reconstruction of an old culvert. Still somewhat bitter that some people who had promised to vote for his candidate had voted for someone else, he commented, "That's the dirty part of democracy." Dore, *Shinohata* pp. 239–241; Iga and Auerbach, op. cit., pp. 556–559.

one knows for sure what a politician spends on these activities a year, but typically an LDP Diet member's reported expenses run five times his government salary, and many observers estimate that their unreported expenditures are seven to ten times as high as their reported expenses.

This discussion of political expenses affirms former Prime Minister Kishi's dictum, "Politics is money." We might also add, "Money is power." Indeed, so important is the role of money in Japanese politics that a politician's fund-raising ability has become one of the principal criteria for becoming a successful faction leader and ultimately securing the post of prime minister. Tanaka's power within the party does not appear to be a product of his own brilliance (he graduated from a vocational school) or his statesmanship, so much as it is a tribute to his prodigious, if occasionally unorthodox, fund-raising abilities.[31]

As we might expect, the Japanese politician's heavy expenses create a virtually inexhaustible need for income that spawns its own set of improprieties. The LDP Dietman typically receives the largest share of his income from his faction leader and his personal support organization (*koenkai*). In turn, the faction leaders and the party as a whole have raised their revenues by annually assessing Japan's big business corporations. Quotas are set for each company or industry depending on its size and income and are paid either to the party's fund-raising association, the Kokumin Seiji Kyokai, or directly to faction leaders. For example, it is reported that at least prior to the new 1975 restrictions, the Japan Steel Corporation had annually contributed in excess of 1500 million yen (over $6 million) to the LDP and its factions.[32] Critics have linked the timing of some contributions to favorable legislation or administrative changes that benefit the donor, but clearly most are regularized contributions aimed at building access and influence rather than payoffs for specific benefits. Nevertheless, these practices contribute to the popular image of the LDP as the servant of big business. Other fund-rais-

---

[31] Takashi Tachibana, "Tanaka Kakuei Kenkyu — Sono Kinmyaku to Jinmyaku," *Bungei Shunju* (September 1976), p. 118.

[32] Frank Baldwin, "The Kokumin Kyokai," *The Japan Interpreter* 10 (Summer 1975), pp. 66–78; Ronald J. Hrebenar, "The Politics of Electoral Reform in Japan," *Asian Survey* 17 (October 1977), p. 994. For the much lower publicly reported figures in 1978, see Chapter 8.

ing techniques that individual politicians may employ on their own behalf include appealing to the small and medium business-men in their districts, assessing such enterprises 10 to 20 percent of the total price of any government contract or subcontract from large companies that they help arrange, and charging constituents up to several thousand dollars a shot for a telephone call, letter of introduction, or personal visit as a go-between on their behalf.[33]

The Japanese distinguish between two kinds of political con-tributions — "surface money" (*omotegane*), which is officially re-ported, and "backstage money" (*uragane*), which is unreported and illegal. Politicians often employ bagmen who stay out of the limelight and arrange the collection and dispersement of polit-ical funds. Reportedly a number of techniques are commonly used to enable politicians to collect some of these backstage monies through technically legal business transactions. For example, com-panies can transfer stocks to a politician at less than market value or at market value prior to an anticipated short-term gain, en-abling him to sell the shares and pocket the increase. Real estate is another vehicle, as land can be sold to politicians and bought back by businessmen at higher prices through dummy companies. Another "rollover" technique is for companies to sell their prod-ucts cheaply to a politician and have them bought back by a subsidiary at higher prices. In addition to using technically legal business transactions to raise illegal political contributions, it is also charged that blatantly illegal practices such as manipulating ledgers are also occasionally employed.[34]

The collusive association of business and politics is nowhere more apparent than in the bidding on government contracts, where personalistic practices often make a sham of what is tech-nically an open competition. For example, it is reported that businessmen frequently get together to divide up a government construction project among their firms. In this process they are fed information as to the type of projects being planned prior to their public announcement and as to the amount of money the government will be budgeting for the project, and in turn

---

[33] Tachibana, op. cit.; Ronald J. Hrebenar, "Money, the LDP and the Symbolic Politics of Reform," *The Japan Interpreter* 10 (Winter 1976), p. 345; Iga and Auerbach, op. cit., p. 560.

[34] Tachibana, ibid.

they pass money to politicians to grease the way for the routine acceptance of their bids. As a result, contracts are frequently awarded almost simultaneously with the announcement of the government project. It could be said that in all walks of life, the Japanese seem to prefer planning everything out beforehand through personal understandings, so that there are no surprises, no unexpected defeats, no loss of face, and each participant gets a piece of the action on a fair-share basis. Hence, the attention given in Japanese culture to *nemawashi* — literally the practice of binding a tree's roots as a preparation long before its transplanting. In a social context, *nemawashi* places an emphasis on laying the groundwork for any transaction by working through personal connections to smooth the way for the deal in advance of a formal decision.[35] While these practices clearly reduce conflict and enhance harmony and personal rapport in decision making, in the political realm they smack of bribery and corruption.

Periodically, when a political scandal breaks and the media attack the various "money politics" practices discussed above, the LDP makes a number of symbolic gestures towards reform. But generally the changes are superficial, and once public interest wanes, the party returns to the same old business-as-usual practices. Some have maintained that the new 1975 restrictions on the size of corporate contributions has had a real effect, in that it has forced the party to collect smaller contributions from a larger number of companies and necessitated greater fund-raising efforts on the part of individual faction members. However, it seems pointless to tighten political funding and campaigning laws when it is well known that politicians commonly report falsified data and that little or no effort has ever been made to verify the data. The pessimistic view would be that these periodic reform efforts have only further inhibited the average citizen from participating in politics, since by now virtually any kind of activity that might involve the voter — from door-to-door canvassing, signature drives, polling, distributing candidate-produced literature, to various kinds of mass rallies and parades for a candidate — are illegal. At the same time, having such rigid laws on the books that are only honored in the breach creates the spec-

---

[35] Tachibana ibid.; on *nemawashi*, see *The Japan Times Weekly*, 12/4/82.

tacle of politicians constantly engaging in illegal activities and contributes to the common mass perception that politics is a dirty, dishonest activity.[36]

In time, the Lockheed scandal may well be viewed as a watershed in Japanese politics. The Lockheed incident was the first occasion on which any politician near the level of a former prime minister had been indicted and prosecuted. The scandal dominated the media for nearly all of 1976, stimulated much interest and discussion among the public, contributed to reform efforts, and seems to have had at least a small, short-term effect on voting behavior in the 1976 election. Still, many are pessimistic about the long-term prospects for any thoroughgoing reform of Japan's structural corruption. It is noted that no aspect of the Lockheed incident would have ever come to light if the American company had not kept official records of its bribery payoffs and reported them publicly in a U.S. Senate hearing. Most Japanese feel that Lockheed is just the tip of the iceberg and that these kinds of practices go on all the time. In a survey conducted nine months after the Lockheed scandal broke, over 80 percent of the respondents expressing an opinion felt that the full story would never be revealed and that the scandal would not result in the cleaning up of politics.[37]

The source of this pessimism can be traced back to Japanese tolerance for these kinds of improprieties. Most Japanese apparently consider favoritism, payoffs, and other questionable practices as inevitable, not only in politics but in other areas of life as well. For instance, in the 1980 NHK Cross-National Survey, 77 percent of the Japanese compared to only 41 percent of the Americans agreed that "in order to get ahead in the world today, you are almost forced to do some things that are not right." And in fact the line between the customary practice of gift-giving and out-and-out bribery is somewhat more ambiguous in the Japanese cultural context. Doctors that receive "gifts" from pharmaceutical companies or music teachers from musical instrument dealers or

36 Each election in Japan is accompanied by a flurry of arrests for illegal campaign practices. Hrebenar, "The Politics of ...," op. cit., pp. 990–992.

37 Hans H. Baerwald, "Lockheed and Japanese Politics," *Asian Survey* 16 (September 1976), pp. 817–829; *The Japan Times Weekly*, 2/5/83; NHK Public Opinion Research Institute, *Dai 34-kai Shugiin Senkyo Zenkoku Chosa: Kekkahyo* (Tokyo: NHK Hoso Seron Chosajo, 1976) pp. 53–62.

school teachers who plan school excursions from travel agents are commonly reported occurrences. At what point does a courtesy call and thank-you gift become a bribe? Some positions in Japanese society attract so many gifts by virtue of the position that the occupants of those offices are frequently deluged with more presents than they can possibly utilize, giving rise to the common practice of selling the gifts back to the department stores they were purchased from at a discounted price. Thus the problem of influence-peddling in Japanese society is not one that troubles only politicians.[38]

The emphasis in Japanese culture on personalism and situational ethics, rather than universal standards, makes it difficult to launch a sustained attack on established corrupt practices. Indeed virtue was displayed by the defendants in the Lockheed case, not in an admission of guilt and a cleansing redemption, but in a willingness to perjure themselves to protect their organizations and superiors. Tanaka still considers himself guiltless. After the prosecution in his court trial demanded a five-year jail term in January 1983, he remained undaunted and continued to expand the size of his faction (reaching one hundred nineteen by the fall of 1983) and gained unprecedented influence (six Tanaka faction members) in the first Nakasone Cabinet, including the installation of a close friend as justice minister. In October of 1983, a verdict was finally handed down by the Tokyo District Court, sentencing Tanaka to a four-year jail term and fining him $2.1 million, the amount of the bribe. However, Tanaka refused to give up his Lower House seat, vowing to fight on and "execute my task in the Diet as long as I live." [39] While Tanaka's intransigent posture may have cost his party dearly (losing 34 seats in the December 1983 HR election), Tanaka himself had no difficulty gaining reelection. Moreover, estimates at the time were that the case would be tied up in the appeals process for at least another ten years before Tanaka would have to spend one day in jail.

Tanaka's days as Japan's "Shadow Shogun" may well be num-

---

38 NHK Public Opinion Research Institute, op. cit., Appendix, p. 46; *The Japan Times Weekly*, 2/26/83, p. 3; 7/9/83, p. 11.

39 Kitazawa, op. cit. pp. 219–220; *The Japan Times Weekly*, 12/11/82, 1/29/83, 2/5/83; *Christian Science Monitor*, 10/20/83, p. 12.

bered. Nevertheless, the system of money politics and power-buying is so entrenched in Japanese politics and society, and so many are involved in it at some level, that the system will be difficult to eradicate. In conclusion, personalistic cultural norms have had a number of damaging effects on the conduct of politics in Japan. In particular, these norms have weakened citizen involvement and contributed to the twin ills of factionalism and corruption.

TABLE 5.5. *Attitudes of Conformity and Passivity*

1. If you think a thing is right, do you think you should go ahead and do it even if it is contrary to usual custom, or do you think you are less apt to make a mistake if you follow custom?

Do what you think is right	31
Depends on circumstances	25
Follow custom	44

2. If community members actively come around to collect contributions, it is better to donate without complaint in order to preserve neighborhood harmony even if you do not necessarily agree with the purpose.

Agree	55
Can't say	24
Disagree	21

3. At meetings in your neighborhood, place of work, PTA, or the like, when opinions are sharply divided, it is better to cut the discussion short in order to avoid bad feelings afterward.

Agree	38
Can't say	30
Disagree	31

4. Suppose you are dissatisfied with conditions in your work place or community. What would you do?

	Work Place	*Community*
Wait and see	44	32
Make a request to a superior or local influential	23	39
Organize and work with other workers and residents to improve conditions	33	29

Sources: Question 1 is from the 1978 National Character Study, Questions 2 and 3 are from the 1976 JABISS Study, and Question 4 is from the 1978 NHK Japanese Values Study. See note 40.

HOLISM IN POLITICS

In the previous discussion of Japan's holistic cultural tradition, it was noted that the concepts of individualism, self-assertiveness, individual rights, and independence were not well developed in Japanese society. In the 1976 JABISS study, for example, only 22 percent of the respondents expressing an opinion agreed with the statement, "Respecting individual rights and freedom is more important than filial piety and the repayment of favors." The emphasis on conformity and dependency in Japanese culture weakens the individual's sense of self-identity and reduces his or her confidence to act without strong group support.

As the first two items in Table 5.5 (p. 192) reveal, a great many Japanese do not believe that one should stand up against one's group even if one is right. In Western societies, of course, there are many examples of those who lack the moral courage to go against the tide, but regardless of their behavior under fire, most are likely to view such a stand as the more virtuous course. In Japan, however, less than one third of the respondents felt that one should do what one thinks is right if it is contrary to custom, and only about one fifth felt that it was appropriate to refuse or even complain when asked to donate to a community project that one did not agree with. The reason for this reluctance to assert oneself is, as suggested by the second and third items in Table 5.5, that the higher virtue in Japanese society resides in the preservation of group harmony. Most Japanese would prefer to go along with a group decision without opposition or, if opinions are sharply divided within a group, to cut off any open confrontation or debate and work out the differences informally, behind the scenes through go-betweens, before a group meeting is reconvened.[40]

Politically this dependency on one's group and weak sense of autonomy means that Japanese citizens frequently lack the self-assurance to involve themselves individually in active participatory roles. Political convictions are often not sufficient by

[40] The 1978 NCS findings are reported in Research Committee on the Study of the Japanese National Character, *Kokuminsei no Kenkyu:* Dai 6-kai Zenkoku Chosa (Tokyo: Institute of Statistical Mathematics, 1979). The reference for the JABISS study is found in note 14 and the 1978 NHK Japanese Values Study in note 18.

themselves to motivate political involvement without the collective backing of one's frame or community. In Japan the strongest expression of citizen participation in politics often takes the form of a citizens' movement organized around a single local community that feels threatened or disadvantaged by some environmental deterioration or government policy. In these situations, the mobilization of community support is so strong and the legitimacy of local interests so respected in Japanese culture, that small communities are sometimes able to bring the government to a standstill, occasionally to the detriment of the broader public interest. For example, the "garbage war" between two Tokyo wards in the early 1970s over the placement of a garbage treatment plant greatly delayed the construction of the much-needed facility. In another example, a group of farmers in the rural community of Narita contested the expropriation of their land and the construction and the opening of the new Tokyo International Airport. The land was designated for the airport in 1966, but it was not until after a series of violent pitched battles in 1971, between the police and the farmers together with their radical student allies, that the land was finally secured. Even after the construction was virtually completed, the airport stood idle for several years until it was finally opened amidst another round of violent confrontations in the spring of 1978.[41]

In contrast to this strong expression of localistic interests, other kinds of interests that cut across communities, such as consumer or class interests, are not as likely to engender citizen participation. Thus civic minded groups designed to promote the common good rather than narrow community interests are not apt to receive enthusiastic support. Moreover, the norms of self-sacrifice of one's personal interests to one's group are not extended to imply that one's group should necessarily sacrifice its interests for the public welfare. Thus in the 1977–78 World Youth Survey, out of the entire sample only 46 percent of the Japanese respondents said they wanted to serve their country, and only 9 percent were willing to sacrifice their own interests to do so. The com-

---

[41] Alan G. Rix, "Tokyo's Governor Minobe and Progressive Local Politics in Japan," *Asian Survey* 15 (June 1975), pp. 538–540; Roger W. Bowen, "The Narita Conflict," *Asian Survey* 15 (July 1975), pp. 598–615.

parable figures for the American respondents were 80 and 54 percent.[42]

As previously discussed, holistic norms are also associated with an unwillingness to make self-reliant choices and a reduced consciousness of individual discretion and responsibility. The discussion of fatalism observed that there is a tendency to view human affairs as flowing inevitably from impersonal forces and circumstances that are beyond the capacity of any one individual to influence. Thus Japanese norms stress adjustment to changing events and a resignation to one's situation. Politically this encourages a low sense of public responsibility, a passive, detached view of politics, and a feeling that nothing can really be done anyway. In contrast, in the West there is more of a sense of conscious choice, of responsibility for what is, and an active striving towards what ought to be, which is reflected in higher levels of involvement and participation on the part of the average citizen in politics, social action groups, and public charities that lie outside of his or her own intimate group.

This passive, fatalistic orientation towards politics appears in the 1977–78 World Youth Survey; 64 percent of the Japanese compared to only 33 percent of the American respondents indicated that, if dissatisfied with society, they would either use their voting right and nothing else or drop out of society and do nothing. Reciprocal percentages displayed a willingness to involve themselves in more active forms of political participation. When those who would only use their vote were asked why they would not take some more active measure, 69 percent of the Japanese respondents indicated that "the problems involved are beyond the reach of individuals." In contrast, only 25 percent of the Americans chose that response. In fact, this expression of fatalistic resignation regarding political affairs was far more widespread in Japan than in any of the other ten nations surveyed, with the next highest percentage (forty-nine) occurring in India.[43]

The last item in Table 5.5 demonstrates that for many Japanese this passive, resigned orientation extends even to one's behavior

[42] Youth Bureau, *The Youth of the World and Japan* (Tokyo: Prime Minister's Office, 1978), pp. 24–26, 60–61.
[43] Ibid., pp. 24–28, 60–63.

within one's immediate environment. Most respondents would either do nothing or simply make a request to a superior or local influential if they were dissatisfied with conditions in their work place or community. Only about one third would organize and work with the other workers and residents to improve conditions. Even in matters of local concern, then, there is a sizable inactive strata. In sum, the cluster of holistic norms that have been discussed inhibit citizen participation in politics, except when the vital interests of one's immediate work group or community are directly challenged.

Another area in which can be seen the influence of holistic norms is in the discrimination against minorities. As discussed previously, there is an intolerance for the maverick and those who do not conform to the expectations of their group. Nonconformists who refuse to change their ways are shut out of the group. This intolerance of nonconformists extends to the treatment of groups who because of their racial origins or other distinctions are considered "different." The largest minority in Japan today is its two million Burakumin.[44] These are the descendants of Japan's untouchable class which were officially designated as "Eta" (literally polluted or dirty) until 1871. Traditionally those who worked with corpses or dead animals were considered unclean; by the Tokugawa era, the Eta had become hereditary outcasts regardless of their occupations. While the government in the postwar period has taken some steps to improve their conditions, they are still discriminated against, ghettoized, and disadvantaged. As an example, companies require that job applicants submit family records, and a prospective spouse's family frequently hire detectives to investigate a candidate's background. As a result, for all practical purposes Burakumin are limited to other Burakumin in matters of employment and marriage.

A Korean community of about 670 thousand faces similar problems. While many of these Koreans today are second and third generation descendants of immigrants who came to Japan in the 1920s and 1930s, they have encountered great difficulties, even in achieving legal rights in Japan. Under Japanese law, only the

---

[44] Chang-do Hah and Christopher C. Lapp, "Japanese Politics of Equality in Transition: The Case of the Burakumin," *Asian Survey* 18 (May 1978), pp. 487–504.

children of Japanese fathers are considered Japanese citizens, and naturalization procedures are extremely difficult and require, among other things, adopting a Japanese name. With the ending of the American Occupation, Koreans were declared resident aliens and required to renew their residency qualifications every three years. With the signing of the Normalization Treaty with South Korea in 1965, Koreans who registered as nationals of South Korea were offered permanent residency, and more recently the same status has been offered to Korean residents loyal to North Korea. Nevertheless, the Korean community in Japan has a long way to go before it achieves equal protection under the law, and Koreans are faced with daily incidents of discrimination in matters of employment, housing, marriage, and other areas of social interaction.[45]

The exclusion of those who are different is apparent in other areas as well — in the treatment of the Ainu (a proto-Caucasian racial minority, mostly in Hokkaido), Okinawans, orphans, children of mixed marriages, and the victims of the atomic bombings at Hiroshima and Nagasaki. This exclusivistic norm can also be seen in the reluctance in the 1970s to admit refugees from Vietnam and Cambodia into Japan. The Japanese people have appeared to be insensitive to the plight of the "boat people," and despite great international pressure, by the end of 1983, Japan was only officially committed to resettling 3 thousand refugees, and it is still unclear whether even that number will find a permanent home in Japan. As the late Prime Minister Ohira noted, "Japan is a free society, but not an open society."[46]

We may say that while Japanese culture provides her nationals with a strong sense of group rights, it fosters a weak sense of the legitimacy of both individual rights and the rights of outsiders. As a result, those who are viewed as outsiders or who deviate from rather narrowly prescribed group expectations and behavior may be treated with indifference, hostility, or discrimination. Resident aliens, including Western professionals, enjoy few legal rights in Japan and have been denied access to public housing,

45 James Lewis, "Strangers at Home: Koreans in Japan," *East-West Perspectives* 2 (Winter 1981), pp. 23–29.
46 Beer, op. cit., pp. 445–448; *The Japan Times Weekly*, 12/6/80, p. 5; Rikio Shikama, "Flawed Japanese Attitudes Towards Refugees," *Japan Echo* 10 (Summer 1983), pp. 34–39.

public employment, state allowances for children, admission to the national pension plan, and loans from lending institutions. The word for foreigner, *gaijin,* literally means "outside person" and as outsiders, foreigners are never fully accepted into Japanese society no matter how excellent their mastery of the Japanese language and customs and are not expected to have the same rights as nationals regardless of how long they have lived in Japan.[47] The same exclusionary treatment awaits Japanese nationals who deviate from the norm, as can be seen not only in the treatment of orphans, atomic bomb victims, and the Burakumin, but also in the treatment of those who detour, even briefly, from the beaten path. The reverse side of the high degree of warmth, support, and security that the Japanese derives from the group, therefore, is the exclusion and rejection of those who cannot or will not fit in.

Another aspect of holism previously discussed is the emphasis on harmony, unity, and conflict avoidance within the group. Because of the enduring hold of these values, the Japanese are perhaps the most diligent people in the world in avoiding conflict. Every effort is made, as self-appointed arbitrators labor tirelessly, to forestall a direct confrontation. The Japanese find such open conflicts intensely disturbing and embarrassing. As a result, within the group one encounters the kind of emotional fretting and bickering and extreme sensitivity to moods and nuances that in the United States one would find only within the family or in dating situations. As Kunihiro states, the Japanese have "an almost abnormal concern about how one's words will affect the other person."[48]

How do these norms of group harmony, unanimity, and conflict avoidance translate into the political realm? Politics, especially electoral politics, is conflict, an open, head-to-head competition for political power. Even here, however, the Japanese from time to time employ a variety of practices aimed at avoiding a direct confrontation or the public display of conflict. For example, Chapter 3 discussed an alternate process the LDP has developed for selecting the party president by negotiation rather

[47] *The Japan Times Weekly,* 3/8/80, p. 5; Beer, op. cit., pp. 449–453.
[48] Masao Kunihiro, "Indigenous Barriers to Communication," *The Japan Interpreter* 8 (Winter 1973), p. 102.

than election. This process was developed long before the public spectacle of large sums of money passing among LDP Dietmen to buy votes in the election became an important public relations problem for the party. The practice was originated to avoid divisive intraparty battles that would leave a residue of bad feeling and hamper decision making.

The greater the intensity of the intraparty conflict, the more likely that the decision will be made by negotiation rather than by vote. The negotiation process enables party elders in the role of neutral arbitrators to find a compromise solution agreeable to all sides in the dispute. In contrast, elections conducted under a majority decision rule produce a winner-take-all outcome. When opinions are severely divided, a decision by majority will grossly violate the norms of unanimity and consensual agreement and bring into question the legitimacy of the outcome itself.

Hiroyuki Kawaguchi speaks of this "strong aversion to decision making by ballot and a predilection for negotiated agreement," and cites as evidence what he calls the erosion of the local government election system through an increase in the number of uncontested elections.[49] Kawaguchi argues that these uncontested elections are the result of behind-the-scenes talks to reach a consensus candidate that can represent all elements in a community. For example, he notes that in 1981 more than half of the mayoral contests fit this pattern of negotiated agreements that are then unanimously ratified by election. Of course, these uncontested elections are most likely to occur in small communities where partisan party divisions are muted or largely absent.

Many intraparty examples, however, could be given of situations where party leaders in conflict situations have sought to avoid a decision by vote. In the fall of 1974, Tanaka's resignation under a cloud of criticism and scandal touched off a bitter succession struggle between Takeo Fukuda and Masayoshi Ohira. With rumors of a party split in the air, the party vice-president and elder statesman, Etsusaburo Shiina, came forward as a self-appointed mediator. He went back and forth among the major contenders and faction leaders and finally was able to win their confidence and maneuver the situation such that he was able to

[49] Hiroyuki Kawaguchi, "The Japanese Method of Settling Disputes," *Japan Echo* 10 (Spring 1983), p. 27.

announce publicly his choice to succeed Tanaka and have it accepted by all factions of the party. His choice was Takeo Miki, neither of the two strong men, but a compromise candidate whose Mr. Clean image was seen as an asset for improving the party's image in the wake of public criticism over Tanaka's "money politics" tactics. Those who personally lost out as a result of Shiina's decision were willing to accept it, because rejecting it would have returned the party to a situation of conflict. Since Shiina's actions were selfless and provided a means of achieving the norm of party unity, his decision carried great moral force within the party.

When a conflict within a party or other organization revolves around questions of personal power, one solution that is often employed to avert a divisive struggle is to take turns. Thus in a period of crisis following the violent May-June demonstrations and the resignation of Prime Minister Kishi in 1960, party unity was preserved by an agreement among key party leaders that Hayato Ikeda would become the next prime minister in return for supporting Eisaku Sato for the office when he stepped down. A somewhat bizarre example of this practice was reported in a 1966 mayoral election in a village in Gifu prefecture. The election campaign between two veteran politicians threatened to split the village apart. The chairman of the village assembly appointed a team of six elder politicians to prevent the situation from getting out of hand. Their solution was to break up the four-year term and have one candidate run unopposed in the 1966 election and then resign two years later and have the other candidate run unopposed to replace him in the ensuing special election.[50]

As these examples suggest, elections within parties and other kinds of organizations are often just ratifications of agreements that have been made among the leadership. This tendency is particularly noticeable in the case of the Socialist Party, which has had unusually severe problems of internal disunity because personal factional feuding has been overlain with intense ideological conflicts. For the Socialists, the preferred technique for resolving the leadership selection issue has been to create a fairly large number of top party positions, including a chairman, a

[50] *The Japan Times Weekly,* 10/26/68.

secretary general, and three vice-chairmen, to permit broad factional representation. Then an agreement is negotiated on a leadership slate that is acceptable to all factions in the party. Finally the negotiated slate is submitted to the party convention for election, preferably by a unanimous vote.

When conflicts are sharp and no negotiated settlement can be worked out prior to a scheduled party election, unusual measures are occasionally taken to avert a showdown by vote. In September of 1968, the thirty-first national convention of the Socialist Party was first extended and then suspended for twenty days because a consensus agreement could not be reached on the new leadership lineup. During the suspension, the outgoing party chairman and his lieutenants labored long and hard to patch up a bitter feud between the Kozo Sasaki and Saburo Eda factions. Ultimately a consensus began to take shape within the party and was used to force the dissenting Sasaki faction to go along reluctantly with the election of Eda to the number two position in the party. A similar rift developed prior to the Socialists' forty-first national convention in September 1977 and once again forced the suspension of the convention until December by which time an agreement on a new leadership slate was finally worked out. The 1977 convention disruption placed the Socialists in the difficult position of having to go into an extraordinary session of the Diet with no officially elected leadership.[51]

Why do Japanese parties and other organizations occasionally go to such extreme measures to avoid resolving internal conflicts by a majority voting decision? One reason is that when conflict becomes open and public, as on the floor of a national convention, it greatly complicates the problem of reaching an agreement. The opponents in the conflict become publicly committed to their positions, and a solution cannot be reached without public retractions and public defeats, which necessarily involve some loss of face. Thus great efforts are made to keep conflicts concealed from external view. Preferably, knowledge regarding the nature of the conflict and the parties involved should be limited to as few participants as possible.

In Western politics, one often hears of the practice of "socializing conflict" — that is political conflicts within a legislature or

[51] *The Japan Times Weekly*, 9/21/68, 9/28/68, 10/12/68, 10/8/77, 12/10/77.

other decision-making body are leaked outside to various social groups and interests, as one side or the other of a dispute carries the controversy to a wider audience in the hope of garnering added strength and thereby gaining the day. In Japan, however, we find the opposite tradition. In prewar Japan and even today, there has been a tendency to privatize conflict and keep it hidden from public view. The effort to conceal conflict, even within political decision-making bodies, often leaves the public uninformed or dependent on the hearsay evidence and guesswork of journalists. Thus the traditional cultural tendency to keep conflict private damages the efforts of public-spirited groups to exercise a meaningful voice in policy-making and the ability of the general public to monitor the activities of their representatives.

The privatization of conflict in Japan is related to the invisible leader phenomenon discussed in the last chapter. Since the positions of the decision makers and the issues involved frequently remain hidden to outsiders, it is often impossible to determine who played a leading role in reaching a settlement and shaping its content. It has been said that leaders are not only invisible in Japan, but missing as well; that is, Japanese history seems largely devoid of the popular heroes and charismatic leaders that have been so prominent in the West.[52] One cause of the absence of popular leaders is found in the exclusiveness of Japanese groups. The general public have been viewed by the party leadership as outsiders who should have no role in the selection of party candidates or party presidents, so that the question of who is recruited to what office has not been so much a function of popular appeal with the general public as internal party politics. Another cause of the absence of leaders with a broad mass following is that personalistic norms inhibit identification with a political leader that one does not have some attachment with. If a leader is not in some way connected with one's geographical area, school, professional association, or union, or does not share some other kind of personal tie, it is believed that the leader will necessarily be looking after the interests of rival groups and interests rather than one's own. Thus both holistic and personalistic norms combine to limit the breadth of mass appeal of political leaders.

---

[52] Joseph A. Massey, *Youth and Politics in Japan* (Lexington, Mass.: Lexington Books, 1976), pp. 21–50.

It has been noted that one reason for the privatization of conflict in Japan is that once a dispute becomes public, it signals the breakdown of the consensual decision-making process, and public disclosure, in and of itself, makes the controversy more difficult to resolve. A second reason is that such external disputes are acutely embarrassing to a group and undermine its standing in the eyes of the world. A group's strength in dealing with other groups is based on its solidarity and commitment or, as the Japanese are fond of saying, its sincerity. A disunified group is an ineffective group and one that can be largely ignored by other groups. During the extraordinary Diet session in the fall of 1977, following the aborted JSP convention that failed to elect a new party leadership, it was noted that the Socialists were pushed around by the DSP and CGP in the proceedings. Moreover, the LDP did not give preference in the management of Diet business to the JSP as it normally has done in recognition of the Socialists' standing as the largest opposition party.[53] At the same time, such open displays of intraparty feuding do not engender public confidence and have been one of the reasons for the Socialists' decline in support at the polls over the last two decades.

A third reason for the elaborate attention to resolving conflict consensually within Japanese groups is that conflict is not only a threat to the harmony of the group, but to its existence as well. When conflict becomes too sharp, intemperate behavior and injured feelings are likely to lead one side of a dispute to withdraw from the group. Nakane argues that the threat of resignation is a common ploy in Japanese groups which is used as a weapon to draw attention to the fact that the group is violating an individual's (or faction's) rights by ignoring its vital interests.[54] If the threat does not elicit the desired result, however, secessions may follow, which in turn are likely to plunge the group into self-criticism to prevent matters from going so far and ending so badly in the future.

A brief history of the internal conflicts within the JSP illustrates this point. In the 1950s the JSP could be described as a Marxist-Leninist party. Indeed the ideological differences between the Socialists and Communists often were difficult to detect and seemed to boil down to the question of whether Japanese mo-

---

53 *The Japan Times Weekly,* 12/10/77, p .5.
54 Nakane, op. cit., p. 77.

nopoly capitalists were the number one enemy of the Japanese people, and American imperialism the number two enemy, or vice versa. The defection of some elements from the party's right wing in 1959 to form the DSP, however, raised the question of whether the Socialists would ever succeed in crossing the one-third barrier in its efforts to rise to the status of the majority party in the Diet. In this context, several elements within the party sought ways to broaden the party's appeal by transforming it from a class party to a national party. Saburo Eda became the leading advocate of this movement with his promotion of the theory of "structural reform" in 1960, a theory developed by Palmiro Togliatti of the Italian Communist Party. The structural reform argument softens Marxism-Leninism by claiming that it is possible to carry out some improvement in capitalistic relations of production and extend real benefits to the working class through peaceful parliamentary means prior to the socialist revolution. In 1962, Eda went further in his efforts to dissociate the JSP from the dictatorship and terrorism of Russia and China by presenting a positive image for Japanese socialism that did not rest simply on a principled opposition to everything the LDP did. Eda's "new vision" for socialism was based on four pillars or goals — the American standard of living, the Soviet social security system, British parliamentary democracy, and the Japanese peace constitution.[55]

While these ideas would seem to provide the JSP with a rational and pragmatic means of expanding its popular base, they were attacked from three sides. First Sohyo, Japan's largest and most militant national labor federation and the JSP's most important organizational support base, feared that diluting the class basis of the party and the rhetoric of revolutionary socialism would weaken labor's voice in politics and its ability to mobilize the work force. Second, the Marxist-Leninist purists in the party, led by theoretician Itsuro Sakisaka, attacked Eda's ideas on ideological grounds as heretical. Third, structural reform and the "new vision" for socialism were too closely identified with the person of Saburo Eda. Thus, to promote these ideas was to pro-

---

[55] See the four articles on the JSP by Fukuo Noda, Yoshihiko Seki, Hiroshi Masujima, and Saburo Eda in the *Journal of Social and Political Ideas in Japan* 1 (August 1963), pp. 39–50.

mote the power of Eda within the party. For the other Socialist faction leaders, Eda was a rival for power. Kozo Sasaki was the leader of the largest faction in the JSP at the time, and while he was identified as left-wing, there are many indicators that his long-standing, bitter feud with Eda was more personal than ideological.

While at any one time there have been roughly five to nine factions in the JSP, during the 1960s the power struggle within the party centered around the Eda-Sasaki conflict. In the 1970s, however, Sakisaka's Marxist-Leninist purists increased their voice in the party through the growth of the Socialist Association, known as the Kyokai for short. By the late 1970s, the confrontation within the JSP had taken on more of a Kyokai/anti-Kyokai coloration, with Sasaki moving closer to the anti-Kyokai camp. The Kyokai also represented a threat to the traditional supremacy of Socialist Dietmen over the party hierarchy, as the Kyokai drew its strength mainly from young party functionaries who did not hold Diet seats. In 1977, the conflict came to a head as the Kyokai's increasing militancy and rude and shabby treatment of Eda at the party's February convention precipitated his withdrawal from the party. That development and the Kyokai's call to revise the constitution to abolish private property and exclude capitalist-oriented parties prompted other elements within the party to launch an all-out attack on the Kyokai. Hideo Den led the attack, labeling the Kyokai a "cancer" that must be irradicated from the party at all costs. Once the conflict had broken open to the stage of mutual public vilification, it was a foregone conclusion that someone would have to secede. In this case, Den lost and bolted the party with several other Socialist Dietmen during the party's forty-first national convention, causing the suspension of that gathering in September 1977.[56]

In an effort to patch up the feud and prevent further defections, the party brought in the popular mayor of Yokohama, Ichio Asukata, who had no previous factional ties, as the new party chairman, and awarded two of the three vice-chairmanships to anti-Kyokai factions. This effort smoothed over party divisions until Asukata, flushed from his overwhelming victory in the first

---

[56] As noted in Chapter 4, it was these combined defections from the JSP in February and September of 1977 that led to the formation of the SDF. *The Japan Times Weekly,* 2/5/77, 2/19/77, 9/24/77, 10/1/77, 10/8/77.

party primary election for the office of chairman in December 1981, asserted his personal authority by forcing his own choice on the party for the number two post of secretary-general. Asukata originally pushed for the institution of a primary to strengthen the power of the office of chairman and weaken that of the party factions that had been responsible for so much of the party's internal problems and dissension in the past. However, Asukata's move upset the traditional factional balance in the power structure and once again set off rumors of a party split, this time resulting in a right-wing boycott of all party executive offices. For an entire year the party carried on under what the press dubbed its "left-wing one-lung executive body." Finally at its forty-seventh convention in December 1982, Asukata bowed to the factions, his man resigned from the secretary-general post, and executive positions were once again parceled out on a factionally balanced basis.[57]

The point of this example is that factional conflict is endemic to Japanese parties and other kinds of organizations of substantial size. The only way these organizations can head off defections or internal disruptions, therefore, is to avoid winner-take-all solutions, maintain a factionally balanced leadership structure in which all elements of the organization are represented, and adhere to a consensual mode of decision making. For this reason, LDP prime ministers in forming their cabinets adhere closer to the principle of balanced cabinets than victory cabinets.[58] That is, even those factions that opposed the prime minister in his bid for the party presidency are represented in the cabinet. Moreover, when the norm of factional balance is violated, loud criticisms and occasionally even rumors of a party split are heard. Despite repeated efforts to abolish factions, they still play a commanding role in Japanese parties as both the source of conflict and the means of controlling conflict.

A final reason for the emphasis on containing conflict in Japanese culture is that when the consensual norms of conflict resolution within groups, organizations, institutions, or communities

[57] *The Japan Times Weekly,* 12/10/77, 12/24/77, 10/24/81, 12/12/81, 2/20/82, 2/27/82, 12/25/82.

[58] Thayer, "The Election of a Japanese Prime Minister," *Asian Survey* 9 (July 1969), pp. 447–497.

are seriously breached, there is a real possibility that the combatants will shift into the normless anomic behavioral domain, with the outbreak of irrational violence. There have been a number of examples over the postwar period where protracted, bitter conflicts within schools, companies, or communities have suddenly erupted in spontaneous, unrestrained violence. Students have kidnapped their administrators, or unionists have subjected company executives to kangaroo court proceedings. In these cases, the unhappy victims are verbally attacked and humiliated by the students or workers en masse; forced to engage in around-the-clock self-criticisms, confessions, and apologies, and frequently subjected to physical abuse. A particularly extreme example of this took place at Yoka High School in 1974, when the Burakumin students and community set upon fifty-two peacefully demonstrating teachers, kidnapped them, and repeatedly beat and tortured them throughout the night. The teachers were so badly beaten that forty-three of them required hospitalization for more than a week, and thirteen of those were hospitalized for over six weeks.[59]

What makes these outbreaks particularly intense is the violation of group norms on both sides — the norms of group loyalty and conformity on one side and the norms of consensually integrating all group interests, including intensely held dissident opinions, on the other. Violence is most likely to follow when, as in institutions or communities, the solution of the conflict by defection or purge is not available. Protracted labor struggles, as in Miike in 1959–60 and Minamata in the 1960s, occasionally have been so divisive that they have led to the formation of second unions, dividing the workers into promanagement and antimanagement unions over the issue of loyalty to the welfare of the entire group (company health) versus the trampling of the vital interests of a part of the group. The Miike strike was particularly intense because of the company's efforts to rationalize the industry in a declining coal market by laying off workers. In the small company town of Minamata, the situation was complicated by the fact that the town's major employer and benefactor, the Chisso Corporation, was responsible for the outbreak of one of the worst epidemics of pollution diseases ever documented, with hundreds

59 Thomas P. Rohlen, "Violence at Yoka High School," *Asian Survey* 16 (July 1976), pp. 682–699.

of victims, some with grotesque, irreversible physical deformities. The issue of company loyalty versus worker rights divided not only the workers but the entire town of 50 thousand inhabitants and led to violent confrontations between the two unions, attacks on outside reporters, scientists, and other investigators, and the beatings of the victims of the disease at the stockholders meetings of the Chisso Corporation on more than one occasion.[60]

A similar kind of confrontation has on occasion disrupted the proceedings in the Diet. Clearly the basic Western institution of representative government, the parliament, was not designed for consensual decision making. Because of the majoritarian decision rule in that body, a consensus is not necessary for a decision to be reached. During most years since 1976, the LDP's majority in the Diet has been so slim that it has had to involve one or more opposition parties in the decision process and hence more consensual procedures, and a more peaceful atmosphere have prevailed. Prior to then, however, the LDP enjoyed a consistent solid majority and, on a number of occasions, legislated its preferences over the strong opposition of the progressive parties. Thus the opposition remained unreconciled to the decisions of the Diet and yet could neither be silenced nor expelled. This situation, then, implied clear violations of holistic norms. On the one hand, the ruling party violated those norms every time it legislated its preferences over the sincere, implacable opposition of the progressives. On the other hand, the opposition parties violated holistic norms every time they cried foul to the press, leaked details of secret negotiations, or maintained the posture of principled opposition, and refused to give ground to the prevailing opinions within the Diet.

These deviations from prevailing social norms governing group behavior undoubtedly exacerbated tensions between the conservatives and progressives in the Diet. On several occasions, tensions have become so high that parliamentary decorum has given way to disruptive, even violent behavior. The opposition parties, and particularly the Socialists, have responded to their condition of

[60] Wakao Fujita, "Labor Disputes," in K. Okochi, B. Karsh, and S. Levine, eds., *Workers and Employers in Japan* (Tokyo: University of Tokyo Press, 1973), pp. 334–343; Donald R. Thurston, "Aftermath in Minamata," *The Japan Interpreter* 9 (Spring 1974), pp. 25–42.

political impotence in the face of the LDP's perpetual majority by developing an array of delaying tactics. A typical example is the practice of "cow-walking" (*gyuho senjutsu*). Roll call votes require each Dietman to walk up to the rostrum through a narrow passageway to cast his ballot. Cow-walking refers to the tactic of rushing into the aisles as soon as the vote is called and blocking movement towards the ballot boxes. That results in slowing the procedure down to a snail's pace so that it may consume two to three hours and is accomplished only with a considerable amount of pushing and shoving in which tempers flare and injuries have occasionally been sustained. The more intense the opposition, the more physical the progressive party tactics may become.[61]

There have been a number of issues in the postwar period that have sharply polarized the government and opposition, most notably those concerning constitutional revision, police powers, educational policy, defense measures and a number of foreign policy issues. On occasion when the ruling party has been committed to pushing a sensitive issue through the Diet, physical confrontations have ensued. The most notable examples here are the 1960 Japan-U.S. Security Treaty, 1965 Japan-Korea Normalization Treaty, and the 1969 University Normalization Bill. In these instances, the opposition was able to bring Diet proceedings to a standstill by submitting multiple nonconfidence motions against various cabinet ministers and Diet officers, calling numerous roll call votes and delaying or aborting committee meetings and plenary sessions by physically preventing the presiding officer from reaching his chair to call the meeting to order. Typically, the LDP would respond with "Pearl Harbor" tactics, catching the opposition off-guard, rushing the rostrum, abruptly changing the agenda, suspending debate, and calling for a final vote on the issue. These "forced vote" procedures usually throw the body into confusion. Sometimes there has been so much chaos and commotion that no one could hear the motion, and the measure was declared passed after-the-fact as a unanimous standing affirmation, even though everyone was on their feet before the motion could be made. After such forced vote episodes, the opposition parties would

---

61 Hans. H. Baerwald, *Japan's Parliament: An Introduction* (London: Cambridge University Press, 1974), p. 109.

generally retaliate by boycotting all Diet proceedings until tempers cooled and some face-saving compromise could be negotiated to normalize relations among the warring parties.[62]

Such outbreaks of violent behavior in politics and other areas of Japanese society are intensely disturbing to the participants and, as the public tends to blame both sides in such disputes, no one wins. As a result, in situations of recurrent confrontations, as between government and opposition, business and labor, or police and protesters, there has been a tendency to ritualize conflict so as to prevent it from getting out of hand. There have developed certain unspoken boundaries over time that limit the levels of physical violence on both sides. For example, street demonstrations in Japan are highly organized and disciplined and rarely lead to spontaneous violence. Even the most intense physical confrontations between police and students are generally limited to water cannons and rocks, so that serious injuries and deaths are extremely rare. There has also been a ritualization of labor-management conflict as well. Strikes are a frequent tactic in labor's annual spring struggles, but they tend to be short, often only several hours to several days, and their starting date and duration are announced well in advance so that management will not be surprised or the public unduly inconvenienced. Frequently strikes are conducted prior to serious negotiations as a demonstration of the workers' commitment and solidarity.[63] In this way strong opposition can be symbolically demonstrated without taking really punitive actions against management that might escalate the confrontation and impede a settlement.

Even in the Diet, it has been reported that the obstruction/ forced vote scenario is often just a play staged by the Diet leadership on both sides for their respective constituencies and hardliners. On occasion, government and opposition leaders have agreed beforehand that the progressives would be allowed so much time to parade their obstructive tactics, perhaps forcing the extension of the Diet session once or twice, in return for ulti-

[62] Hans H. Baerwald, *Japan's Parliament,* pp. 103–120; Baerwald, "The Diet and the Japan-Korea Treaty," *Asian Survey* 8 (December 1968), pp. 951–959; Baerwald, "An Aspect of Japanese Parliamentary Politics," *The Japan Interpreter* 6 (Summer 1970), pp. 196–205.

[63] Tadashi Hanami, *Labor Relations in Japan Today* (Tokyo: Kodansha International, 1979).

mately conceding in the face of a prearranged forced vote. If the opposition leadership is not surprised by the forced vote, the subsequent boycotting of the Diet proceedings and breakdown of communications across party lines can be avoided.[64]

Conflict is probably most difficult to deal with in Japan in those situations in which it is least expected and most disruptive of group solidarity — that is, in small, highly motivated groups. We see this in school and university sports clubs where in many cases the aesthetics of discipline and the standard of unconditional loyalty, as exemplified in the feudal warrior code, still hold sway. A number of instances were reported in the 1970s of beatings, sometimes even to death, of club members for minor breaches of discipline and loyalty. Another example is the ideologically committed radical students' groups on Japan's university campuses. Throughout the 1960s and 1970s there were numerous instances of student factions not only battering each other's heads but also turning inward and brutally attacking members of their own cliques on the suspicion of spying, ideological deviations, or intention of leaving the group. The most shocking of these incidents was the police disclosure in March 1972 that the United Red Army Faction of Japan's "New Left" radicals had tortured to death fourteen men and women members of their group.[65] In a holistic culture, the probability of dysfunctional, irrational violence is increased when sharp, prolonged conflicts emerge within small homogeneous groups and the option of defection is not available.

In sum, holistic norms as well as personalistic norms are reflected in the conduct of politics in Japan. In the case of holism, its influence is particularly apparent in conditioning the kinds of political interests that are most likely to receive strong political expression and in the behaviors associated with efforts to avoid or contain conflict. Holism is also associated with political apathy and a lack of confidence in participating in politics and an intolerance or indifference regarding minority rights and interests.

[64] Ellis Krauss, "Roles and Role Conflict in the Japanese Diet," unpublished manuscript.

[65] Yoshihiro Kuriyama, "Terrorism at Tel Aviv Airport and a 'New Left' Group in Japan," *Asian Survey* 13 (March 1973), pp. 336–346; Beer, op cit., p. 441; Mari Ito Berry, "Evolution and Development of the Japanese Student Movement: The Way of Self-Devastation?" Masters Thesis, Florida State University, 1976.

COUNTERPOINT

The focus of the discussion of Japanese politics in this chapter has been on areas where significant and perhaps puzzling differences appear between Japanese and American behavior. A number of the Japanese practices that have been discussed such as factionalism, corruption, and exclusivistic discrimination would seem to have mainly negative implications and might suggest to the reader that Japan's personalistic and holistic cultural heritage has had a profoundly debilitating effect on Japanese politics. Nothing could be further from the truth. Instead, the differences between the Japanese and American cultural traditions provide their respective body politics with contrasting strengths and weaknesses. If success is judged on the basis of government performance and policy outputs, one would have to conclude that in the Japanese case the strengths far outweigh the weaknesses. Japan's personalistic and holistic norms can be associated with high levels of social cohesion and political stability, effective long-range policy planning, and broad cooperation and compliance in the implementation of important national programs.

Even in the areas that have been focused on, the picture is much more mixed than the one presented above. Democracy is a fragile phenomenon wherever it is found, and one could easily come up with a whole catalog of weaknesses and deficiencies regardless of which advanced industrial democracy one was studying. Since no nation on earth has ever attained the ideal of the democratic form of government, it would be difficult to substantiate a claim that democratic institutions were performing less effectively in Japan than elsewhere. What is interesting in the Japanese case is to observe how a different cultural tradition has led to different kinds of problems and how similar kinds of problems, such as corruption, assume somewhat different forms and have different meanings in contrasting cultural contexts.

Different cultural traditions, therefore, provide systems with different resources, capabilities, and behavioral propensities. It has also been argued that some of the weaknesses in democratic processes in Japan can be attributed to the relative newness of Japan's democratic institutions and the manner in which they were introduced. In the latter case, to the extent that such weaknesses are in fact linked to incompatibilities between traditional norms and modern democratic structures, one should expect to find evidence that the old norms and related behavior patterns are undergoing adaptation and change. Indeed, the most blatant signs of dysfunctions in democratic processes occurred in the early postwar period; and there are many indications of a growing maturity since then, in the area of democratic performance, as familiarity and experience with Japan's postwar political institutions have been achieved.

This chapter has focused on evidence of culturally induced weaknesses in system performance resulting either from a different mix of cultural resources and behavioral tendencies than that found in the West, or in some cases, from actual incongruities between traditional and democratic norms. As such, the chapter has not presented a balanced view by design. It should be clear that the behavior patterns described above do not characterize all cases or all participants. The next chapter will focus on new kinds of values and attitudes that are appearing among broad segments of the Japanese population and the new forms of political behavior associated with them.

By adding into this picture of Japanese political behavior the perspectives presented in the next chapter, the reader will achieve a more complete view of the side-by-side coexistence of the old and the new, the continuities and changes in Japanese politics. A few additional comments are required here, however, to put the above discussion in the proper context. While levels of participation in election campaigns and other kinds of political activities other than voting may appear substantially lower in Japan in most instances than in the United States, it may be that the United States is the deviant case. Cross-national studies report that Japanese participation levels compare favorably with those of several European countries on a number of different kinds of political activities.[66] Also, Japan's personalistic and holistic norms have been associated with high levels of voting and integration into politicized social networks, strong representation of local interests, and frequently strong grass-roots inputs in local decisions.

---

[66] Of course the relatively low participation levels found in such countries as Italy and France issue from very different cultural sources, such as histories of political conflict and partisan polarization. For comparative data *see* Samuel Barnes and Max Kaase, et al., *Political Action* (Beverly Hills: Sage, 1979).

While Japan's input processes do not always operate as they do in the United States, it would be hard to argue that they have brought the Japanese people fewer benefits than a more American-type process would have. The Japanese citizen certainly has a very pragmatic, instrumental orientation towards politics and frequently has been quite successful in extracting from leaders and elites those goods and services he or she desires.

We also should be careful to guard against the possibility of our own cultural perspective blinding us to the realities of Japanese politics. Because Japanese operate through collective institutions and deferential relations with a minimum of public, visible conflict, it might be assumed that they are passive, impotent, or being manipulated from above. What we may miss from our cultural perspective is how effectively the average Japanese citizen can manipulate and work through those cultural norms to gain both group and purely personal, individualistic goals.

Finally, if Japanese cultural norms weaken horizontal mobilization and the strength of national associations, those same norms strengthen community or areal-based organizations. There are many signs that political participation in advanced industrial societies is moving towards decentralized citizens' movements based on local issues and concerns. This is a vehicle of political organization and involvement that is compatible with and strengthened by traditional Japanese cultural norms. The effectiveness of this community-based expression of political involvement can be seen in the rise of and response to several thousand such local citizens' movements in Japan in the late 1960s and early 1970s.

Another theme that has been discussed is the exclusivistic and somewhat unresponsive tendencies of the Japanese political establishment. Increasingly, however, Japanese elites are viewing this popular image as a liability. An important sign of change here is the recent move by both the Socialists and Liberal Democrats to institute party primaries in the selection process for their parties' top leader. These changes seem to be an improvement over the traditional practice of limiting participation to a few hundred Dietmen and party officials. Still, the new rules limit participation to dues-paying members, a total that for the LDP has ranged from around 1 to 1.3 million across its 1978 and 1982 primaries, and that for the Socialists stood at about 62 thousand for its first primary in 1981. One early effect of the primaries has been a growth in the numbers of official members of each party. To date, however, it appears that the winners of these contests simply mirror decisions and factional alliances made at the top.[67] Nevertheless, an important institutional change has been set in place that may in time serve as a vehicle for opening up the Japanese parties for broader participation and provide the Japanese public with a greater voice in leadership selection.

On the other side of the exclusivism issue, one could argue that the greater insulation of the Japanese political elites from shifts in the public mood and the leadership's more in-group, collectivist orientation are sources of strength. In comparison with their Japanese counterparts, American politicians appear too obsessed with the political ramifications of everything they do such that they are always calculating how their every move will go down with the public. Even foreign policy often becomes the captive of potentially dangerous political games aimed at maximizing domestic popular support. In addition, the more individualistic, great-leader syndrome that infects American politics produces a great deal of instability, waste, and inefficiency as each new president, department official, or agency head feels compelled to put his personal stamp on his administration by dismantling old programs and introducing new ones.

In regard to the issue of corruption, it should be clear that American and European politicians are not morally superior to their Japanese counterparts. A kickback scandal forcing the resignation of an American vice-president in the early 1970s or the more recent revelation of bribery within the Dutch royal family are reminders that no culture is free from the corrupting influences of power and money. What is interesting about the Japanese case in this regard is the different meaning and judgment the culture places on influence-peddling. As a result, such corrupt practices are both more widespread and more benign in Japan, because they are less motivated by purely personal self-aggrandizement. Japan's "system of corruption" spreads the benefits rather broadly, and it is clear that the system has brought many resources and positive

---

67 Taketsugu Tsurutani, "The LDP in Transition? Mass Membership Participation in Party Leadership Selection," *Asian Survey* 20 (August 1980), pp. 884–859; *The Japan Times Weekly*, 12/2/78, 1/2/82, 11/27/82.

improvements to local areas. Moreover, as the Japanese media become more vigilant in attacking the gross examples of official misconduct, the system as a whole will undergo change, clarifying the publicly acceptable limits of influence-peddling.

Finally, the discussion of conflict avoidance and consensual decision-making norms suggested that the Japanese often have encountered difficulty dealing with conflict constructively once it has become open and public. It should be noted in this regard that there are signs that open conflict in several contexts is becoming more accepted and routine.[68] Moreover, what appears as a shrill, emotional response with overtones of a life or death struggle is often a ritualized protest. In many cases the opposition parties, within the Diet and elsewhere, have simply manipulated cultural norms to register protest and frustration and gain popular support. Yet the LDP's occasional resort to steamroller tactics in the Diet has never brought into question the fact that the decisions of the Diet are the law of the land. As the intensity of the opposition in the Diet has waned with the rise of the center parties and as the legislators have developed more institutionalized ways of dealing with policy disagreements, conflict in the Diet has increasingly been managed with less emotion and violence than in the past. For example, Ellis Krauss has found that, particularly since the mid-1970s, new leadership roles and procedures have developed in the Diet that are de-emphasizing partisan confrontation and institutionalizing more public and formalized procedures for negotiating differences among the parties. Thus signs of adaptation abound as the Japanese become more accustomed to their postwar political institutions and as attitudes and behavior patterns become better adapted to the workings and democratic intent of those institutions.

[68] *See* Margaret A. McKean, *Environmental Protest and Citizen Politics in Japan* (Berkeley: University of California Press, 1981); Krauss, op. cit.

CHAPTER 6

Political Culture II: Changes in Social and Political Behavior

UP TO NOW, WE HAVE STRESSED the continuities in Japanese society and politics. As important as these continuities are, they must be balanced against the dramatic pace of socioeconomic change that has marked the entire postwar period. The rate of economic growth in Japan since the early 1950s has been much greater than that in the United States or Western Europe. Inevitably these changes are having a profound influence on reshaping social and political behavior. As a result, Japanese political culture today is a blend of continuity and change. To complete the picture of mass political behavior, the focus in this chapter will be on social and political change.

Japan's soaring economic rise from the ashes of defeat, poverty, and economic ruin in 1945 to the exalted status of the third largest economic power in the world in the 1980s could not have been accomplished without fundamental socioeconomic changes. In 1947, 51 percent of the labor force was classified as agricultural, and less than 35 percent of the population lived in cities (shibu). By 1980, only 10 percent of the population was still engaged in agriculture, and over 76 percent lived in cities. The pace of change has been so rapid in Japan that the transformation from a rural,

* Scott C. Flanagan

TABLE 6.1   *The Percentage Distribution of the Work Force by Economic Sector, 1947–1980*

Year	Agricultural Sector	Industrial Sector	Service Sector
1947	51.3	26.7	22.0
1955	41.2	24.4	34.4
1960	33.4	28.2	38.4
1965	24.3	32.8	42.8
1970	16.5	35.7	47.3
1975	12.9	34.9	51.8
1980	10.1	34.3	55.4

Source: Japan Statistical Yearbook, 1947–1981.

agrarian to an urban industrial society has been followed closely by a second shift from an industrial to postindustrial society. The concept of a postindustrial, or information, society suggests a second important change in the development process, one that is signaled by a decline in the proportion of the work force engaged in secondary industry and a rise to over 50 percent of the labor force engaged in tertiary industry. Thus there is a shift from an economy dominated by heavy industry and manual workers to one dominated by the service sector and knowledge workers.[1] As shown in Table 6.1, Japan had crossed the threshold of this postindustrial stage of development by 1975.

SOCIAL CHANGE

The fallout from the rapid pace of urbanization and the changing occupational structure has been felt in many areas. First these changes have been associated with a rise in geographic and occupational mobility. The dislocating effects of this rise in mobility have weakened the solidarity of the residential community, which has long played a key role in socializing successive generations into traditional values, monitoring individual behavior, and enforcing conformity. In some cases the work place has taken on the role of a primary focus of group identification and loyalty. But the reality of the situation is that most Japanese now live in in-

[1] *Japan Statistical Yearbook* (Tokyo: Bureau of Statistics, Office of the Prime Minister, 1947–1981); Daniel Bell, *The Coming of Post-Industrial Society* (New York: Basic Books, 1973).

creasingly large and complex environments in which they are subject to a variety of influences and competing demands on their loyalties, with the result that their identification with and commitment to any one particular group has declined.

A second major change associated with the postwar socioeconomic transformation has been in the role of women and the cohesiveness of the family. Increasingly throughout the postwar period, women have been moving into the labor force. Initially, women were only employed until they were married or had their first child. Even today many companies routinely ease women employees out at age twenty-seven or twenty-eight. By 1982, however, women constituted nearly 35 percent of the work force, and over half of the female population over the age of fifteen were employed, with the majority of those being married women over thirty-five. It is true that working Japanese women still enjoy little job security, have few opportunities for professional advancement, and are paid on the average only half of what men earn. Nevertheless, the attitudes and aspirations of women are beginning to change, and there has been a dramatic decline just over the last decade in the proportion of women who report on opinion surveys that only husbands should work and wives should stay home and take care of the household and children.[2]

Throughout the postwar period the cohesiveness of the Japanese family has been under attack. First there was the transformation from the farm household and the small retail and craftsman enterprises, where the family was the work unit, to large scale enterprises in urban settings where blue and white collar wage earners had to commute long distances to their jobs. Particularly the white collar husbands, who were expected to engage in extensive after-hours socializing with their work colleagues, became nocturnal boarders with only limited interaction with other family members. Still, the bond between mother and children remained, and that has been considered the crucial central foundation of the Japanese family. Now that too is threatened by the increasing movement of women into the work force.

[2] Robert C. Christopher reports that in the early 1970s, 80 percent of Japanese women believed that wives should stay at home, while by 1979 only 36 percent still held that view. Christopher, "The Changing Face of Japan," *The New York Times Magazine*, March 27, 1983, p. 41; Jon Woronoff, *Japan's Wasted Workers* (Totowa, N.Y.: Allanheld, Osmun and Co., 1983).

While many working women are only employed on a part-time basis as pieceworkers in their own homes, there has also been a dramatic surge in the number of day-care centers over the last two decades. By 1980, roughly one fifth of all Japanese children six years of age or younger were enrolled in day-care centers. Traditional Japanese child-rearing practices, as we have noted, were based on the child's close proximity to and dependency on the mother and his insulation from contacts with strangers and outsiders. Several Japanese social critics have warned that the rise in day-care centers is undermining the traditional virtues of dependency on the group and compliance to the expectations of authority figures. These traditional virtues, they argue, are central to social discipline in Japan.[3] If these changes in life-styles and child-rearing practices should have a weakening effect on Japan's vaunted social cohesion, Japan will likely experience some of the harsher forms of social disintegration, conflict, and turmoil that have been visited upon the West.

One final factor that is undermining the solidarity of the family is the skyrocketing costs of land, houses, and apartments in Japan's crowded cities. The economics of overconcentration associated with the growth and shift of the population to a few key metropolitan areas has shrunk the average family's living space. The extremely small size and paper-thin walls of urban residences have forced family members outside the home, often going their separate ways in search of privacy and relaxation.

The socialization of Japan's younger generation is being changed in response not only to changes in women's roles and the cohesion of the family, but also to changes in the educational system. It is well documented that education is one of the most powerful forces for changing cultural values and political attitudes.[4] As a result of the Occupation reforms, the Japanese educational system experienced important changes in the content and context of education in the early postwar period. In content, great stress was placed on teaching the values of individualism and democracy. In context, education in the schools changed from

[3] Christopher, ibid., pp. 81–83; Thomas Nevins, "Who Gets Fired?" *PHP* (March 1983), pp. 19–32.

[4] Gabriel A. Almond and Sidney Verba, *The Civic Culture* (Boston: Little, Brown, 1963); Alex Inkeles and David H. Smith, *Becoming Modern* (Cambridge: Harvard University Press, 1974).

a hierarchic, authoritarian setting to one that emphasized equality and pupil participation.

A second important change has been the tremendous expansion of the educational system across the postwar period. Compulsory education was extended from six to nine years, and the proportion of junior high school graduates going on to senior high school expanded from 30 percent in 1950 to nearly 95 percent by 1980. At the same time, the proportion of the college age population enrolled in institutions of higher learning increased from 9 percent in 1955 to nearly 40 percent by 1980.[5] These rising levels of education among the younger generation have been associated in Japan, as elsewhere, with an expansion of the informed, sophisticated, and politically competent portion of the electorate. The highly educated citizen is less likely to exhibit deferential, conformist attitudes and is more apt to evaluate critically the performance of political leaders and feel confident about participating in politics.

Another social change that is looming on the horizon in Japan today stems from the changes that are now underway in the domestic economic context. Throughout the 1950s and especially the 1960s, the Japanese economy grew at an unprecedented rate. Through the entire decade of the 1960s, the GNP rose in real terms at an average of over 11 percent a year. During this period the Japanese people and the political and economic elites were largely unified behind the goal of building a strong economy through a growth-at-any-cost policy. Economic success, however, has undermined the national consensus on continued growth as the primary goal.

Japanese governments today are faced with a growing diversity of demands for resources that can no longer be easily ignored. More funds must now be diverted for welfare benefits, pollution control, and other measures aimed at improving the quality of life in Japan. There is also a growing need to spend more on research and development, as Japan must increasingly invent technologies rather than import them, as in the past, to move its economy further ahead. In the international arena, Japan's allies

[5] *Japan Statistical Yearbook,* op. cit., 1950–1981; William K. Cummings, *Education and Equality in Japan* (Princeton: Princeton University Press, 1980).

are demanding that it pay a larger share of the defense burden for maintaining security in East Asia. In addition, Japan's neighbors and third-world trading partners are demanding more foreign aid and development funds.

Japan, then, will increasingly have to shoulder more of the costs of success. But at the same time, while the Japanese economy is now strong, its foundations contain certain inherent weaknesses. Japan is poor in natural resources and must import 88 percent of its energy, most of the raw materials for its industries, and even 30 percent of its food supplies. With the skyrocketing costs of energy following the Arab oil boycott and OPEC price hikes in the 1970s, Japan was able to maintain a favorable balance of payments only through an aggressive expansion of exports. Today, however, Japanese trade practices are meeting with growing resistance and threats of protectionism abroad. In the meantime, while labor costs have soared, Japanese industry is now experiencing increasing competition from growing industries in developing countries where labor is cheaper, and not only in labor intensive industries but also in capital intensive industries such as steel. To compete with this threat, Japan will have to phase out some industries and increase automation and productivity through applications of robotics in others.[6]

The changes in the economic context have resulted in lower growth rates. During the 1970s, the Japanese economy grew at only about half the rate it achieved during the 1960s, and real sustained growth rates that average over 5 to 6 percent a year are unlikely in the future. These lower growth rates combined with the dislocation of workers through automation and changes in the industrial structure are likely to lead to rising rates of unemployment.

What will the implications of these changes be for Japan's lifetime employment system? Even now the lifetime employment system is a reality for only about 25 percent of the labor force, an elite class of workers employed in large enterprises. Maintaining this system was feasible in a period of rapid economic expansion when labor was in short supply. The system was sus-

[6] Ronald A. Morse, ed., *The Politics of Japan's Energy Strategy* (Berkeley: Institute of East Asian Studies, University of California, 1981); Ezra F. Vogel, *Japan as Number One* (Cambridge: Harvard University Press, 1979) pp. 9–23.

tained by Japan's dual economic structure in which small and medium enterprises have coexisted with large enterprises through a system of subcontracting. Thus the workers in companies with only thirty to ninety-nine workers enjoy far less job security and only 60 percent of the wages and benefits of workers in firms with over five thousand employees. The denial of job security to women and the early retirement of older workers have been other safety valves that have preserved the system. Now there are growing signs that the system is under stress as declining industries are increasingly resorting to "voluntary" early retirement programs aimed at weeding out older, more expensive, and less productive workers. Moreover, those Japanese workers who are laid off in their forties and fifties are finding much more difficulty in locating second careers than has been true in the past.[7] For those workers on the job, there are smaller bonuses, fewer opportunities for advancement, and increasing worries about whether pension schemes will still be solvent when they retire. As the company's ability to take care of its workers in a changing economic environment weakens, the worker is likely to reassess his dedication and loyalty to the company.

These changes in the socioeconomic environment and socialization experiences in the home, school, and work place are already having profound effects on the attitudes and values of Japanese. Again the signs of change are most apparent among the young. Young workers display less diligence on the job and less loyalty to their company. They are more likely to contemplate changing jobs, more eager to take their paid vacations, and less willing to put in overtime. Managers complain that workers used to work on Saturdays, even without pay, but now the younger workers not only refuse to work on weekends, but will not put in overtime on weekdays without pay. Indeed, a recent survey reported that one of the most common complaints among young Japanese is that working hours are too long and vacations too short. Young workers are also less eager to be enveloped by the company and company life. There are growing sign of a rise in more limited,

[7] Nevins, op. cit., pp. 27–29. A recent survey of 610 major Japanese manufacturing firms reported that the lifetime employment system is becoming a growing burden for many companies, with 72 percent reporting some excess labor and 38 percent reporting that over 20 percent of their employees were redundant workers. *The Japan Times Weekly,* 3/12/83, p. 8.

contractual orientations towards the job among employees in their twenties who increasingly are refusing to live in company dormitories and are withdrawing from after-hours contacts with superiors.[8]

There are also disquieting signs of a rise in an emphasis on self-gratification among the young and rising levels of drug abuse, crime, and senseless violence. Juvenile delinquency has risen 80 percent between 1972–1982, and government White Papers and surveys of teachers and principals have described Japanese students as increasingly apathetic in their studies, prone to lying, lacking a sense of guilt for misconduct, devoid of perseverance, and self-centered. Most alarming from the perspective of Japan's traditional values is the growing incidence of violence against teachers and parents. There has also been an appearance of "thrill violence" with groups of delinquent boys and girls attacking vagrants and other weak victims. Several observers are labeling the younger generation in Japan today a lost generation, one that is out of touch with traditional Japanese values and not yet adjusted to any other cohesive value system. Some young Japanese are now calling themselves "the crystal generation." If this is meant to signify glitter and emptiness, it seems an appropriate label. In fact, many of the current movies and novels popular among this generation reflect the themes of a lack of direction or goals, mindless self-gratification, and a sense of aimless floating.[9]

VALUE CHANGE

Given the difference in cultural starting points, the incidence of crime, drug abuse, and juvenile delinquency in Japan is still much lower than that in the United States and Western Europe, and Japanese workers continue to exhibit more diligence and commitment to their companies; therefore, this discussion of the social changes that are taking place must be kept in perspective.

---

8 Christopher, op. cit., p .87; Robert E. Cole, *Japanese Blue Collar* (Berkeley: University of California Press, 1971), pp. 199–213; Youth Bureau, *The Youth of the World and Japan* (Tokyo: Prime Minister's Office, 1978), pp. 52–55; Hitoshi Kato, "Japan's First Postwar Generation," *Japan Echo* 10 (Spring 1983), pp. 79, 82–84.

9 Alan Booth, "Why Japanese Youth Are the 'Crystal Generation,'" *The Asian Wall Street Journal*, 12/14/82; *The Japan Times Weekly*, 3/5/83, p. 4; 4/23/83, p. 6; *Time*, 8/1/83, pp. 23–24; Robert C. Christopher, *The Japanese Mind* (New York: Linden Press, 1983) pp. 135–136, 162–163.

Japan is still a cohesive, group-oriented society by Western standards, yet it will increasingly have to face many of the problems associated with advanced industrialism in the West. Some Japanese commentators have observed that socioeconomic developments in Japan, both good and bad, tend to mirror those in the United States with a lag of ten years. This fact does not necessarily indicate that Japanese values are converging with Western values. Even where the direction of change is the same, differences in the rates of change may actually widen cross-national differences. Moreover, on some value dimensions, the patterns of change are dissimilar and do not point towards convergence. There are nevertheless a number of changes in the socioeconomic conditions of life that are common to all advanced industrial societies and are pushing an associated cluster of values in a similar direction. The effects on value change of four major changes in life circumstances characteristic of highly developed, mass consumption societies will be noted here.

The first of these is a change from a highly stratified, hierarchic society to an egalitarian one. In comparison with agricultural and even industrial societies, postindustrial societies are characterized by a growing homogeniety of resources and lifestyles that is progressively blurring class distinctions. Blue and white collar wage scales have overlapped increasingly, and both knowledge and wealth have become more equally distributed throughout society as a result of rising levels of education and the growing diffusion of information throughout the mass media.[10] This long-term equalization of life changes, individual resources, and life-styles has undermined the scope and magnitude of authority that one individual can exercise over another. In addition, increasing affluence and institutional guarantees in the form of insurance and welfare systems have weakened personal dependencies on powerful authority figures. As a result, hierarchic and deferential orientations are increasingly being replaced by egalitarian, self-assertive norms.

A second fundamental change in life circumstances is the accelerating pace of change. Traditional, agrarian societies were based on stability, continuity and custom. Whatever had been done in the past was right and whatever was new or different was

10 Yasusuke Murakami, "The Age of New Middle Mass Politics," *The Journal of Japanese Studies* 8 (Winter 1982), pp. 29–72.

suspect. With industrial societies, however, change has become a basic fact of life and traditions and customs are becoming less and less reliable guideposts for successful coping behavior. As a result, values that stress conformity and conservatism are steadily being replaced by those that emphasize independence and innovation.

A third major change in life circumstances is the transformation of human society from a condition of scarcity to one of affluence. The advent of the welfare state has witnessed the enactment into law of an unprecedented set of guarantees against injury, sickness, loss of job, old age problems, impoverishment, and a host of other social ills. For the average citizen living in an advanced industrial society today, there is less objective need to keep one's nose to the grindstone than in any previous epoch in human history. Modern man is no longer confronted with survival imperatives that require disciplining his consumptive urges and storing up a surplus as a hedge against the unpredictable exigencies of fire, famine, and war. As a result, the traditional values of diligence, frugality, and striving for economic success — the so-called Protestant work ethic — have increasingly been supplanted by proclivities towards self-indulgence, immediate gratification, and a growing preoccupation with leisure activities.

The fourth important change in life circumstances is the advance of knowledge, especially scientific knowledge. The advance of knowledge is increasing man's ability to control his environment and understand himself. In most traditional societies, people sought protection from the ravages of nature and unknown threatening forces through religion and the worship of nature and the supernatural. Technology and scientific discoveries have pushed back the frontiers of the great mysteries of life. Science has taught us that sickness is not God's punishment for moral transgressions and that natural disasters are not divine providence but rather are the result of weather patterns which can be predicted and perhaps controlled. Fertilizers, improved grain hybrids, and pest and irrigation control will produce high yields, not prayers to unseen spirits residing in rocks or waterfalls. The decline in mysticism and religiosity have been associated with more permissive attitudes. For example, moral sanctions against premarital sex are less compelling in an environment where contraceptives, abortion, and disease control have largely eliminated the penalties associated with greater sexual freedom. The diffusion of knowledge and scientific advances, therefore, have induced a change from pietism and strict moral codes to more permissive values that are tolerant of a broader range of behavior.

In sum, values are changing in response to four major changes in life circumstances — a growing equality in incomes and life-styles, the accelerating pace of change, rising affluence and economic security, and the advance and diffusion of scientific knowledge. These changes are increasingly liberating people from the constraining conditions of subservience, conformity, scarcity, and ignorance and enabling them to pursue more fully the goal of self-actualization. The result has been (1) a shift in sociopolitical values from an emphasis on authority and conformity to a stress on equality and individualism, and (2) a shift in social-psychological values from austerity and piety to self-indulgence and permissiveness. Politically, the former changes have been manifested in more assertive, participatory orientations and more open-minded attitudes towards minority views and dissident behavior; and the latter have been manifested in growing concerns for a variety of quality-of-life issues and liberal positions on a number of social issues that reflect a tolerance for differing life-styles.

Empirically, since it has been found that these four conceptual dimensions of value change are closely interrelated, they have been combined in a single value scale that labels the old cluster of traditional values authoritarian and the new cluster of post-industrial values libertarian.[11] It has also been found that the shift from authoritarian to libertarian values is largely a product of intergenerational replacement and education. New generations are being socialized under the new kinds of conditions we have outlined. Since basic value orientations tend to be acquired early in life, the changes in life circumstances have had little effect on the values of older generations. Instead, the newer libertarian values tend to show up mostly among the younger generations

11 Libertarian here means an emphasis of those values that stress individual freedom in thought and action — equality, individualism, self-indulgence, permissiveness, and self-assertiveness. The authoritarian-libertarian value change is a similar but more broadly conceptualized type of change from that discussed by Ronald Inglehart in *The Silent Revolution* (Princeton: Princeton University Press, 1977). See Scott C. Flanagan, "Changing Values in Advanced Industrial Societies," *Comparative Political Studies* 14 (January 1982) pp. 403–444.

who have grown up in a postindustrial environment, and among those who have received higher levels of education and are thereby more aware of and open to the changes that are taking place in society.

Because of the rapid rate of socioeconomic change and development during the postwar period, the generation gap is much wider and more visible in Japan than in societies that have experienced lower rates of growth, such as the United States and Britain. As a result, the political effects of this value change are more apparent in Japan than in some other nations. It will be shown that the libertarian value change is associated with important changes in political behavior — higher levels of political interest, efficacy, cynicism, and protest activities — and changes in partisan support — a shift towards the left in issue positions and voting preferences. While the rate of change and the balance between traditional and postindustrial values may differ from nation to nation, the type of change and its political ramifications seem to be a fairly universal phenomenon that is affecting all advanced industrial societies.

There are two other kinds of important value changes taking place in Japanese society today. These are shifts from parochial to cosmopolitan, and from personalistic to universalistic, values. While the authoritarian-libertarian dimension of change exhibits the most pronounced pattern of intergenerational change, the parochial-cosmopolitan dimension is more strongly related to education. In comparison, the personalism-universalism dimension reflects the lowest levels of cleavage and change, attesting to the continuing high valuation placed on particularistic-diffuse relationships in Japan today. Nevertheless, some movement is apparent on all three of these value scales.[12]

In the West, these latter two kinds of value change were associated with the earlier agrarian-industrial transformation. Because of Japan's more recent and rapid emergence from an agrarian stage of development, industrial and postindustrial kinds of

[12] A scale of parochial attitudes was constructed from the first three survey questions reported in Table 5.2 and a personalism scale from the four questions in Table 4.1 (both this volume). *See* Scott C. Flanagan, "Cultural Cleavages, Social Networks and Voting Behavior in Japan," presented at the annual meeting of the Southern Political Science Association, Hyatt Regency Hotel, Atlanta, Georgia, November 6–8, 1980.

value change have become intertwined. Those Japanese who have rejected the parochial, personalistic orientations associated with agrarian societies tend to be the same individuals who have rejected the achievement, work ethic, and hierarchic norms associated with industrial society. The following sections on political behavior and electoral change will identify in sharper detail the combined effects on Japanese politics of the ecological, social, and value changes that have been discussed.

POLITICAL CULTURE AND POLITICAL INVOLVEMENT

Japan's political culture presents something of a paradox in the area of political involvement. The Japanese population ranks very high on media exposure to politics, education, and many measures of political information. These are all variables associated in the United States with high levels of psychological involvement in politics and active participation. The same pattern of associations also holds in Japan, but given the high levels of political awareness, the levels of psychological involvement and active participation in politics seem unusually low, at least by American standards. This phenomenon has led some observers to label Japan a spectator culture.[13] A spectator orientation is one that observes politics from the sidelines with a kind of curious interest, but displays little emotional or personal involvement. To evaluate how appropriate this label is, we must look more closely at the evidence on awareness and involvement.

Japan is a leader throughout the world in the production and consumption of information. The Japanese are avid readers; virtually 100 percent of the population is literate with nearly every man, woman, and child reporting that they read books, magazines, and newspapers. In fact, the per capita publication rate is roughly 25 weekly and monthly magazines and 10 books a year. That is 100 magazines and 40 books for every family of four. The three leading daily newspapers in Japan rank first, second, and fourth in circulation figures throughout the non-Communist world. Comparative circulation figures for 1977 place Japan at

---

[13] Scott C. Flanagan, "The Genesis of Variant Political Cultures," in Sidney Verba and Lucian W. Pye, *The Citizen and Politics* (Stamford, Conn.: Greylock, 1978), pp. 129–165; Mitsuru Uchida, *Seiji Sanka to Seiji Katei* (Tokyo: Maeno Shoten, 1972).

the top with 526 daily newspapers per one thousand population. The next highest figure was 397 for the USSR, with Britain close behind. The corresponding figure for the United States was 287. Television has also completely saturated Japan, with virtually every household having one or more sets. Only one percent of the population report not viewing television, and the average citizen watches 3 to 4 hours a day.[14]

The heavy investment of time in books, magazines, newspapers, and television is not just a mindless search for diversion. The intellectual standards of the written and electronic communications that are utilized are often quite high. In Japan, intellectuals and leading academics are frequent contributors of articles to mass circulation magazines and newspapers. Books, which in the United States would be regarded as limited circulation scholarly works, have on occasion become best-sellers in Japan. The Japan Broadcasting Corporation (NHK) operates two television channels, one of which is devoted to educational and instructional programming and the other of which broadcasts cultural programs of exceptional quality. The popularity of these channels attests to the Japanese thirst for knowledge. There seems to be almost a preoccupation in Japan for lifelong learning and self-improvement, a trait that can be traced to the Confucian tradition of respect for education. The high levels of media consumption are probably further reinforced by holistic norms that stimulate a desire to keep abreast of current trends so as not to stand out or be left out. Little wonder, then, that the term *information society* has become so popular in Japan. Indeed, Japan may come closest to that notion of a society where information is more highly valued than material things.

Exposure to political information through the media also appears to be quite high. For example, 62 percent of the respondents in the 1976 JABISS National Election Study reported that they watched television news programs daily, while 92 percent reported watching at least once a week. Moreover, of the 95 percent that reported reading a newspaper regularly, 85 percent read at least

[14] *Statistical Yearbook* (New York: United National Educational, Scientific and Cultural Organization, 1977); Maureen Donovan, "The Media in Japan," in Bradley M. Richardson and Taizo Ueda, eds., *Business and Society in Japan* (New York: Praeger, 1981), pp. 258–268.

one election-related article during the 1976 HR election campaign. Exposure to political information through the media, therefore, appears to be at least as high in Japan as it is in the United States.

In turning to measures of psychological involvement, however, one finds significantly lower levels in Japan. Table 6.2 shows that 32–38 percent of the American respondents report high interest in politics and elections compared to only 10–17 percent of the Japanese respondents. In regard to the discussion of politics, the comparisons are even more telling; 85 percent of the American respondents report discussing politics at least some of the time compared to only 42 percent of the Japanese. The more recent JABISS study reveals similar low levels of discussion. Only one third of the Japanese respondents report discussing politics with neighbors, friends, and coworkers, and only half with family members.

There is a similar pattern in the more active forms of political involvement. Table 6.3 shows that the Japanese are more likely to belong to some kind of organization than Americans are. Studies have shown that organizational involvement is strongly associated with political participation.[15] The same pattern holds true in Japan, but once again the linkage is somewhat weaker than in the United States, because the Japanese tend to be less active than Americans in their organizations, and Japanese organizations are less likely to discuss politics. Other measures of partisan identification and campaign activities reported in Table 6.4 show a similar pattern of somewhat lower levels of involvement in Japan.

These data must be interpreted with care. Obviously there is considerable political activity in Japan, even though the levels are not as high as typically found in the United States. On many indicators of political involvement and participation, the Japanese compare favorably with a number of European mass publics. Moreover, there are several areas where the Japanese appear to surpass Americans in participation levels. For instance, around 70 percent of the eligible voters in Japan typically turn out to vote

---

15 Norman H. Nie, G. Bingham Powell, and Kenneth Prewitt, "Social Structure and Political Participation: Development Relationships," *APSR* 63 (June 1969), pp. 361–378.

TABLE 6.2. *Levels of Political Interest and Political Discussion in Japan and the United States*

	Interest in Politics and National Affairs						Interest in Elections			
Level of Interest	Japan 1966	U.S. 1967	Japan 1976	U.S. 1976						Japan 1976	U.S. 1976
Very Interested	10	32	17	38						13	37
Somewhat Interested	32	35	31	32						47	42
Little or No Interest	53	24	48	30						37	21
Missing Data	4	9	3	0						3	0
Total Percent	99	100	99	100						100	100
N of Cases	2657	3095	1563	2388						1563	2856

Discusses Politics and National Affairs

Frequency of Discussion	Japan 1966	U.S. 1967
Daily	3	16
Sometimes	39	69
Never	48	15
Missing Data	11	0
Total Percent	101	100
N of Cases	1657	3095

Source: Japan 1966 and U.S. 1967, The Cross-National Participation Study, Verba, Nie, Ikeuchi, et al.; Japan 1976, the JABISS Japanese Election Study; U.S. 1976, SRC/CPS National Election Study. See Chapter 5, footnotes 14 and 16.

TABLE 6.3. *Organizational Involvement in Japan and the United States*

Percentage of Respondents Who:	Japan	U.S.
Belong to an organization	73	62
Are active in an organization	32	40
Belong to an organization in which political discussion takes place	16	31
Were active members of an organization engaged in solving community problems	11	32
Helped form a local group	5	14
Were members of a political club or organization	4	8

Source: The Cross-National Participation Studies, Verba, Nie, et al. See Chapter 5, footnote 16.

in the national HR elections. Even in presidential elections, American turnout figures generally range 10–15 percentage points below the Japanese rates. In Japan, however, high levels of voting participation are not necessarily indicative of high political involvement, as is evident from the fact that turnout levels are highest in Japan's rural areas where they usually exceed 80 percent in national elections and attain even higher rates in local elections. These high rates are an expression of mobilized participation on the basis of social obligations and community solidarity and do not necessarily reflect much interest in national politics.

TABLE 6.4. *Partisan Identification and Campaign Activities in Japan and the United States*

Percentage of Respondents Who:	Japan 67	U.S. 68	Japan 76	U.S. 76
Identified with a party	66	88	60	63
Strong identifiers	12	30	13	24
Attended political meeting	10	8		
Gave money to party or candidate	2	8		
Worked for party or candidate	3	5		

Source: Japan 67, Japanese Election Study, Ward and Kubota; Japan 76, JABISS Election Study; U.S. 68 and 76, SRC/CPS National Election Studies.

Conversely, in the larger metropolitan districts where community ties are weaker, turnout rates often drop below 65 percent.[16]

Japanese voters are also more likely than Americans to have attended a political meeting during an election campaign, as a result of the Japanese campaign practice of organizing candidate meetings on the neighborhood level in local homes and other meeting places. The candidates and various spokesmen and supporters are paraded through a good number of such meetings in a staggered caravan fashion in a single evening. Thus election meetings are more accessible and convenient for the Japanese voter to attend. Moreover, their participation in them may in many cases reflect considerations of social obligations more than political interest. Nevertheless, the practice does provide Japanese voters with a more personal, direct opportunity to meet the candidate and/or his spokesmen than is available to most Americans.

While the cross-national data on participation levels presents somewhat of a mixed picture, however, more subjective indicators suggest that there is a distinct difference in levels of emotional involvement between American and Japanese voters. American presidential elections are extended and massive yearlong media events — from the spring primaries to the hoopla of the summer party conventions to the fall campaigns. In both national and local elections, Americans seem to be more caught up with and fascinated by the electoral process. Absent from Japan are the large number of small political contributions from average citizens, the hordes of unpaid campaign volunteers, the bumper stickers and yard signs.

A measure of this greater detachment from politics is found in the affective distance between citizen and party in Japan. During the postwar period, Japanese have tended to have largely negative images of political parties, national leaders, and politicians in general, and also to have weak to nominal attachments to parties. The differences in the levels of American and Japanese strong identifiers reported in Table 6.4 is one indicator of the weaker Japanese attachments to their political parties. These dif-

[16] Voting rates are reported in the *Japan Statistical Yearbook* and *Chiho Senkyo Kekka-cho* (Tokyo: Election Bureau, Home Affairs Ministry), appropriate years.

ferences were most apparent in the early 1960s, when party loyalties were still very strong in the United States. Since then a party dealignment process has been set in motion in the United States and many European democracies that has narrowed the differences that appear on cross-national public opinion surveys. While the decline in enthusiasm for electoral politics is a fairly recent occurrence in the United States, however, psychological involvement levels have never been high in Japan.

There are, then, some grounds for categorizing the Japanese mass public as one that is high in political awareness but low in emotional involvement. If Japan is in some ways a spectator political culture, however, the galleries are filled with many different types of spectators. This point might be simplified by suggesting that in ideal terms there are two types of galleries, a gallery of traditional and one of modern spectators. Each type of spectator has chosen to sit on the sidelines for different reasons. Seated in the gallery of traditionals, one is likely to find citizens who are older and low in education, women, rural inhabitants and farmers, and small retailers or workers in small enterprises. These individuals have a parochial, deferential, personalistic orientation towards politics and sit on the sidelines because of low levels of interest and psychological involvement in politics. Their interests are centered on local matters, and they tend to be distrustful of distant political leaders and happenings. They prefer to delegate responsibility for political affairs outside their communities to familiar representatives from their hometowns.

Seated in the gallery of moderns one is likely to find those who are younger and high in education, men, urban residents, and blue and white collar workers in large enterprises. These individuals have a more cosmopolitan, self-assertive, issue orientation towards politics. Nevertheless, many of them are found on the sidelines because of their cynicism regarding the possibility of improving the political situation and because, for some, they find few opportunities or channels of participation available to them. Ironically, it is the presence of the traditional gallery, which for so many years enabled the LDP to be returned regularly to office despite its corrupt practices, that has frustrated, disillusioned, and sidelined many of those seated in the modern gallery.

In short, while both types of citizens may choose to sit out the political game, their reasons differ markedly. Moreover, the behavior of the two galleries is starkly contrasting. While the traditionals are likely to sit in stoic silence, the modern gallery is more apt to empty onto the field at unpredictable moments to protest a decision. It is therefore important to note that the kinds of socioeconomic and value changes discussed above have been depleting the traditional and filling the modern gallery. This shift in political orientations is not without important consequences for political participation in Japan.

To clarify this point, the effects of the socioeconomic and value changes discussed above on levels and types of participation must be examined more closely. First, value change has complex and inconsistent effects on participation. All three value-change scales discussed — the authoritarian-libertarian, personalism-universalism, and parochial-cosmopolitan scales — are strongly related, both individually and in a combined traditional-modern value scale, with political efficacy, political interest, and other measures of psychological involvement. Since modern values enhance efficacy and psychological involvement, which in turn are associated with higher levels of participation, this effect of value change should stimulate participation. At the same time, however, the shift towards modern values is associated with an increase in cynism, political distrust, and declining levels of support for the system. This effect of value change reduces the probability of participation in voting, campaign activities, and other forms of conventional political participation. It has been found that these two counteracting effects of value change tend to wash each other out. As a result, none of the more active forms of conventional political participation, such as contacting officials, attending political meetings, or working in campaigns, are related to value change. Moreover, those with modern values are slightly *less* likely to turn out to vote than those with traditional values.[17]

When unconventional political activities are examined, however, such as participation in demonstrations, refusing to co-

[17] These findings and those reported in the remainder of this section are drawn from: Scott C. Flanagan, "Political Involvement, Informal Communications and the Vote," presented at the Conference on Japanese Voting Behavior, Sophia University, Tokyo, Japan, March 27–28, 1981; Scott C. Flanagan and Steven Renten, "Social Networks and Political Participation in Japan," presented at the annual meeting of the American Political Science Association, New York Hilton, New York, Sept. 3–5, 1981.

operate with government directives and other kinds of protest activities, a different outcome is found. Here higher levels of cynicism are positively related to protest activities, so that in this case the two effects of value change have a reinforcing effect on participation levels. As a result, it has been found that modern values are strongly associated with higher levels of protest behavior. These relationships are schematically presented in Figure 6.1. Consequently, value change has been associated with a rise in unconventional forms of political behavior.

A second important impact on participation levels is derived from the various socioeconomic changes that have been described. As discussed below, one impact of urbanization and rising levels of occupational and geographic mobility has been to break down the solidarity and effectiveness of community-based, areal organizations. While involvement in such organizations and associational networks is much lower, membership in community organizations has to some extent been replaced by membership in nonareal organizations, such as labor unions, professional organizations, and a variety of other extracommunity organizations including recreational and hobby groups. Organizations and informal social networks provide individuals with the necessary resources, channels, and motivations for participating in politics.

FIGURE 6.1. *The Relationships Between Value Change and Conventional and Unconventional Participation*

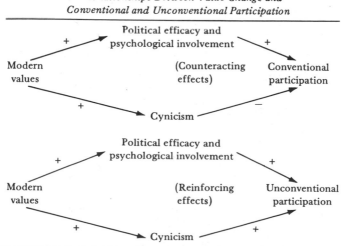

Hence, both formal and informal associational ties, or what will be called network involvement, is an important determinant of levels of participation.

The movement from one type of organization to another, as an outcome of the urbanization process, should have no effect on participation levels because, for example, unions can mobilize participation just as effectively as rural, community-based organizations. However, it has been found that organizations are less dense in urban areas, meaning that there are fewer organizations and organizational memberships in urban areas on a per capita basis. Since urban residents come in contact with fewer mobilizing channels of participation, there is a negative relationship between urbanization and all forms of conventional participation.

It has been shown that across all the various conventional forms of political participation, with the exception of voting, the two strongest predictors by far are network involvement and psychological involvement. In the case of voting, the major difference is that psychological involvement has a weaker, but still substantial, effect and comes in third after age. Older Japanese are much more likely to vote. The central importance of these two variables, network and psychological involvement, on all types of conventional participation suggests a typology of participants based on the standard two by two table, as shown in Figure 6.2.

Those who are high on both network and psychological involvement are labeled *integrated*. Those occupational categories

FIGURE 6.2. *Participant Types by Levels of Psychological and Network Involvement*

		Psychological involvement	
		High	Low
Network involvement	High	Integrated	Mobilized
	Low	Inhibited	Detached

that fall into this classification were found to be executives, professionals, owners of retail and other small enterprises, blue and white collar unionists, and farm owners. The opposite category, those low on both types of involvement, are labeled *detached*. It was found that blue collar nonunionists, their wives and families, and the unemployed fell into this category. The other two categories are in some ways the most interesting. The *mobilized* are those that are low on psychological involvement and high on network involvement. The wives and family workers of farmers and small retailers fall into this category. Conversely, the *inhibited* are those with high psychological involvement but low network involvement. White collar nonunionists, their wives and family members, and students fit this pattern.

As might be expected, the integrated were found to exhibit the highest levels of conventional participation, while the detached were uniformly low. The more interesting finding, however, was that the inhibited scored little better than the detached on all forms of conventional participation. This demonstrates the vital importance of network ties in motivating active participation. In contrast, the mobilized scored as high as the integrated on voting participation, and while fairly low on other forms of participation, still scored higher than the inhibited.

It is important to note that the mobilized tend to live in rural areas and/or be associated with traditional occupations (farmers and the old middle class), while the detached and inhibited tend to live in urban areas and work in modern occupations (blue collar workers and the new middle class). Thus the ecological changes we have discussed are expanding the detached and inhibited categories at the expense of the mobilized category. The net result is a slight depressing effect on the levels of participation, although one might argue that the quality of participation is enhanced. A case in point is a category of voters, dubbed the forgetful voters, that emerged from the 1976 JABISS study. These voters reported that they voted in the 1976 HR election held one to two weeks prior to the interviews, but they had forgotten who they voted for. An analysis has shown that these forgetful voters were substantially lower in psychological involvement than the nonvoters. At the same time, however, they exhibited high levels of network involvement, and clearly that was what motivated their participation.

When we turn to unconventional participation, however, once again we find a markedly different story. Protest activities, as it turns out, are not so much related to the level of network involvement as the types of networks one is involved with. Thus it has been found that unconventional participation is associated with involvement in leftist networks, such as unions, employment in modern occupational environments (i.e., as blue and white collar workers in large enterprises), and the internalization of leftist political ideologies.

In sum, then, value and ecological changes are having a mixed impact on political participation. On the one hand, their impact on conventional forms of participation is either nil or slightly negative. But in the case of unconventional participation, they exert a strong positive effect on increasing involvement levels. The socioeconomic and value changes discussed at the beginning of this chapter, therefore, are having a substantial effect on the mode or form of political participation in Japan.

POLITICAL DISAFFECTION AND POLITICAL STABILITY

Mass political behavior in Japan presents us with a second paradox — the juxtaposition of high levels of political disaffection with high levels of political stability. On a number of indicators of political trust and system support, the Japanese mass public has scored unusually low. While most of the survey evidence available is drawn from the 1960s and 1970s, fragmentary earlier evidence suggests that low levels of satisfaction with politics, at least in comparison with the United States and Britain, have been characteristic of the entire postwar period. Typically it has been found that large majorities feel that government leaders do not understand the people's wishes, are unresponsive to their needs, and run the government for the benefit of big business and other special interests. Distrust of politics and political leaders is widespread, and on the question of overall satisfaction with politics, only 20–30 percent generally express satisfaction, while 65–75 percent are dissatisfied.[18]

Particularly in the area of the image of politicians and the activities of politicians, perceptions appear to be unusually nega-

[18] Scott C. Flanagan and Bradley M. Richardson, "Political Disaffection and Political Stability: A Comparison of Japanese and Western Findings," in Richard F. Tomasson, ed., *Comparative Social Research* III (Greenwich, Conn.: JAI Press, 1980), pp. 6–19.

tive. For example, a 1974 Mainichi survey gave respondents a list of twenty adjectives, half positive and half negative, in the semantic differential format and asked them to identify all those that came to mind when they thought of Japanese politicians. The top five choices in frequency of response were rich, shifty, dishonest, overbearing, and aged. Of course, politicians do not necessarily have strong positive images in other countries, but comparative data reveal that the Japanese image of politicians is far more negative than what is found in many Western democracies. For instance, a similar list of twenty-three positive and negative adjectives given to a sample of British university students found that the top five choices listed in order of frequency were ambitious, intelligent, shrewd, persuasive, and manipulative. Thus even in comparative terms, the Japanese image of politicians is remarkably negative.[19]

Socialization studies have revealed that negative images of political leaders and politicians in general are acquired at an unusually young age in Japan. For example, comparative data from a 1961 Japan-United States survey indicates that the Japanese child's view of the prime minister, while largely positive through the sixth grade, is much less positive than the American child's image of the president. Also, by the ninth grade, 63 percent of the Japanese children regard their political leader as "not a very good person" compared to only 2 percent of the eighth-grade American children. Tadao Okamura in a 1968 landmark study of over six thousand Japanese children in grades 3 through 12 tapped five dimensions of the prime minister's image — liking, honesty, capability, popularity, and wealth. By the fifth grade, he found more negative than positive responses on the dimension of liking, by the sixth honesty and popularity became predominantly negative, and by the tenth grade even the prime minister's competence was viewed more negatively than positively.[20]

19 *The Mainichi Shimbun,* 6/26/74, p. 9; Jack Citrin and David Elkins, *Political Disaffection Among British University Students* (Berkeley: Institute of International Studies Research Series, No. 23, University of California, 1975).

20 Tadao Okamura, "Gendai Nihon ni Okeru Seijiteki Shakaika," in The Japan Political Science Association, ed., *Seijigaku Nempo* (Tokyo: Iwanami Shoten, 1971), pp. 1–68; Tadao Okamura, "Seiji Ishiki no Kitei to shite no Soridaijin-zo," in *Gendai Gyosei to Kanryo-sei* (Tokyo: Todai Shuppankei, 1974), pp. 384–424.

The image of Japanese Dietmen comes off only slightly better in the eyes of Japanese children. Okamura asked his respondents to put a circle around the two things that come to mind when one thinks about a Dietman, listing three positive images (a person who keeps his promises, a great man, and a man who does his utmost for the sake of all) and three negative images (a person who takes money on the sly and does bad things, a person who is arrogant, and a person who tells lies). Through the seventh grade a majority chose both positive images, but by the ninth the positive and negative responses were almost even. Apparently in the first year of senior high school, the negative image of Dietmen rises dramatically and predominates throughout the remainder of the child's secondary education.[21]

As these findings suggest, politics is not viewed as a desirable profession. Few Japanese children growing up aspire to be politicians. Politics seems to be regarded as a necessary evil, a dirty business that requires politicians to soil their hands. When some American academics first encountered Okamura's findings in the 1960s, they were led to question the future of democracy in Japan. From that historical perspective, the Japanese response patterns seemed so much more negative than American responses as to raise the issue of political stability. Yet since the early 1970s, after the question of the governability of democracy had become fashionable in the West, Japanese scholars have been more optimistic about political stability in their country than American and European scholars have in theirs.[22]

There are at least four factors that account for the juxtaposition of high levels of political disaffection and political stability in Japan. First the high levels of political cynicism are a reflection of a number of longstanding problems with the political state of affairs in Japan. Many segments of the Japanese electorate are disenchanted with the corruption, money politics, and unresponsiveness of the LDP establishment, but lack confidence in the Socialists' and Communists' ability to manage the economy and maintain the prosperity and stability of the nation. As the center parties remain too weak to provide a viable alternative to continued conservative rule, it has been impossible to "throw

---

21 Okamura, "Gendai Nihon," ibid., pp. 20–21.
22 Michel Crozier, Samuel Huntington, and Joji Watanuki, *The Crisis of Democracy* (New York: New York University Press, 1975).

the rascals out" and thus to institute comprehensive political reforms.

Cynicism, therefore, seems to be an appropriate, realistic orientation for the Japanese citizen. Are these views aberrant, compared to other democracies, and do they threaten the stability of the Japanese political system? In the context of the mid-1960s, when levels of political trust were high in the United States, Britain, and a number of other advanced industrial societies, many Western scholars probably would have answered yes. Since then, however, events such as Vietnam and Watergate in the United States, economic difficulties, and the effects of postindustrial value change have made high levels of cynicism commonplace in the West.[23] Now we are likely to see cynicism as more eufunctional than dysfunctional, as a sign of a growing political sophistication and vigilance among the public, which is replacing the more naive, trusting orientations of the past.

Second, it is important to distinguish the target of attack, whether the current crop of party leaders and incumbent office holders or the system itself. It has been found that many of the most alarmingly negative indicators of political disaffection are directed at incumbent office holders and politicians in general. These have been shown to be generalized ritualistic attitudes which are not by themselves associated with any form of alienated political behavior. Moreover, while support for political parties and politicians is low, support for the institutions of democracy remains quite high. There is strong support for the maintenance of the constitution, elections, the Diet, and the other democratic institutions of postwar Japan. So long as the principal target of political disaffection remains at the incumbent level, the stability of Japan's political institutions will not be severely threatened.[24]

Third, the high levels of political distrust in Japan are coupled with comparatively low levels of political efficacy. The Japanese citizen is less likely to think that he can do anything about the political problems he sees than the American citizen. The spectator culture tradition of low levels of participation, coupled with

[23] Gabriel A. Almond and Sidney Verba, eds., *The Civic Culture Revisited* (Boston: Little, Brown, 1980); Samuel H. Barnes and Max Kaase, et al., *Political Action* (Beverly Hills: Sage, 1979).

[24] Flanagan and Richardson, op. cit., pp. 3–6, 26–40; Joseph A. Massey, *Youth and Politics in Japan* (Lexington, Mass.: Lexington Books, 1976) pp. 38–48; Hajime Ikeuchi, ed., *Shimin Ishiki no Kenkyu* (Tokyo: Tokyo University Press, 1974), p. 369.

the comparatively high levels of inefficacy, deference, and passivity discussed in the last chapter, provide the Japanese polity with an added cushion of stability. In comparative terms this means that alienated citizens in Japan are more likely to withdraw into political apathy than their American counterparts. To some extent, then, Japan's political culture inhibits the translation of disaffection into active protest behavior.

Finally, local politics is more positively perceived by most Japanese and hence to some extent compensates for the more negative images of national politics. For the more traditionally oriented Japanese, we find that the distrust of politicians in general is offset by positive feelings towards his own district representative. Since local events are his central concern, if politics in the capital is corrupt, he is likely simply to shrug it off. He expects it, but it does not upset him very much, so long as all is well within his immediate environment. For those with modern values, who have been frustrated by the difficulty of affecting any changes in national level politics, municipal and prefectural politics have represented a more promising avenue of political change since the rise of progressive local administrations in the 1960s. There has been turnover and change in partisan control below the national level, particularly in the more urbanized areas of the country. This growth of political competition on the subnational level has led to an increase in the responsiveness of local governments of all political stripes. In addition, the chief executives of municipal and prefectural administrations are popularly elected, instead of being recruited via LDP factional politics as in the case of the prime minister. Surveys show that local and prefectural governments are viewed as being much more responsive to the people. Respondents feel that these lower levels of government better understand and reflect the people's wishes. For instance, one survey of citizen perceptions of government responsiveness found high, positive levels for governors and city mayors; substantially lower, moderate levels for municipal and prefectural assemblymen; and very low levels for the Diet and national government.[25] Additional evidence comes from the 1976 JABISS

[25] Ikeuchi, ibid., pp. 255–261; Tororen Kakushin Tosei Kakuritsu Iinkai, *Ryudoka-suru Tomin no Seiji Ishiki* (Tokyo: Tokyo Shisei Chosakai, 1972); Yoshiyuki Sakamoto, "Chosa — Shimin no Jitsuzo," *Jiyu* (March 1973), pp. 69–75; Bradley M. Richardson, *The Political Culture of Japan* (Berkeley: The University of California Press, 1974) pp. 65–82.

Election Study which reveals that 61 percent of the respondents trust local politics always or most of the time compared to only 41 percent who trust national politics.

All in all, the high levels of dissatisfaction with politics that we find in Japan cannot be taken as a positive sign. These findings point to longstanding and persistent problems with the conduct of Japanese politics. It is also certainly not encouraging to find that the younger generation and those with libertarian and other modern values exhibit the highest levels of cynicism and political dissatisfaction and the lowest levels of patriotism and system support.[26] In other words, the forces of change discussed here are replacing the most supportive elements of the electorate with the most cynical and disaffected elements. At the same time, these findings should not be interpreted as presenting a serious threat to the future of Japan's democratic institutions. Japan's constitution and political institutions are firmly rooted in Japan's contemporary political culture. Moreover, government in Japan has been characterized by a high degree of political stability throughout the postwar period, and that attribute of the Japanese polity is not likely to change in the foreseeable future.

CHANGING PATTERNS OF ELECTORAL BEHAVIOR

In Chapter 3 it was noted that the Japanese party system has undergone a profound change since 1955 which has transformed it from a one-and-one-half party system to a multiparty system. Two phenomena were responsible for this change. The first was the long-term decline in the conservative vote that began in the early 1950s and continued up until 1979. The second was the fragmentation of the opposition vote. The result has been the rise of a number of minor parties at the expense of the two major parties, the Liberal Democrats and the Socialists. This transformation in the party system is a reflection of a realignment that has been taking place among the electorate. Old patterns of voting behavior are being replaced by new ones.

A closer analysis reveals that the realignment of the Japanese electorate is in large part a product of the socioeconomic and value changes discussed earlier. Indeed, it appears that these changes have spawned two types of realignment. The first of these is an *ecological realignment* — a change in party fortunes

[26] *The Japan Times Weekly,* 7/16/83, p. 5; *Time,* 8/1/83, p. 22.

that results from a change in the relative size of one or more social groups or strata.[27] One effect of the societal changes that have been discussed has been to shrink the size of traditional conservative constituencies, a phenomenon that has been largely reponsible for the long-term decline in the LDP vote.

A second type of realignment is *sectoral realignment* — a change in party fortunes that results from a shift in the support of a particular group or strata from one party to another. In Japan, socioeconomic and value change has given rise to new groups and interests that have been unrepresented or underrepresented by the two major parties, a situation has created an opportunity for the minor parties to emerge and carve out new support constituencies. While the evidence suggests that the process of ecological realignment may have run its course, a process of sectoral realignment is still in its early stages, and its outcome is at yet unclear.

In the cross-national voting literature, several different approaches or models for explaining voting behavior can be found. Research on Japan has shown that those psychological models that have dominated the American literature and stressed the importance of party identifications and, secondarily, party and candidate images and issue preferences, are not as appropriate for explaining the vote in Japan. Party identifications and party images are simply not as strongly developed and diffused throughout the Japanese population as they are among Americans. In addition, it has been found that a social cleavage voting model, which has been much in vogue in Western Europe, is also ill suited to the Japanese context. Most of the major social group cleavages that divide European politics, such as divisions of race, language, ethnicity, region, and religion, are either largely absent or have failed to be represented in the party system as issues that divide the parties. The one exception here may be class, since there are several Marxist and social democratic parties that claim to represent the working man. However, on closer inspection this cleavage appears to be more an organizational than a class one, as unionized blue and white collar workers both vote heavily

[27] Scott C. Flanagan, "Patterns of Realignment," in Russell Dalton, Scott Flanagan, and Paul Beck, eds., *Electoral Change in Advanced Industrial Societies* (Princeton: Princeton University Press, 1984).

for the left, while nonunion blue and white collar workers both vote heavily conservative. In fact, it has been generally argued that Japan is more of a status than a class society, meaning that there is great public awareness of the small status differences that distinguish one neighbor from another, but an equally strong perception among most Japanese that they all belong to the same great middle mass of society.[28]

The voting model that has been found most useful in explaining Japanese voting behavior is a social network model. That model stresses the role of both formal organizational and informal small-group networks in shaping individual voting preferences. While such a social network approach can usefully be applied in any democratic society, several aspects of the cultural and social setting enhance the model's applicability in the Japanese case. First, the previous two chapters have argued that Japan is still pervasively a personalistic society in the sense that people do things through known people and rely on chains of connections in their daily lives. Second, there are more extensive and complex hierarchic and lateral communication networks that broaden the reach of interpersonal messages in Japan. Third, Japanese groups, particularly small informal groups, enforce higher levels of conformity on their members than are typically found in most of the industrialized West. Finally, many Japanese organizations have well-developed, institutionalized procedures for transmitting partisan communications, and several culturally reinforced mechanisms for promoting a high degree of conformity in voting for the group's recommended candidate. This social network model is useful for explaining both traditional and newer, more recent voting patterns in Japan.

In order to understand how voting behavior is changing, first traditional voting patterns will be described and then three kinds of effects that socioeconomic and value change are having on the Japanese electorate will be explained. Traditionally, voting behavior was based on community solidarity and patron-client relations. The objective was areal representation, to elect someone

28 For a more detailed discussion of psychological, social cleavage, and social network models of voting behavior, see Scott C. Flanagan and Bradley M. Richardson, *Japanese Electoral Behavior: Social Cleavages, Social Networks and Partisanship,* Contemporary Political Sociology Series No. 06024 (London: Sage Publications, 1977).

who would represent the community and use his office to protect community interests and direct benefits to it.

In rural Japan, the hamlet (*buraku*) has been the basic unit of social organization, a cluster of thirty to seventy farm households whose homes are grouped together in a central area that is surrounded by their land holdings. The Japanese term for village (*mura*) was an artificial administrative unit that included a number of these hamlets and market towns. When elections came to Japan in the prewar period, the hamlets would count up the number of eligible voters living in the community and determine whether they controlled enough votes to elect one of their own to the village assembly. If not, they would get together with the elders of an adjoining hamlet and agree on a joint candidate. In higher level elections, the hamlet would endeavor to deliver its votes in a bloc to a local influential or benefactor who either was a candidate himself or a client of one of the candidates. Again, the decision of whom to support tended to be based on geography, with the idea that a man from one's own area would best represent the area's interests. This pattern of areal representation led to the phenomenon of "mountain voting," in which each candidate's strength peaked in his hometown and declined throughout the rest of the electoral district in proportion to the distance from his hometown.

Areal representation and areal voting are still in evidence in rural Japan today, even in national level elections. Of course the pattern of areal voting is not as sharply defined today as it was in the prewar period or in the early postwar years. Still it has been found that the more rural the election and the lower the level of the election, the more geographically concentrated a candidate's vote is.[29] Also, particularly in local level elections, many examples can still be found of rural communities that are able to mobilize nearly 100 percent of their inhabitants to go to the polls and vote for the community-recommended candidate. Throughout the postwar period there have been numerous stories of this kind of community-based voting in rural Japan reported in the press. An example would be the elders of two hamlets getting together to agree on how long a new bride will continue to vote for the

[29] Scott C. Flanagan, "National and Local Voting Trends," in Kurt Steiner, Ellis Krauss, and Scott Flanagan, eds., *Political Opposition and Local Politics in Japan* (Princeton: Princeton University Press, 1980), pp. 151–168.

candidates supported by her old village after moving into her husband's home in her new village.[30]

It could be argued that voting based on a pattern of areal representation promotes a one-party-dominant system with one permanent leading party. Communities vote in a bloc, and all areas can be hierarchically integrated through patron-client pyramids into a central party power structure. Since the party in power can monopolize the distribution of benefits, all will clamor for linkages with that associational network. The natural competition between neighboring communities over where the school, bridge, or road will be built can be played out through personal and factional competition within the dominant party, without taking the risk of being entirely cut off by gambling on supporting an opposition party.

The decline of one-party-dominance in Japan is closely associated with the decline in this pattern of areal voting. The first of three factors to be discussed that have affected voting behavior is the change in community size. The smaller the community, the more that politics will be conducted on an informal, face-to-face basis, and the weaker will be the tendency for politics to be resolved through formal, impersonal organizations. In small communities, personalism tends to replace partisanship as the basis of political mobilization, both because of the greater degree of proximity and familiarity with the personalities involved and because of the higher value placed on community solidarity. In the small community context, partisan divisions appear to be either irrelevant or inherently threatening to the peace and harmony of the community.

In contrast, as the size of the community increases, its diversity increases, enlarging the number of interests that might potentially come into conflict. Moreover, the larger the community, the more people with similar grievances are brought into close contact. Greater size also reduces the costs of dissent, as conflict becomes institutionalized and depersonalized. These effects facilitate the organization of dissent groups and the articulation of sectarian interests.[31] The process of urbanization, therefore, makes it in-

---

[30] Scott C. Flanagan, "Voting Behavior in Japan: The Persistence of Traditional Patterns," *Comparative Political Studies* 1 (October 1968), pp. 391–412.

[31] Robert A. Dahl and Edward R. Tufte, *Size and Democracy* (Stanford: Stanford University Press, 1973).

creasingly difficult for one party to represent the entire nation, by creating a diversity of interests and facilitating their organization into various functionally specific pressure groups. Such functionally diverse groups are likely to have conflicting interests and therefore to align themselves with competing parties.

With the formation of nonareal associations such as unions, opposition parties acquired an organizational support base. Moreover, in the Japanese context, many of these organizations have proved to be nearly as effective as community-based groups in mobilizing their members to vote for a designated candidate. For instance, many Japanese organizations still adopt the recommendation system (*suisensei*) to mobilize their members to vote in a bloc. The norms of group solidarity and conformity have made this an effective vehicle of mobilization in organizations outside as well as inside the community, especially during the 1950s and 1960s. In addition, large organizations such as labor unions are likely to employ the "organization check" procedure whereby each member is personally contacted in an attempt to assess whether his vote is secure and how many additional votes of family, relatives, and friends he can deliver. Frequently the sense of obligation and commitment is reinforced by inducing union members to sign their names to a *suisensho,* affirming that they, as members of the union, support the endorsed candidate. Such procedures not only solidify partisan support within an organization but also enable large organizations to count and distribute votes among the candidates of a particular party with a fair degree of accuracy. One example of the power of the social networks and influence communications within these organizations to effect voting choice is found in studies of voting patterns among individuals changing their occupations. It has been discovered that as individuals move from one occupational context to another, there is often an abrupt change in the party they vote for that mirrors the partisan coloration of the new occupational setting.[32]

Figure 6.3 demonstrates the impact of the change in occupational environments, from a rural, agrarian to an urban, industrial setting, on voting behavior in Japan. An occupational

[32] Ichiro Miyake, "Party Support: Its Stability and Functions," presented at the Conference on Japanese Voting Behavior, Sophia University, Tokyo, Japan, March 27–28, 1981.

FIGURE 6.3. *Party Support Percentages by Type of Occupational Environment*

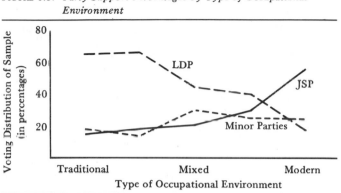

Data base: 1976 JABISS study.

environments scale was constructed by combining type of occupation, the size of the enterprise, and the presence or absence of union ties. Traditional occupational environments are those that are small in scale, in farming, small retailing, and other old middle class occupations, and exclude the intrusion of unions. Modern occupational environments are those that employ blue and white collar wage earners in large enterprises that are heavily unionized. The figure shows that 65 percent of those at the traditional end of the scale voted LDP compared to only 18 percent at the modern end. Urbanization and economic development, then, have created new kinds of occupational environments that are more diverse, larger in scale, and more hospitable to the mobilization of dissent groups. These new occupational environments are associated with more political competition, which in the Japanese context has meant a decline in the dominant party's vote.

In the early postwar period, the growing size and diversity of the working environment benefited mainly the Socialists. More recently, however, new interests have emerged in urban areas that have not been well represented by either of the two major parties. The result has been the growth of the minor parties. In occupational terms, the LDP has consistently attracted heavy support from the farmers and the old middle class, occupational categories that have been declining in size. The Socialists have received their support largely from the working class and the new middle class, but primarily just the unionized portions of these occupational categories. The nonunion portions of these two classes, which constitute nearly two thirds of each, have been poorly represented by either of the two major parties. Recent analyses have shown that two of the minor parties, the CGP and DSP, have been carving out new support constituencies among the nonunion blue collar workers, while two other minor parties, the NLC and JCP, have attracted substantial support among the nonunion white collar workers.[33]

A second change that has affected voting behavior in Japan has been the decline of community. Areal voting based on community solidarity and community recommendations has disproportionately benefited the conservatives, because the positions of leadership in the neighborhood associations and other community organizations are generally dominated by members of the old middle class who tend to be conservative either in terms of their values or their economic self-interests. Also, the kinds of things that communities want — roads, schools, bridges, and other local benefits — can best be satisfied by the ruling party.

Areal voting is based on the cohesiveness of the local community. Naturally as its size increases, its cohesion declines. Moreover, when a community grows, it becomes less bounded, less contained. As a neighborhood community becomes engulfed by metropolitan sprawl, more and more residents are found commuting to work, and educational and recreational facilities, as well as government services, are located outside the community. As community life becomes less bounded, we find a decline in the integration of the community as a cohesive, self-sufficient environment.[34]

Urbanization also is associated with increased geographic mobility. The effect of increased mobility is to weaken the integration of the residents into the community's social networks, which leads to lower levels of participation in the political and social life of the community. In the Japanese setting, mobility increases the citizen's anonymity and defeats the kinds of sanctions that communal groups have traditionally employed to ensure conformity. It has been reported that the solidarity of many

[33] Scott C. Flanagan, "Electoral Change in Japan: A Study of Secular Realignment," in Dalton, et al., op. cit.

[34] Sidney Verba and Norman H. Nie, *Participation in America* (New York: Harper and Row, 1972), pp. 229–247.

established communities in urbanizing areas has been weakened by the arrival of large numbers of newcomers and the erection of high-rise apartments that cater to a highly mobile, transient clientele.[35] Thus many local residents in urban neighborhoods in present-day Japan are simply not available for mobilization by traditional community networks either because of the inability of these networks to integrate effectively many new residents into the mainstream of community opinion or because the greater diversity of interests that have invaded the neighborhood render a holistic, areal mode of representation inoperative.

The decline of community integration in Japan that has accompanied urbanization is associated with both lower turnout levels in voting and a decline in the capacity of community social networks to influence voting choices. It is obvious that residential associations such as the neighborhood associations cannot effectively mobilize masses of newcomers who are only marginally integrated into their communities. Newcomers, therefore, are likely either to fall outside these conservatively oriented associational networks or to attach less importance to their recommendations. As these more mobile residents increasingly slip through these conservative community mobilization networks, their voting patterns become more diversified by default. Clearly not all highly mobile Japanese conform to what has been called the "floating voter" syndrome — i.e., weak attachments to all parties and inconsistent voting behavior. What can be said is that those Japanese who lack integration into the social networks in their residential communities necessarily obtain whatever political socialization and voting cues they receive from other sources outside the community.

A dramatic depiction of the impact of the decline in community on voting behavior is found in Figure 6.4. The community integration scale presented in this figure was constructed from the following variables: home ownership, length of residence, commuting time to work, number of intimate friends in one's neighborhood, and membership and level of active involvement in neighborhood organization (the neighborhood associations, young men's, women's, and old people's associations, and community

[35] Gary D. Allinson, "Opposition in the Suburbs," in Steiner et al., op. cit., pp. 95–130.

FIGURE 6.4. *Party Support Percentages by Community Integration*

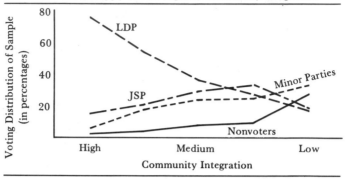

Data base: 1976 JABISS study.

service groups). At the high end of the community integration scale, 75 percent of the respondents voted LDP, while at the low end of the scale only 18 percent so voted. As the level of community integration declines, there is an increase in both the opposition party vote and the proportion of nonvoters. At the lowest level of integration, even the JSP suffers at the hands of apathy and the increased inroads of the minor parties. Clearly, then, in the Japanese political setting, because of the traditional emphasis on areal modes of voter mobilization, the decline in community integration has been directly linked to the decline in support for the conservative LDP and the fragmentation of the opposition party vote.

Several of the newer minor parties are organizationally weak on the grass-roots level and rely mainly on the image of party leaders and candidates and the appeal of their policy positions for specifically targeted urban interests to attract support. Others have tried more aggressively to go after voters who are not well integrated either in the conservatives' community-based networks or in the Socialists' union-based networks. The CGP depends on its close association with Japan's largest new religion, the Soka Gakkai. In addition to the organizational support and ready-made constituency that the CGP receives from the Soka Gakkai, the party has also established a network of Citizens' Livelihood Discussion Centers on the local level where any citizen may come and air grievances. The party then relays these opinions to the appropriate government offices or introduces measures into the local assemblies. The centers also offer free legal aid and provide other kinds of support services for local communities. The CGP describes this system of discussion centers as a "warm hand stretched out to those people discarded by politics." [36]

The JCP is also well organized on the grass-roots level around a hard core of committed ideologues. By deemphasizing ideological issues and focusing on the livelihood concerns of local residents, the Communists have been able to appeal to many different strata of Japanese society, and not simply as a kind of loud protest vote against LDP excesses. The JCP and its affiliated service organizations have sought to attack the distortions in capitalist society by playing the role of ombudsmen for citizens, using their organizations, lawyers, and expertise to apply pressure to redress ordinary citizens' problems with government offices, medical services, environmental pollution, traffic congestion, or other local grievances. For example, the party has organized Democratic Merchants and Manufacturers Associations in many cities to help small and medium businessmen negotiate with the government on tax matters and to provide them with credit, financing, and management consultation services. Small businesmen that are helped in this way usually end up in the support organizations (*koenkai*) of some Communist candidate. The Communists have also established a network of medical clinics and maintain strong youth and women's organizations in urban areas.[37]

A third important factor that is changing voting behavior in Japan is value change. The shift in the direction of libertarian, universalistic, and cosmopolitan values, as discussed above, represents a rejection of traditional Japanese values. The traditional style of politics in Japan, which has been most successfully but not exclusively practiced by the LDP, stresses personalistic ties with the candidate and the dispensing of favors and gifts to individual constituents and local community groups. Personalistic, parochial voters have a narrow, localistic view of politics and seek particularized benefits for themselves, their families, and immediate communities, bestowed either directly by the candidate or indirectly by the local influential who solicits their support for the candidate. The modern, postindustrial value orientation is not only unmoved by this traditional style of politics but highly critical of it. These voters have a different perspective on politics and a different agenda of concerns. They worry about the environment, international peace, the quality of life, and the creation of a more open, participatory style of politics that encourages greater citizen input and holds politicians accountable for corrupt practices.

As might be expected, the long-term intergenerational process of value change is strongly associated with the decline in the support for the LDP. Figure 6.5 presents the association between values and the vote, using the combined traditional-modern value scale. We find that 70 percent of the voters with a traditional value orientation supported the LDP, while only 20 percent of those at the modern end of the scale voted LDP. As values have changed in Japan, there has been a shift in support from the conservatives on the right to the Socialists and Communists on the left.

Value change is associated with the fragmentation of the party system in a slightly different way. In many respects the authoritarian-libertarian type of postindustrial value change represents a new dimension of cleavage that cuts across the traditional left-right, labor-business cleavage. One reason for the emergence of the center parties is that they represent different mixes of stands

FIGURE 6.5. *Party Support Percentages by Value Preferences*

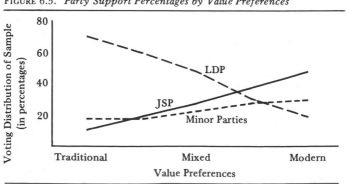

Data base: 1976 JABISS study.

on these two cleavage dimensions from what can be found either on the established right or left. For example, it has been found that the supporters of the CGP lean towards the traditional side in their values but towards the liberal side on economic issues. An even sharper contrast is found among the supporters of the NLC who are strongly modern in values but strongly conservative on economic and foreign policy issues.[38] One reason for the rise of the center parties, then, is that these parties represent different mixes of issue positions and outlooks than those among the established left and right parties.

One effect of value change, then, may be to promote realignment either towards the left or towards certain center parties as postindustrial value cleavages begin to redefine the framework of political competition in Japan. A contrasting effect may be to stimulate dealignment. The decline of authority and conformity associated with the libertarian value change is weakening loyalties to organizations and institutions of every stripe and political hue. Not only are traditional community-based organizations having problems mobilizing the vote, but also progressive nonareal organizations such as unions are encountering increasing difficulties in achieving even modest levels of member conformity to candidate endorsements. The Social Democratic Federation's slogan, "From the politics of pressure groups to the politics of free citizens," reflects the change that is occurring.[39]

A new politics is beginning to take shape in Japan. While the outlines of its agenda of issues and cleavages is not yet clearly defined, the two newest minor parties, the SDF and NLC, may exemplify respectively what the New Left and New Right will look like in Japan in the years to come. The SDF is social democracy without Marxism and virtually without socialism. The party rejects the bureaucratic control, centralized power, and economic inefficiency associated with state ownership of industry and state planning, and instead stresses decentralization of authority, worker self-management, local self-government, and citizen participation. On the other side, the New Right NLC calls for a "new culture" of self-reliant individualism, creativity, and free expression, a greatly increased emphasis on education, and enhancing the

---

38 Flanagan, "Electoral Change in Japan," op. cit.
39 Satsuki Eda, "United Social Democratic Party," in Rei Shiratori, ed., *Japan in the 1980s* (Tokyo: Kodansha International, 1982) pp. 273–290.

quality of life. These libertarian values, however, are coupled with a laissez-faire economic liberalism that advocates a return to the free market mechanism, an end to government subsidies and tax exemptions, and a reform of entitlement programs in line with the principle that social security is the responsibility of the individual, his family, and his company.[40]

The rise of a new politics can also be seen in the appearance of a new style of politics in Japan. The old style politics was based on personalism and paternalism, with important decisions being made through covert factional maneuvering and negotiations beyond public influence and scrutiny. Many of Japan's most effective prime ministers — Yoshida, Sato, Ohira, and others — have been masters of ambiguity, who excelled in obscure public announcements which left their positions vague and maximized their flexibility in factional negotiations and presented opponents with a difficult target to attack. Increasingly, the decline of personalistic and organizational social networks in mobilizing the vote and the rising levels of unattached voters who are more concerned and knowledgeable about politics have forced politicians to change their campaign style. A new breed of politician is emerging, who is a more articulate and accomplished public speaker, with an attractive, friendly media image. LDP faction leader Yasuhiro Nakasone, who became prime minister in December of 1982, perhaps best exemplifies this more popular, forthright political style. However, recent leaders of some of the other parties, such as Yohei Kono of the NLC and Ichio Asukata of the JSP, project similar appealing popular images.

Clearly, then, the Japanese electorate is changing in ways that are profoundly affecting voting behavior. The growth of community size, the decline in community integration, and value change have all been associated with (1) a decline in the size of the conservatives' traditional constituencies — farmers, cohesive residential communities, and traditionalistic voters (ecological realignment), and (2) a rise in the number and strength of the minor parties (sectoral realignment). How the various parties fare in this increasingly altered electoral environment from here on out will depend on how the parties respond to these changes. To

---

[40] Ibid.; Takashi Kosugi, "New Liberal Club," in Shiratori, op. cit., pp. 258–272.

date, the Socialists have not adapted well, and their continued emphasis on Marxism and factional infighting will probably ensure a continuing erosion of their strength.

The LDP, however, being a more pragmatic catchall party, has been showing promising signs of successful adaptation and change. In response to the devastating losses the LDP was suffering in urban constituencies in the 1960s and early 1970s, the party gradually began to formulate an urban policy to address some of the growing problems being encountered by this expanding sector of the electorate. In the 1970s, the LDP strengthened the welfare system, passed tough antipollution legislation, and poured substantial new monies into programs aimed at improving the environment in the cities. These expenditure increases, coupled with an end to the population growth in metropolitan centers, has made a significant impact on urban environments. The LDP, which has made a serious effort to appeal to those groups that traditionally have not heavily supported the party, has made its greatest gains during the 1980s among younger urban voters and blue and white collar workers.[41]

Another factor that bodes well for continued conservative rule is the virtual completion of the process of ecological realignment. In the late 1940s, half of the Japanese labor force was engaged in agriculture. By 1982 that figure had dropped to 9.7 percent, and only a third of those were full-time farmers. While the transfer of the labor force from the secondary to tertiary sector will continue, that change will not necessarily adversely affect the LDP. The decline of agriculture very directly affected the LDP, but that process has been almost completed. Moreover, beginning in 1974 as a result of the energy crisis, the rate of growth of the Japanese economy began to slow markedly. The effect has been to dampen the pace of urbanization and mobility. In addition, the 1978 Japanese National Character Survey found, for the first time in this quinquennial series dating from 1953, a leveling off and, on some items, even a reversal in the direction of value change in Japan.[42] This slowdown in the pace of both economic

41 Murakami, op. cit., pp. 59–67; Michisada Hirose, "The Ingredients of LDP Success," *Japan Echo* 10 (Summer 1983) pp. 56–57.
42 Research Committee on the Study of Japanese National Character, *Kokuminsei no Kenkyu: Dai 6-kai Zenkoku Chosa*, Research Report No. 46 (Tokyo: Institute of Statistical Mathematics, 1979).

and value change in Japan has contributed to a stabilization of the LDP vote.

Finally, the LDP's prolonged grip on the reins of government is reinforced by the absence of a viable alternative to continued LDP rule. A series of public opinion polls conducted between 1976 and 1983 reveal that while substantial majorities of the populace are highly critical of the LDP, associating that party with factional in-fighting, political corruption, unresponsiveness, and catering to the interests of big business, similar large majorities also view the opposition parties as representing narrow interests, hopelessly divided, and incapable of governing effectively. For example, the JSP is still viewed by the public as a party that is too dependent on labor unions and whose policies are too unrealistic. In general, the opposition parties are perceived as being mainly good for criticizing the government, but lacking the competence to govern. On the other hand, while the LDP ranked lowest on charisma in one poll, it was seen as being the "safest" and "most dependable." Not surprisingly, a 1976 NHK survey found that 64 percent of the respondents agreed while only 25 percent disagreed with the statement, "Since there is no other party that we can entrust national politics to, it can't be helped if we entrust political affairs to the LDP." [43]

All of the above factors, plus a short-term shift in issue salience from environmental and welfare to economic and security issues, have contributed to a recent resurgence in the LDP vote. This upswing in LDP fortunes after almost twenty-five years of decline appeared first in the 1979 and 1980 national elections and was sustained in the 1983 HC and unified local elections. The recent LDP rebound from its nadir in 1976, however, does not mean that the party's continued hold on a Diet majority is ensured in the years to come. In the December 1983 HR election, the party suffered a slight decline of 2.1 percentage points in the popular vote below its 1980 HR showing. On a proportional basis, such a drop should have cost the party ten to eleven seats, but because of the erratic and unpredictable effects of the Japanese electoral system, the party won thirty-four fewer seats than in

[43] NHK Hoso Seron Chosa-jo, *Dai 34-kai Shugiin Senkyo*; *The Japan Times Weekly*, 1/17/81, p. 3; 9/24/83, p. 3; Christopher, *The Japanese Mind*, p. 217.

the previous election. Perhaps this decline was caused by only short-term factors, such as popular criticism of Tanaka's refusal to resign following his conviction or Nakasone's efforts to rapidly increase defense spending. In any case, the LDP has stood so close to losing its majority in the Lower House since 1976 that, given the rise in floating, volatile voters, a cluster of unfavorable factors and circumstances in any future election could potentially deny the party a majority, even with the aid of the conservative independents. The likely outcome of such an occurrence, however, would be continued LDP rule in coalition with a small center party. As if to foreshadow that eventuality, the LDP moved into coalition with the tiny NLC following the 1983 HR election, to increase the size of its majority and its control of Lower House committees.

It would appear, then, that at least the steady, long-term cumulative decline of the LDP has been halted. There is also a limit to the fragmentation of the Japanese party system. With the emergence of the SDF, there are now seven nationally recognized parties competing in an electoral system that can logically accommodate only five. The medium-sized, three-to-five member districts in the HR elections mean that even in the largest districts, only five parties can gain representation. The smallest parties will be completely shut out of the Lower House, unless they can rely on a few pockets of unusual strength to win seats in a small number of districts.

Of course the HC National Constituency race provides a much lower threshold of entry, as now only two percent of the vote is sufficient for victory. Also, the shift from voting for individual candidates to voting for parties in the National Constituency, beginning with the June 1983 Upper House election, has created a new spate of virtually one-man parties, as former independent incumbents and hopefuls have attempted to stay in the race by forming themselves into parties. As a result, eighteen parties entered the 1983 HC election, but the high financial deposits required to compete in these elections are likely to make most of these one-man parties short-lived affairs. Moreover, some initial steps have been taken towards a union of the center parties. For example, the leaders of the DSP have for several years been pushing for a unification or some kind of federation of the four center parties — the DSP, CGP, NLC, and SDF.[44] If the center parties could in some way integrate their organizations and support constituencies, they would be a much more effective force at the polls and in the Diet.

Clearly we have been witnessing an unusually volatile period in partisan support patterns throughout the 1960s and 1970s. Up to now, most of the minor parties have been more successful in attracting floating voters than partisan loyalists. Increased volatility in electoral behavior may be a permanent feature of postindustrial politics. However, should the forces of ecological realignment and opposition fragmentation subside, so that the Japanese electorate can become accustomed to a stable slate of contesting parties, it is likely that the new voting patterns of today will in time be reflected in new patterns of stable partisan loyalties. As noted above, there is already some evidence of a sectoral realignment, especially among the urban, nonunion, working, and new middle classes, from support for the major parties to the minor parties.

CHANGING PATTERNS OF PARTICIPATION

Some readers may feel that the image of Japanese politics presented in the last chapter and this one are markedly contrasting — a traditionalistic politics quite alien to the American experience and a postindustrial politics with striking similarities with many of the changes that are taking place in the West. Which one is the more accurate characterization? The answer is, both. Japan is a very complex society undergoing a very fundamental and uneven process of socioeconomic and value change. In the years ahead the new politics increasingly will come to the fore. Yet the role of tradition should not be underestimated. The Japanese people have a very pronounced conservative streak. A recent poll revealed that 73 percent of the respondents felt that their "way of thinking and acting" was conservative to only 22 percent who thought of themselves as reformists.[45] Because of the enduring quality of traditional Japanese norms, incidents will continue to occur in Japanese society for many years to come that will surprise and confuse Westerners. Thus in the study of contem-

---

[44] *The Japan Times Weekly,* 7/9/83, p. 4.
[45] *The Japan Times Weekly,* 1/17/81, p. 3.

porary Japanese politics, both aspects must be kept in mind — the old and the new, continuity and change.

It also must be remembered that the Japanese experience with mass politics and democratic institutions is of a much briefer duration than the American experience. The American polity has experienced many shortcomings and performance failures in groping its way towards the ideal of democracy and, as Watergate has taught us, we can expect more such developmental growth pangs in the future. Japan has experienced special problems because she has been pushed into the postindustrial stage of development before the industrial stage was completed. On the other hand, there may be advantages as well as disadvantages associated with this pattern of rapid change. In the economic sphere, Ronald Dore has argued that because the organizational forms suited for industrialization in a factory setting were not deeply institutionalized, they have been less resistant to adaptation and change to forms more suitable for postindustrial development.[46]

The same may be true of politics. The incomplete development of the mass politics of the industrial era may facilitate the advent of the mass politics of the postindustrial era. The Western literature on electoral change is increasingly pointing to the declining role and function of political parties. As mass publics become more educated and politically sophisticated, parties may actually become impediments rather than facilitators of mass participation. Mass publics in the advanced industrial societies are beginning to demand more input than just the opportunity to cast one vote every three to four years for prepackaged programs. Moreover, the shift from industrial politics to postindustrial politics seems to be associated with a shift from broad social group cleavages to a large diversity of narrow interests and issue groups which are poorly represented by large catchall parties. If parties, which have monopolized mass politics in the West, are going to be forced to share power with other vehicles and institutions of mass participation in the future, there may be less resistance to such developments in Japan.[47]

[46] Ronald Dore, *British Factory — Japanese Factory* (Berkeley: University of California Press, 1973), pp. 375–420.

[47] Scott C. Flanagan and Russell J. Dalton, "Parties Under Stress: Realignment and Dealignment in Advanced Industrial Societies," *Western European Politics* 7 (January 1984), pp. 7–23.

Citizens' movements, initiatives and referendums, ombudsmen and other direct channels to government decision makers, and the bureaucracy are all likely to increase in the future. Also, the problem in the years ahead may not be too little participation but too much participation, as the literature on the governability of democracy suggests.[48] To cope with this problem, several European democracies have been experimenting with neocorporatist models of decision making, whereby extraconstitutional councils of advisors composed of the leaders of the interest groups relevant to a particular policy area are brought together to hammer out an agreement which is then ratified by the parties in parliament. This form of decision making is quite congenial to Japanese cultural proclivities; in fact, such advisory councils are widely employed in Japan, although naturally at this stage of development, the parties in parliament may on occasion ignore their recommendations with impunity. We cannot pretend to see into the future and predict the shape of mass politics to come. But we should not be too surprised if we awake one day to find that the Japanese have leapfrogged us again in yet another area and have become the model for democratic participation for the world.

[48] Crozier, et al., op. cit.; Richard Rose, ed., *Challenge to Governance* (Beverly Hills: Sage, 1980).

CHAPTER 7

Political Recruitment in Japan

THE PROCESS BY WHICH people are selected for roles in the political system is called political recruitment. Not only do these roles involve participation at the mass level, such as activism in political movements or articulation of political interests, but also they involve selection of those to fill roles as the elites who make important political decisions or play a vital part in the management of the major institutions of the political system. The general patterns of mass participation of contemporary Japanese and their political attitudes were discussed earlier in this book. This chapter will consider the recruitment of political leadership, its general profiles, and the political processes which constitute the elite political recruitment function.

Political recruitment touches upon the *motivations* of individuals to become active political role holders, and the relevant *political skills* and *resources* that they possess. Among the motivations which lead someone to enter political roles must be included a wide variety of personal, political, and career-related attitudes. Many commentators on politics feel that simple availability is a very important factor, so that having an alternative occupation which can be left and reentered easily or some other form of economic security is almost essential. The political skills and resources that are needed may include experience in interest

* Bradley M. Richardson

group leadership or the civil service or support by some group of social elites. All of these factors contribute to one's decision to enter politics and to his or her success after entrance.

The nature of selection processes is also a central dimension of political recruitment. Politics is collective activity, and most political decisions including those about political recruitment are made by coalitions within some kind of group. Consequently, most political recruitment is in essence an example of coalition behavior. Coalitions both select particular candidates for elective office and decide who will be chosen for top political positions (such as in Japan where these people are selected from within the parliamentary parties). Access to those who are involved in recruitment coalitions is essential to becoming a candidate, and access to winning coalitions at higher levels of politics is vital in successful entry to high political office.

At the mass level, the political recruitment process is inevitably very loose. Up to a certain point, the most critical element is one's motivation to take an active political role, with selection being virtually automatic. But as one proceeds to elite roles, the selection process itself becomes much more critical. While there are many people who might want to be president or prime minister, few of them are going to be selected as serious candidates, and fewer still will actually become incumbents of these high-level elite roles. At the higher levels of political life, recruitment is based increasingly on such access-determining factors as being attached to a particular political "in-group," having through experience become credible as a loyal and competent politician, and having demonstrated that one has some kind of appeal to the electorate (or to whatever body is making the final selection choice).

WHAT IS A POLITICAL ELITE?

All political systems, whether they be democratic, authoritarian, or totalitarian, have political elites and political masses; however, distinguishing between the two is not always easy. It is easy to conclude that a prime minister, cabinet ministers, and members of parliament are political elites. But what about small town assemblymen? Obviously, it is necessary to be specific when talking about elites so as not to misrepresent or confuse. In order to make clear in which functional areas of politics a specific elite is

TABLE 7.1. *The Hierarchy of Political Roles in Japan*

Prime Minister	1
Cabinet	21
National Diet	763
Prefectural Governors	47
Prefectural Assemblymen	2,825
Local Mayors	3,255
Local Assemblymen	68,017
Government Employees	3,869,121
Political Party Members	(estimate) 6,462,600
Electorate	77,926,588

Source: Compiled from government documents and Asahi Shimbunsha, *Asahi Nenkan* (Tokyo: 1979). The "Government Employees" category includes some persons of very high status, as well as those of lower statuses since national, prefectural, and local civil servants are included in this grouping.

active, so that at least some of the context in which a person is seen as an elite will be evident, such terms as national elite, party elite, interest group elite, and local elite will be used here.

One way to clarify the nature of relative elite and mass status is to examine the hierarchy of easily identifiable, institutional or "formal" political roles found in a given political system. In Table 7.1 it is easy to see that there are very few roles at the top of the political system; in Japan these are the positions of the prime minister and the cabinet. As one proceeds down the hierarchy of roles, the status of elites shifts from that of national top level to national lower level to prefectural elite and so on.[1] At the very bottom level, local elites and ordinary citizens are found fairly close to each other. Thus, some elite roles are considerably more prestigious than others, and there are gradations of elite status throughout the political system.

RECRUITMENT TO THE JAPANESE DIET

The National Diet, consisting of the House of Representatives and the House of Councillors, is Japan's most important legislative institution. To become a member of Japan's Diet requires

[1] Naturally there are also gradations and ambiguities in status within these broad categories. Prefectural governors, for example, are much higher in status than rank-and-file members of the Diet. But party leaders in the Diet outrank prefectural governors.

time and financial resources; political skills; support from a combination of community, occupational, or political groups; and selection through a nomination process and a public election. The relevant personal and political resources are actually very scarce. Moreover, the selection and election process is highly competitive, as is shown in part by the substantially higher numbers of people who run for office in the Diet in comparison with those who actually become members.[2]

One way to look at political recruitment such as selection for Japan's Diet is through examination of the occupations or other social backgrounds of those in political elite status. Information about social backgrounds is easily available, and from it can be inferred some of the criteria for elite selection. It is also possible to make some inferences about the degree of representativeness of particular institutions or the corresponding level of elitism in recruitment processes from data about occupations. As is shown in Table 7.2, six kinds of persons become members of the Lower House of the Japanese Diet more commonly than any others. These categories of members include former government bureaucrats, persons who spent most of their lives in local or prefectural politics, persons with business careers and ties, officials of groups like labor unions and farmers' cooperatives, "professionals" such as doctors and lawyers, and persons whose careers included service as a Diet member's personal secretary. Each of these categories combines certain dimensions of individual motivation and access to nominating processes which accounts for its presence in the National Diet.[3]

As can be seen from Table 7.2, a substantial number of former high-ranking civil servants enter Japan's parliament in each election. Almost one fifth of the thirty-fourth House of Representatives' membership was made up of people who had formerly been employed in elite administrative positions by national or local

[2] In the spring 1980 elections, there were 835 nominees for the House of Representatives but only 511 successful candidates, and many more persons were considered.

[3] It is easy to find information on Diet members' social backgrounds in political handbooks, newspaper articles and public documents. But the information on some individuals is sketchy, and the scholar cannot be sure that the most critical parts of a politician's career are mentioned. Still, findings agree with those of other persons who had studied the Diet earlier, so our judgments seem generally valid even despite the noted problems.

TABLE 7.2. *Occupational Backgrounds of Members of Japan's House of Representatives (1976–79)*

	Liberal Democrats		Japan Socialists	
	N	%	N	%
Ex-Bureaucrats	85	32	9	7
Ex-Local and Prefectural Politicians	98	38	65	52
Business Ties	43	17	9	7
Group Officials	12	5	81	67
Professionals	37	14	28	23
Political Secretaries	27	10	3	2
TOTAL	302 (260)	116%	195 (124)	158%

Source: Compiled from data in Seiji Koho Senta, *Seiji Handobukku* (Tokyo: 1977) and Nihon Seikei Shimbunsha, *Kokkai Benran* (Tokyo: 1978). Percentages exceed 100 because of dual and triple careers. (In all cases we tried to identify Diet members' most important single prior occupation, but this wasn't always possible). Actual numbers of Lower House members are shown in parentheses, while other numbers refer to number of former occupations mentioned in the various biographical sources. Only members from Japan's two largest parties were analyzed for sake of simplicity of presentation.

governments. Most of those in this group were former national bureaucrats from the highest career group in the civil service.[4]

The presence of so many former high-ranking bureaucrats in Japan's National Diet is an extremely important factor in Japanese politics. Their entry into national parliamentary politics also poses interesting questions regarding motivation and selection. Members of Japan's civil service typically retire at an early age. The retirement age at present is normally fifty-five, although quite a few leading civil servants retire before this age. Whatever their specific retirement age, most retiring civil servants still are able and motivated to enter a second career. Consequently, many senior bureaucrats on retirement enter business firms or interest groups, a process which is known in Japan as *amakudari,* or the "descent from heaven." But because of the close link between

---

[4] We chose to study the House of Representatives because in some senses it is the more important of the two houses and because there are somewhat different patterns of recruitment in the House of Councillors due to the larger size of election districts. All of the ex-national bureaucrats in the Diet came from the former category.

politics and administration, a sizable portion enter national politics and make this their second career — including an even higher ratio in the House of Councillors than was shown for the House of Representatives in Table 7.2.[5]

Former bureaucrats have considerable potential political resources which lead them to consider political careers or which make them attractive to political parties as candidates. Many bureaucrats form close relationships with particular interest groups or areas of the country, which can be converted into political resources in the form of electoral support. Members of the civil service also develop close ties with business leaders in some cases, which means possible access to sources of financial support if a political career is chosen. It is also said that a bureaucratic title sits well with the electorate, whose members are motivated to choose people with "experience," according to many opinion surveys.

Whatever the mix of personal motivations, availability, and political resources, former bureaucrats do quite well in elections in Japan. In addition to their considerable numbers in the National Diet, especially in the ranks of the Liberal Democratic party's parliamentary group, former bureaucrats sometimes are elected to prefectural office as well. This is shown by the fact that the governors elected in both Tokyo and Osaka prefectures in the spring of 1979 were former high civil servants.[6]

[5] There are higher proportions of ex-bureaucrats and group officials in the House of Councillors, because the districts in the Upper House elections are larger than those in the House of Representatives contests, and ministerial titles and national group connections are consequently more important to success than local backgrounds. See Bradley M. Richardson, "A Japanese House of Councillors Election: Support Mobilization and Political Recruitment," *Modern Asian Studies* 1 (1967), pp. 385–402.

[6] Other studies have noted the relatively high frequencies of former bureaucrats among prefectural governors, with percentages of the total of all governors accounted for by ex-bureaucrats reaching as high as 67 percent, or thirty-one out of forty-seven prefectural executives, at some times. See Steven R. Reed, "Gubernatorial Elections in Japan," in John Campbell, ed., *Parties, Candidates and Voters in Japan: Six Quantitative Studies* (Ann Arbor: Michigan Papers in Japanese Studies 2, 1981), pp. 139–167. Terry MacDougall also calls attention to the success of former bureaucrats in some big city mayoral elections in "Political Opposition and Big City Elections in Japan, 1947–75," in Kurt Steiner, Ellis S. Krauss, and Scott C. Flanagan, *Political Opposition and Local Politics in Japan* (Princeton: Princeton University Press, 1980), pp. 55–94.

The entry into national political life of former local and prefectural politicians indicated by Table 7.2 is less remarkable than the presence in national politics of former bureaucrats in sizable numbers. For local politicians eventually to seek national office seems like a natural progression, as local politicians clearly have the motivations, skills, and probably the resources to facilitate their movement into national public affairs. Although the scope of national political life is considerably broader than that of local affairs, still many skills are in fact transferrable from the lower to the higher realm of politics. And, quite naturally, access to national political groups and credibility to "gatekeepers" in the national political recruitment process exists for persons successful in local politics. Finally, while former local politicians don't achieve cabinet level positions in proportion to their importance in the Diet, these persons still perform extremely important linkage or representation functions in the Japanese political system.

Many members of Japan's House of Representatives are officials of private groups, being more often the case for parliamentarians from the opposition parties such as the Japan Socialists and the Democratic Socialists than it is for Diet members from the Liberal Democratic Party. Since the two Socialist parties are closely allied with labor union federations, many former group officials who represent the Socialist parties in the Diet come from the ranks of union leadership at the national or regional level. Moreover, the Liberal Democratic Party also has a sizable number of affiliates who have held positions in agricultural groups or in some other sector of organizational activity.

Clearly, former group officials bring both political skills and electoral support bases with them when they enter political life. In fact, many of these former group officials are actually "run" by the groups which support them, in the sense that the relevant interest groups may insist on their leaders' acceptance as party nominees in exchange for group electoral support for the party (see Chapter 8). In a parallel fashion, the groups' own electoral campaigns are often a critical factor in success.

In contrast with the direct way in which labor groups participate in elections, business groups and corporations have relatively more indirect impact. Those people identified as having business ties actually fall within two types: some were formerly corporation officials, whereas others became members of boards of directors or, probably more frequently, "advisors" to companies (an advisor is a special and frequently honorary position in Japanese corporate organization) after they were in political office. Among the first category, there are occasionally examples of people who run for office mainly on the basis of support from the members of their company and its affiliates in a large business group — this situation occurred in the 1977 House of Councillors elections when Mitsubishi group companies and some other groups were called upon by the Liberal Democrats to "run" candidates. But most members of parliament with business ties are supported by other kinds of groups as well as business interests in order to get enough votes to be elected; however, their ties with business are assumed to encourage a flow of money to election campaign coffers. As noted earlier, Japanese elections, like elections in other democratic countries, are very expensive. Since campaigns cost a great deal, political parties, and especially the Liberal Democrats in the Japanese case, value the close ties of many of their members with business, both those provided by election of businessmen and those provided by the close contacts between other persons like ex-bureaucrats with leading business circles, since these provide much of the financial resources needed to finance election campaigns. Although the business ties of the Liberal Democratic parliamentarians and party leaders are best known, the business connections of Diet members of other parties are also significant in certain cases.

A substantial number of professional people are also found in the Japanese Diet. While the legal profession is dramatically less dominant in Japanese life than it is in the United States, still quite a few members of the Japanese Diet are lawyers. Other professionals are also represented, including doctors, dentists, journalists, and educators. As in other democratic societies, professional persons in Japan usually have considerable social status in their communities. Social status is linked both to the motivation to consider an alternative career in politics and to electoral appeal and credibility. People in high status are often already social leaders and feel a sense of responsibility toward involvement in public life. They also know that some people will follow them at election time; furthermore, they have contacts with other community leaders who can help build a local supporters' coalition. Professionals also can reenter their profession in the event that they lose an election and have to leave politics, an option which is no small consideration to those who consider a political career. Finally, most doctors and dentists are also financially independent. As in other free societies, politics in Japan takes much time and money, so that it is comfortable for a candidate to have a career to fall back on when venturing into politics.

One of the most interesting patterns of political recruitment to the Japanese Diet is that in which former personal secretaries of Diet members, some of whom are actually sons of the Diet member whom they served, enter national political life. Actually, the position of private secretary to a political or business leader is a fairly high status position in Japan in its own right, which is shown by the fact that many private secretaries to Diet members have come from other prestigious occupations to this position. In addition, probably few people have better knowledge of politics and are more suited to run for office than many Diet members' senior secretaries (who are always males), since persons in this category have played vital roles in the political lives and electoral campaigns of their former employers. The fact that Japanese politics has a substantial component of residual patron-client relationships also must be remembered; it is certain that many former secretaries are sponsored in politics by their former bosses.[7]

The recruitment patterns and processes found in the Liberal Democratic Party as an example of political recruitment in Japan have been emphasized primarily because this party has dominated Japanese politics for so many years. There are both some differences and some similarities between the recruitment patterns of the Liberal Democrats and those of Japan's other parties. For example, there are more former bureaucrats in the Liberal Democratic ranks, reflecting among other things that party's long rule and proximity to the leading elements of the civil service.[8] As

[7] We use the term "residual" for a special reason: Japanese society is changing rapidly, and social patterns found today are often only a faint residue of earlier tradition. Still, elements of Japanese cultural tradition exist and shape political relationships.

[8] Probably ambitious bureaucrats also look more to the Liberal Democrats than to other parties upon retirement. As long as the Liberal Democrats are in power, access to cabinet positions is possible only through affiliation with the Conservative Party.

was observed earlier, there are correspondingly more people with group connections among the Socialist Party's parliamentarians (see Table 7.2), and also higher proportions of former local and prefectural politicians. (For more information on the representation of particular unions in the Diet, see Table 8.3 and related comments.) These observations notwithstanding, certainly the criteria which influence Liberal Democratic recruitment patterns — motivations, availability, political skills and resources, and access to nominating coalitions — are relevant to recruitment decisions in all Japanese parties.

RECRUITMENT TO THE JAPANESE CABINET

We have shown that members of Japan's Diet, specifically, those of the House of Representatives, come disproportionately from certain occupations, and that the patterns in Diet members' experiences and backgrounds reflect certain plausible combinations of attitudes, availability, and political skills and resources. Since Japan has a parliamentary system, it is natural that the occupational backgrounds of Japan's cabinets and other top political elites would be pretty much like those found in the Diet. Moreover, given conservative dominance of parliamentary politics, intraconservative recruitment patterns should be especially relevant. On the other hand, some kinds of people might be more successful than others at the top elite level, because of their peculiar appropriateness for top positions.

An analysis of the occupational composition of recent cabinets shows the proportions of former bureaucrats holding ministerial positions have been substantially higher even than their representation in the House of Representatives (see Table 7.3). Whereas about 20 percent of the members of the Lower House in the 1970s came from bureaucratic backgrounds, the average proportion of former bureaucrats in core cabinet positions between 1963 and 1983 was 42 percent!

The most dramatic example of bureaucratic dominance of top elite positions has been the prime ministership. Eight of the sixteen post-1946 prime ministers were former bureaucrats. More tellingly, some former bureaucrats had rather long tenures in office with the result that former bureaucrats were in power as prime ministers during twenty-eight of the thirty-eight years since the beginning of the postwar political era. Overrepresentation of

TABLE 7.3. *Occupational Backgrounds of Cabinet Members, 1963–83*

Prime Minister	Bureaucrats	Politicians	Other
Ikeda (1963–64)	7	1.6	3.4
Sato (1964–71)	6	1.9	4.1
Tanaka (1972–74)	6	1.5	4.5
Miki (1974–76)	4	1.5	6.5
Fukuda (1976–77)	3	3	6
Ohira (1978–80)	6	3	3
Suzuki (1980-82)	5.5	1.5	5
Nakasone (1982–)	4	4	4

Source: Figures were calculated from Asahi Shimbunsha, *Asahi Nenkan* for various years and are averages for all cabinets during each prime minister's period in power. Cabinets had twelve major ministerial portfolios during the period of our study; our statistical analysis was concerned with only these positions, since, with only a few exceptions, these positions seemed consistently more important than some other cabinet positions — such as some of the lesser directorships of agencies within the prime minister's office. However, some of the latter positions were also important in some periods, and the decision we made was arbitrary. Where figures include fractions of a position, this means we have averaged backgrounds using data on members of more than one cabinet during a particular prime minister's tenure.

former bureaucrats is the rule in cabinet politics in Japan, as can readily be seen from the data shown for both ministerial positions and prime ministerships. This same trend could also be seen in choices of other top political elites, such as agency heads and ministers-without-portfolio, who are not reported in Table 7.3.[9]

There are some straightforward reasons for the high proportions of former civil servants in recent Japanese cabinets. Liberal Democratic domination of parliamentary politics is one obvious explanation. (The conditions described here also hold for the coalition cabinet formed by the Liberal Democrats and the New Liberal Club in late 1983; the Liberal Democrats are the dominant partner to an overwhelming degree and the New Liberal Club itself is a splinter party formed by dissident members of the Liberal Democratic Party, which means that both the kinds of persons selected by the coalition for cabinet posts and the coalition process itself has not changed greatly.) It is natural that a

[9] The evidence is from our own analysis of top elites' backgrounds between 1960 and 1983, and prime ministerships beginning with Yoshida in 1946.

party in power which had many ex-bureaucrats in its parliamentary contingent should select such kinds of persons for cabinet positions. But up to one half of the cabinet was made up of former bureaucrats at times when a third or less of the Liberal Democrats in the Lower House were former civil servants, so other explanations must also be considered.[10] Presumably former bureaucrats have an edge in top elite recruitment processes because others value their competence and experience. Or else top bureaucrats work their way up into the top levels of the party on the basis of special political resources such as those cited earlier, and simply become successful candidates for high positions in the cabinet and government as a result.

There is an interesting sidelight to the relative importance of former bureaucrats in Japanese cabinet positions. It is often said that one of the "rules of the game" in Japanese cabinet recruitment processes has been that candidates for cabinet positions must have had long service in the Diet. While this is generally true, according to our own calculations, former bureaucrats who attained cabinet positions typically had shorter Diet careers than persons who entered the cabinet from other kinds of backgrounds. Seventy-five percent of cabinet members in 1963–78 from *non*bureaucratic backgrounds had been in the Diet at least seven terms; in contrast, only 51 percent of former bureaucrats had been in the Diet that long. Perhaps this difference in tenures reflects simply the fact that former bureaucrats start their national political careers later in life. However, it also could mean that former bureaucrats achieved cabinet positions faster because of possession

[10] It is important to note that we are comparing the proportions of ex-bureaucrats in the cabinet and in the Liberal Democratic ranks in the Diet across time using other studies, as well as our own evidence from 1976. Also, we have used only the House of Representatives as a basis for comparison of occupational concentrations, because the major share of cabinet members were always drawn from this chamber. For other studies of Diet and top elite recruitment, *see* Robert A. Scalapino and Junnosuke Masumi, *Parties and Politics in Contemporary Japan* (Berkeley and Los Angeles: University of California Press, 1962), Chapter 3; Haruhiro Fukui, *Party in Power: The Japanese Liberal Democrats and Policy Making* (Berkeley and Los Angeles: University of California Press, 1970), Chapter 3; Nathaniel Thayer, "Elections, Coalitions and Prime Ministers," in Lewis Austin, *Japan: The Paradox of Progress* (New Haven: Yale University Press, 1976), pp. 11–30; and Koji Sugimori, "The Social Background of Political Leadership in Japan," *The Developing Economies* 6 (1968), pp. 587–609.

of greater political skills and resources relevant at the national level of politics.

Two other things are important about the occupational backgrounds of Japanese cabinet members in recent years. It was shown above that persons who had been local or prefectural politicians are an important group of Liberal Democratic rank and-file Diet members. But they are actually greatly underrepresented in cabinet positions (see again Table 7.3). Using the other side of the argument that was made regarding the relative dominance of former bureaucrats, it can be assumed that former local politicians, while an important component of the Liberal Democratic Party's Diet representation, somehow lack the attitudes, resources, or skills which lead consistently to top-level positions in Japanese government.

EDUCATIONAL ELITISM AND JAPANESE
POLITICAL LIFE

Because of early establishment of compulsory primary education and employment of meritocratic criteria for selection of students entering leading universities, there has long been a substantial element of egalitarianism in the Japanese educational system. Still, egalitarianism has been paralleled by a trend toward elitism in certain areas of education and related recruitment practices. Before the war, most Japanese tended to rank hierarchically their nation's educational institutions, granting Tokyo and Kyoto Imperial Universities top position, followed by private schools like Keio and Waseda and the other national public universities (such as Kyushu, Tohoku, and Hokkaido). Even high schools were hierarchically ranked in a system that was acutely sensitive to the prestige of top schools and the importance of going to them.

The hierarchical-ranking system has continued in the postwar era, although the identities of the leading high schools and some other aspects of the system pertaining to private universities' rankings have changed. Tokyo and Kyoto Universities are still the leading schools in the country by far, and to graduate from these schools clearly confers top elite status even though graduates from several leading private schools are not far behind, particularly in recruitment outside of politics. Interestingly, the elitism visible in the ranking system and in political recruitment is paralleled to a considerable degree by leadership recruitment practices in old-line large businesses. Thus to a surprising degree, all of Japan's older leading companies recruit their senior executive staffs from these schools. Among the older firms in the Mitsubishi and Mitsui groups, for example, as well as elsewhere among leading firms, one finds that often two thirds of company executives are graduates of schools at the very top of the educational hierarchy.[11]

Elitist *political* recruitment practices are found in many countries. But Japan ranks with Britain and France in the degree to which its most senior political leaders have graduated from a very small number of schools, thus extending educational elitism into politics in a particularly rarified way. Only two of Japan's post-1946 prime ministers were not college graduates. More importantly, all but two of the premiers holding college degrees were graduates of elite public universities, and most in fact came from Tokyo University's law faculty, as well as having graduated in some instances from leading high schools. A particularly good example of educational elitism in Japan was Prime Minister Nobosuke Kishi (1957–60), who was a top graduate of the Number 1 National High School in Tokyo and also first in his class at Tokyo University's law faculty. Other prime ministers have had similar university backgrounds if not grades, and, all in all, graduates of top public universities were in power for thirty of the thirty-eight years of the postwar political era.[12]

Educational elitism is manifested in various other ways in the political recruitment process. As might be expected, a high ratio of cabinet ministers are also leading public and private university

[11] According to a recent study, 47 percent of top business leaders analyzed in 1960 and 44 percent of those studied in 1970 were graduates of Tokyo and Kyoto Universities. *See* Hiroshi Mannari, *The Japanese Business Leaders* (Tokyo: University of Tokyo Press, 1978). Moreover, a recent series extending over two years in the *Nohon Keizai Shimbun* shows even higher concentrations of elite public university graduates in some leading business firms. Thus, 73 percent of Sumitomo Bank's leading executives were Tokyo and Kyoto University graduates, with comparable patterns being observed in other leading former zaibatsu firms. See *Nihon Keizai Shimbun*, February 2, 1981, *inter alia*.

[12] We began our calculations with the first postwar election in 1946 and the first Yoshida cabinet. We also included Tokyo Commercial College (now Hitotsubashi University) as a top public university, even though it has not always ranked quite as high as Tokyo and Kyoto universities, except perhaps in the field of economics.

TABLE 7.4. *Educational Backgrounds of House of Representatives Members, 1976–79*

	LDP	JSP	Other Parties
Tokyo University	32%	10%	15%
Other Public Universities	11%	6%	15%
Private Universities	40%	27%	36%
Other Universities	3%	4%	—
Not University Graduates	14%	53%	34%
TOTAL	100%	100%	100%
NUMBER	260	124	122

Source: Calculated from Seiji Koho Senta, *Seiji Handobukku* (Tokyo: 1977). "Other Universities" includes persons who attended special technical schools or foreign universities.

graduates. Educational elitism is also shown in the bureaucracy, where roughly 80 percent of the members of the upper level of the administrative service have in recent years been Tokyo University graduates.[13]

The Diet itself is somewhat more egalitarian (Table 7.4), in part because of the presence of parties which mobilize from within the trade union movement. But there is a fair degree of educational elitism even within the Diet, especially within the Liberal Democratic Party, the New Liberal Club, and the Japan Communist Party! According to our statistics, most Liberal Democratic Diet members in the 1976 House of Representatives were university graduates — the figure was 86 percent — and within this group, 43 percent, or half of those having college degrees, were graduates of elite public universities. Indeed, 32 percent were Tokyo University graduates.[14] Both the proportion of university graduates and the ratio of elite public university graduates falls off dramatically in the case of the opposition parties, with the ironic exception of the Communist Party. The most egalitarian major party was the Japan Socialists, since only 49 percent

[13] Akira Kubota, *Higher Civil Servants in Japan: Their Social Origins, Educational Backgrounds and Career Patterns* (Princeton: Princeton University Press, 1969), p. 72. In the prestigious Finance Ministry the figure was 92 percent!

[14] Many of the private university graduates were from Waseda, one of Japan's leading private schools, or from other nationally well known schools.

of its Diet contingent in 1976 was university educated.[15] The minority Clean Government Party was similar, in that only 49 percent of its Diet members had graduated from universities. While the Diet shows a strong trend toward educational elitism in some instances, obviously there are also major exceptions to this so-called rule.

GOVERNMENT ELITE RECRUITMENT AND
LIBERAL DEMOCRATIC PARTY COALITIONS

Selection of top governmental and political elites in all countries involves coalition building, i.e., the establishment of an agreement between different groups or individuals in support of a particular political solution. In the United States, before primaries replaced conventions as the heart of the nomination process, supporters of would-be presidential candidates frantically sought to build nationwide coalitions among powerful politicians in different parts of the country. In European multiparty democracies, government elites are often chosen through complex negotiations resulting in coalitions involving several different parties. And in the Socialist bloc, central committees are the product of coalitional politics. Even military junta members are not infrequently chosen in third-world countries by similar processes.

Japan is no different from any other political system in the degree to which coalitions are the heart of elite recruitment politics. However, Japan is an exceptional case among industrialized countries in the degree to which one political movement or one political party has dominated top governmental elite selection. In Europe, multiparty elite recruitment coalitions have been the rule in many countries, while in some countries like Britain and the United States parties have alternated in power. Only West Germany in the 1950s and 1960s, or the Scandinavian countries under Labor or Socialist rule, compare at all with Japan in the postwar

---

[15] This trend in the rank and file membership of the Japan Socialist Party notwithstanding, all of the party's chairmen have been college graduates: three were from Tokyo Imperial University, one was from Kyoto Imperial University, two were from the highly ranked private Waseda University, and one each came from Nihon and Meiji Universities. Among other things, these high status backgrounds reflect the dominance of the party at the elite level by intellectuals who played a major role in founding the socialist movement and in leading the leftist forces even after union officials became a major component in the party's Diet composition. This information was kindly provided by Terry MacDougall.

era, and even these European cases sometimes witnessed broader participation in elite selection than has been the case in Japan. In Japan, the critical elite selection coalitions were formed by parties in the same overall conservative political movement in most years between 1946–55. Since 1955, Japan's prime ministers and cabinets have been selected solely within the parameters of the internal recruitment processes of one party — the Liberal Democratic Party — with the sole exception of the coalition formed in December 1983 between the Liberal Democrats and the small new Liberal Club.

The second important factor about government elite recruitment processes in Japan is the degree to which party *factions* have been the building blocks in coalition processes. Individual party members were contacted and their vote solicited at times in efforts to undermine unity within one or another faction. But the most basic recruitment negotiations always took place between leaders of the different Liberal Democratic Party factions. (Before 1955 conservative parties were the main participants in the coalition process by which cabinets were selected, while in late 1983 both the intra-Liberal Democratic Party factions and the New Liberal Club were involved in cabinet selection negotiations.) In effect, Liberal Democratic Party presidents (and therefore prime ministers), cabinet ministers, and party leaders were all chosen on the appropriate occasions by conclusion of temporary "treaties" between the intensely competitive party factions.

Building a recruitment coalition within the Liberal Democratic Party in the period in question typically proceeded on the basis of very complicated negotiations between faction leaders, a process in which party elders, i.e., leading older members of the conservative camp, sometimes acted as behind-the-scenes negotiators. The coalition-building efforts were often very time consuming, involving as they did a delicate balancing act. The results of the coalition agreement which eventually evolved were also legitimized in a variety of ways, legitimacy being in itself an important feature of political life in Japan as elsewhere. As was discussed in Chapter 3, sometimes leaders were chosen only through private negotiations between faction leaders, sometimes the factional coalition "slate" was put to a vote in a special party convention, and twice national party primaries have been held wherein the voting patterns reflected factional alliances. The intraparty coalition outcome was also at times legitimized by a ratificatory vote in the

Diet in the form of a majoritarian resolution designating a particular prime minister.[16] The overall process we have just described continues to this moment as the method for selecting Japan's top political leaders, except that in the formation of the most recent cabinet in late 1983 the negotiations included both Liberal Democratic factions and the New Liberal Club.

Coalition negotiations within the Liberal Democratic Party begin on the assumption that a minimal winning majoritarian solution must be found, i.e., over half of the party's Diet members or convention participants must support a winning solution. Often the process begins with precoalitions already in place, in the sense that there are already close ties between two or more factions in the form of interfactional alliances. In recent years, for example, the Ohira-Suzuki and Tanaka factions were closely allied, and the Fukuda, Miki, and Nakasone groups also worked together. Although these ties sometimes reflect personal friendships or enmities, they are ultimately political, and the political landscape may change suddenly when it appears to have been prestructured by such alliances. Thus, in the fall of 1982, Tanaka and his faction also supported Nakasone, who had formerly been in the opposing camp.

The heart of the coalition-building process involves complicated and balanced trade-offs between the interests of the different Liberal Democratic factions and their leaders. Faction leaders themselves want to become prime minister, or they frequently want some leading cabinet position if they cannot hold the top post of power. Faction members also want ministerial positions, both for the power and the status thereby conferred, and because these positions become assets in subsequent elections. Every intraparty coalition process therefore culminates in a carefully orchestrated allocation of leading government and party positions to the factions participating in the coalition. A few positions are also often given to members of "opposition" factions, presumably to give the appearance of party unity.

---

[16] When the intra-Liberal Democratic Party selection process came immediately after an election, or in the cases when a new prime minister was selected, a resolution suporting the prime minister's designation was passed in the Diet. At other times, when a cabinet was reshuffled without designation of a new prime minister or when no election was held that resulted in a new Diet, no resolution was necessary.

The criteria for success in these complex coalitional processes are as intriguing as the processes themselves. Coalitions are built around the large and well-to-do factions within the party. But prime minister designates do not always come from the largest or richest faction, even though they usually come from a major faction. If there is any internal guiding logic operative across time in Liberal Democratic coalitional politics, it could be the presence of close ties across generations between former bureaucrats who became party leaders and their own followers. While such a model involves some oversimplification, it is possible to see a series of patron-client type relationships or simply close personal ties linking prime ministers in different generations. For example, Shigeru Yoshida (1946–47 and 1949–54) was patron for Hayato Ikeda (1960–64) and Eisaku Sato (1964–72), while Ikeda himself introduced Masayoshi Ohira (1978–80) to politics. Sato's faction was inherited by his lieutenant and colleague, Kakuei Tanaka, himself prime minister in 1972–74. Moreover, Sato's brother, Nobusuke Kishi (1957–60), was linked with Takeo Fukuda, who became prime minister between 1976 and 1978.

A cultural model which assumes an overwhelming value for close personal ties or relationships between sponsors and their clients may not completely fit modern society or the complexities of political relationships. The former bureaucrats under consideration had often possessed very high ministerial positions in their former civil service careers, were very knowledgable about national politics, had access to business funding, and were credible to such potential veto groups as the business community, all of which were potent political resources whatever the nature of their personal ties. Still, these former bureaucrats with top level ties — only Tanaka was a nonbureaucrat in this pattern — came into politics with access to party leaders and credibility to the "king-makers" of the party, placing them at considerable differential advantage relative to other persons. Moreover, choice of highly talented and successful persons through the vehicle of more or less traditional personalistic channels is not inconsistent. Actually, Japanese patrons and sponsors in nonpolitical spheres appear often to pick the most capable persons to be their clients, thus providing an intriguing blend of traditional structures with meritocratic criteria.

Clearly many factors have influenced success in the highly competitive game of Liberal Democratic factional politics. Some scholars argue that success in the conservative party is based on acquiring experience and credibility, by successively holding high intra-party posts and major ministerial portfolios like Foreign Affairs, Finance, International Trade and Industry, or the Economic Planning Agency. More likely, holding these positions was simply the *reflection* of successful careers predicated on more basic forces, such as the incumbents' skills and connections. Whatever the causal relationships, the importance of the success ladder of ministerial assignments should be noted. Table 7.5 shows the former posts held by various prime ministers, and provides ample evidence of

TABLE 7.5. *Previous Cabinet Portfolios of Japanese Prime Ministers, 1960–83*

Hayato Ikeda (1960–64)
    Finance (4.1)
    International Trade and Industry (2.2)
    Economic Planning Agency (.1)
Eisaku Sato (1964–72)
    Finance (2)
    International Trade and Industry (1)
    Posts and Communications (1.2)
    Science and Technology Agency (.5)
    Chief Cabinet Secretary (.3)
Kakuei Tanaka (1972–74)
    Finance (3)
    International Trade and Industry (1.5)
    Posts and Communications (.5)
Takeo Miki (1974–76)
    Foreign Affairs (3.2)
    International Trade and Industry (1.5)
    Posts and Communications (.8)
    Transportation (1.7)
    Economic Planning Agency (.5)
    Science and Technology Agency (1)
    Environment Agency (2)
    Vice Prime Minister (2.3)
Takeo Fukuda (1976–78)
    Foreign Affairs (1)
    Finance (5.1)
    Agriculture and Forestry (1)
    Economic Planning Agency (2)
    Administrative Management Agency (1)
    Vice Prime Minister (2)
Masayoshi Ohira (1978–80)
    Foreign Affairs (4)
    Finance (2.4)

.TABLE 7.5 (continued)

    International Trade and Industry (1)
    Chief Cabinet Secretary (2)
Zenko Suzuki (1980–82)
    Health and Welfare (1.5)
    Agriculture and Forestry (2)
    Posts and Communications (.5)
    Chief Cabinet Secretary (.3)
Yasuhiro Nakasone (1982–)
    Transportation (1)
    Defense Agency (1.5)
    International Trade and Industry (2.5)
    Administrative Management Agency (2.3)

Source: Compiled from Asahi Shimbunsha, *Asahi Nenkan,* various years. Some prime ministers also held top Liberal Democratic Party posts before assuming the premiership. Years of tenure in particular positions are shown in parentheses.

the presence of "ladders" to success in the ruling party's elite ranks.

Finally, it is important to remember that not all prime ministers have been ex-bureaucrats, so the explanation we have given for bureaucratic dominance doesn't cover all outcomes. A former lawyer and party politician, Ichiro Hatoyama, was premier in 1954–56, Ishibashi (1956–57) had been a journalist, Kakuei Tanaka (1972–74) was a businessman, and Takeo Miki (1974–76) and Zenko Suzuki (1980–82) were both former party politicians. Still, up until now former bureaucrats have played the coalition game most successfully.

OTHER ELITE RECRUITMENT PROCESSES

Selection of persons for top elite positions in Japan's other political parties, such as the Socialist Party chairman and secretary general, often has involved processes much like those we have described for the Liberal Democrats. The major difference has been, of course, that selection of top governmental elites was not usually intermeshed with selection of party executives in the case of the opposition parties. Factions were the basic components of the elite recruitment coalition processes in all parties other than the Clean Government Party, and at times the Communist Party, although, the factions were much smaller and less permanently institutionalized in the case of Japan's smaller parties. Also, ideology played a much larger role in the coalition-building process in the case of the Japan Socialists than it ever has among the Liberal Democrats.

Selection of candidates in Japanese national elections is another vital part of the elite recruitment processes. Once again factions have been important factors, and coalition building is involved. In the Liberal Democratic Party, at least, the party factions are themselves as important in the nomination process as the various units in the party's national organization. The party has a national election council, for example, which supervises granting of the party label to nominees in the individual electoral districts. However, intraparty factions want to run as many candidates as possible in order to maximize their own power base. The result is often intense factional competition over allocations of party endorsements, which dominates the overall party nomination process supposedly run by the election council. Moreover, because there are factions and support groups at the local level who themselves are vying for power, the national factions have to accommodate themselves to local political groups, including local factions, in order to run candidates who have a viable support base in particular areas. The resulting complex negotiations constitute a "vertical" coalition-building process between national groups and local power centers, including not infrequently powerful regional interest groups.[17]

One additional area of elite political recruitment has become important recently and has implications for parliamentary processes and their outcomes. Throughout the 1950s and the 1960s the conservative movement of the Liberal Democratic Party dominated assignments to positions within the Diet. The speakers of both houses were conservatives, even when nominally independents as required by Diet rules, and most committees in the Diet were led and numerically dominated by conservatives. However, as Liberal Democratic majorities dwindled in the early 1970s, more opposition party members were appointed to committee leadership positions, and more opposition members appeared on Diet committee rosters (see Table 7.6). These reallocations of positions represented an accommodation of Diet recruitment pro-

[17] In House of Councillors elections there have also been examples of coalition building between parties and national interest groups, in order to acquire support bases for individual candidates in the pre-1983 system. These patterns as they relate to interest group strategies will be discussed in Chapter 8.

TABLE 7.6. *Party Domination of Diet Committee Assignments, 1973–80*

	House of Representatives			House of Councillors		
	LDP	Opposition	Split[a]	LDP	Opposition	Split
1973 (Dec)	24	0	0	21	0	2
1974 (Dec)	24	0	0	11	7	5
1976 (Mar)	24	0	0	8	9	6
1977 (Feb)	15	6	4	12	7	5
1977 (Sep)	15	5	5	12	9	4
1978 (Feb)	13	5	7	10	8	6
1979 (Feb)	12	5	8[b]	10	7	7[b]
1980 (Sep)	24	0	1	24	0	0

Source: Compiled from Seiji Koho Senta, *Seiji Handobukku,* various. Figures are numbers of Diet standing and special committees on which the Liberal Democrats or opposition parties have a majority of seats.

[a] Split means a committee on which the Liberal Democratic seat totals and those for other parties are equal.

[b] Includes patterns where presence of alternates indicates nondominance by either the LDP or the opposition.

cesses to changes in party representation. They also indicated a corresponding softening of Liberal Democratic leadership styles. Prior to this time, the Liberal Democrats had, at least in the House of Representatives, "arrogantly" (in the words of the opposition parties) allocated committee chairmanships to their own party members on the basis of their own dominance of the Diet. In the House of Councillors, greater attention was given to representation of opposition parties, but, of course, the Upper House is the less important of the two houses of the Diet. In contrast, since the mid-1970s, chairmanships and committee positions in both houses have been assigned on the basis of a process more reflective of the parties' numerical strengths in the Diet. This change in recruitment processes and shift in power within the committees in the Diet has been one of several important changes that have had an impact on Diet deliberations. As Chapter 9 will show, more important bills were amended and/or passed by multiparty coalitions in the 1970s than in the past, as the centers of power become more accessible to the opposition parties. However, after the Liberal Democratic victory in the 1980 general election, conservative party domination of Lower House committees was resumed, while the Liberal Democrats, who already possessed slightly over one half of the seats in the House of Representatives, decided in December of 1983 to form a coalition with the New Liberal Club for the purpose of ensuring conservative control of key Diet committees.

POLITICAL RECRUITMENT AND JAPANESE POLITICS

For three and one-half decades Japan has been dominated by the same political movement. Political recruitment under the conservative movement's hegemony has produced predictable outcomes: during much of this period Japanese prime ministers and cabinets have come from the ranks of a handful of intraparty factions led more often than not by former senior bureaucratic officials. The conservative style has been one of continuity and stability, remarkably so, given the frequent intensity of intraparty factional rivalries. One or another conservative factional leader has ascended to power in a process marked by intense competition, yet a process in which an acceptable solution has always been found. Japan in the postwar era has never experienced "immobilism," or extreme difficulty in forming effective ruling coalitions, and recruitment paralysis of the kind which has affected the elite selection processes of some European countries, notably post-World War II Italy and interwar France. If political stability is a desirable goal, Japan has had stability in its political recruitment processes under conservative rule.

Conservative dominance has also produced social elite dominance, a not unusual state of affairs but one which assumes special importance in the Japanese case. Japan's leaders and cabinets have been disproportionately the products of a highly elitist educational system and similarly elitist bureaucratic backgrounds. The effect on Japanese governance can be assumed to have been profound. Japanese leaders have been the leading graduates of the leading schools, as well as being the top people coming out of highly selective bureaucratic promotion processes. They have thus clearly been competent individuals, whatever their issue predilections and personality traits, and their competence has been salutory for Japan's well-being, however one might feel about other aspects of conservative rule.

As Japan has entered a period in which coalition rule is a reality, the effects of interparty coalition politics on overall governmental recruitment and styles of governance are a live question. However, the most likely coalition outcomes for the foreseeable future would include the Liberal Democratic Party and one or another of the conservative or middle-of-the-road groups, as in the present coalition, thus encouraging a fairly stable solution. Moreover, experience thus far in coalition discussions among Japan Socialists, the Japan Communists, the Clean Democrats, and Democratic Socialists provide little indication that other alternatives, such as an all-opposition party coalition, would be stable. In deed, should an opposition coalition be able to form a government, there is also little indication at present that such a coalition would be a lasting one. Japan, therefore, could have immobilism at some point in the future, should the current trend of Liberal Democratic electoral dominance and stabilization end.

Japan might also have less competent governors in some senses, should conservative rule terminate. While it must be emphasized that leaders of all of Japan's parties are highly intelligent men, having bureaucratic elites run Japan has had some positive as well as possibly negative effects. If, on the negative side, bureaucratic dominance has enhanced the power of the bureaucracy, on the positive side it has permitted highly experienced men to come to power in an increasingly technocratic age. Under conservative rule and the prevailing styles of political recruitment, Japan's postwar leaders have usually been men who at least had a good knowledge of intrabureaucratic politics in an age when bureaucratic decision making is an important component of political processes. Thus, it could be argued that while extending bureaucratic power and economic perspectives into politics in some instances, recruitment of former bureaucrats to high political office in Japan may have also led to better use of the bureaucracy by political leaders. There is no guarantee that leaders from other parties who might rule in the future would have such an advantage.

CHAPTER 8

Interest Articulation
and Aggregation

THE PROCESSING OF SPECIAL INTERESTS is one of the universal functions of political life. Differences between special interests can be found in the simplest of political communities as well as in complex political systems, and in authoritarian regimes as well as democracies. Much of what is generically called politics involves the *articulation* of interests, i.e., their formulation and expression in political communications channels, and the *aggregation* or combination of different interest demands into specific proposals for public action. Indeed, the input and processing of demands for action or protection is the source of a substantial proportion of political issues and the focus of a great deal of decision making in any political system.

Despite the universality of interest articulation and aggregation, the nature and organizational form of interest groups are reasonably varied. Some groups, for example, are expressly formed for the purpose of articulating interest claims to government: these range in size from large organizations like the Japanese repatriates and former landlords' groups to small community-based citizens' protest movements, of which several thousand are believed to have existed in Japan over the past ten to fifteen years. Some other interest groups make claims upon the political system which are outcomes of activities that they engage in outside of

* Bradley M. Richardson

the political sector. Business federations, labor unions, and religious organizations are a case in point in Japan as well as in other political systems: in all instances these large social organizations or institutions exist because they perform important functions for their members, and defending their members' political interests is a spin-off of the group's more general activities. Informal, unorganized, or weakly organized social groups are also involved in the expression of interests. An example of such groups in Japan is the many "discussion groups" of leading businessmen, which are often cited in the Japanese press as having close ties with particular leading politicians. Informal community elites in Japan have traditionally been another of the most common sources of demands upon local and even national government. Moreover, even groups within government such as bureaucrats in a particular ministry or a subsection of a ministry may at times articulate an interest. From this partial description of the different kinds of organizations which develop and articulate interests, some of the complexity of the interest articulation process can be discerned.

The actual articulation of political demands or positions similarly takes many forms. Interests are expressed privately in the ordinary events of daily life, such as in conversations between a farmer and his village clerk, or among members of a business luncheon group which includes some representative of government. At the other extreme, interests are stated openly and in very formal ways, such as when a particular group expresses its position on some important political issue in the form of a petition to the Diet or a publicly disseminated list of annual resolutions or requests for governmental action. Obviously, many intermediate forms of expression are also to be found, as well as combinations of informal, private communications with formal, public statements.

Finally, articulations of demands for action by governments vary substantially in the kinds of persuasions which are used to support claims for assistance or redress of perceived injustices. Many individuals and groups make special efforts to make their requests credible to governments and their citizens, even to the point of arguing that the whole community or nation will suffer if a particular course of action is not taken. Appeals for credibility may cite some other broad principle, such as when Japanese repatriates — individuals or families who lost property and possessions when Japan was forced to give up her overseas empire after World War II — argued that Japan as a capitalist state had a moral obligation to defend the right of private property.[1] Other forms of persuasion include the well-known techniques of offering votes or campaign funds — often very subtly through understandings by the various persons or groups involved about what is going on without a direct open transaction taking place — in exchange for the future favor of consideration of a group's demands. In some cases even more blatant uses of money in exchange for "access" are found (see Chapter 5).[2] Elsewhere, groups may even use extreme methods to persuade governments to accept their demands; for example, they may threaten to close down the economy by strikes or to withhold food supplies. Much less dramatic but still extremely important modes of persuasion rely mainly on cooperative attitudes which develop through long-standing relationships and intimate personal ties between interest groups and government officials. The importance of cooperative links between groups and political officials is indeed often overlooked because more open and confrontational activities and the use of money are more dramatic.

In addition to its complexity, the interest group environment in Japan is a vast landscape. Business is represented by four major groups: The Federation of Economic Organizations, the Federation of Employers Organizations, the Japan Chamber of Commerce and Industry, and the Keizai Doyukai. These groups have different constituencies. The Federation of Economic Organizations represents large businesses, the Federation of Employers Organizations represents big companies as employers, the Chamber of Commerce represents businesses of all sizes, and the Keizai Doyukai is a small group of policy-oriented business leaders. Other areas like labor and agriculture are also represented by multiple groups, among them the large General Council of Trade Unions (Sohyo), which includes the large government employees'

[1] John Creighton Campbell, "Compensation for Repatriates: A Case Study of Interest Group Politics and Party-Government Negotiations in Japan," in T. J. Pempel, ed., *Policymaking in Contemporary Japan* (Ithaca: Cornell University Press, 1977), p. 106.

[2] The recent Lockheed incident, a major *cause celebre* in Japanese politics, is an example of a blatant use of money to persuade.

unions and some industrial unions, the Japanese Federation of Trade Unions (Domei), which represents mainly unions in private industry, and the large Central Association of the Federation of Agricultural Cooperatives. Many other functional interests have representation in Japan, such as doctors in the form of the Japan Medical Association, and small businessmen through the Medium and Small Business Political League. Even local government officials are represented in such groups as the National Governors Association and the National City Mayors Association or other groups of local officials, including associations of heads of local and prefectural assemblies.

Japan's political system is therefore highly pluralistic, at least in a formal, numerical sense. There are hundreds if not thousands of important organized interest groups which regularly petition national government for consideration of their needs.[3] There are also thousands of local interests which sporadically place demands on government for some form of assistance. A significant share of interest generation in Japan also originates in groups within the government itself, such as the ministries of national government and sections within prefectural and local governments.

INTEREST ARTICULATION IN JAPAN

Interest articulation in Japan, like that in any other political system, can best be described as a fairly constant stream of messages directed toward politicians asking for special consideration of individual or group needs. Many studies of interest articulation see these messages as a kind of mechanical "pressure" on political officials. In reality, things are much more complex. Interests provide both pressures and multiple informational cues to government officials. Demands or requests for political help certainly press officials to do things they might otherwise not do. But, politicians and officials are often searching the political system for

[3] Information on the numbers of interest groups comes from various sources. Lists of major interest groups are included in political handbooks, and normally anywhere from thirty-five to nearly one hundred large, national organizations are thus identified. Also consulted was one Dietmember's file of petitions, which contained demands from over seventy "minor" groups not listed in public sources. Estimates of the numbers of local citizens' movements, which came into being to articulate political claims in the late 1960s, run as high as six thousand for the period 1968–72.

ideas about what kinds of issues should be dealt with in order to maximize their own political support. Most politicians recognize that their ability to represent their constituents is of enormous importance to their staying in office, and as a result actively seek out interest demands from individual and group constituents in addition to responding to pressures from groups.

Participation in the interest articulation communications stream we have just identified may be on a one-time basis, intermittent, or constant. Individuals or groups which make a request to government over a short time-span contribute to the overall volume of interest-related political communications, but they don't become important cue givers over the long run for obvious reasons. In contrast, permanently organized interest groups provide many cues to government officials and play a large role in the interest articulation stream. Politicians normally pay special attention to these groups and cultivate their representatives in their efforts to gather information about their own political environments.

Organized groups which represent broad population or occupation sectors tend to be especially important participants in the interest-related communications process and generate a wide-ranging and continuous stream of interest cues. In Japan such groups include some of the groups identified above, such as the large business and industrial organizations, farmers' organizations, trade union federations, pensioners' groups, and groups of professionals, as well as some other groups. Each of the specific interest organizations in these categories typically serves a fairly broad constituency. It is interesting to note that instead of being active on one major issue at a time, as case studies sometimes imply, large organizations in many instances take positions on a large number of issues at any given time. This can readily be seen from the information in Table 8.1 which illustrates the large scope and multiplicity of interests of a typical large organization, using as an example the policy positions of Japan's leading agricultural interest group, the national farm cooperatives.

TYPES OF POLITICAL INTERESTS

Interest groups in Japan ask for many things. The substance of their requests can be classified, and through classification some of the generic qualities of interests can be discerned. Demonstrating what the different general classes of interests are will help show

TABLE 8.1. *1979 Interest Demands of Japan's National Farm Cooperative Movement*

Enhance domestic self-sufficiency in agricultural commodities
Encourage demand for rice
Stimulate production of dairy products
Decrease imports of wheat and rice
Modernize food-processing facilities
Better organize food distribution systems and markets
Continue the government-managed rice supply system
Provide government guidance on crop substitution and conversion
Stabilize producers' prices for agricultural products
Stabilize costs of fertilizer and oil used by farmers
Assist mechanization of agriculture
Reform the agricultural disaster insurance system
Provide more forest land for agriculture
Provide more government investment in land development enterprises
Increase availability of social welfare assistance to farmers
Provide better financial facilities for farmers

Source: Compiled from Zenkoku Nogyo Kyodo Kumiai Chuokai, *Nogyo Kihon Seisaku no Kakuritsu Narabi ni Showa 55 nendo Norin Kankei Juten Shisaku ni Kan Suru Yosei* (Tokyo: 1979).

the similarity of the types of demands which are made by otherwise quite different kinds of interest groups, as well as suggesting how the complex and often confusing world of political issues can be reduced to easily understood patterns. For example, some demands expressed by Japan's interest groups reflect the support of those groups for broad social principles, such as old or new values, or economic principles such as capitalism or socialism. Other group interests are more specific in nature, and, while they may reflect a concern covering many issues for the problems of some large occupational sector like farmers or small businessmen, no specific social value or principle constitutes the binding cement underlying these demands. In the discussion below some examples are given of broad principle-based interests in Japan. There is also a review of non-value-based specific interests, and this category will even be subdivided into different subtypes of more specific interests.

Some of the types of interests articulated by particular groups in Japan are shown in Table 8.2. The support for capitalism and classical liberalism expressed by some of Japan's major business groups is an example of the first general category of interests, i.e., advocacy of broad *social principles* and *goals*. Business groups like

TABLE 8.2. *Patterns of Interests in Japan, 1960–80*

Type I	*Broad Social and Economic Principles and Goals*
Capitalism and Stable Economic Growth —Political stability —Economic stability —Economic growth —Opposition to Communism (in some periods)	Federation of Economic Organizations Federation of Employers Associations Keizai Doyukai* Chamber of Commerce in Japan Specific industry associations
Socialism and Internationalism —Social welfare programs —Neutral and Internationalist Japan	Sohyo
Postwar Constitution and Guarantees of Rights —Opposition to Constitution revision —Favor right to strike for civil servants —Favor defense of civil rights against enhanced police power proposals	Sohyo Soka Gakkai*
Imperial System and Old Constitution	Seicho no Ie* Japan Shinto Shrine Agency

Type II	*Special Assistance to Specific Interest Groups*
Grain price supports and general agriculture support	Federation of Agriculture Cooperatives
Development of government land improvement programs	National Land Improvement Association
Support for specific recessed or developing industries	Specific industry associations Medium and Small Business League
Pensions and compensation for service or loss of life or property or injury in World War II	Military Pensions Association Japan Association of Bereaved Families Association of Repatriates
Establishment of special credit facilities	National Farmland League Medium and Small Business League Federation of Agricultural Cooperatives Federation of Environmental Hygiene Enterprises
Opposition to regional development	Local citizens movements
Distribution of tax revenues to local governments	National Governors Association National Mayors Association

TABLE 8.2. (continued)

Type III	Regulation of Behavior of Other Groups
Control of industries' pollution of the environment	Local citizens movements
Regulation of community morals	Japan Mothers League Federation of Womens Clubs
Control of military personnel off-base activities	Military Base Area Countermeasures League

Note: Substance and spin-offs of broad value commitments are indicated in notations beginning with a dash (—). An asterisk (*) indicates names of groups for which there is no suitable English translation. Groups listed in the right column are those that have particular interests, as can be seen, sometimes more than one group espouses the same interest.

Japan's large Federation of Economic Organizations have upon occasion openly and directly advocated in their statements of their general political principles that Japan should be a liberal capitalist society. By this they have meant that Japan should have a capitalist and not a socialist society and economy, and one in which the role of government is constrained relative to the initiatives of the private sector. Elsewhere, support for classical liberal concepts of capitalism can be seen in the stands of different groups on particular issues. For example, Japan's business groups have upon occasion indicated their preference for a laissez faire economy by opposition to bills which would have extended ministerial powers to intervene in industrial decisions. Even though Japan's major business groups have accepted indicative economic planning and believe the government should promote economic stability and growth, opposition to too much government interference in business affairs is still widespread, especially among strong industries whose economic condition is healthy. Preservation of a free capitalist economy is thus the "bottom line" for Japan's business community.[4]

Japan's labor union federations, Sohyo and the Domei, in contrast, would prefer a more socialist form of society, much like

[4] Business advocacy of a laissez faire economy may seem especially ironical, since many sectors of the Japanese business world have asked for special government assistance on occasions. The student of Japanese politics is faced with the same contradictions between espousal of general laissez faire principles on the one hand and a multitude of requests for special governmental intervention on the other that characterize the positions of business groups in all industrialized democracies including the United States. Moreover, busi-

their respective allies, the Japan Socialist and Democratic Socialist parties.[5] There have been major internal differences like those between and within the leftist political parties on precisely the kind of socialism desired, with specific union federations and even some of their component unions differing fairly sharply on these central principles. Nevertheless, the union movement in general has been united in its desire for broader social welfare programs and in its defense of the working class and other groups seen as being underprivileged, even while also differing with regard to the optimal scope and pace of socialist change that they envision as desirable for Japan.

The Japanese labor union movement has also defended other broad principles, including those expressed in the postwar constitution regarding civil rights and local autonomy. Many Japanese conservative politicians supported constitutional revision in the 1950s and early 1960s, and at that time labor federations like the General Council of Trade Unions were adamant in their defense of the postwar institutions, which among other things had extensive guarantees of civil rights. Even after this aspect of the constitutional issue had dwindled in importance during the late 1960s and 1970s, the labor unions remained on guard against the remaining forces of revision, in part because their own right to organize and bargain collectively was established in the constitution and related legislation. Some labor unions have also strongly opposed efforts to expand police powers or to enhance central administrative control over the educational system at the expense of local autonomy in these areas. The unions have also argued that the constitutionally guaranteed right to strike should be extended to government workers.

---

ness is far from homogenous as case studies of both foreign and domestic policies demonstrate. *See* Ogata, "The Business Community and Japanese Foreign Policy," in Robert A. Scalapino, ed., *The Foreign Policy of Modern Japan* (Berkeley and Los Angeles: The University of California Press, 1977), pp. 175–203; and Eugene J. Kaplan, *Japan: The Government-Business Relationship* (Washington: United States Department of Commerce, 1972), pp. 120–128. Indicative economic planning is planning of economic activity which lacks inbuilt sanctions for non-compliance, such as those found in Communist societies.

5 At present it is not completely accurate to call the Sohyo an "ally" of the Socialist Party, since some member unions have supported other parties or coalition slates in recent elections. The statement is nevertheless accurate for most of the postwar era prior to the late 1970s.

Other groups have also taken positions on the constitution and related issues which reflect their attachment to general principles. *Seicho no Iie*, a Buddhist religious organization, and the National Shinto Shrine Agency currently advocate return to a Japanese style constitution just as did earlier conservative groups. Among other things, these two groups favor an enhanced status for the emperor, presumably something like the concept of imperial rule outlined by the Meiji Constitution. These same two groups have also supported a bill which would make Japan's monument to its war dead, the Yasukuni Shrine, eligible for government financial support; in addition, they have favored a retention of the imperial era system under which Japan's calendar is calculated on the basis of the rule period of specific emperors.

THE QUEST FOR GOVERNMENTAL ASSISTANCE AS AN INTEREST

A highly visible and recurring type of political interest in Japan, which is considerably more specific than broad principles, consists of demands by organizations and communities for some kind of direct *governmental support*. These specific requests for governmental help take many forms. Some interest groups have desired governmental intervention in the marketplace in the form of price supports. Other groups have requested government subsidies for particular projects, while still other interest organizations have advocated government establishment of special credit facilities to serve a particular occupation's needs. Some other kinds of specific public assistance requested by groups include pensions and compensation for persons who suffered in some way during World War II or during the subsequent reversion of Japanese territories to former owners.

Intervention in economic markets has been desired by Japanese farmers and specific industry organizations. Like their counterparts in North America and Europe, Japan's leading agricultural organizations have wanted government to ensure that farmers receive incomes equal to those of urban workers. In annual demands to government, agricultural groups in Japan have used income parity formulae and other arguments to seek support for artificially high rice and other farm commodity prices.[6] Liberal

6 Michael Donnelly, "Setting the Price of Rice: A Study in Political Decisionmaking," in T. J. Pempel, ed., *Policymaking in Contemporary Japan* (Ithaca: Cornell University Press, 1979), pp. 143–200.

Democratic governments, which have been heavily dependent on the farm vote, have accommodated most requests by farmers for price subsidies, although in some cases at a lower price level than that advocated by large agricultural interest groups such as the Agricultural Cooperatives Federation's national executive.

Particular Japanese industrial organizations have also at times supported market intervention in the form of protectionist policies regarding foreign imports. In the 1950s, and in some product areas throughout the 1960s, Japan had higher import tariffs on many products than many other industrialized nations. Japan also had quota restrictions on many imported manufactured products, which limited the volume of permissible imports. These protectionist controls helped Japan develop its own native manufacturing industries without serious threats from foreign competition. Import restrictions also helped conserve foreign exchange needed for vital raw materials imports. Trade liberalization programs have by now nearly eliminated all protectionist measures in Japan's foreign trade. However, some farm products such as meat and citrus fruits are still protected, because of vociferous demands by agricultural organizations. Also, trade frictions still exist between Japan and the United States over the existence of so-called nontariff barriers, which are said to be a form of protection based on use of existing laws and regulations, like those pertaining to automobile safety and food sanitation.

A second form of governmental assistance widely desired by functional interests in Japan has been provision of special credit facilities for firms or households in particular economic sectors. Banks would not always make loans to farmers and owners of small businesses, who often fell in higher risk categories than their large corporate customers. Reflecting these difficulties in obtaining credit, agricultural and small enterprisers' groups like the Medium and Small Business Political League repeatedly sought governmental help, with the result that special credit facilities supported by the government now exist for small companies, farmers, and enterprises in the environmental hygiene sector (restaurants, barber shops, butchers, and other similar businesses whose activities are regulated under environmental sanitation laws). These special credit arrangements are not dissimilar in form from those provided small businesses in the United States and Europe, and reflect special problems peculiar to small businesses in all modern industrialized societies. However, the especially large size of the small business sector in Japan's dual economy as well as the economic and political importance of the residual agricultural sector have made the small economic unit credit issue especially important in Japan. Reflecting this imperative, Japanese government lending to small business has recently been four times the levels of support for large industries; interestingly, it was also three times the size of the United States government's loans to small business.

Groups concerned with government pensions and other forms of government compensation for their members have constituted another kind of specific interest category in Japan. Many of the individuals and families who suffered as the result of Japan's involvement in World War II banded together to seek governmental aid. These have included former soldiers, families that lost husbands and sons in the war, and persons who lost property when Japan's overseas territories in China and Southeast Asia were lost as a result of defeat. Other groups, including retired civil servants and former members of Japan's Self-Defense Forces, have made claims, fueled at times by rising inflation, for better pensions. Former landowners, who lost holdings through government appropriation during the postwar Occupation-sponsored land reforms, also sought assistance, and eventually won compensation for part of their losses through a sustained political campaign in the late 1950s and early 1960s.

Government assistance in the form of subsidies and grants-in-aid, i.e., direct governmental financial assistance, have been sought by many large and small interest groups in Japan, including the important national leagues of governors, mayors, and prefectural and local assembly chairmen. Because Japan has a tradition of centralized public finance and administration, thousands of local interest groups or coalitions regularly turn to Tokyo for aid to finance school and road construction projects or other local public works. Inauguration of special government programs, such as the land improvement program called for in postwar legislation, has also resulted in appeals for support for local projects. In addition to the many requests for local assistance, national interest groups like the agricultural cooperatives and the national organizations of local government officials have also requested governmental subsidy packages for programs in such fields as agricultural extension and worker training.

INTERESTS AS DEMANDS FOR REGULATION OF BEHAVIOR

Some Japanese interest groups, rather than expressing support for diffuse principles or demanding specific governmental *assistance,* have asked political authorities to *regulate* the behavior of others in order to achieve some desired state of affairs. The most conspicuous example of interest groups' requesting governmental regulation in recent years has been the fight against environmental pollution and regional industrialization. Hundreds, and perhaps even thousands, of local neighborhood and community groups have asked local, prefectural, and national authorities to regulate the pollution-creating practices of industrial plants or to abandon plans to create new industrial zones, which could lead to new sources of pollution and other kinds of damage to the environment.

National groups, including the labor unions and consumers' groups, in turn echoed concerns at the local level and demanded central government action in the antipollution field. Groups of local residents have also asked for controls on noise at major airports, or opposed their construction for these and other important reasons such as reluctance to sell cherished farmland. Other examples of government corporations being asked to regulate their own behavior occurred when local residents in several areas complained about the noise and vibration from the Japan National Railway's high speed "bullet" trains routed through their neighborhoods, or opposed new construction of similar lines which would run through their communities.

Many other national and local groups have regularly petitioned the government for regulation of behavior which they deplore. Women's and community groups, like the Federation of Womens Clubs and the Japan Mothers' League, for example, have often tried to control prostitution and licentiousness in districts near American bases, while at the national level women's groups were the main force behind legislation outlawing prostitution in 1956. Women's groups have tried at other times to regulate other aspects of behavior, for example, by opposing sales of toy weapons as part of their general opposition to war. In a parallel fashion groups including the labor unions and the Soka Gakkai have denounced corruption in politics and have endorsed anticorruption legislation. And the Buraku Liberation League has defended the interests of persons in traditional outcast occupations by urging an end to discrimination in employment and other areas of behavior. While groups which have sought to control the behavior of others have not always been successful — the mixed record of campaigns against regional industrial development is a case in point — this category of interests is nevertheless an important part of the Japanese political landscape.

INTEREST GROUP RESOURCES: MEMBERS, ORGANIZATION, MONEY

Interest groups have a variety of resources which may be mobilized in the search for access to politicians and officials. For example, groups with large memberships can offer support from blocs of voters in exchange for reciprocal support for their interest claims. In recent years, quite a few important Japanese groups have mobilized voting blocs, with varying degrees of success, with precisely this purpose in mind.

Japan's largest mass groups, i.e., groups with large memberships, are in the agricultural sector. The Federation of Agricultural Cooperatives with a membership in 1979 of over 7 million is one of the largest mass interest groups in the world, even though its membership is down from 15 million in the mid-1960s as a result of declines in the farm population. The agricutural cooperatives' national organization is actually an association of several major cooperative federations in the areas of production and sales, purchases, and credit. Collectively the cooperative federations claim to include every farm family in Japan in at least one of their organizations. Traditionally, the farm cooperatives have leaned toward the Liberal Democrats in both national and local elections. However, in recent years, the cooperatives have assumed a more independent posture reflecting the increasing political diversity of its own membership. Since many farmers now work in regional industries established as the consequence of Liberal Democratic development plans, as a result they come under the influence of the opposition parties and labor unions. Moreover, even the staff members of the cooperatives federation are now reported to be heterogeneous in their political orientations, since they are unionized like their white collar counterparts in other large organizations and corporations, and therefore come under the influence of opposition political movements.

A second very large interest group in the agricultural sector in Japan is the National Land Improvement Association (NLIA). The NLIA was formed as a direct response to a governmental policy decision, namely the National Land Improvement Law of 1949. This important legislative bill provided funds for irrigation projects and other local programs for land development and improvement of land productivity. The NLIA, which is a much looser organization than the farm cooperatives, serves only one function in contrast with the cooperatives' multiple-functionality. However, the NLIA has effectively mobilized its membership on various occasions and supported winning Liberal Democratic candidates, usually its own officials, in several recent House of Councillors elections.

Some pensioners' groups, or groups of people who suffered as a result of World War II, are also quite large and have at times been able to use their memberships as political resources. For example, the Federation of Repatriates, which was active in the 1950s and 1960s, had a claimed membership of around 3 million at certain times, while the membership claims of the Association of War-Bereaved Families were actually twice this number in some periods. Veterans and other pensioners' groups have had considerably fewer claimed members in comparison with these "giants," yet still qualified as mass groups with reported memberships varying between 300 thousand and 700 thousand persons. Typically the pensioners' groups and the associations of those who claimed damages as a result of the war appear to have been fairly loosely organized. Consequently, national leaders couldn't always count on effective mobilization from the different organizations' memberships in the face of competing claims from other groups or local elites and others who supported particular candidates. Still, most of these groups, and especially those with large memberships, were able at one time or another to send one or more of their officials to the Upper House, as well as providing effective support for local conservative candidates in some constituencies.[7]

---

[7] Our inference that these groups were weakly organized stems from an analysis by John Campbell of the repatriates' failure to maximize the votes of

TABLE 8.3. *Membership of Sohyo Affiliated Unions and Diet Seats of Union Officials, 1974*

Union	Membership	Diet Seats
Japan Teachers' Union (Nikkyoso)	600,000	29
National Railway Workers' Union (Kokuro)	225,000	17
Communications Workers' Union (Zentei)	200,000	10
Local Government Employees' Union (Jichiro)	1,071,000	8
Telecommunications Workers' Union (Zendentsu)	271,000	7

Source: Sankei Shimbun, p. 3, May 26, 1974. Reprinted by permission.

Japan's labor unions appear to have been effective in using their memberships as a political resource in several important cases (even if they supported the losing side in national elections). Some Japanese labor unions have had major internal schisms — a recent split within the teachers union between supporters of the Communist and the Socialist parties is an example. Also, the relationship between the union locals, which in Japan are organized around firms rather than industries, and the relevant national federations is extremely varied and complex. However, instances where unions have been relatively successful in mobilizing at the polls are not hard to find. As can be seen in Table 8.3, various Sohyo affiliates typically were successful in having several of their officials elected to the Upper and/or Lower Houses of the Diet. This success serves as a witness to their effectiveness in vote mobilization. However, these data also show that there is no simple link between size alone and effectiveness, as

their claimed membership in both Upper and Lower House elections in the 1960s. By weak organization, we mean that either the internal links between national and local groups were ultimately not effective, or else some members had fairly fragile connections with the group. *See* John Campbell, "Compensation for Repatriates," in T. J. Pempel, op. cit., pp. 128–132; *See also* Haruhiro Fukui, *Party in Power: The Japanese Liberal Democrats and Policymaking* (Berkeley and Los Angeles: University of California Press, 1970), pp. 192–195, for a similar analysis of the influence of the repatriates' groups.

some smaller unions apparently mobilized their members more effectively than some large federations. These variations in successful mobilization once again raise the question of what differences between organizations encourage differential degrees of success in vote mobilization.

Some unions associated with the Japan Federation of Labor (Domei) also have fairly large memberships, even though the industrial unions in the Domei group are considerably smaller than the very large government employee unions affiliated with Sohyo (Sohyo also has several industrial union affiliates). Domei affiliated unions such as the auto workers, electric power workers, and textile industry workers regularly have sent winning candidates to the House of Councillors under Democratic Socialist "colors." The Domei unions were also important in House of Representatives district contests at times, particularly where their support was concentrated, as in the case of the Toyota auto workers.

There are a number of interest groups in Japan which could hardly be called "mass" groups in terms of size of membership, yet which occasionally have mobilized sufficient votes to succeed at the polls. Included in this category of "semimass" groups have been the Medium and Small Business Political League (believed to have around 300 thousand members), the Japan Communist Party oriented Democratic Merchants and Manufacturers Association (believed to have 200 thousand members), groups of farmers specializing in one type of product, such as the Association of Citrus Fruit Producers, and professional groups such as the Japan Medical Association and the Japan Dentists Association. These groups didn't always have the capability to mobilize the roughly 600 thousand votes necessary for success in the House of Councillors national districts under the election laws operative until the 1983 election; however, they were successful in this constituency at times and were also important elements in coalitions of groups electing candidates in the House of Councillors local districts and House of Representatives constituencies. Actually, press analyses of individual candidates' support coalitions in many districts claim that local or prefectural elements of these national organizations were contributors to candidates' voting blocs, along with other groups such as local union affiliates and prefectural agricultural cooperatives federations.

In discussing the success of different groups at mobilization of voting blocs, it has been noted that groups probably varied in their effectiveness at getting out the vote. The effectiveness of organizations in mobilizing their supporters is a complex matter, but variations in organizational form could be an important variable. Most of the large interest organizations we have been discussing are *"peak"* organizations. They are thus *national federations* whose constituent members are actually other *federations* at either the national or local level. Their component national or local federations are made up in turn of local units, and the local units in many cases themselves may have individual members, as in the case of what we have called mass groups, or individual companies are members, as in most business groups. Some peak associations like the Federation of Employers' Organizations and the Japan Housewives Federation also have direct members; in other words the members of these large organizations include companies, and individuals as well as federations. It can't be said with certainty just how big a difference exists between the multi-tiered peak organizations, which some scholars argue are less effective at mobilization, and those groups with simpler organizations and direct memberships (for some interesting variations in organizational type, see Table 8.4). Other factors such as the scope of services performed by different groups — compare the multi-functional farm cooperatives with the narrower activities of the pensioners' groups — may also influence the appeal and effectiveness of organizations. Also those groups where members are involved more in group activities may be more successful in commanding their members' loyalties at election time. Leadership, too, may be a variable: some influential interest groups like the Japan Medical Association have had strong leaders at times. But it is easy to accept the popular idea that large, peak associations or even their component federations do not always find electoral mobilization of their memberships an easy matter.[8]

---

[8] Another group of factors affecting how well groups mobilize their members in elections could be the extent to which issues which group members care about are at stake in an election. Also the degree of ideological unity and commitment could be a variable, with more unified and "ideological" memberships being more prone to follow group leaders at election time. An additional consideration affecting mobilization appears to be the degree to which a group's leadership is united behind a particular candidate. In most elections the Japanese newspapers identify several instances where there were factional splits within groups on such matters. *See* Bradley Richardson, "A Japanese House of Councillors Election: Support Mobilization and Political Recruitment," *Modern Asian Studies,* October 1967, pp. 385–402.

TABLE 8.4. *Japanese Interest Groups: Organizational Characteristics and Membership*

Group Name	Type	Group Members	Corporate Members	Individual Members
Federation of Economic Organizations (Large corporations)	Peak-membership	110*	793	
Japan Federation of Employers Organization (Large and small employers)	Peak-membership	88*		28,629
Japan Committee for Economic Development (Large company presidents)	Membership			895
Japan Iron and Steel Federation (Large iron and steel companies)	Membership		50	
Japan Fisheries Association (Large fisheries and federations of small fishermen's cooperatives)	Peak-membership	161	208	45
Japan Housewives Federation (Shufuren)	Peak-membership	461		535
National Assembly of Consumers	Peak	55		
All-Japan Mayors Association	Membership			646
All-Japan City Assembly Chairmen's Association	Membership			646
Central Union of Agricultural Cooperatives	Peak	8,331+		
General Council of Trade Unions (Sohyo)	Peak	50#		
Japan Confederation of Labor (Domei)	Peak	31#		

Source: Information is from group publications or was supplied directly during interviews with persons in group secretariats. * = industry associations, + = cooperatives federations, and # = union federations. The membership base of particular groups is shown in parentheses where a group's name does not indicate the nature of its constituency.

The groups shown in this table were selected to demonstrate some of the variations in types of major groups in Japan; this is *not* a listing of all major groups.

Large memberships which can be mobilized at the polls constitute an important category of political resources for some interest groups. Another well-known potential source of political influence is money, and some Japanese interest groups make heavy monetary "investments" in candidates and parties, presumably to safeguard their interests. The most important examples of the use of money in Japanese politics have been the large, regular transfers of funds from business interests to the Liberal Democratic Party and its factions (Table 8.5). Political contributions

TABLE 8.5. *Contributions to Japanese Political Parties and Factions from External Groups 1976–78 (in 000 yen)*

Political Parties	1976	1977	1978
Liberal Democratic Party	7,284,660	7,908,170	8,285,080
Democratic Socialist Party	815,500	679,340	817,950
Japan Communist Party	109,000	117,000	194,970
New Liberal Club	129,000	136,340	176,490
Japan Socialist Party	166,110	153,680	5,980
Liberal Democratic Party Factions			
Ohira Faction	594,110	535,800	698,290
Fukuda Faction	678,900	610,120	616,360
Nakasone Faction	330,800	207,780	287,950
Tanaka Faction	300,830	301,730	199,210
Miki Faction	145,760	119,130	80,470
Leading Corporate and Industrial Association Contributors (1978)			
Japan Synthetic Textiles Association	100,000		
Japan Iron and Steel Association	100,000		
Tokyo Stockbrokers' Association	98,790		
Japan Automobile Manufacturers Association	90,000		
New Japan Steel Corporation	82,400		
Kobe Steel Corporation	81,000		
Nippon Kokan Corporation	80,490		
Kawasaki Steel Corporation	80,260		
Steel Materials Makers Club	80,000		
Shipowners Association	80,000		

Source: Material assembled from public sources and given to the authors by the late Fusae Ichikawa and associates. Political parties and factions listed here include only major groupings (the Clean Government Party is excluded as it did not report having received any contributions). Contributions to Liberal Democratic factions are independent from gifts to the Liberal Democratic Party, thus reflecting the imporance of the factions. Only the leading ten contributors from a longer list of corporate and business association donees are reported here. The value of the yen in 1976–78 fluctuated between 293 and 200 yen per each U.S. dollar.

are typically made both by industry association (*gyokai*) level federations, such as the Japan Iron and Steel Association or the Japan Automobile Manufacturers Association, and by individual corporations (see Table 8.5 for specific examples of leading contributors in 1978). The peak business associations themselves do not give money. Still, most industry federations and companies giving money to the Liberal Democrats and occasionally even to other parties are affiliates of the major peak business organizations, and organizations like the Federation of Economic Organizations are said actually to allocate the contributions of the business community among their different industrial organization members at times. Their collective contributions can thus be assumed to constitute a plus for businesswide interests, in addtion to the more direct implications of the fragmented pattern of business sector contributions for advancement of particular industrial associations' or firms' own specialized political concerns.

The steady flow of finances from business interests to the Liberal Democratic Party and its major factions constitutes an important political resource. There is no effective way to separate out the role of financial gifts alone in the often cited close relationship between business and the Liberal Democrats. Shared beliefs on many issues, exchange of personnel, and intimate personal ties all play an important part in the party-business relationship, in addition to the contribution of financial support.[9] However,

---

[9] There is no simple way to say what business wants as an "interest" because there are so many different constituencies within the business sector. At one level, big business supports the idea of a laissez faire economy, perhaps more nowadays than in earlier periods. But many industrial groups have sought government intervention, too, when the times and the issue suited them. Perhaps more than anything else Japanese business wants political stability under a non-Socialist government. A recent study of the links between business and politics in Japan has suggested that the relationship is declining in importance, and also qualified the often readily assumed significance of social ties between important politicians and leading businessmen and their various formal and informal groups. While we accept the importance of these qualifications, it is also clear that business and the Liberal Democrats still maintain many channels of communications and that the business sector is the main source of funds of the conservative political movement. *See* Gerald L. Curtis, "Big Business and Political Influence," in Ezra Vogel, ed., *Modern Japanese Organization and Decision Making* (Berkeley and Los Angeles: University of California Press, 1975), pp. 33–70, for a study of the possibly declining role of business contacts in Japan in general.

the importance of the heavy money flow cannot be underestimated, constituting as it does the very life blood of conservative finances.

There are other interest groups in Japan that provide political funds for the parties of their choice. Among the other visible money flows besides that from business to the conservatives are the transfers from the Sohyo federation unions to the Japan Socialist Party, and a similar movement of funds from the Domei federation affiliates to the Democratic Socialist Party. In some years the contributions from some union federations equaled those from some of the top business groups which give to the Liberal Democrats, although there are fewer well-to-do labor union federations than wealthy industrial groups and corporations with the result that the Socialist parties receive much less outside support than do the Liberal Democrats. Other interest organizations, such as the Repatriates Association, the Japan Medical Association, and the Federation of Medium and Small Businessmen also make contributions to party campaign funds or have done so in the past, according to analyses of political finances in Japan. However, as Table 8.5 shows, the scale of interest group financial support for parties is actually fairly small in most cases, with the exception of business contributions to the Liberal Democrats. Only one party in the opposition camp, the Democratic Socialist Party, is at all comparable in relative scale of funding to the conservative party, as the Democratic Socialists receive gifts from labor unions and also contributions from business. Although money is clearly an important political resource in Japanese politics, it is distributed very unequally among the various interests and parties.

DIRECT GROUP REPRESENTATION IN THE
DIET AND ADVISORY COUNCILS

Interest groups seek access to decision-making centers in a variety of ways. Direct participation by interest group representa-

---

See also Joji Watanuki, "Kodo Seicho to Keizai Daikokuka no Seiji Katei," in Nihon Seiji Gakkai, *55 nen Taisei no Keisei to Hokai* (Tokyo: Iwanami Shoten, 1979), pp. 159–162 for an assertion of the importance of such ties in one specific Japanese policy-making process, the formulation of industrial policy during much of the postwar era.

tives in public processes is not uncommon in many countries, although the form of these contacts varies. In several European political systems, close ties between interest groups and parties result at times in group officials being elected to parliaments. In a few cases, special corporate legislative bodies were even established in the past to provide direct occupational group representation in parliaments.[10] Interest groups also participate in administrative commissions and councils in many countries.

Direct representation is an accepted mode of interest group participation in Japanese politics, and a substantial number of Diet members are officials of large interest groups or formerly held such positions. The logic by which large groups support candidates, including their own officials, in national elections, has already been described in the discussion of group resources. Mobilization of the vote by interest groups has been important to both of Japan's major political camps for many years, while groups themselves are anxious to improve their political position by supporting candidates. Because of the intertwining of party and group interests in interest-group vote mobilization, it is even hard to tell whether the original initiative for group officials' candidacies came from the groups themselves or from the side of the parties, which are ever anxious to gain voting blocs.

Whatever calculus brings interest group officials into parliamentary politics, direct Diet representation is a visible and potentially important dimension of Japanese interest group politics. The Japanese labor union movement has been heavily represented in the Diet, as discussed above, though it was not affiliated with the ruling party (see Table 8.1 again). A substantial number of private group officials also became members of the Diet under Liberal Democratic colors in recent years. For example, according to our own analysis (see Table 8.6), at least 15 officials representing a variety of interest groups were successful Liberal Democratic nominees in national district contests in the 1974 and 1977 House of Councillors elections. An additional 20 interest group officials were Liberal Democratic Councillors from the local district races in this same period, while there were 11 group officials among the 256 conservative party members of the House of Rep-

---

[10] Italy under Fascist rule and Spain under Franco are fairly recent examples of use of corporate parliamentary bodies.

TABLE 8.6. *Interest Group Representatives Elected from the House of Councillors National District and Affiliated with the Liberal Democratic Party, 1974–80*

Name	Organization
Kobayashi	National Land Improvement Association
Okuda	Military Pensions Association
Eto	National Travel Agents Association
Sakomizu	Retail Tobacco Merchants Association
Otani	Bereaved Families Association
Ueda	Japan Rivers Association
Shimoto	Japan Nurses Association
Kajiki	National Land Improvement Association
Kusanoki	New Japan Federation of Religious Associations
Tamachi	*Seicho no Ie* Political League
Tokunaga	Bereaved Families Association
Nishimura	National Association of Special Postmasters
Takeuchi	Military Pensions Association
Fukushima	Japan Medical Association
Horie	Self-Defense Forces Veterans Association

Source: Sankei Shimbun (various dates), *Asahi Shimbun* (various dates), and Jichisho Senkyokyoku, *Sangiin Giin Tsujo Senkyo Kekka Shirabe* (Tokyo: 1974 and 1977).

resentatives after the 1976 election.[11] Altogether some 46 members of the Liberal Democratic contingent in the Diet in 1978–80 were consequently group representatives. This figure included 14 members from agricultural groups, 2 representatives from religious groups, 5 parliamentarians from pensioners groups, and 25 members from other groups including groups representing the medical organizations and small business.

Direct representation in the Diet was most likely an advantage for some interest groups, since their members could sit on Diet

[11] The disparity between interest group representation in the Liberal Democratic Party membership in the Upper House and that for the Lower House is readily apparent from these figures. This difference reflects the nature of the Japanese electoral system before the recent introduction of proportional representation in the Councillors national district contests. Specifically, the larger size of districts in House of Councillors contests encouraged candidacies by group officials. Large groups provided the only kind of organizational base in national constituencies and in large prefectural districts that transcended regions.

committees concerned with group problems.[12] However, the Diet has not played a strong role in policy-making at all times and on all issues, and group representatives for this reason probably had more impact on policies as articulators of interests than as legislators. Still, membership in the Diet gave former group officials inside access to the upper level policy-making councils of their parties. Diet membership also provided direct access to the institutionalized communication channels which exist on a permanent basis between parliamentarians and their counterparts in particular government ministries. Some symbolic legitimacy or credibility for group interests may have also accrued from Diet membership, in the sense that group officials who were also Diet members could speak as government officials in a variety of settings rather than merely as group representatives. However, it must be remembered that these and other advantages of Diet membership were probably much more important to group officials who were Liberal Democratic affiliates than to former group officers attached to other parties.[13]

In addition to participation in the Diet, many Japanese interest groups and corporations have had direct political representation through their officials' membership on advisory councils (*shingikai*) which are attached to government ministries and agencies. At present there are 162 advisory councils connected with different ministries and various agencies within the Japanese government. Some ministries like International Trade and Industry or Welfare, which have many interests as "clients," have more councils (see Table 8.7 for a summary of the council system and

[12] An examination of the membership of a recent Lower House Transportation Committee showed heavy representation of association officials from transportation industry groups. Also, several advisors to taxi and bus companies could be seen on the Committee; these members probably acquired advisor positions — which are potentially significant to group and company access — after they were elected.

[13] Interestingly, comparison of earlier studies of the Diet with our own data indicates a long-term decline in the number of interest group representatives in the national parliament, which may reflect new partisan divisions among group memberships in some cases, as well as a parallel effort by different parties to appeal to group followings or to capture particular occupational sector memberships, both of which processes might result in divisions within groups with regard to party support and a reletedly diminished capability to mobilize voting blocs of sufficient size to permit success at the polls.

TABLE 8.7. *Advisory Councils to Japanese Ministries, 1979*

Ministry	Number of Councils
Prime Minister's Office	33
Justice Ministry	7
Foreign Ministry	1
Finance Ministry	14
Education Ministry	13
Welfare Ministry	21
Agriculture and Forestry Ministry	13
International Trade and Industry Ministry	20
Transportation Ministry	10
Postal Ministry	5
Labor Ministry	13
Construction Ministry	9
Home Affairs Ministry	3

Source: Gyosei Kanricho, *Shingikai Soran* (Tokyo: 1979).

the numbers of councils attached to each major government organ) than ministries like Foreign Affairs, which have fewer interest group relations. (The Prime Minister's Office has the largest number of attached councils simply because it houses many government agencies which themselves are linked with groups.) Each of the many advisory councils typically has several interest group representatives, in addition to members from the academic world, corporations, and other kinds of backgrounds, as can be seen in the case of the composition of some selected councils attached to the Ministry of International Trade and Industry (Table 8.8). There are two other important things that can be observed from the patterns of memberships on MITI councils. Business groups are well represented, therefore supporting the general point that the advisory councils provide potential access channels for private interests. Yet business representation on MITI councils accounted for only half of council composition on the average — even though in some cases like the important Industrial Structure Council, business interests were indeed more dominant.

Even though advisory councils provide some kind of access channel to the bureaucratic ministries for private groups, it is actually difficult to determine just what kind of influence members of advisory councils have, since the role of these councils

TABLE 8.8.   *Representation on Selected MITI Advisory Councils, 1979*

Council Name	Business Groups	Corporations	Professors	Other	Total
Industrial Structure	27	24	11	20	82
Industrial Technology	3	7	5	9	29
Export-Import Trade	42	22		5	69
Factory Planning	7	1	4	22	34
Aircraft and Machine Industry	27	12	6	19	64
Information Processing Industry	4	7	1	14	26
Textile Industry	17	2	1	7	27
Coal Mining	5	8	6	17	36
Small-Medium Industry Stabilization	17		3	10	30
ALL MITI Councils (37)	246	173	111	321	851

Source: Calculated from Gyosei Kanricho, *Shingikai Soran* (Tokyo: 1979).
"Other" includes representatives of labor unions, agricultural groups, research
centers, professionals, and the government.

varies with time and across issues and councils. The most publicly visible and active council has been the Rice Price Advisory
Council attached to the Ministry of Agriculture. Farm groups
have used the Council to argue vociferously in support of higher
price supports on many occasions. Still, this council was at the
center of the rice-price process at times, while at other times it
played a more peripheral political role.[14] Moreover, the functions
of different advisory councils seem to vary. Many of the councils
apparently exist mainly to legitimize positions proposed by the
ministries and agencies themselves. In contrast, some councils are
influenced by particular interest groups, such as was the case for
the repatriate league; consequently, those councils assume an important role in political debate and provide an important point
of access in the interest articulation process. And in the most minimal sense, membership on the many advisory councils attached
to the Japanese government provides some kind of symbolic access and official role for the participating groups.

[14] See Michael Donnelly, loc. cit.

CLIENTELISM AND REPRESENTATION OF INTERESTS

It is popular to view interest groups as acting in a one-way direction to pressure parties and government officials, but the actual quality of relationships between groups and the officials they seek to influence is mixed. Groups and parties become interdependent through exchanges of electoral support and funds for advocacy of group causes. Likewise, interest groups and ministries or governmental agencies may become interdependent through use of advisory councils both for group access and/or for legitimization of ministry policies. Political officials, it will be remembered, also look to groups for cues as they seek to predict and understand their own political environment.

To perceive the interest group-government relationship as simply confrontational is therefore oversimplified; there are also elements of interdependence, manipulation, and cooperation at many points. Nowhere is the potential for cooperative relationships between groups and government more apparent than in the clientelistic relationships which develop between particular ministries and interest groups which fall under their jurisdiction. Each bureaucratic ministry in Japan has a responsibility for supervision of some broad economic sector or area of activity. For example, the Ministry of Agriculture, Forestry, and Fisheries is concerned with problems in the farm sector and the forestry and fisheries industries; the Ministry of International Trade and Industry is responsible for both large and small scale manufacturing; and the Finance Ministry supervises the banking, insurance, and securities industries. Each of these ministries, as well as most of Japan's other bureaucratic organs, regulates behavior in its area of jurisdiction. Each ministry also typically promotes governmental assistance programs designed to help economic units, groups, and citizens within its area of responsibility. In the process of regulating and serving particular economic, occupational, or welfare sectors, the ministries on many occasions take positions which are similar to those of the interest groups operating in their areas of responsibility. The policies of the ministries and the interests of the relevant organized groups thus coincide to a considerable degree, since both at times seek to ameliorate conditions within a particular social or economic sector. For example, farm groups and sections within the Ministry of Agriculture,

Forestry, and Fisheries both want land development and other programs which enhance agricultural productivity, while auto-makers and the Ministry of International Trade and Industry both want a healthy domestic auto industry, even though some auto makers are still fairly independent in their attitudes on issues like ministerial control over company organization and plans.

In addition to congruities of interest, close working relationships between groups and relevant ministries can often help cement clientelistic relationships. For example, it is often said that the administration of farm programs by the agricultural cooperatives brings them in sustained contact with officials of the Agriculture, Forestry, and Fisheries Ministry. In Japan, inevitable tendencies toward ministerial clientelism induced by common interests and close ties are further enhanced by exchange of leading personnel between the ministries and the groups they supervise. Japanese civil servants retire early, as was noted in Chapter 7. Many retired bureaucrats go to work in interest groups and corporations, thus becoming human bridges between organized interests and their former employers. In the process, those ex-officials bring with them considerable knowledge of bureaucratic politics and close personal ties with former bureaucratic colleagues.[15]

Clientelism appears to be a real force in Japanese interest politics; however, not all political relationships under the clientelist umbrella are necessarily congenial. Manifestations of ministerial paternalism are clearly visible on a regular basis, such as the Ministry of Agriculture, Forestry, and Fisheries' defense of quotas to protect Japanese farmers. At the same time, the Ministry and farmers may not agree on rice price supports in a given year.

---

[15] According to Japanese newspapers, some interest groups also even hire Tokyo University graduates so that "old boy" ties can be used to develop close working relationships with former schoolmates in the civil service. Actually personal ties are an important part of Japanese interest politics at many points. An intriguing example of this fact is the presence of groups of friends and advisors of particular politicians whose existence becomes highlighted when the person in question becomes prime minister. The late premier Ohira, for example, was linked with at least nine such informal groups with whom he met on a regular basis according to Japanese media accounts. *See Zaikai*, various issues, fall 1979. Nevertheless, we are persuaded by recent analysis of such private ties to downplay them somewhat as a major category of business-government interaction.

Comparable examples of both congruities and differences of opinion between interests and ministries within an overall clientelistic relationship can be seen in industry, education, and medicine. Accordingly, clientelism can be inoperative and irrelevant in some specific policy debates, just as it is a viable political force in others.[10]

PETITIONS AND PUBLIC ACTIVITIES

A variety of situations, including interest group representation in national legislative and administrative bodies and clientelistic relationships and exchanges of leading personnel, provide private interests with potential routes of access to policy-making centers in Japanese politics. The substance of group interests is communicated through these channels by private discussions and statements in the chambers of government. Interests are also articulated in Japan through more public modes of communication, including public statements, petitions, rallies, and demonstrations.

The use of petitions (*chinjo*) is probably the most common public form of interest group communications with political actors in Japan. Petitions are also the most traditional form of articulation, having originated in imperial China before being imported to Japan. Thousands of petitions are submitted each year to government officials ranging from requests for minute adjustments in ministerial regulation of gasoline station operations, to expressions of broad ideological views on Japan's foreign policies. In some years the number of petitions may be even substantially greater; for example, in 1962 alone members of the National Farm Cooperatives Federation sent an estimated 4 million postcards and petitions to government offices and members of the Diet! The targets of petitions to national government range from the prime minister and cabinet members to specific units of particular ministries and rank-and-file members of the Diet.

Most large interests groups express their demands in statements

[16] Relations between MITI and the computer industry are a case in point. The government traditionally has had close ties with the leading electronic firms and at times has promoted development of the domestic industry by protectionist barriers and other supportive policies. Still, manufacturers of computers have opposed some of MITI's policies even while accepting the ministry's tutelege in other areas. *See* Ira Magaziner and Thomas S. Hout, *Japan's Industrial Policy* (London: Policy Studies Institute, 1980), pp. 82–87 as well as Eugene Kaplan, op. cit., pp. 77–102.

in the media, in annual policy papers and resolutions, and in organizational publications, in addition to submitting vollies of petitions to government officials and parliamentarians. The Federation of Economic Organizations, for example, contributes a steady stream of observations on appropriate remedies for Japan's general economic problems similar in content and scope to the government's own voluminous economic plans and broad policy statements. The positions of the Federation of Economic Organizations are expressed in organization press interviews as well as in a wide array of Federation publications made available to politicians and officials, the media, and the general public. Some other interest groups have less visibility, but all major groups make frequent statements to the media or publish materials which communicate their demands to whatever audience can be reached.

Many Japanese interests groups also utilize public rallies and marches to underscore their claims for political consideration. Labor unions and student groups, some of which have held strong views on economic and foreign policy and university autonomy, have been noted for the frequency and occasionally the violence of their demonstration activities vis-à-vis both national and local authorities. The struggle over ratification of the United States-Japan Security Treaty in May and June of 1960 was the largest public demonstration in postwar Japanese history; according to some estimates, at least 300 thousand persons demonstrated in front of the Diet building on various days over a three-week period. The participants were union members and students, as well as persons from some other groupings and backgrounds. Unions also frequently mix economic and political goals in their annual spring general strikes (known as *shunto*) or in demonstrations on other occasions. Students have a long tradition of political demonstration participation in Japan and were especially active during the 1960s but less visible in the 1970s.

Many other interests participate in demonstrations and rallies, as is witnessed by the frequent ritual in Tokyo's governmental district of long lines of flag and poster-bearing demonstrators. Many farm groups and other interests assumed to be fairly tame in their political styles demonstrate on a regular basis, and public demonstrations appear to be as much a legitimate mode of interest articulation in Japan as they are a last resort of frustrated radical groups and movements of the left or right. Among the groups cited in various case studies of Japanese policy-making as engaging in demonstrations, national conventions, and rallies designed to attract public attention are farmers, former landowners, and repatriates. The farm groups are by far the most unruly through, among other things, occasionally conducting sustained sit-ins outside the Liberal Democratic Party headquarters during particularly tense rice-price negotiations.[17]

INTEREST AGGREGATION IN JAPAN

Japan has a multitude of interest groups which have approached government through different channels with a large number and variety of requests for help. Local communities have traditionally turned to prefectural and national governments for financal aid, and typically sent delegations to their Diet member or the national ministries to ask for help when funds were needed for a new school or some other local public works project. Pollution and antidevelopment groups mobilized their resources at the local level, and asked for regulation of the behavior of polluters or for abandonment of regional industrial expansion plans. Mass groups have approached the political parties in the Diet, whose rank-and-file members then became carriers of interest demands to the parties' decision-making bodies; in addition, such groups have approached party or bureaucratic elites directly to request resolution of their problems. Meanwhile, business groups have regularly submitted lists of policy recommendations to party and government organs, while corporation presidents have mentioned their needs to governmental colleagues in informal "discussion group" meetings in Tokyo's prestigious hotels and restaurants. Other interest group representatives have presented claims directly in Diet committees or in government advisory councils.

The interests articulated by local and national groups or individuals are handled by the political system in different ways. Demands from different interest sectors may be combined into pro-

---

[17] Strikes and general strikes have not been used as political interest weapons in Japan as much as in some European countries, even though political goals are often articulated during strike actions, especially by public workers. For references to demonstrations and rallies by farm groups, repatriates, and former landowners see the case studies on these groups by Donnelly, Campbell and Fukui cited elsewhere in this chapter.

gram packages. Alternatively, the requests of some groups may be denied, while others are favored. Action on a request may be deferred or even passed on to another decision center. The term interest aggregation refers to the process which results in either a combination of demands or in decisions to accommodate, reject, or defer some demands. Interest aggregation is believed to take place primarily during early stages in policy processes, as specific interests are combined into alternatives to be considered by final decision makers, i.e., leading government ministries or the National Diet.

There are many decision points where interests are aggregated in Japan's political system. Requests for local financial support are usually dealt with by prefectural governments or in sections within particular ministries, or even by means of agreements involving several ministries, such as between the Construction and Education ministries when school construction projects are the concern. The amount of support that is allocated will then be added to the project list submitted with a particular ministry's annual budget request. This is an example of fairly "low level" aggregation. In other instances, aggregation decisions may be made at higher levels of the bureaucracy and government. For example, the positions of national business groups on tax policy matters may be discussed in advisory councils, at the ministerial level, or in cabinet meetings where decisions on tax and fiscal policy are considered from the point of view of their macroeconomic consequences. Other interests may be processed at other points within the political system. Thus, the demands of mass groups for pension increases or farm price supports may be considered at a variety of decision points, such as in advisory councils or within the policy councils of the Liberal Democratic Party. In each of these cases, aggregative decisions are often made as the proposals of groups are weighed against other alternatives on the basis of their objective or political merits.

Three variables are critical in determining where aggregation of interest group demands occurs. The jurisdictional competence of particular ministerial and governmental bodies is often the main determinant of where a particular interest group demand is handled. MITI's functional bureaus, for example, deal specifically with the problems of particular industrial sectors, and demands from interests in these sectors typically go through the first stage of processing in the appropriate MITI bureau. A second factor affecting where aggregating decisions are made is the scope of the demand. Some demands require either a minor expenditure of governmental resources or a trivial concession in the application of some law or ministerial regulation. Other requests require either the passage of a new major law or the expenditures of large sums of money for important projects. As the scope of demands increases, decisions can no longer be made at lower or intermediate levels of governmental ministries, and then the higher level decision makers and institutions become involved.

The kind of political resources mobilized in support of a particular demand is also a factor affecting where aggregating decisions are made. Demands from small, local groups can be considered by one or another element of the bureaucracy, or they may even be dealt with initially by a representative in the Diet or some local governing body. Large groups tend to mobilize broad support in the Diet and within political parties, and well financed groups tend to have contacts with or influence the opinions of senior politicians and government officials. When major political resources are mobilized, intermediate level aggregation is difficult, and unaggregated demands move to final decision points for consideration by top political elites like the prime minister and his cabinet.[18]

In summary, when the political resources allocated in support of a demand are small, when the scope of the demand is narrow, and when a single governmental section can handle the demand, aggregation occurs at an "early" stage in the decision process. On the other hand, when important political resources are involved, when the demand itself is broad in scope, or when the demand exceeds the scope of competence of a lower level governmental unit, aggregation at the early stages of decision processes is difficult, so that decisions are often postponed to later and "higher" stages of policy-making. The three factors affecting aggregation timing and location often seem to co-vary and mutually reinforce

[18] Rice price subsidy processes provide good examples of deferral of aggregation until later stages of decision making, in that failure to aggregate demands within the Liberal Democratic Party often led to party-government confrontations on the rice price issue and negotiated settlements between the two sides which involved Japan's top political leadership.

each other in "pushing" demands toward earlier or later consideration in the decision process.

These general tendencies having been noted, it is important to realize that one of the distinctive features of Japanese politics is the apparent frequent inability of the ruling Liberal Democratic Party to aggregate effectively interest demands within normal party channels. John Campbell, in an analysis of Japanese budget politics, has noted that often the ruling party submits unaggregated lists of budget demands to the Ministry of Finance and central executive elite.[19] It would appear from this evidence that the party's internal decision-making bodies are unable to make effective aggregating decisions on budget issues in situations where there is substantial pressure either from the rank-and-file members of the parliamentary party on behalf of different interests or from the various party subcommittees which are often de facto captives of particular interests. This same tendency is shown in other policy arenas. Groups like the repatriates and former landowners, for example, were successful in having special committees established within the Liberal Democratic Party's policy-making organs which favored their positions, and these groups in turn "lobbied" the party's leaders on behalf of the groups' interests. At times the same process was repeated through the capture of Liberal Democratic policy subcommittees on farm policy by agricultural interests. In cases of this kind, the party's internal organs and leadership became a transmission belt for the articulation of interests, rather than vehicles for interest aggregation. Whether this state of affairs is typical of political parties elsewhere is not known, yet it seems clearly to reflect frequent patterns in Japanese politics. Indeed, it is tempting to consider the Liberal Democratic Party's limitations with regard to interest aggregation as reflection of the parochial tendencies of Japanese political culture, in the sense that there may be a tendency for political bases to be built through separate contacts with multiple groups whose interests are mutually exclusive and which at times are articulated with such irresistible pressures that intraparty mediation of interests is impossible. It may be, however, that this is the nature of the links

[19] John Creighton Campbell, *Contemporary Japanese Budget Politics* (Berkeley and Los Angeles: University of California Press, 1979), pp. 128–132.

between catchall parties and private groups in other societies as well.[20]

INTERESTS IN JAPAN: CORPORATISM OR PLURALISM

There are many examples of interest group successes in Japan. Pensioners' groups have received aid in the form of specific legislation or administrative increases in their allotments, farmers have received price supports and protection from foreign competition, and business interests have successfully resisted MITI pressures. There are also many examples of only qualified success or even of failure. Groups don't always get what they want, or they may be unsuccessful for many years before getting any kind of assistance.

Specific group successes or failures can be identified; however, there is no easy way to gather comprehensive evidence on the general outcomes of Japanese interest politics. Still, there is a strong impression made of the general "style" of interest politics in Japan, and through this a relative sense of strength and vitality of interests in that country. On one hand, several specialists have argued that Japan's interest politics are corporatist in nature. Proponents of the corporatist theory of Japanese interest politics argue that close relationships between Japan's ministries, Liberal Democratic Party leaders, and business and agricultural interests have inhibited competition and assertive definition of interests by specifically labor unions which are denied the access granted to other groups. In effect, only interests having close ties with the bureaucracy and ruling party are seen as being successful. The corporatist "school" also sees strong controls being imposed on interests by Japan's economic ministries in both the prewar and postwar eras, and postulates that a state of dependence exists between interest groups and the ministries which regulate them or provide them with subsidies and help. In summary, corporatism implies intimacy and interdependence with, and vulnerability to,

---

[20] There is a certain parochial nature to the internal organization of the party as well, and as Campbell and others have recognized, it is hard for top-level party organs to ignore the positions of the particular policy committees and subcommittees within the party or other groups, in addition to the presence of pressures from interests which are well represented in the party.

governmental control, as well as favored access to certain groups.[21]

In contrast, students of Japanese politics whose works support a pluralist interpretation describe the proliferation of interest groups in Japan and frequent sharp differences of opinion between interests and government, which serves as evidence for the existence of an open, assertive, and vital interest process. The dramatic struggles over farm prices can be argued to indicate a degree of independence more characteristic of pluralism than corporatism, as does the resistance by automobile, steel, and computer corporations to MITI pressures to cooperate in mergers or other kinds of action desired by bureaucratic officials.[22]

The response to this controversy is that the information presented in this chapter indicates that Japanese politics includes elements of both corporatism and pluralism. A kind of "structural corporatism" can be seen in the close ties existing between some private interests and the bureaucracy through participation in advisory councils, hiring of former bureaucrats, and other kinds of clientelistic relationships and informal links. These close relationships can be assumed to indicate favored access in many cases. Likewise, the degree to which ministries have appeared to influence industry decisions about technological innovations, investments, production, and pricing has, in some instances, been striking evidence of vulnerability to government influence, which is another indicator of a corporatist kind of relationship.

Yet the evidence on many political processes and from different

---

[21] For a study that emphasizes the corporatist nature of Japanese interest group politics, see T. J. Pempel and Keiichi Tsunekawa, "Corporatism without Labor? The Japanese Anomaly," in Philippe C. Schmitter and Gerhard Lehmbruch, eds., *Trends Toward Corporatist Intermediation* (Beverly Hills: Sage Publications, 1979), pp. 231–270. Actually, the Pempel and Tsunekawa argument is much more detailed and complex than our necessary over-simplification would indicate. Furthermore, definitions of corporatism range from those that emphasize authoritarian relationships between government and economic groups to those that place more stress on simply the presence of group participation in government councils or other examples of institutionalization of government-group relationships. See other chapters in Schmitter and Lehmbruch, op cit., and earlier works by Schmitter cited therein for discussion of the development of the corporatist school.

Works by Chalmers Johnson cited in Chapter 9 also give example of close government and group ties that approximate some definitions of corporatism.

[22] Pluralist analyses of Japanese politics include Haruhiro Fukui, "Economic Planning in Postwar Japan: A Case Study of Policy Making," *Asian Survey* (1972), pp. 327–348, and Magazines and Hout, op. cit.

time periods is actually contradictory, and there is considerable support for characterization of a large part of contemporary Japanese interest group politics as pluralistic. Japan was a relatively more controlled economy for the first decade or so after the end of World War II, and corporatist relationships were more evident in this period between business and government. More recently business-government relationships have been more open and complex. Moreover, the very openness and assertiveness of position-taking, both that between different interests groups and that by groups which are aligned against the government, in broad sectors of Japanese politics throughout the postwar era are themselves a strong argument for acceptance of the pluralist view of interest group relationships with government in Japan. On any given major issue in Japanese politics, several important groups typically argue among themselves for different solutions. In addition to intergroup competition, government policies in many areas are opposed by private groups, even those in the business sector; for

TABLE 8.9   *Recent Patterns of Interest Group and Interest Group-Government Competition in Japan*

Issue	Favor/Accept	Oppose
Protection of Japanese Farm Products*	NACCA	FEO
General Consumption Tax Proposal*	FEO	NCC, GJSPA, CED, GCTU
More Regulation of Polluters	GJSPA, GCTU	
Special Tax Consideration for Doctors	JMA	CED
Increase in Corporation Taxes	GCTU	CED, FEO
National Railways Fare Increases*		NCC, CED

Source: Interest group publications and newspaper accounts.
Abbreviations are as follows:

NACCA = National Agricultural Cooperatives Central Association
FEO = Federation of Economic Organizations
NCC = National Consumers' Convention
CED = Committee on Economic Development (Keizai Doyukai)
GJSPA = Great Japan Sea Products Association
JMA = Japan Medical Association

* Indicates a position favored by the government or some section of the government.

example, macro-economic policies and fiscal initiatives are almost universally commented upon or even opposed by interest groups such as the Federation of Economic Organizations or other leading business organizations. Business and farmers' groups and other interest organizations also address foreign policy issues at many points and often oppose government actions. Also, Japan's labor unions frequently take strong and highly visible positions on a variety of political issues. Table 8.9 demonstrates this point with some examples of recent interest-group position-taking and opposition to government proposals on a few major issues. Among other things, it will be noted that different interests are allied with each other in varying ways on different issues, which is a sign of an open, pluralistic political system. Comparable evidence could be shown from hundreds of earlier issue conflicts.

The scale of open claim activity persuades us that there is ample pluralism in Japanese politics, at least at the verbal level. On balance, evidence of the articulation of interests would indicate that there have been elements in Japanese politics of both widespread pluralism and of corporatism, particularly in the area of structural ties, depending on the time and the specific policy arena and issue. However, a complete evaluation of this central and important feature of Japanese political life requires evidence on policy-making process and outcomes in Japan's political system, which follows in the next chapter.

CHAPTER 9

Policy-Making
in Japan

POLICY-MAKING IS the most basic and pervasive activity of governments. Policy-making involves rule-making in the Almond functional approach in its broadest sense, as well as related functions
such as goal setting. Public policies themselves take the form of
official positions on issues, collective decisions, laws and governmental regulations. Public policies resolve domestic conflicts, set
collective goals, and provide for internal order and regulation of
many activities which affect the welfare of the general public.
Public policies are also made which provide for or seek to provide
for external security and orderly relationships between nations.

Public policy-making is intimately related to other political
functions. The personnel who play a dominant role in policy-
making are recruited by the structures and through the processes
identified in Chapter 8. Interest articulation and aggregation functions similarly contribute to policy-making as they feed inputs of
various kinds into the public policy-making process through a
variety of channels.

Public policy-making also directly involves most of the structures of government and the political system above and beyond
their performance of other kinds of functions. As we shall see, political parties, in addition to recruiting political personnel, articu-
ting interests, and in some cases aggregating interests, play an
tive and direct role in policy formulation. Interest groups are

Bradley M. Richardson

also frequently directly involved in policy-making. Actually, the line between the more or less continuous functions of interest articulation and aggregation and public policy-making is not always clear.

PUBLIC POLICY-MAKING IN JAPAN: THE CORE QUESTIONS

Since policy-making is the central activity of political systems, identifying how governments make policy decisions is of basic importance in the study of any country's political life. Indeed, the central question of "Who Governs?" has dominated political inquiry for many centuries. In answering this question, we have essentially two kinds of models of politics to guide our analysis. One is an institutional model, which stresses the importance of the formal institutions and processes of government. A second approach is more "informal" in its concerns, in that the importance of noninstitutional sources of power and influence and informal political structures is emphasized. Both models are important.

The institutions of government are important structures in Japanese policy-making processes. In Japan this includes at the national executive level the prime minister and his cabinet, which we will call the *central executive elite*. The constitution charges this central executive elite with important public policy-initiation functions within the Japanese government system. In other words, the constitution expects the political executive to lead in policy-making.[1]

The postwar Japanese Constitution of 1946 also provides that a legislative body play a major role in public policy-making in Japan. The constitution thus empowers the two houses of the National Diet — the House of Representatives and the House of Councillors — with the function of making laws. According to the basic constitutional document, which was based on western political traditions, the Diet is the repository of the people's will. As such, this institutional structure is supposed to have the last word in all policy decisions which result in passage of laws.

---

[1] According to the Constitution, the central executive elite is given extensive leadership powers. It is empowered to submit bills, report to the Diet on national affairs and foreign relations, exercise control and supervision over administrative branches, manage foreign relations, conclude treaties, administer the civil service, prepare the budget, enact cabinet orders, and declare general amnesty.

The national administrative bureaucracy, including the twelve line ministries and the many agencies and commissions affiliated with the Prime Minister's Office is, like administrative "branches" in other democratic systems, mainly supposed to implement public policy. Reflecting this philosophy, the bureaucracy has no assigned role in the Japanese Constitution.

The provisions of the Japanese Constitution and related laws affecting the operation of the Japanese Diet and other central institutions suggest a kind of model of the policy-making process.[2] In this model, members of the Diet and the cabinet as a collective body are both empowered to initiate legislation, as we have seen. Furthermore, the Diet is expected to debate, amend, and *pass* bills which are proposed to it by the cabinet or suggested by members within the parliamentary body itself. The legislation produced by this familiar textbook model of government in turn empowers the bureaucratic ministries to carry out the dictates of the law.

The formal institutional, or textbook model, of policy-making is important in Japan, as the major political institutions do channel policy processes, and as the formal rules of the constitution and supplementary legislation are carefully adhered to. But, for many reasons, some of which Japan shares with other modern governments and some of which are idiosyncratic, the policy-making reality also departs substantially from the general model implied in the formal documents. Initiation of legislative proposals is diffused throughout the administrative bureaucracy, in that ministries supply many of the ideas which lead to legislative proposals passed by the Diet. Moreover, political parties, which are not discussed in Japan's basic institutional documents, also play important roles in political processes, either directly by participating in decisions about public policies or indirectly by providing the bases of power and competition which play an enormous role in the political life of any country.

There is nothing unusual about the interjection of bureaucratic initiative into the policy process. Nor is it surprising that political power is shaped and molded by political parties, as party leaders

---

2 The role of legislation or other rules implementing the Constitution is often understated in political science analysis. In Japan the *Rules of the House of Representatives* and the *Rules of the House of Councillors* are extremely important bodies of legislation which perform the function of guiding the day-to-day processes within the national Diet.

and intraparty groups struggle for influence within their own parties, or by extension of those efforts they seek to influence the directions taken by the total political system. The presence of these important political forces calls our attention to the less formal side of politics, in effect the arenas of power that are shaped by the ongoing forces of political competition. Consequently, any balanced analysis of policy-making should reflect both the institutional and noninstitutional factors which influence how public decisions are formed.

In the search for the effects of the less formal forces of politics on public policy processes in Japan, various models of informal politics can serve as reference points. Are Japanese policy decisions dominated by a single, inner circle of powerful persons who hold high positions in government, the major political parties and interest groups, according to the elitist interpretation? Or are Japanese public policies the product of open, competitive bargaining between multiple centers of power, according to the pluralist interpretation? Or are Japanese policy processes more like the corporatist model introduced in the last chapter, in which various interest groups are believed to be closely linked to the centers of power, yet with policy-making being somewhat more decentralized than elitists would argue?

The alternative models of politics — the institutional approach and the various interpretations of informal power relationships and behavior — can be brought down to earth by examining the roles played by different political structures in Japanese policy-making. By examining the role played by the central executive elite of the Japanese government and the Japanese parliament it can be seen how formal institutions and their incumbents influence policy-making. From these concerns one can turn to look at how political actors outside the formal institutions, such as political parties, contribute to policy-making processes, emphasizing the way in which parties operate within the framework of Japan's party system. Then one can also observe the contribution of the Japanese bureaucracy which, while a part of the government institutional framework, still derives influence from informal traditions.

As the roles of different structures and actors are observed and then analyzed to form some basic policy-making *patterns*, it wi be seen that no simple model of politics fits Japanese reality. Both institutions and informal sources of power are important, and the real political world mixes elements of corporatism and pluralism.

POLITICAL CULTURE AND POLICY-MAKING:
CONSENSUS AS A FACTOR IN JAPANESE POLITICS

Constitutions and empowering legislation are public, formal devices which allocate authority and provide for the procedures which governmental policy-making should follow. The pursuit of power and ideology conflicts, moreover, contribute much of the substance of policy-making. A nation's political culture — including the values and attitudes which indicate how political actors should behave — also is believed by many scholars to affect policy-making in important ways.[3] There are, it is argued, in any particular political system many informal expectations and ideas about what is fair and how things should be done which affect the process of public policy-making by influencing the behavior of persons in government, political parties, and interest groups. Often these political cultures are admixtures of traditional values concerning appropriate social behavior, and both traditional and modern ideas about proper modes of governance.

One of the dominant norms of Japan's political culture, which is believed to influence strongly how policies are made, is the concept of consensus, or harmony. In a variety of settings ranging from the nuclear family to multinational corporations, Japanese people try to patch up differences and avoid open conflict more than many other peoples. Where actual surface agreement is reached, consensus can be said to exist in substantive terms; however, a procedural side of consensus also exists. In this case the Japanese have developed many rituals which tend to smooth ruffled feelings and promote a sense of participation in decisions even in circumstances where people in reality differ greatly.

The norm of consensus in Japan has historical origins. Traditional Japanese village life abounds with examples of decisions in which careful adjustment or management of opposing opinions results in at least a surface appearance of harmony. Imported Con-

3 Political culture is discussed extensively in Chapters 5 and 6.

fucian ideas about the importance of social harmony also encouraged consensus as a goal in Japanese social groups, and many aspects of Japanese behavior still reflect Confucian precepts in some residual way. Thus, both the model for behavior inherited from traditional rural society and a cultural norm which is still relevant to some degree in Japan encourage the maintenance of consensus as a decision-making rule.

Despite its importance in Japanese life, consensus is probably more a property of small group processes where interaction is frequent and interests are fairly homogenous than a norm which regulates behavior in less intimate and homogeneous settings. Since national politics often involves large organizations and heterogeneous interests, as well as small groups, the relevance of the cultural norm of consensus to the behavior of national political actors is somewhat problematical, even in the face of widespread assumptions about its importance in Japanese political life. Actually, the norm of consensus appears to be operative in policy-making in a fairly qualified way. Among other possibilities, consensus appears to have at least the following five meanings in the context of actual political policy-making processes:

(a) The call to form a consensus is frequently used as a culturally legitimate political tactic by leaders who seek to attract opponents of their policy goals into joining an affirming coalition — this type of behavior can be seen frequently in the appeals for unity.

(b) An outraged claim that consensual norms have been violated by an arrogant majority is a form of protest used by frustrated minorities and is similar to calling "foul" where rules of good sportsmanship are supposed to prevail. In a sense, this was probably the origin of frequent breakdowns of parliamentary processes in some periods when the Liberal Democrats were accused of being autocratic in their dealings with the opposition.

(c) Consensus is a ritualized process or procedure in which as many as possible of the individuals and groups interested in a policy outcome are at least informally consulted. Actually, a great deal of effort is often spent to make each relevant participant in Japanese decision-making situations somewhat satisfied. The satisfaction may be purely symbolic, in the sense that a person or group is merely recognized as having a legitimate view, even if is one which is ultimately not accepted. Or the satisfaction may be substantive in varying degrees, in that some portion of a particular political actor's positions may be accepted. The main purpose of consensus as a procedure is to give the participant a feeling of being involved in the final decision, so that whatever the outcome of a policy process, the decision can be called a "consensus" in some way, and therefore be seen as legitimate. An example of the operation of consensus as a procedure is the extensive informal consultation between ministry officials, Liberal Democratic Party policy groups, members of parliament from relevant committees, and persons representing relevant private interests, that occurs when particular policies and bills are being formulated within the bureaucratic ministries. This kind of policy-making process, which involves extensive behind-the-scenes negotiations, is not completely atypical of policy-making in other political systems. Still, the Japanese case is different in regard to the degree of emphasis placed on consensual procedures.

(d) Consensus may be one of the considerations that lead Japanese bureaucrats to form small policy working-groups, which bring together on a fairly intimate basis individuals from a variety of interested administrative units.[4]

(e) Consensual norms may be the underlying principle which often led the ruling Liberal Democrats to withhold bills particularly objectionable to the opposition or to withdraw or postpone deliberations on similarly problematic legislation in order to appease opposition parties and pave the way for passage of important bills on the conservative agenda, a process discussed in detail later in this chapter. Alternatively, this widespread practice in Japanese politics may have been simply a pragmatic response to the intensely conflicted parliamentary politics of the 1950s and 1960s. Still, pragmatism of this kind may have been reinforced by a desire to avoid too much open conflict in Japan's parlia-

---

4 Small working groups are seen within ministries when task forces are set up to coordinate policy-making across various divisions and within the Cabinet itself, when special groups are called together to coordinate policy-making in such areas as the economy. While a need for coordination across administrative boundaries and accommodation of political interests in different organizational entities usually motivates formation of these working groups, is also possible that Japanese turn to small, face-to-face groups to resolve problems more often than people from some other cultures.

mentary processes, resulting in consensual norms and pragmatism being intermingled as motivations for particular patterns of ruling-party behavior.

Having denoted these possible manifestations of consensual norms and processes in Japanese politics, it is essential to appreciate that all of Japanese political life is not devoid of open conflict. Open confrontations between political parties and factions is frequently intense and matches the reputed ferocity of competition among individuals in Japanese society and companies in the Japanese market. Japan, then, is a society like most others, in that there are actually contradictory tendencies within both general and political cultures. Consensus can be an important fact in Japanese politics, and particularly within relatively smaller and relatively more homogeneous settings; elsewhere, in larger, more heterogeneous environments, it becomes less relevant, or has only limited applications.

One final note on the implications of consensual decisions in Japan should be made. Many observers of Japanese society are aware that conflictual opinions, while consistently understated in many small group situations, actually are communicated in various ways. In other words, differences are acknowledged and expressed in more subtle ways in the face of the imperative in many situations of attempting to preserve surface harmony. Just how important these subtleties are in the sometimes bloody combats of political life remains to be seen. But it seems likely that consensus as a goal governing all behavior is sometimes overemphasized or misunderstood in interpretations of Japanese society and politics, where in reality, effective methods for expression of differences within the context of superficially harmonious relationships actually exists.

THE CENTRAL EXECUTIVE ELITE:
POWERS, VULNERABILITY, AND POLICY ROLE

Like the chief executive of any industrialized nation, Japan's prime minister in theory has substantial political powers. He is entitled by the constitution to appoint the members of his cabinet, limited only by a clause requiring that a majority of cabinet members must be selected from the national parliament. The prime minister and his cabinet are also empowered to propose legislative bills, i.e., to give impetus and take initiative in the poli making process. The prime minister with his cabinet is also empowered to run the enormous administrative branch of two million persons in its task of implementing legislation. Like the American president, the Japanese prime minister functions as chief executive or head of government; but different from the American president, he is, according to the constitution, responsible to the national Diet. Thus as noted in Chapter 3, the prime minister of Japan can be removed from office by the Diet, if his political support in that body wanes. This is a fundamental institutional fact of life that makes the chief executive of Japan sensitive to the need to maintain a viable base of political support at all times.

Since for over two decades the prime minister of Japan has also been the leader of a permanent majority party, or head of the predominant party in a two-party coalition, as at present, it might be anticipated that his powers and influence are particularly extensive. Yet like chief executives elsewhere, the Japanese prime minister is in fact enormously restrained in the exercise of his powers by the forces of ongoing politics. Because the prime minister is chosen mainly by a coalition of Liberal Democratic Party factions, his freedom of action is restricted by the endless play and counterplay of factional politics. Like the political game elsewhere, Japanese elite politics — and in this case Liberal Democratic factional politics — involves frequent power moves by ambitious senior politicians. Typically, these manipulations focus on the recruitment process and involve attempts to place members or leaders of particular factions in leading positions. Factional in-fighting, though, spills over into the policy-making process at times, particularly when a prime minister takes a firm public stand on an issue which is controversial. Liberal Democratic factional coalitions, involving an unremitting struggle of ambitious and powerful leaders, are potentially volatile. The vulnerability of the prime minister, and the related vulnerability of his cabinet as well, to being pushed out of office in the factional game, is sufficient to restrict considerably their freedom of choice in policy matters.

The prime minister is also limited in his freedom to initiate policy by the presence of numerous policy-oriented opinion groups (see Chapter 3) within the Liberal Democratic Party itself. A major split over China policy, in which two organized policy groups held diametrically opposed positions, clearly limited the scope of prime ministerial initiative in this important foreign policy area for many years, particularly in the 1960s.[5] The presence of "hawk" and "dove" groupings within the majority party has had similar effects on prime ministerial initiative in a number of policy areas, including decisions on defense and foreign policy-making. The existence of leagues of Liberal Democratic Diet members affiliated with institutionalized interests in agriculture and other areas also potentially restricts the range of action of the prime minister and his cabinet. The prime minister himself may be in agreement with one or another of the policy groups in his own party; yet where groups exist whose members oppose his thinking, his freedom of policy-making action is obviously restrained. Underlying this restraint on his freedom of initiative is the basic fact of his dependence on an intraparty coalition of groups for his very existence in office, augmented at present by the desirability of maintaining the coalition between the Liberal Democrats and the New Liberal Club by not offending the latter group.

Groups outside the Liberal Democratic Party also potentially limit the prime minister's range of alternatives in policy-making as well as that of the members of his cabinet. One of those groups, actually many groups in reality, is the administrative bureaucracy. While the prime minister and his ministers are nominally heads of the administrative branch, they are in many ways also the prisoners of the ministries and their officials. There have been numerous accounts of tugs-of-war in relationships between ministers and the officials in their ministries, but perceptive observers say that the norm is for ministers, whose terms are often short, to be dominated by their subordinates.[6] The prime minister and members

---

[5] The differences we mention are the traditionally pro-Taiwan orientation of the Liberal Democrats' Asian Problems Studies Group and the preference for relations with Peking of the Afro-Asian Problems Group. *See* our earlier discussion of these and other policy group differences in Chapter 3 and Haruhiro Fukui, *Party in Power: The Japanese Liberal Democrats and Policymaking* (Berkeley and Los Angeles: University of California Press, 1970), especially pp. 254–262. These and other groups are still active at times, and their positions are relevant to political elite behavior, depending on the issue at stake.

[6] This is the view of John Campbell, who notes, however, that many factors influence the degree to which a minister is able to assert his own preferences and influence the decisions of the permanent bureaucrats who in theory work for him. Among the relevant considerations are a minister's expertise in ministries' areas of business, the stature of the ministers as politicians in the Liberal Democratic Party, and even the personality and assertiveness of

of the cabinet are actually enormously dependent on the bureaucracy for information, advice, and cooperation in handling the myriads of details involved in policy-making and implementation. Little of the job of running the affairs of a major, industrialized country could be accomplished without the help of experts in the administrative branch. Consequently, cooperative relationships with leading persons and groups within the bureaucracy need to exist for effective governance to be maintained.

Other groups, including powerful interest groups and the opposition parties, also exercise important checks on the policy-making initiative of the Japanese central executive elite. On several occasions the opposition parties have effectively vetoed positions taken by the executive elite, while interest groups like the farmers have upon occasion taken such strong positions as to force a reluctant prime minister to give in to their demands. Suffice it to say that the constitutional policy-making powers of the Japanese prime minister and cabinet are severely constrained by politics both inside and outside the ruling party and by the need for cooperation from other political actors. These restraints on executive power common to all pluralistic democracies have been enhanced in some periods by the Japanese cultural norm that leadership should not be too autocratic in style. This norm appeared to be at work in the favorable press reception of Prime Minister Ikeda's "low posture" in comparison with the frequent condemnation of the less conciliatory political style of his predecessor, Nobusuke Kishi. Taken together, an impressive array of informal forces potentially limit the exercise of the constitutional power of the policy-making initiative possessed by the Japanese central executive elite.

Despite the restraints on their freedom of action, the Japanese central executive elite still plays extremely important roles in public policy-making processes. Among these roles is that of policy "broker," by which is meant a person or group that plays a pivotal role in negotiating a decision from among alternatives

---

particular appointees to ministerial positions. See John Campbell, *Contemporary Japanese Budget Politics* (Berkeley and Los Angeles: University of California Press, 1977), pp. 151–152. For an entertaining example of the shock of subordinates when a minister was especially assertive on matters of appointments of a key subordinate, see Chalmers Johnson, *MITI and the Japanese Miracle: The Growth of Industrial Policy, 1925–75* (Berkeley and Los Angeles: University of California Press, 1982), pp. 261–262.

advanced by opposing groups. Alternatives in most policy areas are proposed by a substantial number of political actors. The bureaucratic ministries are a rich source of ideas and proposals, and in some instances competing programs are proposed by different ministries. Likewise, the Liberal Democratic Party Policy Affairs Research Council (and its subcommittees) and other leading formal organs within the dominant party also submit policy proposals on many issues. Positions also may be advanced by various Liberal Democratic Party informal policy groups, interest groups (sometimes in their capacity as direct participants in advisory councils), Diet members' groups affiliated with interests, and, more significantly in recent years, the opposition parties. Some disputes over policy directions between different political actors have to be resolved informally through negotiations, a situation that occurs where important ministries disagree or where a major difference of opinion erupts between the administrative bureaucracy and the ruling Liberal Democratic Party. In both of these instances, the prescribed institutions and routines of Japanese government provide no easy method for resolution of the conflict. If, for example, the leading organs in the Liberal Democratic Party oppose solutions advanced by some of the bureaucratic ministries, as has occurred frequently in conflicts about rice price supports, the prime minister or some small group within the central executive elite typically acts as broker, or arbiter, in the negotiation process.[7] In this process, solutions are arrived at by informal behind-the-scenes discussions between at least some of the various parties involved. The role of the executive elite as a policy broker in such a process is a subtle and a complex one, which involves the exercise of great manipulative skill and extremely delicate use of the prime minister's influence, with the result that

[7] Such was the role of Prime Minister Ikeda and his cabinet in the 1961 rice price negotiations, according to Michael Donnelly in "Setting the Price of Rice: A Case Study in Political Decision Making," in T. J. Pempel, ed., *Policymaking in Contemporary Japan* (Ithaca, NY: Cornell University Press, 1977), pp. 171–172. But Donnelly reports that Ikeda's successor, Prime Minister Sato, was forced on other occasions to capitulate to Liberal Democratic and farm group demands for higher prices, while at other times Sato was able to hold the fort against pressures from these groups. In these two types of scenarios the premier was either vulnerable to pressures, or able to exercise firm leadership, and in neither situation could be seen as playing an arbiter's or broker's role.

his leadership is not open and explicit even though his authority may be considerable in such situations.

A second role of the executive elite in Japan involves ratification of decisions made elsewhere, typically within the bureaucratic ministries. The *ratifier* role is assumed under two kinds of circumstances. The executive elite ratifies decisions by other groups when decisions are not major ones and when they fall clearly within the jurisdiction of a particular ministry or agency. In this case, the ministry in question consults with the prime minister or a cabinet member about the decision; in some instances, consultation is merely a ritual. Elsewhere consultation represents an effort to ensure that the substance of the decision fits overall major policy orientations. Whatever the motive for the consultation, the executive elite role is basically one of ratifying or approving a policy decision made elsewhere with little actual involvement in the policy-making scenario. Examples of ratificatory decisions are abundant, such as when a prime minister agrees with the decisions of the Defense Agency on new weapons choices or when the cabinet approves the International Trade and Industry Ministry's policies on long-term research and development targets.[8]

Ratification by the central executive elite also occurs when major policy initiatives are taken by especially powerful ministries without direct elite involvement. There is probably no pure case of complete dominance of a particular policy-making arena by one or another ministry; still, influence is highly relative. Some ministries, particularly Finance and the International Trade and Industry, do appear at times to make independent decisions on economic policies, where by tradition, jurisdictional competence, or expertise, their influence is very great. In such situations the prime minister and his cabinet follow the policy set by the ministry in question rather than independently creating policy directions. Such has been the general relationship between the cabinet and Ministry of Finance on microeconomic

---

[8] For the Defense Agency example and use of the term "ratifier" to describe the role we have assigned to leading executive bodies, see Bradley Richardson, "Policymaking in Japan: An Organizing Perspective," in T. J. Pempel, op. cit., pp. 239–268. The comment on MITI and cabinet relationships comes from recent newspaper accounts of "R and D" planning processes.

policies like the routine allocation of budget funds to different ministries.[9]

So far the role of the central executive elite in Japan seems to be fairly passive, at least in comparison with popular political myths and constitutional theory. However, there are situations in which the prime minister does provide strong and positive executive leadership. Most of Japan's postwar prime ministers have committed themselves to a major foreign or domestic policy goal at some time. In some instances, such as Kishi's plan to amend the U.S.-Japan Security Treaty, Hatoyama's rapprochement with the Soviet Union and Sato's desire to normalize postwar relationships with South Korea and have Okinawa revert to Japanese control, the relevant commitments to a policy goal can be seen as signifying the desire of an incumbent prime minister to make an impact on history through completion of at least one major political task in the foreign policy area. In other instances, as in Ikeda's resolve to double incomes or Tanaka's proposal to remodel the Japanese archipelago, prime ministerial objectives also reflected strong commitment to a particular policy goal. Some Japanese prime ministers have also had strong views on Japan's fiscal priorities, as John Campbell documents, and as a result have intervened in budget-making decisions dominated normally by other political actors.[10]

Thus, on certain occasions, postwar Japanese prime ministers exhibited strong leadership on major policy issues. In addition, in a variety of small issues, prime ministers and cabinet ministers have taken similarly strong positions depending on both their

[9] See John Campbell, op. cit., pp. 43–70 (Chapter 3), which discusses the annual process of microbudgeting, where the Ministry of Finance has considerable say as to allocations to specific ministries, even though politics also intervenes at times to force ministry concessions to outside pressures. In this context Campbell also describes a norm of balance (*baransu* in Japanese), which means that efforts are made to equalize increases in allocations to different ministries. This norm may still be one more example of the ideal of consensus at work in national political processes in Japan.

[10] Intervention by the Liberal Democrats and the central executive elite is especially visible in macrobudgeting decisions, i.e., those decisions where national economic directions are at stake. Even here the role of particular prime ministers has varied, but especially strong and determined leaders have apparently single-handedly forced their ideas on the Finance Ministry by such tactics as Kakuei Tanaka's practice of calling middle-level ministry officials to task for particular decisions. Tanaka was called a "computerized bulldozer" as a result. See Campbell, op. cit., especially pp. 160–162.

own personal style and the political situation of the times. The policy scenarios following the major elite policy commitments in several instances actually reveal in a stark manner the character of the political forces constraining the actions of the Japanese central executive elite. In the case of issues such as Yoshida's commitment to limited rearmament, Hatoyama's normalization agreement with the Soviet Union, Kishi's revision of the U.S.-Japan Security Treaty, and Tanaka's normalization of relations with the People's Republic of China, strong opposition to the prime minister's positions came from within the Liberal Democratic Party or conservative movement itself. In some cases, the opposition from elements within the conservative camp reflected ideological difference within the party, such as the intense intraconservative divisions over China policy.[11] But in some cases, factional power struggles were also the underlying source of the strong opposition made to prime ministerial issue initiatives, such as in the intraparty struggles over the security treaty.[12] In each of the cited policy processes, the intraparty opposition was sufficiently intense as to indicate the perils facing a Japanese prime minister who considers making a strong commitment to a particular policy position. Japan is not a unique example of the inhibiting effects on central executive elite independence that come from the opposition of other political actors. However, in the Liberal Democratic Party setting of recurring factional struggle and fragile factional coalitions, the risks of assuming strong leadership roles are substantial. Indeed, much of the dynamism of Japanese elite politics as portrayed by the Japanese press stems from the almost constant internecine struggle for power within the conservative movement.

THE ADMINISTRATIVE BUREAUCRACY

According to most democratic theory, the administrative part of government is supposed to be subordinate to the legislature and the central executive elite. The latter two structures are expected to provide popular representation and responsible lead-

[11] Haruhiro Fukui documents the intraparty conflict on China policy particularly dramatically in his study of Kakuei Tanaka's moves to normalize relations with China in "Tanaka Goes to Peking: A Case Study in Foreign Policymaking," in T. J. Pempel, op. cit., pp. 60–102.

[12] See, among various sources, Robert A. Scalapino and Junnosuke Masumi, *Parties and Politics in Contemporary Japan* (Berkeley and Los Angeles: University of California Press, 1962), Chapter 5.

ership, while the administrative bureaucracy, it is argued, should mainly implement the expressed policies of the elected organs of government.

Reality, however, is quite different from theory in most contemporary industrialized democracies. The administrative branch of government is often strong and somewhat independent from legislative and central executive control. Laws which empower particular components of the administrative bureaucracy to perform specific tasks are numerous and actually have a kind of constitutional function, as they create important institutions and assign to them major functional jurisdictions. In the late 1970s, for example, Japan's well-known Ministry of International Trade and Industry (MITI) had functions assigned to it by 109 separate laws (Table 9.1). This group of laws provided the ministry broad powers, including the authority to establish certain specific sections within the ministry, oversee the health of some industries, regulate prices and market operations in some economic sectors, provide for product quality control and regulation of patent rights, and regulate conditions of employment and aspects of the environment in certain industries. MITI's authority over the economy and industrial development has declined somewhat recently relative to the early postwar eras, yet this ministry remains as a good example of the considerable power given to administrative bureaucracies by legislative acts.

In addition to the importance and scope of empowering legislation, administrative bureaucracies have permanent staffs, in contrast with the institutionalized impermanence of the political branches of government. Bureaucracies also develop highly valuable, specialized competence in particular areas of governance. The knowledge required to regulate the aviation industry (in Japan the job of the Transportation Ministry), plan multibillion dollar budgets (supervised by the Ministry of Finance), and develop high technology defense systems (the responsibility of the Defense Agency) is an example of the expertise which civil servants must develop to carry out their jobs. In contrast with many bureaucrats, members of legislatures and central executive groups have much less opportunity to develop expertise on complex aspects of the economy or technology. Both the politicians' vulnerability in elections and the perhaps inevitable gap in expertise between elected officials of government, whose jobs require them

Table 9.1. Ministry of International Trade and Industry Empowering Legislation

	Institution Building	Structural Control and Development	Market Control	Quality Control	Conditions of Employment	Environment and Consumers' Interests
General Purpose	2	6		3	1	2
Foreign Trade	2		1	3	1	
Retail Trade			3			5
Utilities and Energy		7	5			3
Mining	2	3	2			2
Chemicals and Fertilizer	1		1			
Manufacturing	1	4	3	2	1	1
Medium and Small Enterprises	2	20	1		1	1
TOTAL	10	40	16	8	4	14

Source: Compiled from The Ministry of International Trade and Industry Handbook (Tokyo: 1975). Figures are number of empowering laws in each functional and substantive area. Functional areas are as follows:

Institution Building: Laws that established ministries and other administrative or research organizations.

Structural Control and Development: Laws that call for development of a particular industry or region or provide for regulation of enterprise organizations or regulation of plant locations.

Market Control: Laws that call for regulation of transactions, prices, and market operations.

Quality Control: Laws that provide for production standards enforcement and patents regulations.

Conditions of Employment: Laws that regulate insurance and safety conditions.

Environment and Consumers' Interests: Laws that provide for environmental controls or consumers' protection. Sixteen of the laws affecting MITI's powers were difficult to classify and were omitted from this table.

345

to be generalists in at least relative terms, and bureaucrats, who are more often specialists in some policy areas, result frequently in de facto dependence of the former upon the latter for advice on complex technical issues.[13]

In Japan, the tendency toward comparatively strong bureaucratic influence common to all modern political systems is enhanced by tradition. The Japanese bureaucracy has been a strong influence in government continuously since its formal inception in the late nineteenth century. A strong administrative branch was anticipated in the Prussian-inspired constitution of 1889, wherein ministers-of-state were politically responsible to the emperor rather than to the Diet. While the Diet at times was actually quite assertive, and the principle of transcendental or upwardly responsible cabinets could not always escape the realities of party politics, modern Japan has consistently had a strong bureaucracy. The Japanese bureaucratic ministries were especially dominant in the early development of Japan's modern economy and military establishment, as they were subsequently during the era of Japan's military expansion and involvement in a major war in the late 1930s and early 1940s, with the result that they became accustomed to leadership.

Another feature of Japan's recent political tradition has influenced the position of the bureaucracy. Because Japan's leaders anticipated that the bureaucracy would play an important role in political centralization and modernization, the top levels of the administrative branch were staffed from the late nineteenth century on by an elite educated specifically for government service in Japan's leading universities. Recruitment of the top products of an elitist educational system (detailed for the postwar era in Chapter 8) in itself reinforced the influence and status of the bureaucracy during the prewar period and continues to do so today.

One way to evaluate the role of the bureaucratic ministries in Japan's contemporary policy-making process is to determine the

[13] The vulnerability of elected officials may reach a peak in the lack of familiarity of some cabinet ministers (appointed from the parliament) with their ministries and the complex tasks which the ministries are expected to fulfill. John Campbell notes amusingly that ministers rotate so often in Japan's frequent cabinet reshuffles that they may hardly have ample time to learn their way around ministry buildings. See op. cit., p. 151.

extent to which they dominate rule-making. Domination can occur in two ways, either through control over the initiation and drafting of legislative proposals by the bureaucratic ministries or through the formulation of bureaucratic rules and policies which implement laws and control economic activity and other aspects of life in Japan. It is often argued that the Japanese bureaucratic ministries do in fact dominate legislative processes through their role in drafting proposals for new laws. This argument is based on statistics, such as those shown in Table 9.2, which demonstrate that a substantial ratio of the legislation considered by Japan's parliament is originated by the cabinet rather than on the floor of the National Diet. Thus, even though the proportion of cabinet bills has declined over time, which is in itself an important trend (see below), cabinet bills have over the past three-and-a-half decades consistently accounted for somewhere between three fifths and two thirds of all the bills dealt with by the national parliament. Since cabinet bills are usually drafted somewhere in the bureaucracy and are often formulated at the initiative of the bureaucratic officials themselves, these kinds of data seem persuasive evidence supporting the bureaucratic domination thesis.

Nevertheless, assumptions about bureaucratic control based on these very simple statistics must be qualified. The fact that bureaucratic officials do draft legislative proposals certainly gives them a great deal of influence over the content of legislation, enabling them to shape legislative proposals on the basis of their

TABLE 9.2. *Cabinet Bills Compared with Parliamentary Member Bills, 1946–79*

Years	Cabinet Bills	Member Bills	Ratio of Cabinet Bills to Total
1946–55	2,204	835	72.5%
1956–69	2,574	1,218	67.9%
1970–74	624	315	64.0%
1975–79	437	329	57.0%

Source: Calculated from Naikaku Hoseikyoku unpublished documents. The figure under "Ratio" indicates the proportion of all bills accounted for by cabinet bills. Time periods were chosen on the basis of party system information.

own perceptions of complex problems and solutions. If the idea for a new law (in addition to the fact of drafting the bill) actually originated within a ministry, then the chances for bureaucratic domination are indeed great. It also seems likely that the ministries dominate legislative processes in which the objective of bills is control over some technical aspects of the economy, such as mine safety, patents, and licensing of new plants. However, where proposed bills affect ruling Liberal Democratic Party concerns, opposition party commitments, group interests, consumer problems, or important "macroeconomic" decisions, some or all stages of decision processes are more often highly politicized, with the result that the ministries have more of a relative or qualified influence over process outcomes, even though legislative bills still may in fact be drafted within ministerial bureaus.[14] In other words, where there are strong external political pressures, these influence the substance of legislation more than in the less politicized cases, even though the bureaucracy still prepares the bills which are introduced to the Diet after cabinet approval.

In contrast with the complexities inherent in the legislative process, where initiative taking can be fairly complex, the ministries' function of administrative "legislation" is a less ambiguous example of bureaucratic influence. The Japanese bureaucratic ministries actually formulate a large volume of rules as a result of their more general responsibility for policy implementation. In the modern political context, implementation implies carrying out the dictates of legislative bodies, since it is the most important function of administrative branches in any democratic political system. However, in Japan as elsewhere, the line between implementation and policy-making initiative is often invisible. The major economic ministries, for example, legislate extensively through their emission of ministerial ordinances and other kinds of rules; the cabinet collectively performs a similar legislative function, utilizing the vehicle of cabinet ordinances and rulings. An even more subtle device for enforcing ministerial policies, called "administrative guidance," is used by the bureaucratic ministries in Japan. The term administrative guidance re-

[14] It will be noticed that there is a trend of decline in the ratios of cabinet bills as a percentage of all bills. Probably this potentially important theme reflects the growing emphasis on limiting cabinet legislative proposals to bills which will not offend the increasingly powerful opposition parties.

TABLE 9.3. *Legislative vs. Ministerial Output, 1946–76*

Years	Number of Laws	Number of Ordinances	Ratio (Laws: Ordinances)
1946–55	2417	3525	1:1.5
1956–69	2371	5298	1:2.2
1970–74	649	1964	1:3.0
1975–76	168	707	1:4.2

Source: Calculated from data provided by the Naikaku Hoseikyoku. Time periods were chosen on the basis of changes in the party strengths within the National Diet and/or changes in the number of parties where these could have affected the style of parliamentary politics (see text below for relevant discussion of these matters in recent times).

fers to a wide variety of practices through which national ministries persuade or try to persuade the private sector or lower levels of government to comply with the policies by the use of the broad powers embodied in legislation which established the ministry. (Since administrative guidance involves the extension of powers granted under existing legislation and the weight of ministerial authority to persuade groups, companies, and lower levels of government to follow ministerial policies, whether it is a legitimate use of administrative powers is questioned both in Japan and abroad.) [15]

The volume of direct ministerial "legislation" is substantial. Comparison of the numbers of Diet laws with the frequencies of administrative ordinances over the postwar era shows both the importance of the latter as well as a dramatic increase in the potential legislative role of the bureaucracy in recent years (Table 9.3). It is important that these administrative laws, while not necessarily violating the spirit of related empowering Diet legislation, are themselves frequently very broad in scope and of comparable impact to the empowering laws themselves. While similar

[15] Many observers feel that this is a major and distinctive aspect of bureaucratic practices in Japan and so broad in scope as to indicate ministerial dominance of many private sector decisions and initiatives. For a particularly lucid and persuasive account reflecting this position see Chalmers Johnson, "MITI and Japanese International Economic Policy," in Robert A. Scalapino, ed., *The Foreign Policy of Modern Japan* (Berkeley and Los Angeles: University of California Press, 1977), pp. 253–255.

examples of bureaucratic legislation exist in other industrialized democracies, the relative scope of bureaucratic law-making through the ordinance power seems very great in Japan.

The broad influence of the Japanese ministries has led many observers of Japanese politics to ascribe almost mythical, monolithic power to the bureaucracy in influence over policy. Actually, the bureaucratic ministries are far from a monolithic unity, and while very powerful, their influence is circumscribed in many instances. The nature of these limitations must be understood in order to put the role of the bureaucracy in proper perspective. examples of interministerial differences of opinion on issues are numerous, and these differences are one of the forces which effectively limit the power of the bureaucracy as a collective unity. For example, the Ministry of International Trade and Industry and other ministries and political actors have been divided on major policy alternatives on numerous occasions (some of which are outlined in Table 9.4, while many other examples of interministerial differences can be found at any recent time in Japan.[16]

The interministerial differences of opinion are issue-based as well as jurisdictional, so that some interministerial conflict stems from different policy orientations in different ministries or agencies. For example, the interests of the Ministry of International Trade and Industry in some periods in promoting stronger Japanese industries through restrictions on competition between firms or promotion of mergers between companies were in most cases opposed initially by the Fair Trade Commission, whose job is to combat monopolistic concentrations of economic power.[17] Elsewhere, as in a major controversy between MITI and the Ministry of Posts and Telecommunications, the core issue was which administrative unit would supervise Japan's emerging telecommunications equipment industry.[18]

[16] Inter- and intraministerial conflict indeed seems a chronic feature of the Japanese political landscape, as accounts of army-navy and intraservice rivalries before and during World War II would indicate. See Yale C. Maxon, *Control of Japanese Foreign Policy: A Study of Civil-Military Rivalry 1930–45* (Berkeley and Los Angeles: University of California Press, 1957), pp. 21 and 98–102.

[17] The Fair Trade Commission and MITI struggles are discussed extensively in Johnson, op. cit., pp. 282 and 298 ff.

[18] See Eugene J. Kaplan, *Japan: The Government-Business Relationship* (Washington: U.S. Government Printing Office, 1972), p. 97.

TABLE 9.4. *Interministerial Cleavages Involving Japan's Ministry of International Trade and Industry and Other Administrative Units*

Disputing Actors	Issue
MITI-Bank of Japan	Proposed creation of an automobile industry in Japan
MITI-Fair Trade Commission	Company mergers and cartel policy
MITI-Finance Ministry	Use of special tax incentives for certain industries
MITI-Welfare Ministry	Pollution problems and responsibility
MITI-Postal and Telecommunications Ministry	Jurisdiction over the information industry
MITI-Transportation Ministry	Jurisdiction over oil pipe lines

Source: Japanese newspapers and magazines and policy writings cited in the text.

The differences of opinion between ministries with regard to certain issues, visible in the short run in specific policy processes, may actually reflect long-term differences of near ideological nature in many instances. For example, the Ministry of Finance which is responsible for collection of revenue and preparation of the annual national budget, is consistently very conservative with regard to expenditures of money or restrictions on revenue such as accrue from tax benefits for particular industries, whereas other ministries are more expansive in their financial proposals. Similar long-term differences in basic attitudes have existed at times within ministries as well as between ministries, as when the domestic faction of MITI placed major emphasis on domestic industrial development, which included support for protectionist foreign economic policies, while the international faction accepted liberalization of trade barriers in accordance with international practice and the logic of international trade politics.[19]

Whatever the substance and origins of interministerial and

[19] The ideological factionalization of internal MITI politics is discussed in Chalmers Johnson, op. cit., pp. 227–229, and in Johnson, *MITI and the Japanese Miracle*, pp. 280–281. For a revealing discussion of interministerial politics in the budget process, see John Campbell, op. cit., especially Chapters 2 and 3.

intraministerial conflict, these opinion differences belie the existence of a monolithic bureaucracy which runs a "Japan Incorporated." [20] A more realistic view is that the Japanese administrative bureaucracy, and especially the major economic ministries such as Finance, MITI, Transportation, and Construction, is very influential in policy-making at the same time as it is highly pluralistic internally.

THE NATIONAL DIET

The 1946 Constitution grants Japan's National Diet the power to make all final decisions on legislation in its capacity as the "highest organ" of the state. On the basis of this broad grant of authority and of supplementary legislation which outlines the functions and capabilities of the Diet, there are several roles which the Diet and its members can play in the legislative process. Diet members can initiate legislation, debate alternatives, amend bills, and pass laws. Because of the strength of the administrative bureaucracy as well as the dominant position of the Liberal Democratic Party within the Diet — which meant that in many cases bills that were submitted by the ministries and cabinet and which were also supported by the Liberal Democratic Party were passed automatically — some observers feel the Diet's main function over recent decades has been to "ratify" without amending the many legislative proposals initiated by the cabinet and the bureaucracy.[21] In reality, the roles played by the Diet and its members have been much more substantial than this version of Japanese politics has argued.

Data introduced earlier in Table 9.2 demonstrated that typically between 57 and 72 percent of the bills considered by most Diet sessions originated outside the Diet. This trend supports the idea that the bureaucracy is dominant. An even more dramatic testimony to the dominance of the bureaucracy is the fact that 80 percent of all cabinet bills in 1946–79 passed the Diet in some

[20] The term "Japan Incorporated" was initiated by Western observers of Japan's great strength as a trading power, who attributed this strength to the leadership of ministries like MITI and the close relationship they felt to exist between Japanese government and business interests.

[21] One of the proponents of this view is T. J. Pempel in his "The Bureaucratization of Policymaking in Postwar Japan," *American Journal of Political Science* 18 (1974), pp. 647–664.

form and became law in contrast with only 15 percent of member bills. In other words, most cabinet-sponsored bills drafted within the bureaucracy were successful and actually passed the national parliament, in contrast with a substantially higher failure rate for member bills. On the basis of this information alone, which is often cited in discussions of Japan's parliament, it would appear that the Diet's role is subordinate to that of other institutions.

A closer look at the activities of the Diet in the 1970s suggests some qualifications to this pessimistic view of the parliament's role in policy-making processes. For one thing, the ratio of cabinet bills submitted to the Diet has declined in recent years, while that of member bills has increased (see again Table 9.2), even though the former were still passed far more often than the latter. It is not clear whether this means that the growing strength of the opposition parties documented elsewhere in this volume has resulted in the parties' proposing more legislation relative to the cabinet's output or whether the bureaucracy and cabinet have become more timid with regard to submission of bills to the Diet which might result in controversy (thereby lowering the number of cabinet bills submitted, which would inflate the proportion of members' bills).

Member bills are also generally not quite the insignificant phenomenon they have been thought to be by some Japan specialists. Actually, there are various kinds of member bills. Just as in the American Congress, many member bills deal with important local interests or problems, such as proposals for regional development plans. Other member bills deal with very important national issues. On a number of occasions in recent years, opposition parties sponsored member bills which presented their versions of desired legislation as a way of countering objectionable government proposals. According to our analysis, at least 20 percent of all major government legislation in the 1970–74 period was matched by opposition member bills. Often this tactic resulted in government-Liberal Democratic Party accommodation to opposition stands through amendment or withdrawal of government bills.

In addition to the growing numbers of member bills in recent years, there is other important evidence contradicting the idea that the Japanese Diet is merely a "rubber-stamp" parliament. In preparing this chapter, we conducted a series of primary analyses of Diet policy-making which demonstrate that the Diet played a substantially more active role in legislative processes than has been thought by many observers of Japanese politics. The findings can be summarized as follows:

(a) The Japanese Diet has in recent years taken significant action on as many as two thirds of the major bills submitted to it by the cabinet and ministries. Confining the analysis for the moment to the years 1970–74, twenty-one bills, or 40 percent of the important bills considered by the Diet in the five year period (see Table 9.5), were actually amended in committee or in general sessions of one or the other or both houses of the Diet. So the Diet does actually amend bills much more than most accounts of Japanese politics (based on simple statistics about passage or failure, which do not include information on amendments) would suggest. Furthermore, an additional nine bills were withdrawn from Diet deliberations in this period as the result of strong opposition party pressure, a process which will be called the de facto veto later in this chapter.[22]

(b) A similar analysis of Diet processes in the subsequent period of 1975–79 showed the same patterns already indicated for 1970–74. Moreover, while an extension of the study of how bills were processed backward in time to cover the years from 1960–69 showed more examples of Liberal Democratic domination of Diet processes and fewer examples of amendments than was the case in the 1970s, still the Diet was an active participant in legislative processes on several important occasions, and many bills were withdrawn because of opposition pressure. (Specific examples from either the period of the late 1970s or that of the 1960s are not shown here for the sake of brevity, but some of them will be reported later in the discussion of the opposition parties and in the conclusion where Japanese policy-making is summarized.)

---

[22] The information on major bills is from our analysis of chapters on the national Diet in Asahi Shimbunsha, *Asahi Nenkan,* 1960 through 1979, wherein the editors of the yearbook selected issues for discussion on the basis of their general visibility in the media. We have emphasized the 1970–74 patterns here, because we felt that the early seventies was an especially interesting period of transition toward emphasis on new social issues in which all of Japan's political parties had a strong interest and a time when the shifting strengths at the polls of Japan's major parties began to affect their relative standings on Diet committees.

TABLE 9.5. *Disposition of Major Cabinet Bills in National Diet, 1970–74*

Bills Passed Without Amendment by Liberal Democratic Majority

1970	Farmland Reform Law
1970	Agricultural Cooperatives Reform Law
1970	Defense Laws (3)
1972	Okinawa Reversion Supplementary Laws (5)
1973	Defense Laws (2)
1973	Tsukuba University Establishment Law
1974	Special Tax Law Providing for Subsidies to Local Government Entities

Bills Amended in the National Diet Deliberations

1970	Anti-Pollution Basic Laws (11 separate bills)
1970	Anti-Pollution Criminal Code*
1971	Middle and Old Aged Workers Employment Law
1972	Budget
1972	Air Pollution Prevention Law
1972	National Environment Preservation Law
1973	National Railways Fare Increase Law
1974	Petroleum Supply Laws (2)
1974	National Life "Stabilization" Law
1974	School Principal Position Law

Exercise of "DeFacto Veto" by Opposition

1971	Health Insurance Fee Increase Law
1971	Immigration-Emigration Control Law
1971	National Government Administrative Reform Law
1971	Yasukuni Shrine Law
1972	National Railways Fare Increase Law
1972	National Health Insurance Fee Increase Law
1974	Yasukuni Shrine Law
1974	Alcohol and Tobacco Price Increase Law
1974	Postal Rate Increase Law

Source: Asahi Nenkan (Tokyo: 1971 through 1975). The term "de facto veto" means that bills were withdrawn after strong opposition pressures. Figures in parentheses are numbers of law proposals in legislative packages.
* Amended by extraparliamentary pressure from business interests.

(c) Information provided by the Naikaku Hoseikyoku (Cabinet Legislative Bureau), an organ of the Japanese government, indicated that on the average, only 56 percent of all cabinet bills submitted to the Diet between 1960 and 1980 passed without being amended, postponed, or shelved. Importantly, the figure for passage of cabinet bills declined from 58 percent in the 1960s to 53 percent in the 1970s, thus confirming the importance of shifts in issues and the relative strengths of different parties in the parliament in the most recent decade of Japanese politics. As can be seen from these data on cabinet bills in general, which look beyond the mere fact of "passage" or "failure," the image of the Diet as something more than a passive body, indicated by detailed analysis of major bills, is once more confirmed.[23]

The evidence suggest that the Diet as a collectivity is a more active body in Japanese public policy processes than is often assumed. Diet members as individuals also have somewhat unanticipated inputs into policy-making even before bills get to the Diet. The standard process of local interest articulation involves Diet members as representatives of local demands in meetings with ministerial officials, who incorporate some of these demands in subsequent budget proposals. "Sub-governments," which are coalitions that cross institutional boundaries and involve Diet members, government officials, and interest group personnel in long-term defense of particular policy interests, also exist and provide a basis for Diet member inputs into the prelegislative drafting process which goes on within the ministries.[24] Because of these practices, as well as the more assertive role we have reported for the Diet, it is probably reasonable to say that the Japanese Diet functions more or less like legislative bodies in other democratic countries, with probably the important exception of the United States where the tradition of an activist legislature is stronger.[25] National legislatures do not play as central a role in

[23] We are indebted to Akira Kuroda, formerly of the Naikaku Hoseikyoku and a senior civil servant, for assistance in this analysis and for providing government compilations on Diet processes.

[24] The concept of subgovernments was introduced by Douglass Cater in *Power in Washington* (New York: Random House, 1964), p. 50, to describe the informal alliances between interest groups, Congressional committees and their leadership, and elements of the administrative bureaucracy in the American political system. John Campbell has been the main scholar to apply this concept to Japan; see *Contemporary Japanese Budget Politics*, pp. 123–128 and 268–272.

[25] While the Japanese rate of successful cabinet bills might still seem fairly high in isolation, it is interesting that 85 percent of the bills passed by Britain's House of Commons in 1976 originated in the cabinet and that most of the amending that went on was the result of interventions by government ministers rather than ordinary members of parliament. See *The Economist*, August 7, 1976, and November 27, 1976. (This does not mean that the bureaucracy initiated all bills but does indicate that the House of Commons is comparable to the Japanese Diet as regards to the sources of legislative inputs.)

policy-making as democratic theory and constitutional arrangements would suggest, but they are also not the passive bodies that proponents of a bureaucratic dominance theory of policy-making would argue. Our discussion below of the special legislative functions of Japan's opposition parties will further reinforce this observation.

The Diet also performs one additional, major function as a legislative body above and beyond its role, and that of its members, in processing legislation. Through open debates and interpellations both on pending bills and on other important policy issues, members of the executive elite and leading bureaucratic officials are regularly pressed to defend their policy positions and decisions in the forums of the Diet. The most active and public forum for Diet members' interpellations are Budget Committee meetings and plenary sessions in both houses, both of which are regularly reported in the national media. While it is impossible to indicate precisely the impact of the public debates on specific policy outcomes, participation in interpellations by opposition party members as well as Liberal Democratic Party backbenchers is an important check on the executive and administrative components of Japan's government. Indeed, as the experience of the Diet during interpellations on the Lockheed scandal in 1976 will testify, the role of Diet members and opposition parties in interpellations of the government and conservative party leadersthip can become so great as nearly to paralyze the normal legislative process.

THE LIBERAL DEMOCRATIC PARTY

Political parties play complex roles in policy-making processes. Far from being simple in structural and functional terms, parties and their internal organs may actually perform policy-making roles at a variety of points and in different forms. In the case of Japan's Liberal Democratic Party, such intraparty groups as the party's executive elite, the formal party policy-making organs, intraparty policy groups, intraparty leader factions, and rank-and-file Diet members have each made important inputs into policy-making, depending on the issue and the phase of policy processes. Because the Liberal Democratic Party and its predecessors have dominated Japanese politics for so long, these elites and groups within the conservative party have also assumed particular importance in that country's policy-making. Moreover, chronicling the roles played by these intraparty groups should help in understanding the internal processes of other political parties in Japan, since there are some structural similarities shared by almost all Japanese parties. Knowledge of this kind would be particularly important if the Liberal Democrats at some time in the future have to give up the reigns of government to other parties or have to participate in a coalition with other parties, as at present, since the internal processes of Japan's other parties would plausibly be more central to national policy-making under such conditions.

As leaders of a permanent majority party, the Liberal Democratic elite — the vice president (when such a position existed), the secretary general, the heads of the executive and policy councils, and the heads of the party's Diet policy, national organization, and party discipline councils on some occasions — typically has interacted very closely with the central executive elite, i.e., the prime minister and his cabinet. The party elite also has been subject to some of the same political pressures which affect the central executive group, particularly those originating within the party, which is above everything else a "catchall" party including and representing many diverse opinions and interests. For this reason, the roles of the party elite in policy-making have resembled those of the central elite, in that their freedom of action has on occasion been constrained by intraparty pluralism. The party elite has thus been called upon to play a role of broker between intraparty groups, and members of the Liberal Democratic leadership at times have had to give in to rank-and-file pressures and ratify decisions made by lower level organs within the party. Like their counterparts in the central executive elite, party leaders have also spoken out independently on some issues.

Intraparty pluralism has also affected the efforts of the policy and executive councils of the Liberal Democratic Party to promote specific policy stands or aggregate different positions. As discussed in Chapter 8, the party's positions on annual budgets often take the form of unaggregated and unranked lists of demands from different interests.[26] Apparently the diversity of interests represented within the party has been so substantial, and sufficient numbers of these interests have had such strong rank-

---

[26] See again Campbell, op. cit., pp. 128–133.

and-file or policy-council subcommittee support, that decisions on which budget proposals merited higher and lower priorities were not or could not be made by the party's leaders while still preserving their positions and the organizational integrity of the party. Likewise, strong pressures within the lower ranks of the parliamentary party for raising rice prices have meant that the normal elite level decision-making processes of the party's policy council have been influenced by ad hoc efforts from below to manipulate the upper level officials of the party to accede to lower level demands. Thus, on many instances the Liberal Democratic Party's rank-and-file within the Diet have been very powerful vis-à-vis the party's elite and established policy-making organs. Organized as members of the leagues of Diet members in support of agriculture and other interests, the party rank-and-file have succeeded in raising rice prices to a point dramatically above world market levels; thwarted efforts by other Japanese interest groups to liberalize farm imports from America, Australia, and elsewhere; promoted the interests of such groups as the former landlords and repatriates; and provided inputs to party decision making on many other issues.[27]

The presence of informal policy groups, such as the Asian Problems Research Association and the Afro-Asian Problems Research Association, the now defunct Seirankai, the Hirakawakai, and other groups described in Chapter 3, has been another major component of intra-Liberal Democratic Party policy pluralism. Differences of opinion among intraparty policy groups on relations with the two Chinas was one of several factors in a continuing debate on various aspects of Japan's China policy in the 1960s.[28] The same policy group antagonisms also provided stumbling blocks to Premier Tanaka's initial attempts at rapprochement with Peking in 1972 and to Prime Minister Fukuda's later

[27] See John Creighton Campbell, "Compensation for Repatriates: A Case-Study of Interest Group Politics and Party-Government Negotiations in Japan" and Michael W. Donnelly, "Setting the Price of Rice: A Study in Political Decision Making," in T. J. Pempel, op. cit., pp. 103–142 and 143–200. See also Haruhiro Fukui, *Party in Power*, Chapter 7, pp. 173–197. The party elites themselves are vulnerable to the pressures active in their own election districts, and since many of these are rural, their own behavior may be strongly influenced by forces which coincide with pressures from intraparty groups.

[28] See Haruhiro Fukui, op. cit., Chapter 9.

continuation of these efforts, which culminated in a peace treaty with the People's Republic in 1978.[29] The now defunct Seirankai and other intraparty groups concerned with security policy have not had as great an effect on party elite choices and on Policy Council actions as did the two China policy groups. Still, the presence of hawk and dove groups advocating different directions in security policy and other issues has been a complicating factor in Liberal Democratic policy-making.

The Liberal Democratic Party factions and their leaders have been only occasional participants in policy-making. Liberal Democratic Party factions generally do not have a strong ideological coloring, even though leadership elements in some of the factions have had reputations for being hawks or doves. Lacking cohesive opinions on most issues, the factions and their leaders refrain from involvement in policy matters, or otherwise are indifferent *qua* factions because of other kinds of preoccupations. However, when political recruitment becomes entangled with policy processes, the factions or their leaders on occasion express policy opinions. Like politicians in other political systems, Japanese Liberal Democratic Party faction leaders, especially those who see themselves as candidates for top party positions, often are motivated to choose the substance of their policy stands primarily on grounds of political expediency. It is on such occasions, and particularly when the prime ministership is at stake, that factional politics becomes a part of the policy-making process in Japan.

Policy group pluralism internal to the Liberal Democratic Party is a major factor characterizing and determining that party's overall participation in policy-making processes. Still, the leadership and formal policy groups within the party do exert influence at times. Prime Minister Sato generally held the line against rank-and-file pressures for higher rice prices in 1968 and subsequent years, and in doing this apparently buttressed the ability of the party's leaders to take a more determined position in their own right.[30] But many pressures also flow up from below, either from the explicit policy factions within the party or from groups of rank-and-file party members.

---

[29] See Haruhiro Fukui, "Tanaka Goes to Peking," in T. J. Pempel, ed., *Policymaking in Japan*, pp. 60–102.

[30] Michael Donnelly, "Setting the Price of Rice," in T. J. Pempel, op. cit., pp. 195–199.

The collective influence of the Liberal Democratic Party on national policy-making during the 1960s and 1970s was probably less consistently and visibly influential in Japanese policy-making than its status as a permanent majority party would lead observers to believe. On the one hand, the prime minister and ministers who ran Japanese government came from the Liberal Democratic party and thereby provided a major source of party influence over government policy formation. But these same party members sometimes came to represent their own ministries in party government donnybrooks, so influence in any simple sense was not always afforded through the party's access to executive positions. Meanwhile, in a mechanical sense the party's parliamentary group was able to dominate Diet processes in many instances since the party's rank-and-file parliamentarians almost always voted as a bloc. Indeed, once internal divisions within the party on particular issues were overcome, the Liberal Democrats had the necessary votes to railroad legislation whenever necessary, although for a variety of reasons that wasn't always done. But intraparty pluralism was so great on some issues that it took a long time for the necessary unity to be achieved, with the result that complex coalitions involving elements of the party and other political actors often emerged in this process.

A second source of the party's power potentially existed in its close ties with the bureaucratic ministries and big business — the links provided by the recruitment of former bureaucrats to high positions and through the partial consensus and financial ties existing between the party and business interests. In reality, however, this array of relationships was almost infinitely complex and not the simple reinforcing triad of power that is sometimes portrayed. In many cases, the party leadership and organs did provide independent policy pressures, such as when the Party's Special Committee on Okinawa Problems became a major actor pushing for faster and more generous treatment of the Okinawan reversion problem in the late 1960s vis-à-vis a recalcitrant bureaucracy.[31] Elsewhere, the most conspicuous role of the Liberal Democrats was that of acting as an intermediary between the bureaucracy and business, or the party was simply consulted by

31 Bradley Richardson, "Policymaking in Japan," in T. J. Pempel, op. cit., pp. 256–257.

bureaucrats in the drafting of laws.[32] It is thus impossible to trace a relationship of consistent party domination on most policies including the important arena of macroeconomic and microeconomic issues, even though the party's many policy groups generally have had open or informal inputs into bureaucratic decision-making processes, which in turn produced the legislative proposals that were submitted to the Diet. Moreover, at times the party's organs have been used by bureaucrats as sources of support in interministerial struggles for influence; in other words, the close and continuous relationships between the party and officialdom led ministerial officials to cite party support for their positions in order to enhance their own credibility or to ask party policy groups and individual party politicians to help them in persuading other components of the bureaucracy to accede to their positions. Perhaps the best way to summarize the party's contribution in many issue areas is to note that it was at some level an inevitable partner in complex, coalitional politics involving the party's own internal organs, the central elite, elements of the bureaucracy, and leading interest groups, and to note also that patterns of influence were complicated and seldom unidirectional.

Still, in some policy scenarios the Liberal Democratic Party or some of its internal elements has played a more central role. The conservative party and/or party and interest group coalitions have overcome ministerial and central elite resistance in some dramatic confrontations over rice prices and over compensation for repatriates and former landlords. So in situations where issues were usually comparatively simple and highly politicized, and where powerful outside alliances or pressures existed, the party as a distinct political actor was a forceful component of Japanese policy-making processes.

THE OPPOSITION PARTIES IN THE EARLY POSTWAR ERA

The Liberal Democratic Party numerically dominated Japanese parliamentary politics throughout the late 1950s and the

[32] One of the best discussions of Japanese macroeconomic policymaking in which the complexities of the party's relationships with other leading political actors is clearly detailed is Haruhiro Fukui, "Economic Planning in Postwar Japan: A Case Study in Policy Making," *Asian Survey* 8 (1972), pp. 327–348.

1960s by maintaining a substantial although slowly declining majority in the Diet. As a result, in spite of the complex roles played by conservative party politicians and organs in "establishment" coalitions on various issues, its capability to dominate Diet processes was, in terms of potential, fairly clearcut. It was only after 1976 that the forces of the opposition in the Diet approached parity with those of the ruling Liberal Democrats. Up until that time, Japan's opposition parties were a vocal voice within the Diet at the same time that their junior status clearly had the potential of reducing their impact on policy outcomes in many cases. As the result, many observers of Japanese politics have argued that the role of the opposition was confined until recently to that of ritualistically expressing contradictory opinions.

Nevertheless, on quite a few occasions the opposition parties or their members were still active participants in policy-making. For example, individual opposition members of the Diet participated as members of Diet committees specializing in specific functional areas in consultations with counterparts in the ministries much as did rank-and-file Diet members from the Liberal Democratic Party. There were also occasions when opposition party leaders and even rank-and-file parliamentarians reportedly discussed issues freely with their counterparts in the majority party, even when the parties' formal stands were less conciliatory.[33] Finally, there were examples of subgovernment coalitions which involved interest groups, bureaucratic ministries or their internal divisions, and the opposition parties. Such was the case when a committee of the National Mayors Association representing the interests of coal-mining areas succeeded in tandem with the government, the Ministry of International Trade and Industry, and the Japan Socialist Party in getting legislation passed which provided for funding for the rehabilitation of municipalities in the mining districts

---

[33] A more complex interpretation of the role of opposition parties and also a perspective on the Diet which complements our own argues that the opposition cooperated with the conservative camp in the Diet to amend bills both during the multiparty period from 1946 to 1955 and during the "low posture" role of Hayato Ikeda (1960–64). This position differs at points with the bureaucratic dominance theory of Pempel and others (see footnote 21). See Shigeo Misawa, "An Outline of the Policy-Making Process in Japan," in Hiroshi Itoh, *Japanese Politics: An Inside View* (Ithaca: Cornell University Press, 1973), pp. 12–48.

(which has suffered because of the long-term decline of Japan's coal-mining industry.)[34]

Affirmations of the impotency of Japan's opposition parties before the mid-1970s also ignore the importance of the de facto veto power which the opposition camp and its allies sometimes exercised over government policy initiatives. The de facto veto actually resulted from a particular set of recurring circumstances in which the price for the opposition parties' good behavior in the Diet was withdrawal of a bill they opposed. It was the habit of the opposition parties, when they were dramatically opposed to a particular proposal, to filibuster or otherwise obstruct Diet processes and so bring normal parliamentary procedures to a standstill. When, as also occurred repeatedly, the Liberal Democratic Party or government had other legislation they wanted to get through the Diet and were prevented from doing so by opposition party blockage of normal legislative processes, negotiations were conducted between the governing and opposition parties which, on quite a few occasions, resulted in an interparty treaty by which bills objectionable to the opposition camp were withdrawn in favor of opposition party support for "normalization" of Diet procedures.

The scenario of the de facto veto occurred on several occasions in the early 1960s when bills calling for enhanced police powers were brought before the Diet. Similar situations involving the de facto veto occurred in the 1960s in repeated withdrawal of bills to compensate former landlords for losses during the early postwar land reform, when the bills in question were strongly criticized by the opposition parties. Other important bills in the 1960s, such as legislation relating to Japan's affiliation with the International Labor Organization, budget bills, a political funds reform bill, and some educational administration legislation, were withdrawn, or deliberation was postponed, sometimes repeatedly, in a similar exercise of the de facto veto. On one occasion in 1958, the Liberal Democratic Party also withdrew a legislative proposal when the opposition parties were joined by the media and popular movements in the denunciation of a particularly repugnant bill which

---

[34] This example of a subgovernment coalition which included a party from the opposition camp was provided by Terry MacDougall. The law in question was passed in the early 1960s.

called for expanded police powers. Actually, a similar practice to the one observed in earlier periods has been visible even in the recent era of increasing intercamp parity. As noted in the review of major legislative processes in the early 1970s, eight out of fifty important bills in a four-year period were withdrawn in processes reflecting the operation of something like the de facto veto rationale.

In addition to their exercise of a de facto veto, the opposition parties, contrary to folklore about their persistent opposition to all conservative initiatives, joined the ruling Liberal Democrats in support of legislation which favored their own constituencies, such as coal-mining industry related legislation in 1961, 1963 and 1967, and bills which raised public employees' salaries in 1961, 1968, and 1969. Also, the opposition parties joined in support of general interest legislation like the fifteen disaster relief bills which were passed in the 1961 Diet.

Nevertheless, although the role of the opposition parties was a more qualified one than is usually asserted, much opposition party activity in the 1950s and 1960s was in fact ritualistic opposition. Indeed, on one occasion in 1966, the Japan Socialist Party rank-and-file insisted that the party oppose one ruling party proposal on the grounds that the party should do this to compensate for previously cooperating with the Liberal Democrats. Moreover, stiff opposition resistance to some legislative proposals was not always successful in overcoming the dominant Liberal Democrats, even when the opposition parties were supported by the media and mass movements in the streets. The most famous example of Liberal Democratic intransigence was its dictatorial handling of the opposition at the time that the United States-Japan Mutual Security Revision Bill was railroaded through the Diet in June 1960.

OPPOSITION PARTY ROLES IN
QUASI-COALITION DIET POLITICS

The reduction of the Liberal Democratic Party majority to a very narrow margin since 1976 has resulted in some important changes in the style of national policy-making that have further enhanced the political clout of Japan's opposition parties relative to their role in earlier periods. The reallocation of parliamentary committee assignments mentioned in Chapter 8 is one manifestation of this change, although the situation has returned since 1980 to one of greater conservative dominance. Softening of the central elite and the Liberal Democratic Party posture in favor of co-operation in the Diet exemplifies this trend toward new patterns of behavior in the parliament.

Some dramatic changes have taken place in actual policy processes that reflect the trend toward more flexible and complex behavior on the part of all parties within the Diet. In addition to a continuing trend in which many important legislative bills are amended within the Diet, and some bills objectionable to the opposition like the Yasukuni Shrine Bill were withdrawn or postponed, interparty coalitions became more common in the late 1970s. Thus, the opposition parties have crossed over to support government bills on a number of important issues in recent years, as is documented in Table 9.6, which shows that interparty coalitions have become increasingly common between the Liberal Democrats and middle parties (Democratic Socialists and Clean Government Party) while, in a few cases, even the leftist Japan Socialists and Communists have joined in the passage of important legislation. Actually, as noted above, this trend toward greater flexibility and cooperation started even before the period beginning in 1976, which will be referred to as quasi-coalitional government, because that is the point after which the Liberal Democratic strength was almost reduced to complete parity with that of the opposition camp. As conditions increasingly favored softening of conflict and cooperation between parties, the frequency of interparty coalition behavior increased. In addition to the changes in relative party strengths in the Diet, the shifts in the issue environment in the 1970s discussed in Chapter 4 undoubtedly also contributed to more cooperation between parties and camps in the parliament.

PATTERNS OF POLICY-MAKING AND CONFLICT

Day-to-day events reported by the media often are sufficiently dramatic or so dominated by personalities that politics gives the impression of a series of more or less unrelated experiences. The seeming idiosyncrasy of specific events and issues is perpetuated in many historical accounts of politics and studies of particular "cases" of policy-making. Nevertheless, underlying the seeming idiosyncrasies of specific issues is often a fabric of continuity,

TABLE 9.6. *Interparty Coalitions in the Japanese Diet, 1970–78*

Year	Legislative Issue	Participants
1970	Anti-Hijacking Law	All parties
1970	Aviation Reform Law	All parties
1971	Okinawa Reversion Agreement	LDP, DSP, CGP
1973	National Health Insurance Fees Law	All parties
1974	Petroleum Supply Law	All parties
1974	School Principal Position Law	All parties
1974	National Life Stabilization Law	LDP, DSP
1976	Budget	LDP, DSP
1976	Telegraph and Telephone Rates Law	LDP, JSP
1977	Tax Law Reform Law	All parties
1977	Budget	LDP, NLC, DSP
1977	Territorial Waters Extension Law	All parties
1977	Fisheries Waters Delineation Law	All parties
1977–78	Japan-Korea Continental Shelf Agreement and Related Laws	LDP, DSP
1977	Anti-Monopoly Law Reform	All parties
1977	Supplemental Budget	LDP, NLC, DSP, CGP
1977	National Health Insurance Law Reform	LDP, NLC, DSP, CGP, JSP
1977	National Railways Fare Law	LDP, NLC, DSP
1977	Assistance to Unemployed Persons in Special Industries Law	All parties
1978	Budget	LDP, DSP, CGP, JSP, JCP
1978	Narita Airport Security Law	All parties
1978	Supplemental Budget	LDP, DSP

Source: Our analysis of informaiton in Asahi Shimbunsha, *Asahi Nenkan* (Tokyo: 1971 through 1979). Support by all parties often reflects that proposed legislation is simply not controversial.

which when discerned provides meaning to events which might otherwise seem to have little significance beyond specific policy scenarios.

The struggles of Japanese politics can be related with only a small degree of arbitrariness to three modal patterns of policy-making and political conflict.[35] Each one of these patterns is an ideal type, in the sense that reality is never quite as simple nor as

[35] The discussion of modal patterns which follows depends heavily on analysis in the introductory (authored by Haruhiro Fukui) and concluding chapters (authored by the editor) of T. J. Pempel, ed., *Policymaking in Contemporary Japan* and various other sources on Japan's policy experience cited earlier.

tidy as these models taken from reality would suggest. In addition, there are some instances of overlap between the three modal patterns. However, once these qualifications are made, the basic patterns themselves stand out with a kind of stark clarity, and each represents a certain clustering of political actors, decision-making roles, lines of antagonism, and webs of influence.

Long-standing differences between Japan's major parties over ideological and quasi-ideological issues underly one of the modal patterns of Japanese policy-making. Differing as they have done — and still do, although much less intensely — over the role of business, the autonomy of local entities and university faculties, the rights of citizens and unions, the nature of international conflict and related security arrangements, the rights of the consumer in a postindustrial society, and the welfare obligations of the state, Japan's major parties and ideological camps have often confronted each other in the definition of governmental policies. This struggle has abated with the onset of quasi-coalition government. Still, the themes of intercamp conflict, the first example of a modal patten, are one of the dominant threads of Japan's political life in recent decades, and continue in the present in a qualified form.

The central patterns of intercamp policy-making are shown in Figure 9.1. Proposals for policy action in this arena were generally initiated by the central executive elite in some form. Some of the ideas expressed by central elite members did initially come from within the bureaucracy or the policy and executive councils of the Liberal Democratic Party (see the lines of influence indicating these alternative paths in Figure 9.1).[36] But the prime minister and/or his cabinet in most cases took the initiative in proposing or strongly supporting policy directions, either expressing their own personal political commitment or acting as articulators of more-or-less majoritarian preferences inside the Liberal Democratic Party and/or the bureaucratic elite. (However, minority policy group and factional resistance was also great at times within the ranks of the majority party itself — note once again the lines of influence in Figure 9.1 — and caused elites to alter direction or

---

[36] For example, the income-doubling commitment of Hayato Ikeda's premiership was actually based on policies proposed within the bureaucracy before they were embraced by Ikeda.

FIGURE 9.1. *Modal Patterns in Contemporary Japanese Policy-making*

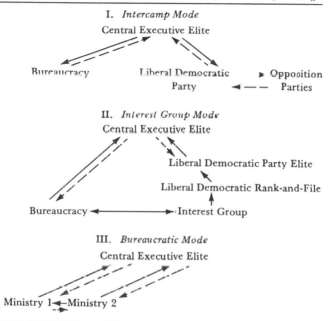

I. *Intercamp Mode*

Central Executive Elite

Bureaucracy   Liberal Democratic   ▸ Opposition
Party   ◂ ─ ─ Parties

II. *Interest Group Mode*

Central Executive Elite

Liberal Democratic Party Elite

Liberal Democratic Rank-and-File

Bureaucracy ◂─────────────▸ Interest Group

III. *Bureaucratic Mode*

Central Executive Elite

Ministry 1 ◂─ Ministry 2

Note: Solid lines indicate dominant patterns of influence, dashed lines indicate alternative lines of influence (or counterinfluence), and two-headed arrows indicate patterns of intimate interaction or coalition in which unidirectionality of influence cannot be attributed.

procrastinate even while maintaining some of their initial policy preferences.)

Whatever the specific lines of initiative and influence within the central elite-bureaucracy-Liberal Democratic Party, i.e., establishment, sector, the major conflict in intercamp policy-making was focused on confrontations between the conservative camp and the opposition parties, and the most common battleground was the National Diet. There, in deliberations over proposed legislation or treaties which required ratification, or in interpellations about the directions of bureaucratic and executive policy-making, the conflict was intense and often sustained over a substantial period of time. Indeed, it is this intensity of parliamentary conflict, at least in the 1950s and 1960s, as well as the substance and lines of participation, which marks intercamp policy-making as a major modal pattern. The ideological issues were central, party and camp loyalties were intense, and the very ideological nature of the conflict permitted little or no compromise, a factor which in itself further fed the intensity of conflict. Only in recent years has this conflict declined markedly in intensity through the overlapping processes of (1) the softening of government-Liberal Democratic positions, (2) the approach to parity in power between the Liberal Democrats and Japan's other parties, and (3) the reciprocal softening of the opposition resistance, coupled with (4) some decline in ideology, (5) hope by the middle-of-the-road parties for participation in government, which encouraged them to take even more moderate views, and (6) a shift of the issue environment away from security and defense questions to greater concern for quality of life problems and other less divisive concerns.

The second modal pattern in Japanese policy-making is that of interest-group related processes. Interest groups did have a role in intercamp conflict at times, inasmuch as the defense of union, consumer, and teachers' rights was so closely related to opposition ideology. Still, policy-making resulting from group demands was on many occasions different in its patterns from intercamp processes. At least in the case of interest groups not affiliated with the opposition, a relatively stable pattern of group-stimulated intra-Liberal Democratic Party and intrabureaucratic interactions can be discerned. This pattern of party-group relationships can be seen in the accounts of farmer, repatriate, and former landlord pressures in the 1950s and 1960s, which were cited in this and the last chapter. Recently the demands and tactics of farm groups opposed to liberalization of Japan's protectionist quotas on such products as meat and citrus fruits have taken the same pattern.

The politics of interest group linked policy-making in Japan is made complex by the presence of subgovernments which include interest group representatives, rank-and-file Diet Members, many of whom are from the Liberal Democratic Party, and officials from the bureaucratic ministries. The commonality of interests and stable interpersonal relationships within these subgovernments in agriculture, construction, and elsewhere not only blurred the lines of initiative and influence but also clouded the overall picture of policy-making involving major organized interests. However, once this area of complex interaction is recognized, the remainder of interest group policy-making is relatively clear in at least its modal patterns.

In contrast with the fairly dominant role of the central executive elite in intercamp policy-making processes, the central elite was typically much more passive and reactive where interest group politics were concerned. Interest groups tended to push their causes upward through the Liberal Democratic hierarchy in the case of mass groups like farmers, former landlords, and repatriates, or else they attempted to influence the party's elite laterally in the case of elite groups like big business. In the case of mass interests, the upward movement, operating through rank-and-file Diet members and lower level policy organs within the majority party, often resulted in the Liberal Democratic Party's own senior policy groups and elite having to take up the group cause. Liberal Democratic parliamentarians were also organized in Dietmember leagues to advance the cause of a particular interest in many instances, which presumably helped make their positions more visible in order to gain leverage over the senior elements of the party. In the final stages of policy-making relating to group interests, the Liberal Democratic Party elite — the secretary general and the chairmen of the party's executive and policy councils were probably the most important consistent members of this group — often faced a recalcitrant bureaucratic elite (as representatives of party-group coalitions) in impasses over policy alternatives. The cabinet ministers who represented the bureaucracy were themselves leading members of the Liberal Democratic Party. However, holding a position as head of a ministry often led to representation of the bureaucratic side vis-à-vis that of Liberal Democratic Party and its supporting groups. In cases where subgovernmental ties did not result in ministerial sponsorship of a group's claims or in those instances where group demands involved a large expenditure of government money — something which Finance Ministry officials and even some other bureaucrats were loathe to encourage — a kind of standoff occurred between Liberal Democratic advocates of group interests and their cabinet minister opponents. In policy-making scenarios of this kind, the central executive elite, usually the prime minister himself or his chief cabinet secretary, acted at times as a broker and sought to promote reconciliation between the two sides. The prime minister's own relative neutrality with regard to interest group demands facilitated his playing such a role, whatever the motivations for his neutrality may have been.

In addition to the difference in the roles typically played by the central elite and other actors, conflict patterns in interest group policy-making processes were different from those in intercamp confrontations. The stakes for groups and their members were often great, and at times tempers flared in demonstrations and sit-ins by interest group members. However, other actors in the process such as the central executive elite and the camps in the Diet were usually much less committed than in the case of intercamp processes. As a result, there was less conflict between the parties in the Diet in the interest group mode, except in cases like that of compensation to former landlords in which camp ideologies and interest group issues overlapped.

Intrabureaucratic policy-making, the third visible, modal pattern in contemporary Japanese policy-making, was in itself both a separate policy-making pattern and often a component or early stage of intercamp and interest group policy-making. The difference between the bureaucratic mode and the other kinds of policy-making patterns lay in the location of the initiative for policies. Several ministries or even one ministry tended to be so important in the process as a whole, or in some phase of the process, that their presence stood out relative to the role of the bureaucracy in other policy scenarios. The budget is a case in point. However politicized the budget may have become, the various ministries and agencies, and especially the Ministry of Finance, always played a big role in budget initiatives and decisions, and actually dominated budget-making during much of the time.

Actually, it may be most reasonable to perceive the bureaucratic mode as a cluster of sub-types which may in reality vary in terms of the degree of involvement of other actors and the roles other actors play. Whether a specific scenario involved bureaucratic monopoly of policy-making via ministerial legislation or initiation of legislative proposals, or whether bureaucratic activity was the first stage of a lengthy process involving camp or group conflict, various patterns in bureaucratic policy-making actually existed. In some cases, specific ministries initiated policies which were in turn ratified at some point by the central executive elite. Alternatively, components of the bureaucracy were themselves urged to take a particular policy course by the central executive elite, but then dominated the remainder of the policy process. Or, in certain cases, the central elite or leading elements of the conservative party acted as an arbiter-of-last-resort in conflicts between particular ministries, or at times played no visible role in what were essentially ministry dominated processes.[37]

POLICY-MAKING IN JAPAN

Analysis of policy-making roles and overall, modal patterns of policy-making in contemporary Japan has shown a fairly complex political process in which political actors often deviate from the roles assigned them in the constitution or in institutional theories of politics. Moreover, some actors were present whose participation was obviously not anticipated in the formal institutional format. From this it can be seen that in Japan as elsewhere, the participation of political parties has a great deal to do with how power is distributed. The distribution of power in turn defines how roles are played by such political actors as the central executive elite, the parties in the Diet, and the various factional and policy-group inside parties. Moreover, the frequent participation in political processes of activist and powerful bureaucratic ministries (unanticipated by the formal constitutional documents) further affects how power is distributed and thereby how outcomes are determined in policy processes in a variety of ways.

One of the central questions of Japanese politics is the degree to which the different models posed by elitists, pluralists, and corporatists actually fit political reality. From the evidence about limitations on the power of executive and party elites stemming from the imperatives of coalitional politics, it seems reasonable to reject the elitist approach without detailed consideration. The corporatist and pluralist approaches, in contrast, merit more attention.

Corporatism, it will be remembered, implies that private inter-

[37] Because there were so many different subtypes of bureaucratic policy processes, it is hard to make precise statements about conflict in this mode. There were intense struggles between ministries at times, as documented earlier in this chapter, and some may have been as intense as the conflicts generated in the Diet during intercamp struggles and the tensions between groups and parties or ministries. But bureaucratic conflict is often less visible and less publicized than other kinds of political conflict, so it is more difficult to assess.

ests are closely tied to government centers of power — in Japan presumably the Liberal Democratic Party and central executive elites, and the bureaucratic ministries — thereby gaining special treatment, while also possibly being vulnerable to control and manipulation by these power centers. Pluralism implies a more open relationship between private interests and core political actors, one characterized by more flexible patterns of coalition formation and competition.

In the last chapter it was shown that Japan had some elements of both corporatism and pluralism. This chapter introduces further evidence of the mixed nature of Japanese political processes involving both interest group-government relationships and interest group ties with central political actors like the Liberal Democratic Party. We would like to pull the relevant points together here, and supplement them with some additional important distinctions drawn from the monographic and press materials used as evidence for this chapter. The discussion focuses on patterns of policy process participation and influence and the nature of policy-making outcomes. Confining comments to the relationships between business and government which probably best fit the corporatist model, we conclude as follows:

(a) In some areas of broad economic policy-making, such as in the formulation of national economic plans, there has been a kind of "limited" pluralism, in the sense that (i) different ministries, the Liberal Democratic Party, and business groups all have inputs into policy processes, (ii) their inputs are conflictual at times, and (iii) the resulting pluralistic participation, however, is limited by the absence of effective participation from the opposition parties and mass interest groups including the labor unions.

(b) In industrial policy-making within ministries, there were usually fewer visible indications of pluralism in decisions about industrial plans and policies and even more limited participation, but differences of opinion still emerged at times in both the formulation and implementation of these programs.

(c) Where economic ministries like MITI provided assistance to weak industries, as in the early 1950s, or recessed industries, as in the late 1970s and early 1980s, often the ministries did provide favored access to private interests while also providing strong leadership. Weak or recessed industries at times went along with government initiatives or at least major portions of government programs as they were interlaced with such help as special tax benefits and government loans. In this kind of policy scenario relationships did at times resemble the corporatist model, depending on the specific time and industrial program.

(d) Where industries were strong and economically viable, there was much greater resistance to government intervention, and therefore more pluralism. For example, as Japan's major industries became more sure of themselves after the initial years of high growth (wherein they had achieved better financial and market positions), there was much more of a desire to be left alone by the government ministries. Also, in cases where the ministries tried to make structural changes in industries by attempting to induce firms to merge into smaller numbers of competitors, there was also often strong resistance from the side of private business. Finally, where there have been differences of interest between different industrial sectors, administrative policies don't always work very well. For example, recent efforts by the Ministry of International Trade and Industry to support the petroleum refining industry by permitting higher prices brought angry rebuttals from industries which purchased petroleum products, whose main interest lay in obtaining raw materials cheaply.

From the above summary it can be seen that even where the institutional relationships which best fit the corporatist model cited in Chapter 8 existed, still the actual patterns of policy-making were mixtures, and neither the pure corporatist nor the pure pluralist model fit all policy experiences and situations. Somewhat similarly, as other areas of Japanese policy-making and policy outcomes are examined, it can be seen that private interests affiliated with the establishment Liberal Democratic Party have received mixed treatment in actual policy scenarios over the years in which the ruling party has dominated Japanese government, while interests linked with the opposition camp have not always been denied. Once again the patterns do not fit a simple model:

(a) It is true that agriculture, the bulwark of Liberal Democratic voting support, has been favored through a variety of policies, such as price subsidies and protection from foreign imports. Even opposition from such powerful groups as Japan's big business federations have so far failed to deter the Liberal Democrats from its supportive stance toward agriculture. But in policy-making areas like the annual rice price settlement, some government ministries and the farmers have at times had sharply different views. Elsewhere, the Liberal Democrats have also represented the interests of business in a variety of ways over the years, especially in their defense of business's broadest interests in political and economic stability, the defense of capitalism (in some periods), and, relatedly, opposition to Communism and Socialism, even while the government-business relationship in many more concrete economic policy-making scenarios was at times conflictual. Thus relations between Japan's conservative governments and its most consistent long-term support groups have been characterized by somewhat mixed patterns.

(b) It is also true that the Liberal Democratic Party pushed many bills through the Diet on the basis of their numerical majority, which included legislation strongly opposed by the opposition parties and their affiliated interest groups. Most prominent among these examples of conservative party or camp arrogance were the railroading of bills and treaties related to defense and international security arrangements. Conservative-party supported budgets were also pushed through the Diet in most years in the 1960s in the face of opposition resistance, although opposition to these bills was not so intense as it was on security issues. Still, the opposition parties and the interests they represented were far more successful than might have been expected from their legislative vulnerability in some periods. First, there was the de facto veto, which resulted in the withdrawal or postponement of many bills which the opposition disliked. Secondly, even in the 1960s during the period of greater conservative strength, the opposition participated in legislative decisions which favored its own constituencies, such as the many bills passed to help coal miners and coal-mining regions and legislation which raised public employees' salaries. (Most public employees were members of unions which supported the opposition parties.) Later, in the 1970s, there were numerous examples of bills which were amended in response to opposition initiative and opposition participation in legislative coalitions supporting particular legislation. (On at least two occasions, the Liberal Democratic Party even departed from its tradition of bloc voting, with some Liberal Democratic Diet members voting with the opposition.[38]

The patterns of Japanese policy-making have been mixed, whether the issue be corporatism vs. pluralism in a simple sense or the broader consequences of a dominant party system. Overall, a great deal of pluralism can be seen in policy processes in contemporary Japan. Pluralism can be seen in intrabureaucratic processes — even though it is not always present — and in intra-Liberal Democratic policy scenarios, interest group politics and intercamp policy-making. Although one actor or a coalition of actors is the ultimate winner in each policy contest, the overall patterns of Japanese policies have been those of give-and-take between multiple actors. No one group or small coterie of groups dominated all of Japanese policy-making in the periods that have been surveyed, although participation in policy-making was sometimes confined to establishment or corporatist channels. Rather, influence is shared in a complex and variable ways across different policy areas and individual decisions. Moreover, while particular actors did not always play their roles according to the constitution or democratic theory, the fabric of Japanese policy-making was one of checks-and-balances between competing groups having different interests, goals, and ideologies. It is this pluralism itself which is the hallmark of modern democracy far more than rigid adherence to one or another institutional format, and it is through demonstration of such a degree of pluralism that contemporary Japanese policy-making resembles in substantial degree that of other industrialized nations, even though differing at times in terms of the form of relationships existing between private interests and Japan's strong bureaucratic ministries and through the presence of a dominant party system.

Having established that pluralism is a central feature of Japanese political life in the postwar era should not blind us, however, to the fact that outcomes of policy processes were somewhat one-sided in the broadest sense. Decisions on social policy in postwar Japan reflect the partial exclusion of the left and labor

---

[38] The bills where some Liberal Democratic Party's Diet members defected were the Public Election Law amendments of 1974 and the Anti-Monopoly Law Revision bill of 1977.

unions, particularly in the early years, even though political processes were open usually and there was substantial pluralism. Thus postwar Japanese policies were quite different from those of European nations where socialist governments or socialist participation in ruling coalitions led to development of comprehensive social welfare and security systems. In dominant party Japan, many policies favored conservative opinions just as some European nations tended to favor leftist ideas; in each case an important political force was excluded from participation in some outcomes even though pluralism otherwise prevailed. Chapter 10 will portray these tendencies in social policy in detail.

Outputs and Outcomes

POLITICAL OUTPUTS ARE the product of governmental processes: the instruments of political outputs include policy statements, legislation, and administrative policy, while the substance of outputs ranges from allocation of government budget resources to conduct of foreign policy. Because Japan has had more of a tradition of state guidance than laissez-faire liberalism, it could be expected that the outputs of Japanese governmental processes would be very wide ranging and interventionist. In effect, government outputs could be expected to be more important to Japan's economy and society than the outputs of a more classic liberal type of government.

Outputs are government actions. In contrast, outcomes represent the combination of political outputs with more general societal and economic processes. *Outputs* in the area of the economy include economic planning and monetary and fiscal policy designed to provide for stability or growth, or tax concessions for favored industries and the like. *Outcomes* are the actual production figures resulting from the combined impact of policy and traditional economic incentives and behaviors. Outcomes also include the broader social and physical consequences of economic activity, such as population movements, urban crowding, industrial pollution, consumer affluence, and rising educational levels.

Usually it makes sense to talk about outputs and outcomes in

* Bradley M. Richardson

static terms. Outputs are seen as the direct consequence of governmental processes, and are described separately from the outcomes to which they may contribute directly or indirectly, whereas outcomes are discussed much as a separate and consequent domain that *follows* governmental output activity. Comments on outcomes note the importance of feedback loops, by which outcomes produce more problems for government processes, but these feedback loops are seldom traced in any great detail.

Because the outputs-outcomes-feedbacks linkage was particularly visible and dramatic in Japanese political processes in the past three decades, special attention will be paid to the feedback problem. The outputs in two phases or segments will be studied, stressing first the actions of government in the 1950s and 1960s, and secondly the outputs of the Japanese political system since 1970. Between discussion of the two phases of outputs, this chapter will look at outcomes as they emerged from the first phase of outputs and produced problems which were dealt with in the second phase. This approach will emphasize the importance of economic growth policies in the 1950s and 1960s, the positive and negative results of growth policies represented by outcomes in the late 1960s and early 1970s, and the actual adaptations made by government to some of these problems in the outputs of the 1970s.

WHAT THE JAPANESE GOVERNMENT DOES

Political output instruments can take a variety of forms. A statement by the Japanese prime minister that Japan will follow a particular kind of foreign policy may constitute an output in lieu of any immediate follow-up legislation or administrative action. In other words, in the short run, policy statements are often outputs, even though over the long run, they would be expected to have some tangible expression in specific executive, legislative, or administrative policy actions. Executive decisions are themselves political outputs: in the Japanese case specifically, the cabinet and ministerial ordinances and rules on such important matters as economic or foreign trade policy.[1] Legislative outputs are obviously an important component of overall govern-

---

[1] Conclusion of treaties and international agreements are another output of the Japanese executive branch, but treaties must also be approved by the Diet.

mental outputs as well; at present in Japan as elsewhere, they provide both broad outlines for administrative action and at times specific solutions to narrow problems.

Because of the tradition of bureaucratic rule in Japan, it is necessary to stress the importance of ministerial outputs in Japanese political processes. Ministerial outputs take the form of ordinances, or notices, which are bureaucratic rules much like those found in other political systems. Ministerial outputs also include administrative guidance, a process by which bureaucratic agencies persuade or threaten other political and economic actors to seek compliance with particular goals.

Three other kinds of government output instruments should be mentioned. These are budgets, plans, and court decisions. Budgets are in many ways the heart of the government processes, in that they allocate the financial resources necessary to keep government operations going, while also paying for some kinds of public investments, subsidies, and other external programs. Plans have a special place in Japanese government outputs. Japanese government offices have used long term economic plans and other types of planning to indicate major goals and to lay the basis for more specific government outputs and policies. The Japanese government has made economic plans, defense plans, construction plans, and a multitude of other kinds of plans, all designed to provide an overall framework for subsequent policy decisions. Indeed, planning is one aspect that distinguishes Japanese politics from the less consciously structured approaches to broad policy problems and future needs found in politics in the United States. Finally, the Japanese court system itself produces government outputs in the form of important decisions. Although litigation among private persons and corporations is not as important an instrument for conflict resolution in Japan as it is in the United States, Japan still has an active system of justice and processes by which decisions on legal principles and review of government actions can be made.[2]

Like all governments of large, complex, industrialized societies, the Japanese government emits a large volume of specific outputs

[2] Most legal experts agree that Japan's court system has not played anything like the role of the American federal courts in independently defining constitutional law and evaluating the performance of the national legislature on the basis of constitutional principles.

— 5,698 laws, 11,144 executive and ministerial ordinances, and 475 treaties were registered in the years 1946–76, along with an unknown number of bureaucratic communications, uses of administrative guidance, and relevant court decisions. Because the volume of specific outputs is so great, the focus here will be mainly on the broad trends in government outputs visible in major decisions and output instruments. Still, it is important to keep in mind what the specific instruments of outputs are and also how large their volume is, in order to appreciate the actual nature and scale of the operations of a modern government.

The laws, ordinances, foreign treaties, uses of guidance, and court decisions which constitute Japanese government output can be classified into certain generic kinds of output actions which are independent from the particular types of instruments employed. Looking at these broad classes makes it easier to understand what government actually does. In order to explore these generic output patterns, the laws passed between 1946 and 1976 have been classified into different categories of government action as follows:

(a) *Institution Building and Survival.* Governments enact laws and ministerial ordinances in order to establish the very institutions which are used to make and implement government policies. After Japan's core political institutions were transformed by constitutional change in 1946 — in itself a major output — there was a flurry of implementing legislation which detailed the specific rules for operation of the Diet and other institutions. In a parallel fashion, laws were subsequently enacted to establish new ministries like International Trade and Industry and Home Affairs, while other acts were passed to provide for creation of new suborgans of existing ministries. While there were more examples of important institution building in the period just after the end of World War II, institution building continues to the present as a major output of Japanese governmental processes.

Government institutions also have to survive. To do this, laws and regulations governing the selection, support, and behavior of public personnel have to be enacted. These include provision for the civil service, establishment of recruitment and promotion criteria, regulation of the operations of the bureaucracy, and such nontrivial matters as provisions for pensions for civil servants (which may be an important motivating factor in development of a quality administrative elite). Civil servants have to be paid regularly, offices have to be maintained, supplies must be replenished, and new government buildings have to be built from time to time; accordingly, substantial government outputs in the form of budgetary allocations for salaries and maintenance are necessary for the very survival of day-to-day governmental operations.

(b) *Government Outputs and the Provision of Services.* In many nations, governments are the providers of such major services as transportation and public housing, with the importance of government activities in these areas growing as economies become more complex and societies become more urban and more mobile. The conduct of foreign policy and the establishment of armed forces to provide for collective security are other examples of services performed by most governments.

Since the nineteenth century, many governments have in addition played a very large role in the education of young people, which is another kind of service output. Likewise, provision for economic stability and social welfare has become part of the natural service obligations of government in response to the insecurities of modern industrialized urban life. The provision and maintenance of roads, sewers, waterways, and other kinds of social capital is another form of government service, and one which probably has been found in every kind of traditional and modern political system.

(c) *Government Regulation.* Governments regulate a great deal of economic and social activity. Particular professions and occupations whose members' activities affect the public good, like doctors and restaurant owners, are usually regulated in some way. So, too, may be the conditions of work, the behavior of businessmen with regard to formation of monopolies or cartels, the standards of safety in certain occupations, the polluting activities of car owners and companies, and even the internal organization of private groups. At present, it isn't really known whether the Japanese government regulates more activities than other modern governments. However, more of the legislative output of the Japanese Diet was concerned with regulatory activities than with any other kind of legislation.

(d) *Help for Specific Groups.* In an earlier section, it was noted

how pleas for special help was a generic category of interest articulation. In a parallel fashion, the provision of help is an important political output class. Specific groups ask for and get supports for incomes, special credit facilities, special pension and
health insurance plans, and various items. This form of government output is nowhere near as large as regulation in terms of
numbers of visible laws, in part because many group requests are
for services or regulation of some kind of behavior, so that the
relevant laws were put into these categories on the basis of the
evaluation of their nominal intent. Still, help to groups is important, and controversies over group assistance generated some
of the major legislative conflicts that occurred in Japan's postwar
experience.

(e) *Goal Setting as a Government Output.* Some political philosophies reject the idea that governments should intervene in
economic activities or set national social and economic goals.
This is the central core of traditional laissez faire liberal approaches to the relationship between the state, the economy, and
private groups. Alternative philosophies of governance or political cultures call for government direction of the economy and
society: the most extreme form of such a belief system is that
which advocates totalitarian governance. In the Japanese case,
the contemporary government's commitment to engage in long-
range goal setting issues from several sources: the traditional belief that the state should intervene broadly and regulate many
aspects of life, the perceived need to use state power to further
the goals of economic development, and perhaps even a cultural
preference for institutionalization of many unpredictable aspects
of life. The Japanese government is heavily involved in establishment of long-term goals, as the existence of a number of very
visible outputs, including national economic plans, is witness.

Table 10.1 displays the actual frequencies of laws passed in
the different categories just discussed during most of the postwar
era. Of the various types of legislative outputs, regulation was
by far the leading category and accounted for nearly 40 percent
of all postwar legislation. Legislative outputs relating to institution building and the conduct of government were second in
importance, in that roughly 30 percent of the laws passed since
World War II fell in this category. As can be seen in Table 10.1,

TABLE 10.1. *Japanese Legislative Outputs, 1946–76*

Period	Institutions	Services	Regulation	Group Support	Goal Setting
1945–50	149	51	134	5	19
1951–55	86	66	120	4	25
1956–60	40	45	72	0	14
1961–65	48	34	49	1	22
1966–70	30	34	63	1	9
1971–76	41	21	55	1	15
Total	394	251	493	12	104

Source: Analysis of 1,254 laws identified in Kokuritsu Kokkai Toshokan, *Nihon Horei Sakuin* (Tokyo: 1976). Each law was given one of forty-seven specific codes, and then specific coded groups were summed according to the general classification scheme identified in the text. Some examples of content are as follows:

Institutions: Basic laws establishing institutions and public corporations, tax system legislation, public administration legislation

Services: Education, pollution control, public works, resolution of economic crises, aid in natural disasters, welfare state programs

Regulation: Regulation of economic activities, safety and health, patents and trade marks, criminal activities

Group Support: Laws which specifically identified programs designed to benefit a particular private group directly, such as the legislation for former landlords' and repatriates' compensation

Goal Setting: Legislation promoting economic and regional development, energy resource development, technological innovation, and occupation reforms

both regulation and institution building were especially important during the early postwar era when the government was rebuilding the political system, moving into new areas of activity and changing practices to fit the postwar political environment. Legislation supportive of goal setting was numerically less significant than that in other categories, perhaps because goal setting is an intermittent activity followed by many implementing laws or administrative actions. The main message of Table 10.1 is simply to denote the actual nature of the Japanese government's legislative output during the period covered by this book. The variations in legislative emphasis across time also serve as an interesting supplement to our discussion below of the overall trends in Japanese policies since the early 1950s, which is based on more conventional indicators of government outputs such as data from budget schedules.

JAPANESE POLITICAL OUTPUTS 1952–69:
CONSOLIDATION AND HIGH GROWTH

Japan's economy was heavily damaged during World War II: plants and facilities were damaged or destroyed, and work was disrupted by mobilization and flight from the cities. Much of the initial output of Japanese government after the end of the war was concerned with repair of the economy. A fair amount of the early postwar government outputs were also related to occupation reforms of the economic, social, and political systems. In contrast, the decade of the 1950s was generally a period of consolidation and building for the future in both the domestic and foreign policy realms. The 1950s also witnessed the beginning of a sustained period of government-stimulated economic growth which was to continue and accelerate in the 1960s.

Throughout the 1950s and most of the 1960s, the Japanese government was supportive of economic growth, at times at the expense of alternative policies. A variety of government instruments was developed to foster growth, and several alternative policy commitments which would have been competitive with growth were rejected. Probably the one most important contribution by the Japanese government to the support of economic development during this period was its commitment to "cheap government." Because of this emphasis, not only were taxes in Japan held to a lower rate than in most other industrialized countries, but also outputs on social welfare programs and defense were markedly lower than their counterparts in other comparable political systems.

As the figures in Table 10.2 indicate, Japan in the 1960s had the lowest level of taxation of any major industrial power. In 1965 total taxation in Japan (excluding social security contributions) amounted to 18 percent of gross domestic product, in contrast with 27–35 percent for the United States, Britain, Germany and France.[3] Public expenditures from the annual budgets in Japan also carried out the theme of "cheap government." In the

---

[3] Figures from earlier periods show an even lower level of government expenditure relative to gross domestic product. According to data in Hugh Patrick and Henry Rosovsky, *Asia's New Giant: How the Japanese Economy Works* (Washington: Brookings, 1976), expenditures were only 11 percent of GDP in 1952!

TABLE 10.2. *Government Revenues and Expenditures as a Percentage of GDP, Selected Countries*

	Japan	France	West Germany	Italy	United Kingdom	United States
Current Government Expenditure (as % of GDP) 1960	13	30	28	27	29	25
Outlays on Social Security (as % of GDP) 1965	6	17	19	17	14	8
Outlays on Defense (as % of GDP) 1965	1	6	4	3	6	7
Tax Revenues (as % of GDP) 1965	18	35	32	27	32	27

Sources: Government expenditures and taxes: calculated from United Nations, *Yearbook of National Accounts*, 1980. Social Security: Harold Wilensky, *The Welfare State and Equality* (Berkeley: University of California Press, 1975). Defense: Gabriel Almond and G. Bingham Powell, Jr., *Comparative Politics* (Boston: Little, Brown, 1978). Taxes: OECD, *Revenue Statistics of OECD Member Countries, 1965–79* (Paris: 1980).

1950s and 1960s government outlays on current account represented only 13–14 percent of gross domestic product in Japan, whereas in other industrialized countries they ranged as high as 30 percent. One major reason for these differences were the lower Japanese outlays on social programs and defense. In the mid 1960s Japan spent roughly one third of the amounts committed to social programs by European countries, and a little less on social welfare outlays than the United States. Moreover, after a long debate in the early 1950s over choices between defense outlays and economic development, Japan's government committed itself to a restricted defense-force concept, which was reflected by subsequent defense outlays that hovered around 1 percent of national income and remained at this level throughout the postwar era. In contrast, the United States spent around 6 percent of its

GDP on defense in this period, while other countries in the NATO alliance spent between 3 and 6 percent on their military efforts. Lower outlays on these two main items, social welfare and defense, were a sizable component of the total difference between Japanese government expenditures and those of other large, industrialized countries in the relevant periods (see Table 10.2).

Much of Japanese economic policy during the postwar era was directed toward encouraging high levels of savings and investment. Low government overhead was one way to facilitate savings and investment, in that less was extracted from national income and allocated to public expenditures than in other industrialized nations. The Japanese government also encouraged low interest rates in most periods, which was another factor favoring high investment ratios.[4] A cultural disposition to save was further encouraged by liberal tax exemptions for savings deposits. As a result of these supportive policies, savings and investment in Japan ran substantially higher than their counterparts in other industrialized nations. By the late 1960s, the OECD estimated that gross fixed investment in Japan averaged 38 percent of gross domestic product each year; the comparable figures for other major industrialized countries ranged between 16 percent for the United States and 26 percent for France.[5]

Japan's government-run Fiscal Investment and Loan Program (FILP) and related government banks have also played a special role in Japanese investment and economic development. The FILP is a government administered program which funnels monies from nonrevenue sources into government designated investment projects of many different kinds. The FILP has ranged in size between 27 and 52 percent of the Japanese government budget. However, since most of the FILP's funds come from postal savings and other nontax sources, the program cannot strictly be

[4] Economists point out that economic stability was not a major goal of monetary policy in much of the postwar era, and that higher interest rates were introduced only when the economy heated up and higher imports relative to exports threatened Japan's balance of payments.

[5] Patrick and Rosovsky, op. cit., especially Chapter 11 by Philip Trezise and Yukio Suzuki. See also Tsunehiko Watanabe, "National Planning and Economic Growth in Japan," in Bert. G. Hickman, ed., *Quantitative Planning of Economic Policy: A Conference of the Social Science Research Council Committee on Economic Stability* (Washington: Brookings Institution, 1965), pp. 233–251.

compared with the budget even though some of its uses of funds are comparable to budget funding elsewhere.

The FILP has invested in a variety of fields including roads, railways, ports, housing, and other social and industrial infrastructure projects as well as making some direct loans via institutions such as the Japan Development Bank to industries for development. In 1955 through 1962 between 11 and 21 percent of the FILP's funds were designated for basic industrial development. Since that time the FILP's direct role in funding economic growth in the large, medium, and small business sectors has steadily decreased, and currently the FILP spends only 2.5 percent of its substantial funds on direct support of industrial growth.[6]

The Japanese government also endeavored to promote economic growth through other macroeconomic policies and by means of microeconomic programs aimed at development of specific industries. Japan initiated indicative economic planning in the 1950s; indicative plans set economic goals but do not provide sanctions for non-compliance. Through consultations involving the major economic ministries and representatives of business and other private interests, large scale development plans, buttressed by elaborate statistical references, were developed to guide public and private economic activity. Economists discount the direct effects of planning on economic growth, in part because there was no tidy fit between planned and actual growth.[7] Still, five major plans were created by the Economic Planning Agency between 1955 and 1967, roughly the time span of our first output period (see Table 10.3 for plans and their general goals), and both the lengthy discussions of goals and the statistics which were accumulated and published to support the planning activity may

[6] United States General Accounting Office, *Industrial Policy: Japan's Flexible Approach* (Washington: 1982), pp. 18–20. Among the designees of FILP funding are Japan's many public corporations. The presence of FILP means that Japan's government's public role in the economy is greater than budgetary figures would indicate. However, on the tax side Japan still fits the concept of cheap government. Moreover, some of the FILP funds include revenues and supports for state run railways and other services which are typically not reported in budgets in other countries. So the presence of FILP means that the Japanese government is more important to the economy than would initially appear, although this importance cannot always be measured in terms comparable to practices in all industrialized countries.

[7] Patrick and Rosovsky, op. cit., pp. 533 and 559.

TABLE 10.3. *Japanese Economic Plans, 1955–67*

Name of Plan	Plan Period (fiscal years)	Aims	Major Policy Objectives
Five-year plan for economic self-support	1956 –60	1. Strengthen industrial foundation; 2. promote trade; 3. raise level of economic self-support, and reduce outflow of foreign currency; 4. promote development of national land; 5. promote science and technology; 6. nurture medium-size and smaller companies; 7. increase job opportunities, and improve social welfare system; 8. promote healthy fiscal and financial policies; 9. stabilize prices; 10. stabilize national living standard and foster restraint in consumption	On foundations of economic stability, move to realize full employment and economic self-support
New long-range economic plan	1958 –62	1. Expand exports; 2. strengthen capital accumulation; 3. improve basic sectors for economic development; 4. raise sophistication of industrial structure; 5. modernize agricultural production structure; 6. improve labor situation and national living standard	Maintain economic stability and achieve continuous economic growth at as high a level as possible, steadily raising national standard of living and moving toward full employment
National income doubling plan	1961 –70	1. Fill out social overhead capital; 2. raise sophistication of industrial structure; 3. promote trade and international economic cooperation; 4. raise capability levels of human resources, and promote science and technology; 5. ease the two-tier economic structure and achieve social stability	Achieve substantial increase in national standard of living and progress in achieving full employment; to accomplish those aims, move toward sharply expanded, stable economic growth

Medium-term economic plan	1964 – 68	1. Promote trade and raise sophistication of industrial structure; 2. raise capability levels of human resources, and promote science and technology; 3. modernize industrial sectors with low production levels; 4. promote mobility and effective use of labor; 5. raise quality level of national life and promote social development in other ways such as improving the living environment, improving social overhead capital, and reducing environmental pollution	Rectify imbalance in domestic economy by bringing lagging aspects of industrial and daily living sectors to par level with general economic growth, thus achieving overall harmonious economic development
Economic and social development plan	1967 – 71	1. Stabilize; 2. make economy more efficient; 3. promote social development; 4. put into order the structure needed for realizing long-term economic growth; 5. improve overhead social capital	Establish position of Japan's economy in changing international society, and build basic structure needed for Japanese to enjoy standard of living fitting for such position, thus moving toward realization of balanced, well-rounded social development

Source: Economic Planning Agency, various documents.

have had a substantial effect in raising consciousness about economic goals in both the public and private sectors. The activity of government indicative planning itself may thus have made some important contributions to the thinking and motivations of political and economic actors, even if the plans themselves did not relate directly to public outputs and private outcomes at all times.

Specify industry "rationalization" and development policies and the foreign trade policies of the Japanese government also represent an effort to promote economic growth and shape its directions in specific industries. In a battery of special programs aimed at Japan's steel, electrical power, shipbuilding, machine building, automobile, petrochemical, electronics, and some other industries, the Ministry of International Trade and Industry orchestrated a wide range of supports to encourage rapid development and competitive viability in international markets. Incentives like accelerated depreciation allowances for equipment purchases, special reserve funds for export market development, and deductions from income earned overseas were all designed to foster growth and strong exports. Controls over raw materials and technology imports also permitted allocation of critical materials and processes to industries slated for development, particularly in the 1950s. Mergers were also encouraged to support growth of large firms with healthy market positions, although this is one area of industrial policy where private sector resistance to government programs was particularly pronounced.

Despite the wide range of policy attention to industrial development, the amounts of aid given to different industries varied considerably. The sectors most favored were shipping, power, coal, iron, and steel. Meanwhile the government role in industry "guidance" declined steadily from the early 1950s onward in terms of the share of public resources actually allocated to industry support. Because of this decline and the fact that politics more than economics lay behind the enormous amounts of funding provided the coal and shipping industries in some periods, while highly successful industries like optical goods, consumer electronics and automobiles were given very little in relative terms, not all of the industrial supports can be seen as rational and successful from an economic point of view. Finally, the government did play a direct role in technology development, although actually at a lower rate than occurred in most other major industrialized countries.[8]

In addition to seeking to promote economic growth, the Japanese government followed policies of political and foreign policy consolidation in the first decade of the postwar era. As one example of "consolidation," the 1946 Constitution withstood onslaught by revisionist forces from within the Conservative camp (see Chapter 3). From the late-1950s on, the constitution was gradually accepted by even the conservative forces which had sought its revision, partly because resistance from groups in the opposition camp effectively prevented revision and in part because other higher priority concerns occupied the attention of Japan's leaders. Meanwhile, administrative practices were revised in some cases along lines to conform more to Japan's centralized tradition, a position preferred by many conservatives and bureaucrats. Thus, various of the Occupation reforms were amended in "reverse-course" policies which saw a partial recentralization of police and educational administration and relaxation of the Occupation-period Anti-Monopoly Law.[9] Towns and villages throughout the country were also merged into larger administrative units, following the apparent Japanese principle that "bigger" is more efficient. Both preservation of the constitution and reverse-course policies resulted in a consolidation of polit-

[8] For information on technology funding see Patrick and Rosovsky, op. cit., p. 656. Qualifications regarding the rationality of Japanese industrial policy are based on the discussion in Patrick and Rosovsky, op. cit., Chapter 11 and by the author's own ongoing research, portions of which are reported in United States International Trade Commission, *Foreign Industrial Targeting and its Effects on U.S. Industries, Phase I: Japan* (Washington: USITC Publication 1437, October 1983).

Japan's inventory of industrial policy supports also included protection from foreign imports, particularly in the 1950s and the early 1960s. This system and its subsequent abandonment are discussed in Chapter 11.

[9] The Anti-Monopoly Law was patterned in part after the United States' antitrust legislation, and was relaxed in the 1950s and thereafter as the government encouraged industrial concentration and cartels for the sake of high growth. *See* Kozo Yamamura, *Economic Policy in Postwar Japan* (Berkeley: University of California Press, 1967) and the same author's "Structure Is Behavior," in Isaiah Frank, ed., *The Japanese Economy in International Perspective* (Baltimore: Johns Hopkins University Press, 1975), pp. 67–93.

ical and administrative practices, even though their inspiration came from different political philosophies.

Japan's foreign policies during the 1950s and 1960s also stressed resolution of the problems left over from the country's defeat in World War II, as well as adaptation to the postwar environment, and included expanded participation in the international community, development of a free-world oriented security system, and efforts to expand overseas economic activities. For example, reparations agreements were signed with Japan's former enemies in Southeast Asia, which resulted in shipments of Japanese capital goods to countries which later became important overseas markets. The total cost was roughly one billion dollars.[10] In an event hailed by the domestic press, Japan became a member of the United Nations Organization in 1956, thus becoming a legitimate participant in the most important organization for international cooperation. Membership was especially symbolic for the Japanese, since Japan's departure from the prewar League of Nations in 1933 had been widely condemned in other countries. Japan subsequently became a nonpermanent member of the UNO Security Council in 1958, and joined other international organizations like GATT in the 1950s and 1960s.

National security was a major problem for Japan's political leaders in the 1950s. Anti-Communism was rife in some circles within the conservative movement. Still, various factions in the conservative camp argued stridently over security options. Some conservative leaders favored an expanded domestic defense effort. This position was partially opposed by the Yoshida wing of the conservative movement, and was total anathema to the opposition forces, which held a vital one third of the seats in the Diet after 1955, thus preventing any effective moves toward revision of the constitutional restrictions on military forces. The outcome of the struggle over security options was a decision to establish a limited defense force while continuing to rely on the already established mutual security arrangements between Japan and the United States. A tentative security force had been begun under

[10] The countries to which major reparations payments were made after Japan's independence were Burma, the Philippines, Indonesia, and South Vietnam.

Occupation tutelage after the outbreak of the Korean War. These forces were reorganized and renamed several times, and finally became the tri-service Self-Defense Forces in 1954; from then on, Japan had an established defense effort. However, following the limited forces concept, arms budgets were restricted to around 1 percent or less of the gross national product in most years, the total force size was to be under 300 thousand persons, and main emphasis was placed on technological improvements in arms through a series of plans which articulated major defense goals much in the style of indicative economic planning (see Table 10.4 for examples of Japan's defense plans and related force figures). The limited defense concept that was developed in the 1950s is still viable, even though very recently there have been some expansions of this idea. Currently, Japan ranks ninth in the world in absolute military expenditures because of her considerable wealth as a nation (see Table 10.13), and seventeenth in size of forces because of her large population. Still, defense budgets are modest as are also recruitment levels: in the 1960s, for example, Japan had just under four persons per one thousand in the working-age population in her military forces, in contrast with eleven and twelve persons respectively in Germany and Britain and twenty-five persons in the United States.[11]

Expansion of overseas trade opportunities and support for industries which could contribute to high domestic economic growth and be competitive in some foreign markets were central components of Japan's economic and foreign policies in the 1950s and 1960s. Since Japan needed imported raw materials to fuel her domestic economy, export trade expansion became a goal of policies designed to provide enough foreign exchange to buy raw materials imports. The quest for markets motivated initial moves for economic rapprochement with the People's Republic of China that anticipated political relationships by nearly two decades. Meanwhile, economic dependence on the United States in the form of high levels of trade reinforced political and security ties even while also contributing to strains in the bilateral relationship at times. Meanwhile, a desire to expand foreign markets,

---

11 Gabriel Almond and G. Bingham Powell, Jr., *Comparative Politics: System, Process and Policy* (Boston: Little, Brown, 1978), p. 298.

Table 10.4. *Japanese Defense Plans, 1958–76*

Item (FY)		1st Buildup Plan (1958-60)	2nd Buildup Plan (1962-66)	3rd Buildup Plan (1967-71)	4th Buildup Plan (1972-76)
Self-Defense Official Quota		170,000 men	171,500 men	179,000 men	180,000 men
GSDF					
	Units Deployed Regionally in Peacetime	6 Divisions 3 Composite Brigades	12 Divisions	12 Divisions	12 Divisions 1 Composite Brigade
Basic Units	Mobile Operation Units	1 Mechanized Combined Brigade 1 Tank Regiment 1 Artillery Brigade 1 Airborne Brigade 1 Training Brigade	1 Mechanized Division 1 Tank Regiment 1 Artillery Brigade 1 Airborne Brigade 1 Training Brigade	1 Mechanized Division 1 Tank Regiment 1 Artillery Brigade 1 Airborne Brigade 1 Training Brigade 1 Helicopter Brigade	1 Mechanized Division 1 Tank Brigade 1 Artillery Brigade 1 Airborne Brigade 1 Training Brigade 1 Helicopter Brigade
	Low-Altitude Ground-to-Air Missile Units	—	2 Anti-Aircraft Artillery Battalions	4 Anti-Aircraft Artillery Groups (another group being prepared)	8 Anti-Aircraft Artillery Groups
MSDF					
Basic Units	Anti-Submarine Surface-Ship Units (for mobile operation)	3 Escort Flotillas	3 Escort Flotillas	4 Escort Flotillas	4 Escort Flotillas
	Anti-Submarine Surface-Ship Units (Regional District Units)	5 Divisions	5 Divisions	10 Divisions	10 Divisions
	Submarine Units	1 Flotilla	2 Divisions	4 Divisions	6 Divisions
	Minesweeping Units	—	2 Flotillas	2 Flotillas	2 Flotillas
	Land-Based Anti-Submarine Aircraft Units	9 Squadrons	15 Squadrons	14 Squadrons	16 Squadrons
Major Equipment	Anti-Submarine Surface Ships	57 Ships	59 Ships	59 Ships	61 Ships
	Submarines	2 Submarines	7 Submarines	12 Submarines	14 Submarines
	Operational Aircraft	(Approximately 220 Aircraft)	(Approximately 230 Aircraft)	(Approximately 240 Aircraft)	(Approximately 210 Aircraft)
ASDF					
Basic Units	Aircraft Control and Warning Units	24 Groups	24 Groups	24 Groups	28 Groups
	Interceptor Units	12 Squadrons	15 Squadrons	10 Squadrons	10 Squadrons
	Support Fighter Units	—	4 Squadrons	4 Squadrons	3 Squadrons
	Air Reconnaissance Units	—	1 Squadron	1 Squadron	1 Squadron
	Air Transport Units	2 Squadrons	3 Squadrons	3 Squadrons	3 Squadrons
	Early Warning Units	—	—	—	—
	High-Altitude Ground-to-Air Missile Units	—	2 Groups	4 Groups	5 Groups (another group being prepared)
Major Equipment	Operational Aircraft	(Approximately 1,130 Aircraft)	(Approximately 1,100 Aircraft)	(Approximately 940 Aircraft)	(Approximately 490 Aircraft) (Approximately 900 Aircraft)

Note: Parenthesized numbers of operational aircraft denote total numbers of aircraft including trainers.

The numbers of units from the 1st to 3rd Buildup Plans are as of the end of each plan period.

which led to strong Japanese interest in relationships with many third-world countries, was one of the motives for beginning a Japanese foreign assistance program that resembled at lower levels economic aid efforts by other advanced countries.[12]

THE PERFORMANCE OF THE JAPANESE ECONOMY

Economic performance is one of the best examples of sociopolitical outcomes in postwar Japan, since production levels in the economy reflect a combination of social and economic forces supplemented by political outputs. Japan's economic performance since World War II is also independently important, since it is one of the truly dramatic trends in recent world economic history. Starting with an economy drastically disrupted by World War II and more dependent on certain foreign raw-material sources than that of any other major power, Japan in some years registered the highest annual growth rates ever experienced in the world's major industrial nations. While Japan made major strides in growth before World War II, the performance of the economy in the 1960s was nothing short of phenomenal.

Trends in the gross national product — an estimate of the total value of a country's economic production and services — provide a good beginning point to measure Japan's recent economic success. In 1960 (more or less the beginning of the high growth period) Japan's estimated GNP was $39 billion. By 1978 the GNP figure had reached $963 billion, a twenty-four fold increase over the 1960 figure (see Table 10.5). By 1980 Japan's nominal GNP was believed to be slightly over $1 trillion.[13] As can be inferred from these figures, Japan experienced very high growth rates in some specific years. The peak years in this trend were 1968 and 1969, when 13 percent growth was observed, which

---

[12] Between 1957 and 1970, Japan lent nearly 2 billion dollars to various developing countries under seventy-three separate loan agreements. The credits were used in most cases for specific projects involving shipments of Japanese goods to the destination countries. See Japan Institute of International Affairs, *White Papers of Japan, 1970–71* (Tokyo: 1971), pp. 363–71. By the late 1970s Japan was third, following France and the United States, in total volume of foreign aid being given annually by the advanced nations of the "north" to the poorer nations of the "south." See Foreign Press Center, *Facts and Figures on Japan* (Tokyo: 1980), p. 41.

[13] See explanatory note in Table 11.5 for cautionary information relevant to this estimate.

TABLE 10.5. *Absolute and Per-Capita Gross Domestic Product, Selected Countries, 1960–1978*

| | *Absolute GNP (in billions of US dollars)* | | | |
	Japan	*United States*	*West Germany*	*Great Britain*
1960	39	504	71	72
1965	89	688	115	100
1970	203	992	186	124
1975	498	1,549	421	234
1978	963	2,156	642	315
1980	1,040	2,626	824	519

Per-Capita GDP-GNP (in US dollars)

	Japan	*United States*	*West Germany*	*Great Britain*
1960	458	2,804	1,325	1,358
1963	704	3,142	1,687	1,585
1970	1,961	4,789	3,055	2,198
1975	4,499	7,148	6,781	4,082
1978	8,382	9,880	10,481	5,658
1980	8,902	11,536	13,383	9,280

Source: All figures on absolute GNP are from Keizai Koho Center, "Japan 1981: An Economic Comparison" (Tokyo: 1981), p. 9, and are based on United Nations estimates. 1960–77 per-capita data are from United Nations *Statistical Yearbook,* and 1978 and 1980 per-capita information is taken from Keizai Koho Senta, op. cit. Because of differences in the calculation of GNP and GDP data, cross-time comparisons are not totally valid between the 1960–75 series, which are GDP estimates in the case of the per-capita data, and the figures for 1978 and 1980, which refer to GNP trends. However, important long-term trends are not grossly misrepresented, and cross-national comparisons at each time point are valid. Figures for 1960–75 were also standardized to reflect changing prices across time and changing exchange rates between countries, but those for 1978 and 1980 are probably nominal (i.e., unstandardized for inflation) estimates. Inflation in Japan was considerable between 1975 and 1978, so this was one kind of distorting influence on cross-time comparisons. Also, the increased value of the yen in the late 1970s inflated Japanese figures when converted into dollars, thus leading to some problems for cross-national comparisons in those years relative to earlier periods. The substantial upward movement in both absolute and per-capita figures between 1975 and 1978 is thus a reflection of both real changes as well as shifts in prices and exchange rates.

was a figure dramatically higher than growth rates in other economies in that period.[14]

When the Japanese figures are compared on a per-capita basis with those from other industrialized countries, some of the drama of Japan's economic success can be seen even more clearly (Table 10.5). In 1952, Japan's per-capita GNP was $188, roughly one-twelfth that of the United States and one-half that of West Germany.[15] By 1960, Japanese per-capita GDP had grown to $458, while by the mid-1970s it was well over $4,000 and nearly 60 percent of American and German levels. By 1978, because of changes in currency values, the Japanese figure soared even closer to the levels registered in the United States and West Germany, according to United Nations data (Table 10.5). Some enthusiastic observers even claimed that Japan's economy passed that of the United States in per-capita income sometime in 1978 or 1979, although subsequent information showed this was not the case, with Japanese per-capita GNP remaining slightly below that of the United States throughout 1978–80.[16]

Increases in crude steel production are another excellent indicator of postwar growth in Japan. Japan was unique in the non-Western world before World War II by virtue of its then high levels of industrialization relative to other countries outside of Europe and North America. Japan, which grew dramatically in this period, by the 1930s had built up one of the world's few major industrialized economies. In 1936 Japan's crude steel output was 4.5 million tons. By 1960, at the beginning of the high growth period, the figure for Japan — which no longer included the product of Japan's large steel mills in Manchuria — was 22 million tons. In 1973, Japan reached its peak steel output at 119

[14] The average annual growth rate in Japan in the years between 1963 and 1974 was 8.4 percent. In the United States, annual growth percentages were only 4 percent in these years, and in West Germany the relevant figure was 4.4 percent.

[15] The 1952 figures were shown in Patrick and Rosovsky, op. cit., p. 4; in the same year, per-capita GNP in the United States was $2,181, and in West Germany it was $643.

[16] Ezra Vogel, in *Japan as Number One: Lessons for America* (Cambridge: Harvard University Press, 1979), p. 21, claimed that Japanese per-capita GNP had already surpassed that of the United States, only to be proven wrong by subsequent figures.

million tons. Since then, Japan has ranked third in the world in crude steel behind the United States and the USSR.[17]

Gross domestic product and crude steel figures provide good basic indicators for Japan's overall economic performance. The GDP estimates indicate the general shape of economic growth, and crude steel is the most basic of industrial commodities because of its use in many other industrial products. Still, these general performance figures do not tell the whole story, since quite a bit of Japan's postwar success has been due to the growth of specific industries; in the 1950s and early 1960s these industries included shipbuilding and steel; then later, automobile, electronic, and machine tool industries were added to the list.

The automobile industry is a particularly striking example of Japanese success. In the early postwar era, Japan's automobile production was very small, actually miniscule in comparison with the United States and the large, established automobile-producing centers in Europe. In 1960 Japan produced only 165 thousand automobiles and 308 thousand trucks. By 1970, however, automobile production had increased to just over 3 million units, and by 1980, the figure was actually just over 7 million, which represented a forty-two-fold increase in production over an eighteen-year period. As a result, by the late 1970s, Japan's auto industry was producing at a level which was roughly 60 percent of that in the United States, and in 1980 Japanese production actually exceeded that of its recessed American counterpart.[18]

The dramatic performance of the Japanese economy reflected in industries like steel and automobiles is generally believed to be at least partially attributable to government policy. Tax incentives and other instruments required by key-industry development plans undoubtedly helped facilitate growth by creating favorable conditions for investment in long-term capital improvements in some industries. The steel industry alone went through two major renovation plans in the postwar era and, as a result, has the most modern equipment in the world. In a similar way, the Japanese automobile industry has reached higher levels

[17] In 1980, for example, Japan produced 111 million tons of crude steel, while the United States produced 124 million tons; and the USSR produced 149 million tons. Keizai Koho Center, op. cit., (Tokyo: 1981), p. 21.

[18] The sources are *Nihon Kokusei Zue* (Tokyo: 1979), p. 338, and Keizai Koho Center, op. cit., p. 20.

of automation than industries in other countries because of heavy investments in robots and other types of automated equipment. Investments in improved facilities has in turn facilitated rapid and dramatic increases in labor productivity, resulting in Japan's leading the industrialized world in productivity increases in most recent years. Japanese government development of industrial zones adjacent to deep water ports has also reduced raw materials costs significantly, sometimes to one half of comparable costs in countries like the United States, which are more dependent on land transportation. Finally, the government's control of the banking system facilitated economic growth through maintenance of very low interest rates.

Japanese economic and industrial performance is also due to variables less subject to the direct control of government. Japanese company organization and goals seem to be different from those in the West, apparently more often facilitating corporate emphasis on long-range planning and investment. Labor practices are also different in Japan. Although the image of the Japanese worker as a docile, highly motivated producer may be overdrawn, Japan's culture and its permanent employment system in the large corporation sector and enterprise unions certainly encourage development of workplace discipline and strong company loyalties in many instances. Improved process technologies such as the highly touted "just in time" auto parts supply system have also likely made a big contribution to production efficiency. A very high national savings ratio is of vital importance to capital investment and growth, as was noted earlier, providing the money actually needed for capital expansion. Finally, Japan's highly developed educational system is undoubtedly a major factor encouraging growth. On the supply side, it provides for a high level of literacy and exposure to basic mathematics and science information, thus ensuring a high quality labor force, other things being equal. On the demand side, mass education is one of the many factors in the complex of forces involved in the development of a modern communications system and the related consumer-market development.

JAPANESE HIGH GROWTH AND STRUCTURAL CHANGE

Economic development and the high growth experience in Japan between the late 1950s and the 1970s had profound consequences for Japan's social structure. As the economy grew primarily in the industrial and services sectors, the population of Japan's major urban areas expanded. In 1950 only 25 percent of the population lived in cities over 100 thousand in population; by 1975 the figure had grown to 55 percent through emigration to both regional and large cities.[19] In a related trend, the proportion of people in agriculture declined from 45 percent in 1950 to 12 percent in 1975. Thus, by the mid-1970s Japan had followed the trend in other major industrialized nations toward urbanization and abandonment of agricultural occupations. While Japan's farm sector is still larger than the 3–4 percent of the work force found in Britain and the United States, it did shrink dramatically in size and economic importance in the postwar boom period, falling below 10 percent in the 1980s.[20] A further spinoff of these important population movements and occupational changes was the suburbanization of Japan's major urban areas. In the decade of the 1960s alone, the total population in prefectures such as Chiba and Kanagawa outside of Tokyo, and Hyogo and Osaka outside of urban parts of Osaka and Kyoto, grew by as much as 72 percent.[21] These population movements had profound

---

[19] Some part of this figure is falsely inflated because a large number of new cities were created in the late 1950s by mergers of smaller units. Still, one can examine populations in these newly formed cities and in major established cities and see dramatic evidence of urbanization during the periods in question.

[20] The cited population movements did not denude the rural areas. Rather sons and daughters, and even husbands, went off to work in the cities, while other family members stayed home in many cases. Also, new cities could be found in formerly rural areas with resulting occupation structure changes. Probably one third of Japan's population actually lives today in what were once rural areas, either in actual farm communities or in regional cities and towns that have grown up around them.

[21] The following population data from typical metropolitan and suburban prefectures illustrate the trends we have been discussing (population figures are in millions of inhabitants):

Prefecture	1950	1960	1970	1975
Tokyo	6.3	9.1	11.4	11.7
Saitama	2.1	2.4	3.9	4.8
Chiba	2.1	2.3	3.4	4.1
Kanagawa	2.5	3.4	5.4	6.4
Osaka	3.8	5.5	7.6	8.3
Hyogo	3.3	3.9	4.7	4.9

The source is Prime Minister's Office, *Statistical Yearbook*, various years.

consequences, some of the specifically political results having been mentioned earlier in the discussion of changing electoral trends (Chapter 6). Concentration of more and more of the population in the cities and suburbs also meant that Japan's already high urban population densities became even higher than they had been previously in some areas as more and more high-rise apartments were built. Meanwhile, former rural areas were transformed almost overnight into high-density urban and suburban districts in ways even more dramatic than in Europe or the United States.

A second major consequence of high economic growth occurred in the labor sector. Japan had traditionally been an economy with surplus, underemployed labor in the rural sector and probably even in some urban settings. High growth changed the labor market dramatically and ultimately produced a labor shortage which became noticeable in the late 1960s. The change in the labor market in Japan is hard to trace by using unemployment figures, since these typically disguised hidden unemployment — i.e., people living on farms who had never been employed and who accordingly didn't appear in labor force statistics. However, the effects on wages and incomes induced by labor shortages, union pressures, and other factors were themselves visible and dramatic. In 1968, for example, the average monthly wage in all industries employing more than thirty people in Japan was only $154; one decade later, in 1977, the figure was $818.[22] The gains in comparative wage levels between Japan and other countries were similarly dramatic; as Table 10.6 demonstrates, average wages in Japan were roughly one ninth of those in the United States in the early 1950s, while by the late 1970s they were approximately 80 percent of the American levels. Strong gains were also registered relative to the wage level of other countries, with the result that wages in Japan were higher than those in France, Italy, and Britain by the late 1970s.

The result of changes in Japan's labor market and wage levels, as well as of the sharing of profits with permanent employees by Japan's major companies in good years, was a dramatic increase over time in average family incomes in the employed sector in Japan. In 1965 the average income for households whose head

[22] Source is the same as for Table 11.5.

TABLE 10.6.   *Comparative Wage Levels, 1955 and 1977*

	1955	1977
Japan	100	100
United States	913	122
Germany	202	116
United Kingdom	542	60
France	199	61
Italy	145	53

Source: Japan Federation of Employers' Associations, "Conditions of Labor Economy in Japan" (Tokyo: 1978).

was an employed person was 65 thousand yen per month; in 1978 the same figure had risen to slightly over 300 thousand yen. Even when inflation in prices is considered — the Tokyo consumer price index rose from 443 to 1,224 in this period — a major trend of increase can be seen in Japanese household incomes in these years. Moreover, when these figures are added to a related trend toward redistribution of incomes downward among income groups (Table 10.7), the profound nature of change in both aggregate and shared affluence in Japan can be seen. As general income levels moved upward, more people at the lower levels of the income structure did better, to the degree that some economists

TABLE 10.7.   *Income Distribution in Japan, Selected Years*

Percentage of total income received by persons in:	1939	1955	1972
Lowest quintile	6.3%	6.6%	8.4%
Second quintile	8.0%	11.1%	13.4%
Third quintile	10.2%	15.3%	17.8%
Fourth quintile	20.4%	23.1%	27.2%
Fifth quintile	55.1%	43.9%	38.2%
Top 5 percent	36.8%	17.7%	12.9%
Top 1 percent	20.2%	5.8%	4.6%

Source: Martin Schnitzer, *Income Distribution: A Comparative Study of the United States, Canada, West Germany, East Germany, and Japan* (New York: Praeger, 1972), pp. 224 and 228. Reprinted by permission.

TABLE 10.8. *Household Ownership of Home Appliances and Electronic Equipment in Selected Countries*

	Japan	United States	United Kingdom
Color TV Sets	98%	72%	55%
Refrigerators	99%	99%	75%
Washing Machines	98%	78%	73%

Source: Economic Planning Agency, *Kakei Shohi no Doko* (Tokyo: 1979),
cited by Yoshi Tsurumi in Bradley Richardson and Taizo Ueda, eds., *Business
and Society in Japan* (New York: Praeger, 1981), p. 135. Data are from the
late 1970s, and figures represent proportions of all households which owned
appliances or equipment.

feel that Japan is currently the most egalitarian of the industrial
ized countries with regard to income distribution.

THE BENEFITS OF HIGH GROWTH AND AFFLUENCE

High-growth related changes in the labor market and in wages,
as well as increased household affluence in the rural as well as in
the urban sectors, had some dramatic effects on consumption and
on some aspects of the quality of life in Japan.[23] A series of what
the Japanese have called "booms" in enthusiasm for purchase of
new automobiles, homes, and appliances swept Japan along with
the increases in incomes and purchasing power. As Table 10.8
demonstrates, Japan recently has achieved higher rates of diffusion of some appliances and home electronic equipment than
even the United States, while also surpassing some European
countries in all relevant statistics. More Japanese homes had color
TV sets than any other country for which there is information.
The same was true for washing machines. And more Japanese
homes than British had refrigerators, with the Japanese levels in
this instance being almost identical to the American ones.

By the late 1960s more and more Japanese were also buying
automobiles and individual homes in what came to be known as
the *mai ka* (my car) and *mai homu* (my home) booms. In 1961

[23] Ministry of Agriculture figures show that farm household incomes gradually increased in absolute terms and also relative to urban households. By
1968 farm households were receiving 92 percent of the average incomes received by workers' families. Japan Institute of International Affairs, *White
Papers of Japan*, 1970–71, p. 141.

there were 2,100,000 motor vehicles in Japan; by 1977 the figure was 33 million, a nearly sixteen-fold increase.[24] A large part of the increase resulted from purchases of automobiles by families, athough the number of trucks also increased as the economy needed more and more transport capability. In housing, 233 thousand new private homes were built in Japan in 1960. By 1965, the figure was 377 thousand and by 1976 the total of new homes built in Japan peaked at 712 thousand.[25]

Japan's growing consumer affluence in recent years was also reflected in the field of culture and education. More newspapers were published per population in Japan than in the United States even before the period of Japan's affluence, but recently Japan also surpassed most other major industrialized nations on this indicator of cultural achievement.[26] It is important to realize that the statistics for newspaper publication in Japan do not include a large number of tabloid newspapers, such as exist in countries such as Great Britain, as an inflating factor in newspaper publications data. The Japanese newspapers are also relatively centralized, and thus provide a large amount of national news coverage. One Japanese newspaper, *Yomiuri Shimbun,* has the highest circulation of any newspaper in the non-Communist world, with over 8 million copies being sold each morning throughout Japan, while the second largest newspaper, *Asahi,* produces just over 7 million of its own morning edition. Magazine publication rates are also high in Japan, as is the publication of books; in 1978, 2.6 billion weekly and monthly magazines were published, and slightly over 1 billion books.[27]

Japan has long had a highly developed education system, as mentioned earlier. School attendance has been compulsory through the ninth grade since World War II and was required through the sixth grade before that time. One of the major effects of postwar high growth and affluence has been a sharp increase

[24] *Nihon Kokusei Zue,* pp. 468–469.

[25] Op. cit.. p. 124.

[26] UNESCO, *Statistical Yearbook,* 1977. Japan had 526 newspapers per one thousand persons in the population, and was surpassed only by Sweden which had 572 daily general interest newspapers per one thousand persons.

[27] Foreign Press Center, *Facts and Figures of Japan* (Tokyo: 1980), p. 138. It should be borne in mind that some of Japan's weekly magazines resemble the tabloid press in other countries.

TABLE 10.9. *Changes in Education, Health Care, and Mortality*

	1955	1960	1965	1970	1975	1980
Ratio of high school entrants to middle school graduates	52%	58%	71%	82%	92%	94%
Ratio of college entrants to high school graduates	10%	10%	17%	24%	38%	38%
Nurses (per 100,000 people)	133	129	134	121	179	199
Hospital beds (per 100,000 people)	569	728	881	1015	1040	1099
Mortality rate	7.8%	7.6%	7.1%	6.9%	6.3%	6.2%
Life expectancy (Male)	63.9	65.3	67.7	69.3	72.7	73.4

Source: Mombusho, *Mombu Tokei Yoran, 1981* (Tokyo: 1981), pp. 140–141; Prime Minister's Office, *Japan Statistical Yearbook, 1981* (Tokyo: 1981), pp. 592, 622, and 954; Koseisho, *Kosei Hakusho, 1981* (Tokyo: 1981), p 596.

in the numbers of students attending high school and a virtual explosion of matriculation in junior colleges and colleges (see cross-time trends in Table 10.9). As a result, Japan now ranks third after Canada and the United States in the proportions of the population having already received a college education. Perhaps even more dramatic are the figures for persons who go to college in the appropriate age brackets. In the United States it is 45 percent. Japan is a close second with 38 percent. In contrast, the figure for West Germany is only 20 percent; Germany is representative of the residual elitist educational tradition of other European countries in this regard.[28]

High growth and affluence also had some profound effects on health care, mortality, and the proportion of older people in the Japanese population. Health care facilities measured in very crude statistics on the ratios of nurses and hospital beds to the population (see Table 10.9) increased substantially during the high growth period, as did the number of doctors. Qualitative improvements in diagnosis and treatment were also made in this

[28] *Nihon Kokusei Zue*, p. 492, based on Ministry of Education figures.

period. Because of these changing conditions and other effects of
affluence, such as more heat in homes, improved diets, and better
access to medical facilities, mortality rates declined and life expectancy increased in Japan in recent years. In the mid-1950s,
life expectancy for males was sixty-four years and for females
sixty-eight years; a decade later, it was seventy for males and
seventy-six for females; and in 1980, it was seventy-three for males
and seventy-eight for females. As a result of these changes, the
proportion of the population over sixty years in age grew from
8 percent in 1950 to 12 percent by the mid-1960s, while fore-
casts for the future called for substantially higher ratios of older
people in the population by the end of this century.[29]

NEGATIVE CONSEQUENCES OF GROWTH AND IMMUTABLES

Not all of the spin-offs of high growth in Japan in the 1960s
were positive. Japan is a crowded nation with extremely little
space. Population movement to the cities and development of regional industrial centers in the 1950s and 1960s brought further
concentration to already overcrowded areas. According to the
most recent figures, Japan has 306 persons per square kilometer,
and ranks with Korea, Indonesia, the Netherlands, and Belgium
as one of the most heavily populated places on earth. But as in
all countries, population concentration varies between different
parts of the country. In Hokkaido, which to some people looks
like the American Midwest, there were 70 persons per square
kilometer in 1977. In contrast, in Tokyo prefecture, which is
made up of both a highly urbanized metropolitan district and
some rural and mountainous areas on the periphery, population
density in 1977 was 5,420 persons per square kilometer, a figure
dramatically higher than the national average.[30]

Overcrowding was one major consequence of high growth
about which not very much can be done beyond some further
regional deconcentration of industry and related service centers.
Crowding placed growing pressure on urban transportation facilities and on social capital — roads, parks, sewers, and water

[29] Foreign Press Center, op. cit., p. 24, based on Ministry of Health and
Welfare publications. One estimate predicts that people over sixty-five will
constitute 19 percent of the population by the year 2010. See *Japan Times
Weekly*, September 17, 1983, p. 6.
[30] Op. cit., pp. 38–39 and 71.

mains — which were already inadequate by comparative standards. Crowding has also contributed to widespread pollution problems and housing shortages.

While Japan has one of the best urban rapid transit systems in the world, and made many improvements in train lines in the 1960s and 1970s, urbanization and growth meant no end to overcrowding of trains and long commuting times. Statistics do not really serve as good indicators of this problem. The fact that people living as far as one hour and a half from Tokyo must scramble to get standing space on trains leaving their local stations during the rush hour is better evidence. Roads were much like urban transit; even though Japan's government has spent a great deal of money on highway construction in recent years, Japan's roads are still inadequate in that the proportion of paved roads in Japan ranks substantially below that for other major industrialized countries (see below). Simultaneously, as people moved to the cities and suburbs, Japan's waste disposal and utilities systems were hard put to keep up with demand. Compared with other industrialized countries, Japan lags in sewage disposal facilities: in 1973 only 31 percent of Japanese homes had flush toilets, in contrast with figures above 90 percent in Britain, the United States, France, Sweden, and West Germany. Also, only 27 percent of homes in Japan were connected to sewer lines, whereas the figures for other countries were substantially higher. Obviously, the urban-rural distribution of homes affects these figures somewhat, with conditions in Osaka and Tokyo being much better than the national average.[31] Finally, Japan's cities had relatively little space for parks, and the growth of urban populations brought even lower ratios of park land per-capita than had been the case previously. In 1976, there were only 1.6 square meters of park space per resident in Tokyo, compared to 80 in Stockholm, 46 in Washington, 30 in London, and 19 in New York[32]

Deficiencies in transport and social capital were matched by a growing pollution problem which surfaced in the nation's attention in the late 1960s. With most of its population and all of its industrialized centers concentrated on only 20 percent of its land, Japan by the early 1970s had the highest concentration of indus-

[31] Op. cit., p. 114.
[32] Op. cit., p .103.

trial output and energy use per kilometer in the industrialized world (Table 10.10). The figures were substantially higher than in Europe, which is comparatively crowded, and incredibly higher than in the more sparsely populated United States. Japan actually had severe water pollution problems at earlier times, including even in the nineteenth century. But the painful fact of overcrowding of her urban, industrial districts became particularly obvious by the late 1960s and early 1970s, as high growth brought more factories, cars, and homes to the country's most heavily populated areas and even began to spread the polluting influences to remote parts of the islands through regional industrialization and growth. As trees died and as birds fled the cities and as people suffered from air, water, noise, and even "sunshine pollution" — the shutting off of direct sunlight by construction of high-rise apartments — a myriad of local citizen movements opposed to pollution and regional growth sprung up around the country.

One of the immutables of Japan's physical setting is the shortage of usable land and space. The unfortunate land-population ratio is reflected very directly in pollution problems. It is also at the root of severe overcrowding and astronomical land prices; neither of these problems were new to Japan, but during the high growth period they became much more acute. In 1963, the average dwelling had just under four rooms and a total area of 72.5 square meters (roughly 24 by 27 feet). Thirteen years later there

TABLE 10.10.   *Industrial   Concentration   per   Square   Kilometer,   Selected Countries*

	G.N.P. (10^6 \$U.S.)	Industrial Output (10^6 \$U.S.)	Energy Consumption (10^3 TEP)	Number of Cars
Japan	6.05	1.93	4.12	303
United States	0.32	0.08	0.36	26
United Kingdom	1.04	0.25	1.00	72
France	0.87	—	0.47	47
Italy	0.81	0.20	0.66	72
Sweden	1.67	0.37	1.09	65
Netherlands	3.10	0.58	2.38	138

Source: Data are from OECD reports from 1973–75 and were reported by Frank Upham in Bradley Richardson and Taizo Ueda, eds., *Business and Society in Japan* (New York: Praeger, 1981).

had been only minor changes in the size of homes, although construction of slightly larger homes and shrinkage of family size resulted in more space per person. Whereas each person had a little over 7 square yards of space in 1963, by the mid 1970s the figure had increased to roughly 11 square yards, and by 1980 it was 16 square yards.[33] While this growth was salutory, Japan was still an extremely crowded place by comparative standards, and population pressure on housing was a constant problem. In the early 1970s, land price inflation considerably exceeded general inflation trends. In comparative terms, both land and housing prices were and remain extremely high in Japan. In 1979 one square meter of residential land in Tokyo cost on the average $43 thousand, which was roughly the cost of a typical lot in an expensive suburb in many cities in the United States in the same year. Even in remote areas like the southern island of Kyushu, a square meter in Japan cost roughly $15 thousand. Meanwhile, the cost of houses soared to an average of $61 thousand in 1979; as a result, many married couples were unable to purchase homes until their mid-forties, if indeed they were able to buy them then. Because of the chronic shortage and high cost of homes, demand for public housing in Japan was consistently high despite considerable national and local expenditures on housing over the years. For example, applications for housing units in public projects ranged from eight requests per one vacancy to eighty-five requests for one vacancy in Tokyo in the early 1970s (with the different ratios depending on the cost and type of housing). Housing therefore joins other social capital investments as a major lingering problem for government in Japan.[34]

JAPANESE POLITICAL OUTPUTS 1970–79:
QUALITY OF LIFE AND OVERSEAS ADJUSTMENT

In the 1970s Japan continued to have "cheap government" in comparative terms. In 1978, for example, tax revenues were 24 percent of GNP in Japan. In the same period, revenues in the

[33] Prime Minister's Office, *Japan Statistical Yearbook*, (Tokyo: 1975), p. 431, and (Tokyo: 1981), p. 459.

[34] Foreign Press Center, op. cit., pp. 110–111. Figures on public housing demand in Tokyo are from Japan Institute for International Affairs, *White Papers of Japan*, 1973–74 (Tokyo: 1975), p. 109; the 85:1 ratio between demand and supply occurred with regard to public housing units which were for sale.

TABLE 10.11. *Government Outlays on Social Security Programs, 1960–78*

	1955	1965	1975	1978
Total Budget Outlays (in trillions of yen)	1.0	3.7	20.8	34.3
Social Security and Welfare Outlays (in trillions of yen)	.1	.5	3.9	6.7
(as percent of budget)	11%	14%	19%	20%
Social Insurance Subsidies (as percent of social security budget)	12%	40%	59%	61%

Source: **Prime Minister's Office,** *Japan Statistical Yearbook,* various, and Shinsuke Kishida (ed.), *Zusetsu Nihon no Zaisei* (Tokyo: Toyo Keizai Shinposha, 1978), p. 97. Reprinted by permission.

United States were 28 percent of national product, in Britain they were 37 percent, and in Sweden the figure was 50 percent.[35] Yet a shift in emphasis toward greater public fiscal involvement had occurred: a 6 percent increase in the ratio of taxes to GNP could be seen between 1965 and 1978 as the Japanese government sought to cope with the problems of pollution, urban housing shortages, social capital inadequacies, and an aging population. (Actually portions of programs designed to ameliorate Japan's quality-of-life problems were financed through the FILP. But more budget monies were also spent over time in these funding areas as well as in pump-priming expenditures to combat the mid-1970s recession.)

Nowhere were the changes in fiscal priorities more evident than in outlays on social security and related programs. Whereas the Japanese budget itself increased 34-fold between 1955 and 1978 — the 1955 figure was one trillion yen while expenditures for 1978 were 34.3 trillion — outlays on social security and welfare programs increased nearly 70-fold in the same period (Table 10.11). Within the overall outlays on social programs there were also important internal shifts in emphasis: expenditures on general assistance to the aged increased 121-fold during the period in question, while outlays on social insurance, including government medical insurance contributions, increased a staggering 335-

35 Keizai Koho Center, op. cit., p. 65.

fold. Because of these changes, social insurance expenditures moved from 12 percent of all government social welfare outlays to 61 percent in the 1955–78 period, while the share of social security and welfare programs in the total budget doubled. The ratio of social security and welfare outlays to gross domestic product in Japan also roughly doubled to 13 percent by 1978, in comparison with figures for the 1950s and 1960s. The changes in emphasis on social security and welfare programs in Japan were further reflected in comparative figures on social welfare commitments, even though Japan continued to lag behind the United States and European programs in this area. Net transfer payments were 11 percent of gross national product in Japan in 1978, in contrast to the higher figures of 15 percent for the United States, 22 percent for West Germany, and 26 percent for France. Thus the gap between Japan's social programs and those of some other major industrial nations was narrowing. (In reality, per-capita payments in some program areas in Japan were already more or less equivalent to those in the United States, so that the slight comparative lag in proportions of overall transfer payments to GNP between these two countries reflects in part the still smaller ratio of older people in Japan's population in the 1970s relative to that in the American case.)

There were two causes of the relative increases in social security outlays. Government health insurance programs were expanded in the early 1970s as part of a move toward greater government concern for quality of life and welfare issues, this increase being one example of the new programmatic emphases. Also, the population itself changed in composition, so that more older persons were seeking medical services under the expanded programs. (Inflation was a factor in the overall increase of the budget as well as the increases in social security outlays specifically, and for that reason the expansion of the relative share of social security outlays rather than the absolute increases is emphasized.)

These changes in fiscal program emphases in Japan were made largely without raising tax rates. However, tax revenues and social security contributions did increase substantially in Japan by the 1970s, partly because of higher incomes and partly through hikes in contribution requirements, with the result that combined taxes and social security contributions had reached 24 percent of GDP in Japan by 1978, in comparison with 34 percent in the United States, 38 percent in Germany, and 40 percent in France.[36] Thus, while Japan continued to have "cheap government" in comparative terms, new social commitments were reflected in expanded governmental extraction of economic wealth.

Pollution policy was another example of emphasis on quality-of-life concerns in reaction to the negative spin-offs of high growth. The first governmental responses to pollution problems in Japan were limited and tentative, given the government's commitment in the 1950s and 1960s to growth and industrial expansion. But by the end of the 1960s, as a result of a combination of dramatic pollution cases in the courts, demands by local anti-pollution movements, opposition party and media pressure, increasing bureaucratic concern (from as early as 1965), and probably the sheer size and therefore visibility of the problem, government action on the pollution problem was forthcoming.

In a series of major antipollution laws passed in 1970, the government sought to implement pollution standards that were eventually among the highest in the world in some respects. Also, an agency was created within the Prime Minister's Office in 1971 to implement antipollution measures and deal with other environmental problems at the national level. Even though the accomplishments of Japan's antipollution programs have been uneven, not only have major strides been made in improving air standards, but also water pollution has been ameliorated in some areas.[37]

Quality-of-life problems have been addressed in other ways as well, such as through expanded outlays on public works. The composition of public works outlays actually tells a more accurate story regarding these efforts than levels of overall expenditures on public works, which were designed at times to support growth or stimulate employment as well as provide for social capital improvements.[38] The expenditures on water systems and sanitation

[36] Shinsuke Kishida, *Zusetsu Nihon no Zaisei* (Tokyo: 1978), Toyo Keizai Shinposha, p. 91, and OECD, *Revenue Statistics of OECD Member Countries 1965–79* (Paris: 1980), p. 43.

[37] For a concise discussion of Japan's antipollution measures and their consequences, see the contribution by Frank Upham in Bradley Richardson and Taizo Ueda, eds., op. cit.

[38] Perhaps the term "quality of life" is a misnomer in the Japanese context, since many Japanese programs were designed more to catch up with the

facilities in the national budget are one example of quality-of-life-oriented public-works outlays, although some of these facilities also certainly supported industrial expansion. Budget funding of this category increased from .7 percent of the public works budget in 1955 to 13 percent by 1978. Public housing outlays also increased from 4.5 percent in 1960 to 11 percent in 1978 in response to obvious need. Expenditures on road improvements, which served both industrial expansion and the needs of private vehicle owners, increased in the middle and late 1960s, only to decline in the 1970s under pressure from other categories. As a result of these various outlays, public water service was extended to 89 percent of all homes by 1977 in contrast with only 38 percent in 1955; sewers served 27 percent of all housholds instead of the 1960 figure of 11 percent — a large comparative lag but a major domestic increase — and the proportion of paved roads to all roads increased from 2 percent in 1955 to 37 percent by 1977. However, while the improvements were substantial, Japan still lagged behind most industrialized nations in provision of relevant services and social capital levels, as shown earlier. Moreover, the pressure of population and affluence was so great, that in a few areas conditions in Japan actually declined for a while despite absolute improvements. For example, in 1955, there were 11 meters of paved road for every automobile; by 1971 the space had declined to 6 meters, or slightly more than the length of a car, despite extension of the length of paved roads. However, later road-paving efforts remedied this shortcoming, so that each vehicle now has 32 meters of paved road.[39]

Inflation was a problem in Japan in the 1970s much as it was

---

necessities of life than to improve the quality of life in some highly self-conscious sense. But the term "quality of life" still has international connotations which help communicate what was a real reorientation of Japanese public policies. The stimulus of the progressive local government movement to raising both public and national government awareness of quality-of-life issues should also not be overlooked. In certain cases local governments led the way in social capital improvements or in social program development. *See,* for example, John Creighton Campbell, "The Old People Boom and Japanese Policy Making," *Journal of Japanese Studies* 5 (1979), pp. 321–357.

[39] Figures quoted in this paragraph were taken or calculated from Japan Institute of International Affairs, *White Papers of Japan,* 1973–74 (Tokyo: 1975), Table 1-10-2, Foreign Press Center, *Facts and Figures of Japan* (Tokyo: 1980), pp. 52 and 114, and *Nihon Kokusei Zue* (Tokyo: 1980), p. 468.

elsewhere in the world, and concern for dampening rising prices augmented other forces for change in government economic priorities. Domestically induced pressures on prices were present during the high growth era because of stimulated demand. The oil crisis of 1973 added enormously to whatever secular domestic forces for inflation already existed. As a result, very high inflation rates were registered in 1973 and subsequent years, as can be seen from Table 10.12. Inflation in Japan was especially dramatic in 1973–74 after the first oil shocks but abated somewhat in response to restrictive government monetary policies in 1973–75 and to other factors. Still, structural pressures for wage increases from Japan's government employee unions, wage demands in the industrial sector, and other forces continued to push prices upward; moreover, government outputs were only temporary palliatives for the inflation problem, as stagnation set in and fiscal and monetary expansion became the policy after 1975. As a result of the relatively high inflation rates in Japan throughout the mid-1970s, Japanese government economic policy outputs in this period shifted away from primary concern for long-term growth to a much greater preoccupation with price controls and management of business cycles.

Indicative economic planning continued in Japan even though the four plans from the mid-1960s on came to stress economic stability and quality of life as much as or more than absolute economic growth. However, the Japanese economy still grew in most years in real GDP terms, even though growth rates in the 1970s were considerably lower than those of the 1960s. Meanwhile, foreign trade, which had prospered during the high growth period, continued to flourish in the 1970s. In 1955 Japan's total foreign

TABLE 10.12. *Annual Increases in Consumer Prices in Selected Countries, 1973–78*

	1973–74	1974–75	1975–76	1976–77	1977–78
Japan	30%	18%	16%	16%	8%
United States	13%	12%	8%	9%	12%
Great Britain	20%	36%	31%	35%	21%

Source: United Nations, *Monthly Bulletin of Statistics,* May 1979. Percentages are increases in the consumers' price index relative to the previous year.

commerce was 4.4 billion dollars. By 1970 foreign trade had grown to 38 billion dollars, and in 1978 the figure was 177 billion dollars. Japan's share of total world trade simultaneously increased from around 3 percent in 1960 to 6 percent in 1970. However, Japan's share of world trade was still just 7 percent in 1980 after inflation in oil prices and enormous growth in the value of petroleum trade both changed the structure of world commerce and depressed markets in other economies.[40] Japan's trade success was predicated both on internal growth, which increased demand for both producer and consumer imports, and on external market conditions in which some Japanese products did exceedingly well.

The long-term growth of Japan's foreign trade was, however, a mixed blessing. While expanded trade levels permitted Japan to import the raw materials necessary to fuel high growth and satisfy new food preferences among the Japanese population, and also to pay its huge oil bills in the 1970s, the success of Japanese products like color television sets, automobiles, and high quality steel produced adverse reactions in other countries and created problems for the government. At several points in the 1970s, Japan became involved in intense disputes with the United States and other countries as businessmen and politicians abroad accused Japan of maintaining import barriers. Because of trade liberalization Japan had reduced or eliminated most of its quotas and tariff barriers, and accusations from abroad focused on alleged nontariff barriers like inspection procedures and government procurement policies in this period. In some cases, as in textiles, steel, and color television sets, foreign resistance resulted in government-led reductions of exports from Japan. Elsewhere, as in the United States-Japan automobile crisis of 1980–82, similar results were obtained. And, in some cases, notably in the steel, aluminum, chemical fertilizer, synthetic textiles, and shipbuilding industries, the government also had to develop antirecession policies to deal with industrial slowdowns resulting from either declining world markets (coupled with slowdowns in domestic demand in some cases as overall growth rates declined), overseas competition from newly industrializing nations like Korea and Taiwan, increased imported energy costs, or politically imposed "voluntary" trade reductions

40 *Nihon Kokusei Zue* (Tokyo: 1980), pp. 140 and 171.

on Japanese exports. In effect, the government became involved in energy cost reduction and other remedial programs involving labor force and facilities reductions, promotion of antirecession cartels, and provision of special recovery loan funds in efforts to restructure industrial priorities in industries which, according to MITI, employed one out of every five of Japanese workers.

Although Japan has always been heavily dependent on foreign raw materials to supply its industries, many have marveled at Japan's economic success in the face of such a pronounced native shortage of industrial minerals and energy sources. In recent years, for example, Japan has imported 99 percent of her iron ore needs, 92 percent of copper requirements, 78 percent of her lead inputs, and 99.8 percent of her oil needs, which supplied about three fourths of Japan's overall energy requirements.[41] Japan's foreign trade policy has long been oriented toward securing stable sources of foreign raw materials and maintenance of export levels sufficient to pay for these needed imports. As the Japanese economy grew, and imports of ever larger volumes of foreign raw materials became necessary, the concern for having secure foreign sources of supply accelerated. The oil crisis brought further realization of the importance of secure sources of supply, and in a symbolic, as well as real, shift in priorities the Ministry of Foreign Affairs announced in 1973 that henceforth raw materials supply stabilization would be a guiding force in Japan's overall diplomacy. In a related series of events, Japan signed agreements with the USSR on (a) natural gas development in the Yakutsk basin in 1973, (b) development of Siberia in 1974, and (c) rights to offshore oil deposits near Russian Sakhalin in 1975. Similarly, Japan made loans to oil-rich Abu Dhabi, lent money for development of natural gas in Indonesia, and signed an economic cooperation agreement with Iran, followed later by a government-supported oil refinery project in that country. Division of rights over offshore oil deposits in the East China Sea and elsewhere subsequently became major issues between Japan and the Republic of Korea, the People's Republic of China, and the Republic of China government on Taiwan as all of the countries in the Northwest Pacific realized the urgency of their energy needs.

[41] Keizai Koho Center, *Some Data About Japanese Economy in Comparison with Foreign Countries* (Tokyo: 1979).

The developing economic ties between Japan and the Soviet Union were symbolic of the extent to which economics typically operates as a major determinant of Japan's foreign policy. Security and defense were not ignored. Japan continued her mutual security ties with the United States, supported development of a technologically advanced military program, and recently even permitted modest increases in defense expenditures. Still, Japan continued to spend much less on defense in the 1970s and early 1980s than other large nations (Table 10.13). And like other free-world countries that have also developed defense programs to meet perceived Communist bloc threats to their security, Japan simultaneously endeavored to expand its trade with Asian countries in the Socialist bloc as well as with other countries. In the context of shifts in the world environment and pursuant to Japan's chronic quest for markets and sources of raw materials, Japan's relations with her largest Communist neighbor, the People's Republic of China, improved markedly in the 1970s. After the United States renewal of its relationship with mainland China in 1971–72, the Japanese government under Prime Minister Kakuei Tanaka initiated its own policy of rapprochment. This

TABLE 10.13. *Japanese Defense Expenditures Compared with Other Countries, 1977*

Country	Rank	Absolute Expenditures	Per-Capita Expenditures	Expenditures as: % GNP	Expenditures as: % Budget
USSR	1	$127 billion	$ 492	11-13	
United States	2	$113 billion	$ 523	6	24
China (PRC)	3	$23-28 billion			
West Germany	4	$16 billion	$ 263	4	23
France	5	$14 billion	$ 256	4	20
Great Britain	6	$11 billion	$ 201	5	11
Iran	7	$7.9 billion	$ 227	12	16
Saudi Arabia	8	$7.5 billion	$1,005	18	24
Japan	9	$6.1 billion	$ 54	1	6
Italy	10	$4.4 billion	$ 78	3	8
Egypt	11	$4.3 billion	$ 112	37	25
Israel	12	$4.2 billion	$1,178	35	32

Source: Shinsuke Kishida (ed.), *Zusetsu Nihon no Zaisei* (Tokyo: Toyo Keizai Shinposha, 1979), p. 241. Reprinted by permission.

resulted in a normalization agreement signed in Peking in the fall of 1972 — which brought inevitable problems in political relations with the Nationalist government on Taiwan even though Japan's profitable trade with that area continued. Subsequently, trade and air agreements were also signed with the People's Republic, official visits at various levels were exchanged, and in 1978 Japan signed a peace treaty with Peking. Throughout this period and later Japan and the People's Republic increased their mutual trade as China sought materials and assistance for economic development and as Japan negotiated for Chinese oil and coal.

The quest for resources and trade motivated more than closer economic ties with oil and gas producing nations, and exploration of mutual economic interests between Japan and its Communist neighbors, the People's Republic of China and the USSR. In the 1970s Japan participated in several conferences and international agreements on sharing of sea resources. Domestically, a variety of programs were put into force as a response to the energy crisis and rise in oil prices. Like other countries Japan began to explore other energy possibilities involving both old and new technologies and promoted domestic conservation through the customary instrument of long-term planning. In the decade of 1975–85, hydroelectric facilities were to be nearly doubled, nuclear power facilities were to increase nearly five fold in total capacity, domestic coal and oil production from relatively limited reserves would increase slightly, and liquid natural gas production and imports would increase, as would also imports of coal. However, even if all of these measures succeed, which is not certain, Japan would be importing more oil in 1985 than she did in 1975, meaning that supplies of oil must be available, a situation which Japan cannot control except through cooperative foreign policies toward producing countries. Japan must also export enough to pay for needed energy imports — the cost of crude oil imports alone rose from $2 billion in 1970 to $23 billion in 1977 — as well as for other raw material necessities.[42] Export expansion will consequently be a continuing necessity for Japan even though the world opportunities for trade growth in

[42] From Japan Institute of International Affairs, *White Papers of Japan*, 1971–72 (Tokyo: 1973), p. 67, and *Nihon Kokusei Zue* (Tokyo: 1980), p. 152.

many industrialized economies may shrink through intensified product competition and economic stagnation. Moreover, though Japan uses substantially less energy than most other industrialized countries — Japan used roughly three-quarters as much energy per capita in 1976 as did Britain and France, one-half as much as West Germany, and one-third as much as the United States — Japan's energy dependence will still strongly influence economic trends and government policy outputs for the foreseeable future, just as it has in the recent past, and in earlier periods, of Japan's modern century.[43]

GOVERNMENTAL OUTPUTS AND SOCIETAL OUTCOMES

We have seen that Japan's recent experience illustrates clearly the interaction between government policies and economic outcomes, and outcomes and subsequent public policies. In the 1950s, and even more in the 1960s, Japan stressed economic growth through supportive policies including "cheap government." Government policies and other factors resulted in Japan's having extremely high rates of economic growth in the 1960s, which in turn brought affluence to many Japanese as well as important changes in Japan's urbanization levels and population age structure. When the negative spin-offs of high growth became clear in the form of overcrowding, high land prices, inadequate social capital, and enormous pollution problems, the Japanese government changed its priorities to favor more attention to quality-of-life issues. This series of events and other related trends brought important shifts in emphasis on welfare program outlays and other budgetary measures, and made Japanese government somewhat more expensive in terms of budget expenditures than had been the case earlier — although still substantially cheaper than government in Europe and the United States. Meanwhile, the oil crisis produced enormous problems for resource-dependent Japan in the form of both a concern for present and future energy supplies and, at times, galloping inflation. As Japan looks to the future, government outputs will probably be concerned with

[43] From Japan Press Center, op. cit., p. 71. This observation will hold true even should petroleum prices drop further, although a return to cheap oil (which seems improbable at this time) would obviously reduce some of the intense pressure on Japan.

energy, price stability, limited growth, and international competitiveness (even though current pressure from abroad has actually led MITI to stress import promotion.) While the Japanese government has shown itself adaptive to new problems, it remains to be seen how far new government outputs can be developed to meet problems which are in some cases increasingly out of its control. It is also clear that the cost of government will be a major problem for Japan as in other countries. In the 1970s Japan became dramatically dependent on deficit financing through sales of government bonds, and by the end of the decade the per-capita national debt was close to that of the United States. By the late 1970s and early 1980s, tax increases and administrative reform were being considered as measures to decrease deficit financing dependency and to pay for the increased debt interest load. This trend, in turn, means that Japanese government will probably have strained financial resources in the future just at a time when it must deal with emerging problems like the increased welfare load imposed by an aging population and the need to develop new energy sources. Just as for other industrialized nations of the world, Japan's problems for the latter 1980s appear awesome.

At the beginning of this chapter it was hypothesized that Japan might take a more interventionist stance politically than some other countries because of its tradition of a strong bureaucracy and the recency of its government-led modernization experience. In reality, the picture is rather complicated. We have seen that Japan spends less on government through collection of tax revenues than some other major industrial powers, in part because cheap government was seen as a means to rapid capital accumulation and high economic growth, so that Japan appears less interventionist in certain quantitative terms than some other industrialized countries. Still, Japan had indicative economic planning, while many other societal problems were also approached by detailed government planning and intervention to a degree not found in many Western industrialized nations. Also, Japan's "second budget," the Fiscal Investment and Loan Program, results in a substantial increase in government's economic role even though this program does not depend on tax revenues. In addition, the Japanese government appears to regulate as much economic and social activity as other free governments. Like European nations, but unlike the United States, most railways, a substantial porition of air transport, and all telecommunications are owned by the government or run by government corporations, as are also the salt and tobacco industries. Clearly, in qualitative terms, Japan is more like the interventionist European countries even though its lower outlays on social welfare and some social capital facilities give a contrary appearance.

CHAPTER 11

The Capability of the Japanese Political System

THE PAST CHAPTERS have discussed the institutions, political parties, and groups which are the main structures of Japan's contemporary political system. It has also been shown how these central political actors and structures perform in important functional arenas and core political processes. It is equally important to examine and evaluate how the Japanese political system performs as a whole entity; that is, how capable it is of effective governance. Is the Japanese political system legitimate in the eyes of the public and important political groups? Has the Japanese government been capable of extracting sufficient political resources to finance its own needs and meet the costs of its commitments? Has Japanese political leadership been able to direct authoritatively the country's economy in ways which produce positive outcomes? Have various Japanese administrations been able to resolve recurring political issues and basic societal problems? Finally, has the Japanese political system been stable in the postwar era yet capable of adapting to new challenges? And will it be able to meet current and future problems and needs as these emerge?

These core questions of political system capability will be addressed in this chapter. In so doing evidence cited earlier on political system performance in different functional areas will be

* Bradley M. Richardson

424

utilized, this time evaluating this performance against various normative measures of capability or effectiveness. Because a new set of questions will be addressed while still using evidence already provided about various dimensions of Japanese politics, this chapter will serve simultaneously as a critique of Japanese governmental performance and as a summary of many of the main points of earlier chapters.

CAPABILITY AS LEGITIMACY

Legitimacy has been a concern of students and practitioners of government for many centuries. Generally the term means elite and popular acceptance of ongoing political institutions and practices. Legitimacy can also be seen as the absence of major anti-system movements or parties. Governments are considered legitimate when they have the support and the trust of their citizens and when no important political group is dedicated to the overthrow and elimination of the present system. Typically, at any time the degree of legitimacy a particular government and political system enjoys is relative — systems are more or less legitimate — and legitimacy varies over time.

Postwar Japanese government has enjoyed a fairly high degree of legitimacy, yet there are many countercurrents in attitudes and behavior which indicate some ambiguity in contemporary patterns of legitimacy. There is also some difficulty in precisely measuring legitimacy.

Mass political attitudes toward the institutions of contemporary government are one clue to the state of legitimacy in Japan. In their answers to simple questions about approval of democracy and acceptance of the importance of democratic political processes such as elections and institutions such as political parties, contemporary Japanese seem to support their political system. Democracy is seen by pluralities as probably the best form of government, and most people who answer these kinds of political culture questions endorse the idea that elections are essential to popular government and that political parties are an important guardian of democratic rights.

The Japanese are also active participants in ongoing political processes in at least some frames of reference, and many observers of politics feel that participation is a valid indicator of acceptance of the legitimacy of these processes. Voting levels are high in

Japan relative to those in some other countries including the United States, interest in some kinds of media accounts of politics — a kind of pseudoparticipation — is relatively high in comparative terms, and some forms of campaign participation approximate levels found in other industrialized democracies. However, the Japanese talk about politics less often than some of their counterparts in similar foreign democracies, and even their media interest and exposure suffer in comparison with people in other industrialized countries at times. If participation means acceptance, Japanese rate higher in the easier forms of participation such as voting than in the more difficult and time-consuming areas of face-to-face political communication and even the more difficult forms of media involvement, such as reading about politics in newspapers. Moreover, Japan's comparatively high levels of voting and campaign participation probably reflect the effects of mobilizational efforts by candidates and groups and duteous attitudes toward civil obligations to a marked degree, so that the actual meanings for legitimacy of the voting act are less than completely clear. Finally, while Japanese citizens approve of the role of political parties in the abstract, their overall levels of party support are lower than those in many other advanced democratic systems, and disenchantment with all parties has been a growing phenomenon among the younger members of the electorate. Consequently, the implications that can be drawn from these complex patterns of participation, support, and motivation are somewhat ambiguous. Japanese do participate in politics in important levels but for complicated reasons and more often in easy forms of behavior than in more time- and energy-consuming participatory acts.

Mass attitudes of trust and cynicism toward political regimes and satisfaction and dissatisfaction with governmental performance provide still another indicator for the state of acceptance of a particular political system. As mentioned earlier, young Japanese tend to be very cynical toward political leaders and institutions and in increasing degrees as they advance toward adulthood. Comparative studies also show typically that Japanese youths are more dissatisfied with the performance of their government than young people in both other industrialized systems and third-world countries. While some of the cynicism and dissatisfaction prevalent among young Japanese may be a manifestation of "pop" alienation, it does not indicate a mood of acceptance of government;

moreover, massive attitudinal disenchantment among Japanese youth is paralleled by fairly widespread distrust in national politics among adults in contemporary Japan. Although levels of political cynicism in Japan were surpassed in some years by those in the United States after the American Watergate experience, in general Japan ranks higher than many other industrialized nations in the amount of citizen dissatisfaction with ongoing politics and in distrust of the motivations of political leaders and the degree of responsiveness inherent in national political processes.

The frequency of distrust and dissatisfaction in national government in Japan appears in turn to be related to a more general value cleavage in contemporary Japanese life. People with traditional attitudes toward a wide variety of institutions and situations tend to indicate more allegiance to government in the form of greater trust and satisfaction than do persons who espouse more modern social viewpoints. Traditionalists are generally older people, residents of rural areas and graduates of elementary schools. Thus it might be assumed that trust in government, and even satisfaction with political performance, is the product of less critical, duteous orientations toward government inculcated at earlier points and correspondingly consonant with older views of appropriate morality and social behavior. In contrast, persons with modern attitudes and manifesting cynical attitudes toward government are usually younger, more urban, and generally higher in educational attainment. Apparently exposure to schooling in the postwar democratically oriented system encourages higher levels of political idealism, which in turn lead to pessimism and frustration when normative expectations and political performance are compared. This is a rather simplistic explanation of the complex learning and imitation behavior embodied in cultural diffusion processes. But the link between cynicism and modern attitudes is a significant one, just as the relationship between more traditional attitudes and political trust is important.

So far it has been suggested that Japanese display acceptance of the government in the form of formal attitudes, yet simultaneously reject the political system by showing at times marked distrust in political leaders and institutions and fairly substantial levels of political dissatisfaction and rejection of political party affiliations. What these contrasts mean is far from self-evident. There are contradictions in most countries between formal attitudes toward government, which are typically measured by interview questions that tap ideas learned in school courses on civic "ethics" and therefore which represent expressions of current societal ideals, and the more reality-oriented attitudes identified in questions about trust-distrust and satisfaction-dissatisfaction. Still, the gaps between formal acceptance and distrustful rejection in Japan are fairly large, which could mean that there is a reservoir of discontent which could be tapped by antisystem movements at some point in the future. And if it is remembered that participation in politics indicates somewhat ambiguous patterns of meaningful involvement, it cannot really be said that the overtly measurable indicators of mass political legitimacy are strong in contemporary Japan.[1]

Measured against the ambiguity in popular attitudes toward current institutions and political processes, the patterns of contemporary political allegiances of Japanese citizens indicate a more optimistic view of popular political legitimacy. It is true that fewer Japanese than Americans and British are psychological followers of Japan's major political parties, which could, like the participation tendencies, indicate only partial politicization into supportive frameworks. Yet it is also important to observe that very few Japanese support parties which could be seen in any sense as antisystem movements. Actually, there are no antisystem parties in the literal sense in contemporary Japan. No party now advocates a radical change in Japan's basic political institutions, at least in the sense of arguing for an alternative to parliamentary democracy. But there is one party which had some kind of broad antisystem orientation in the past — this is the formerly revolution-oriented Japan Communist Party. Although the Japan Communists have not explicitly advocated institutional change in recent years, still, they at times advocated dogmas or ideas which could have been a crystallizing point for mass antisystem resentments of a broadly focused kind. Moreover, growth in their popular support in the past decade might be read as an indicator of some concrete manifestation of the high levels of political cynicism found among contemporary Japanese. Actually, an attitudi-

[1] See Bradley M. Richardson, *The Political Culture of Japan* (Berkeley and Los Angeles: The University of California Press, 1974), Chapters 2 and 3, for evidence relative to the gap between formal acceptance of institutions and parties and pessimistic evaluations of their actual performance.

nal link can be found in survey data on the relationship between cynicism and party support which would support this inference. Still, survey data also show that substantial majorities of the Japanese electorate dislike the Communists and would never consider voting for them. So even the growth in support for this "party of antisystem potential" is by all indicators a limited phenomenon, and one that is even at best a weak and somewhat ambiguous indication of antisystem expressions, given the nature of this party's more recent moderation in public appeals.

There is also some evidence from attitudes toward political protest and actual protest behavior which indicates real limits in the potential for meaningful antisystem behavior in contemporary Japan. On the one hand, truly massive organized political demonstrations are a commonplace in Japan. Student organizations were able to turn out large numbers of members and followers in the past on such issues as the U.S.-Japan Security Treaty, the Vietnam War, and student rights. Antiwar and antinuclear groups have also mobilized many very large demonstrations and meetings, while labor unions and farmers' groups produce regular demonstration extravaganzas in Tokyo's government quarter whenever issues affecting their interests or ideologies emerge. Still, these demonstrations have a strong element of institutionalization despite their often discordant tune: they are in many cases ritualized behavior led by groups which strongly support Japan's current institutional arrangements however strongly they may oppose the conservative government and its policies or however intensely they may feel regarding their own interests and points of view.[2]

At the attitudinal level, the evidence on protest participation and protest approval indicates that few Japanese have actually participated in protest movements, even though more persons would consider protesting than have actually participated. Moreover, although the protest activities of major groups like unions

---

[2] For a discussion of the institutionalized nature of much demonstration activity in Japan see Bradley M. Richardson, "Movements and Political Stability," in Bradley M. Richardson and Taizo Ueda, eds., *Business and Society in Japan* (New York: Praeger, 1981), pp. 179–184.

It is also important to remember that most popular movements in the postwar era, and especially the larger and more visible ones, have been leftist in orientation. Even though the extreme left wing has become much smaller in recent years, it is probably still larger than the extreme right wing, which represents a major change from Japan's prewar history.

and farmers are perceived by the citizenry as expressions of legitimate grievances, at the same time, poll data usually indicates abhorrence for use of violence in demonstrations and condemnation of the violent tactics of some movements. These tendencies are somewhat similar to the attitudes of other electorates on these kinds of issues. Yet in the Japanese case they ring especially true as indicators of overall tendencies in society, for the simple reason that there have been remarkably few instances of political violence in recent years in Japan in comparison with the United States and Europe.[3] Underlying this important aspect of Japanese political life is undoubtedly an overall tendency toward enhanced social control, as noted by so many observers of Japanese society, which is expressed in a true conservatism and conventionalism in attitudes toward extreme behavior or extreme departures from contemporary political formulae.

Japanese government is therefore relatively legitimate, in part because of the strength of pressures for conformity in Japanese society and because of the degree of ensuing social control that discourages widespread extremism and violence. Some of the same conventionalism may lead to rejection of the Japan Communist Party, the only significant party having a nuance of an antisystem potential at any time in the postwar era. At the same time, Japan has been a society which has experienced very rapid social change, a fact which is expressed in contrasting values endorsing both tradition and modernity, which themselves encourage attitudes of alternatively political trust and legitimacy among some social groups and political distrust and dissatisfaction elsewhere. Thus, mass attitudes regarding the legitimacy of the contemporary political system are somewhat ambivalent as the result of rapid social and value change, even though the overall homogeneity and conventionality of Japanese society supports general acceptance of contemporary political forms and solutions.[4]

---

[3] Even though Japan's Red Army Faction has become internationally famous, much of its terrorism has been conducted outside of Japan. In addition, no postwar Japanese prime minister has been assassinated or been the target of an assassination attempt (although a leading Socialist politician was assassinated in 1961), and Japan has not had waves of terrorist kidnappings such as have occurred in Europe.

[4] Remember that system distrust in Japan may be more regime than institution oriented, because of long rule by just one political movement.

Japan's overarching social homogeneity has also meant that there have not been the kinds of social cleavages which have divided some European societies so sharply as to undermine the efficacy and therefore the legitimacy of government. Japan is religiously and ethnically homogeneous by and large, and neither ethnicity nor religion is a major political issue, in addition to the fact that levels of religiosity are low and that internicine religious conflict is itself subdued. Furthermore, in contrast with many countries, political conflict between social classes has been relatively limited. Even though class-based issues have been a constant theme in party differences, social class has not been a major divide which promoted recurring crises and large-scale mass movements of the variety seen in various European countries within the past century.[5] Indeed, the only political issue which has seriously challenged the legitimacy of Japan's postwar political institutions was the debate over the constitution itself, which was most prominent in the 1950s and early 1960s. And, while there were in this experience differences on certain basic aspects of Japan's postwar political formula, such as the role of the emperor, the status of the Upper House, and the legitimacy of the antiwar clause, much of the basic document and related institutions were excepted from controversy. From this it can be concluded that postwar Japan's institutions have been accepted in general by the elite political actors. There is further evidence in support of this positive view of institutional legitimacy at the elite level in the relatively strong commitment to keeping parliamentary processes alive shared by all political parties even in the face of periodic stalemates, and in the totally peaceful methods of succession of political executives throughout the postwar era (itself something of a contrast with the more turbulent 1930s).

CAPABILITY AS EXTRACTION OF
RESOURCES AND AUTHORITATIVE DIRECTION

The legitimacy of a democratic political system and government is based on its acceptance by a nation's citizenry and on its

---

[5] See Scott C. Flanagan and Bradley M. Richardson, "Japanese Electoral Behavior: Social Cleavages, Social Networks and Partisanship," *Contemporary Political Sociology Series* 2 (Number 06–024), 1977, for evidence on the low saliency of class attitudes in Japan and citations of related explanatory literature.

support by important political parties and groups. Some writers on politics have even seen legitimacy as providing a flow of energy which enables governments to do their work effectively.[6] Although measurements of legitimacy are at times elusive, support for governments is still very important as it enables them to ask groups and individuals to obey laws and regulations or to behave in certain ways desired by the government.

However, governments and political systems are not altogether passive in the relationship that exists between them and private groups and citizens. Governments and their leaders affect the degree to which they can command allegiance through their own use of political skills and manipulation of the overall political forces with which they must deal. If political leaders are skillful, they are able to rule effectively and extract resources from the economy for allocation toward political ends.

Measured against this standard — the ability to extract resources and rule authoritatively — the Japanese government has demonstrated fairly high levels of capability in comparison with many other governments in the world. It has been able to extract an adequate amount of resources from the private sector in the form of taxes to support governmental commitments in some periods, and it has used authority creatively for economic development and regulation of private sector behavior at times. Yet the record of Japanese government is not completely unblemished in this area of capability, and important qualifications to this general picture must be noted.

Several factors contributed to this satisfactory level of extractive capability. Early decisions to limit expenditures on defense and social programs were particularly important, while a rapidly expanding revenue base contributed substantially to Japan's fiscal viability once economic growth began to accelerate. The choice in the early 1950s to establish only a modest national defense effort meant that one of the major burdens on fiscal resources common to many developed and less developed countries was dramatically limited in the Japanese case. Instead of spending as much as 4 or 5 percent of gross national product on military forces, as is the typical case in most other large industrialized nations, Japan

[6] See David Easton, "An Approach to the Analysis of Political Systems," *World Politics* 9 (1957), pp. 383–400.

made the decision to restrict its outlays to 1 percent or less of gross national product. Simultaneously, Japan did not choose to develop its public social welfare system beyond early postwar levels until the late 1950s, and even much later where certain programs were concerned. In the earlier part of the postwar era, conservative governments felt that major portions of Japan's social welfare needs should be met privately within companies or through the trickle-down effects of economic growth. Commitment to expansion of public social security programs came later.

Both reduced military outlays and lower expenditures on social programs than were typical for most other advanced industrialized democracies meant that Japan had a lower fiscal burden in the 1950s and 1960s than would have otherwise been the case. At the same time, as Japan's economy began to grow by the end of the 1950s and during the high growth era of the 1960s, the government was able to extract rapidly increasing revenues without raising taxes. In a process similar to the effects of rapid industrialization elsewhere, the tax base increased substantially via economic growth. Expenditures on roads, harbors, and other kinds of industrial support systems by necessity increased as part of the overall infrastructure expansion which accompanied high economic growth. Typically, this did not pose problems for national expenditures because of the lower outlays required in other potentially competing areas and use of funds from non-revenue sources such as the Fiscal Investment and Loan Program. Although this is oversimplifying what was at times a complex process of adjustment of fiscal priorities, it is fair to say that Japan's extractive capability in the 1950s and 1960s was adequate for the country's assessed public expenditure needs. Indeed, in certain senses it was more than adequate, as a series of tax cuts during the 1960s serves witness.

This seemingly rosy scenario came to an end in the 1970s. Economic growth slowed down after the 1973 oil shock, and the government was faced simultaneously with a much slower expansion of its tax base plus a perceived need to stimulate the economy through higher expenditures on public works. In addition, a decision to expand Japan's public social security outlays in the late 1950s and commitments to expansion of other public social programs later began to place much heavier burdens on budgets than had hitherto been the case. The simple effect of increased programmatic commitments was amplified in some years by very rapid inflation, which increased the costs of pension and other programs. Moreover, as Japan's population began recently to age rather rapidly and fewer families were supporting their older members within their homes than was the case in the past, the demand for social programs also increased.

Faced with both slowdowns in the expansion of its revenue base and new expenditures, the Japanese government needed substantially more revenue by the mid-1970s than it was currently receiving. Rather than raise taxes, a short-run solution was found in deficit financing through sales of government bonds to financial institutions. By the end of the 1970s this fund-raising method was obviously becoming increasingly costly to the Japanese government, particularly in terms of current and anticipated interest payments. Reacting to increasing interest costs and the enormous absolute size of the government debt, Japan's government began to consider increasing taxes by means of a proposed value-added tax. However, because of intraconservative party disputes over this policy and opposition from other parties and interest groups, the plan to introduce this new revenue source was abandoned. Although later some adjustments to corporate tax laws were made which produced relatively minor increments of increased revenue, recent Japanese governments have been loathe because of obvious political costs to consider the issue of increasing taxes in any substantial way and have considered alternative techniques to promote fiscal balance, such as by planned reductions in the size of the civil service and other kinds of proposed administrative reform.

Since Japanese governments were unable or unwilling to make adjustments to tax laws sufficient to prevent continued heavy deficit financing of budgetary outlays, deficits were running at roughly 30 percent of the budget in 1979–80. Therefore, it cannot be said that the Japanese government has shown itself capable of extracting sufficient resources to finance its commitments in recent years. While many governments throughout the world are experiencing similar fiscal problems, the Japanese case has been a more extreme example of rapidly increasing deficit financing than has been typical abroad. Thus, while many governments are currently facing an "extraction crisis," the situation in Japan is probably more acute than that in some other countries.

Clearly, the Japanese government has been relatively more capable of extracting sufficient resources for its needs in some periods than in others. In some other areas of state activity, the use of governmental authority to regulate private behavior has been more consistently effective in terms of at least gross indicators. Like all governments, Japanese public authorities regulate extensive areas of private group, corporate, and citizen behavior. As reported in an earlier chapter, regulation accounts for a great deal of the Japanese government's legislative activity. While it cannot be determined precisely whether or not the Japanese government regulates more areas of behavior than other governments, certainly the government does a great deal of regulation, and it appears that government rules are obeyed. This situation reflects a tradition of bureaucratic regulation enhanced by extensive social control.

The Japanese government has also played a role vis-à-vis economic development and control of foreign trade which appears to have been qualitatively different at times from practices in many other industrialized countries. In the immediate postwar era a number of measures were taken by the Diet and/or the bureaucracy to control foreign trade and the use of foreign currency. Later some of these controls and other postwar measures were extended or altered to provide for targeted development of certain industries and for careful marshaling of foreign exchange resources to assure allocation of imports to areas supportive of development. During the 1950s and early 1960s Japanese tariffs on imported goods were higher than those of other industrialized countries; there was also an extensive import quota system and import and export licensing designed to insure ministerial control over foreign trade. Imports of capital and foreign technology were also rationed so as to encourage maximum development opportunities in industries selected for growth by Japanese bureaucrats. Japan's Ministry of International Trade and Industry was the main architect of these efforts, although the Ministry of Finance was also involved in matters involving foreign exchange and foreign capital. Other ministries like the Ministry of Transportation, which was concerned with development of the shipping and shipbuilding industries, also participated at some points in the ministerial planning process. Specific industries were encouraged to develop by inducements such as tax concessions, governmental research and development assistance, and government bank loans accompanied by sanctions such as licensing of plant site locations (in addition to controls over imports of raw materials and technological processes). The industry development programs at the ministry level were part of a broader planning process which involved indicative economic plans originated by the Economic Planning Agency.

This seemingly broad-scale effort to induce particular industries to develop and to protect them from foreign competition and capital during the developmental process was dubbed "Japan Incorporated" by some foreign observers. Use of this expression serves to heighten the image that Japan's government made unusual efforts to control and direct its economy. Even though economists tend to discount the actual impact of government planning activities and industrial development programs, the scale of government economic intervention on behalf of coordinated industrial development seems to indicate a high level of government authoritative capability in some private sectors relative to many other societies.[7]

We accept the assessment that the Japanese government played a dominant political role vis-à-vis the private economic sector at many points in the postwar era. At the same time, a few qualifications to the idea that Japan was and continues to be "super-capable" at economic policy-making are in order. First, it is important to note that from the very beginning of efforts to structure Japan's economy along lines that would encourage key industry development and high growth, the policy-making process was always highly pluralistic. Corporations and business groups fought the government over the basic plans and over ministerial strategies at many points, and different ministries disagreed strongly at times over policy matters. Different ministries also pursued contradictory policies at some points, and in a few instances different sections of a single ministry promoted contradictory policies. So "Japan Incorporated" was never monolithic in the way sometimes perceived overseas, even though Japanese planning may have been more successful (or less unsuccessful)

[7] See Gardner Ackley and Hiromitsu Ishi, "Fiscal, Monetary and Related Policies," in Hugh Patrick and Henry Rosovsky, eds., *Asia's New Giant: How the Japanese Economy Works* (Washington: Brookings, 1976), p. 232–235.

than its European counterparts.[8] Second, it is appropriate to separate government economic policy-making into two distinctive eras: a control period running roughly up until the mid-1960s and a persuasion period extending from that date.[9] Actually, that dividing line is too arbitrary, but in the earlier years, ministries acted much more independently and with a broader battery of controls (including protectionist foreign trade regulations) than has been the case in the later period. Liberalization of Japan's external trade practices began in 1962 and gained momentum during the late 1960s and early 1970s. Abandonment of the elaborate trade control system deprived relevant ministries of some of their specific powers which could be used to target development. The Japanese bureaucracy still uses a variety of techniques, especially government bank loans and "R and D" support (plus occasional tax concessions), to stimulate industrial development, even though there has been a major decline in specific industry support programs after the mid-1960s and government funding of "R and D" as a proportion of GNP is about one half that of the United States and European countries. Moreover, decisions are made these days in a less arbitrary manner than was the case earlier, and the ministries have turned more and more to use of coordinating committees (the advisory councils discussed earlier) for participation in policy-making or at least legitimization of decisions. Specific ministries also have leaned heavily on particular firms to limit competition through mergers, or to reduce capacity in distressed industries. But the ministries appear these days to lack the far more substantial capability they had in the 1950s and early 1960s to intervene and influence private economic decisions.

CAPABILITY AS FUNDAMENTAL CONFLICT
AND PROBLEM RESOLUTION ABILITY

The ability of governments to cope with problems and conflict, particularly that reflected in long-term issues, is one more dimension of their capability. There have been many areas of conflict between parties and groups in post-World War II Japan. Some of

[8] See Stephen S. Cohen, *Modern Capitalist Planning: The French Model* (Berkeley and Los Angeles: University of California Press, 1977).

[9] See Chalmers Johnson, *MITI and the Japanese Miracle: The Growth of Industrial Policy, 1925–1975* (Stanford: Stanford University Press, 1982).

these conflicts and the problems they raised were of relatively short duration and idiosyncratic nature, and therefore not of permanent significance to political decision makers. Many issues raised by interest groups fall within such a category. Even though they were sources at times of dramatic differences of opinion, their transitory nature meant that they did not pose long-term problems for government. Even where group pressures such as the repatriates' requests for compensation and the former landlords' desire for help were of longer duration, the demands of the groups were still relatively narrow, i.e., they were not part of a larger class of basic problems which dominated the attention of policy-makers and protagonists over time.

In contrast with the multiplicity of narrow and sometimes short-term individual, group issues which have been important sources of conflict in Japan in the past three decades, some issues are related to systemwide patterns in disagreement or broad common problem areas which have persisted across substantial time periods. These more basic problem areas include such issues as institutional consolidation, economic and infrastructure development, quality-of-life problems, foreign economic competition, national security and related interbloc relations, and resource and energy dependency. In discussing these major problem areas, it will be interesting to see whether the Japanese political system was able to resolve these problems in a more or less satisfactory way and whether the conflicts between parties and groups generated by the problems abated or continued.

Altogether thirteen areas of fundamental divisions of opinion or basic needs can be identified from postwar Japan's political experience. These long-term, divisive issues or problems are outlined in Table 11.1, along with an indication of the way in which the specific problem or issue conflicts were resolved. In looking across the different areas of fundamental conflict, it can be seen that three kinds of outcomes typically prevailed: (1) some issues were resolved; (2) some issues and problems were partially but not completely resolved; and (3) resolution of some problems was delayed for long periods of time or not satisfactorily accomplished in the period under consideration.

Looking at the different issue clusters on the basis of the speed and degree of their resolution tells something about the capability of the Japanese political system. A government is assumed to demonstrate more conflict resolution capability in issue areas or problem areas where satisfactory conclusions emerged from political debates and attempts at compromise. Still, it must be noted that the ideological nature of differences over some particular issues clearly affected the ability of governments and politicians in postwar Japan to find a satisfactory resolution or compromise, and presumably the same observation holds true elsewhere. The deeper, ideologically based issue conflicts were the hardest to resolve. Other restraints such as the nature of Japan's physical endowment also affected the political system's ability to provide solutions. For this reason, governmental capabilities to resolve basic issue conflicts and find solutions to central problems must always be seen as relative and as being affected by other conditions and factors.

Out of the matrix of basic issues and problems outlined in Table 11.1, three were brought to satisfactory conclusion. The first of these was economic development policy and foreign trade liberalization. Although there was considerable debate among ministries, political parties, and interested groups over Japan's early postwar economic policy directions, Japan's political system was able to forge enough agreement on an industrial development policy which laid some of the foundations of high economic growth, and the policy was successfully implemented in many areas. Moreover, as part of this policy process, a secondary issue "spun-off" as foreign countries began to criticize Japan's reliance on protectionism to develop strong domestic industries. Reactions to these criticisms provoked a strong internal debate on the issue of trade policy liberalization, but this issue too was eventually resolved by governmental actions which over a period of time dismantled the trade quota and high tariff system.

Resolution of the economic development and trade policy issues was facilitated by the comparatively narrow range of differences between concerned political actors and the nonideological nature of the dispute. The ministries which developed these policies were also some of the strongest components of the Japanese political system at the time, and they had both prestige in the eyes of the groups with whom they were dealing and a substantial battery of sanctions and rewards which could be used to persuade other political actors to follow their lead or resolve their differences, at least part of the time. Some of the same circumstances

TABLE 11.1. *Problem and Conflict Resolution in Japan, 1952–80*

Conflict or Problem	Resolution or Nonresolution
Institutional "Crises" Debate over Constitution revision	Postponement resulting from lack of a two-thirds majority necessary for amendment and study of problem followed by nonresolution
Proposals for reverse-course administrative changes Debates over internal security laws and University Control Bill	Bills passed by conservative movement over protest Efforts to change police control not generally successful because of intensity of opposition; University Control Bill passed as a result of wide societal condemnation of university disruptions even though interparty differences
Infrastructural Development Need for better roads, ports, and overall transport system improvement	New freeways in metropolitan areas, new high speed railways, new industrial parks and harbor projects, many developed by creation of new public corporations
Quality-of-Life Shortcomings Popular antipollution movements and damage claims, antiindustrial development movements	Multiple pollution programs enacted and enforced; attention to amenities increased in budgets, although problems never completely solved; some regional industrial centers postponed
Economic Growth and Response to Foreign Economic Competition Key industry development plans Early protectionism and industry support Resistance abroad to Japanese exports Competition from newly industrializing countries, falling demand	Domestic debate but implementation in most areas Foreign and domestic pressures lead to trade policy liberalization Voluntary restrictions on export levels Various structural recession policies including reduced capacity programs and personnel relocation

Petroleum and Resource Dependency

Oil shock — Efforts to conserve energy, promote alternate energy sources, and stabilize country-of-source relations

Need for mineral resources — Efforts to develop extraction and overseas processing arrangements in producer countries and related diplomatic efforts to maintain "positive" relations with relevant nations

National Security and Interbloc Relations

Debate over appropriate security effort levels and constitutional legality — Decision to have limited defensive effort and security tie with U.S., but intraconservative discord and twenty years of intense opposition from left

Differences on People's Republic of China relations — Twenty-year debate with periods of government postponement of decisons facilitated smooth development of Japan's industrial infrastructure consisting of roads, industrial parks, and harbor expansion projects which was able to proceed rapidly during the 1960s because of a low level of disagreement. Initially, there was virtually little or no disagreement over infrastructure development as it provided generally needed facilities, construction industry projects, and jobs in many parts of the country, and only occasionally was there localized resistance to land purchases. Subsequently, expansion of industrial zones became more controversial, as did also expansion of high-speed rail facilities. Still, in at least the 1960s the need for infrastructural development was aggressively addressed by national authorities, and issues were subsequently resolved, in part because of the prevalence of a general national consensus on the need for growth.

The University Control Bill of 1969 was another example of a solution developed in a mood of relative national consensus. This time many people and groups felt that resolution of the student demonstration problem was important and necessary. There was intense debate over the control bill since some university faculties and leftist party groups felt that absolute university autonomy should be preserved. Yet the national mood favored some kind of solution to the problem, and the bill providing for national intervention in university disputes after a waiting period represented a concession to the forces opposing university control measures. It was a matter of importance that the issue was resolved, with the existence of a generally consensual environment facilitating this resolution.

By far the most typical political outcome of basic issue conflicts and fundamental problems facing Japan's postwar political system was partial resolution, i.e., solutions which addressed part of a problem or resolved part of a controversy without satisfying all interested groups and parties. There were several reasons for the more limited nature of this class of governmental solutions: in some instances the policies proposed by the government were compromises in situations where no solution fully satisfactory to all parties could be achieved. Elsewhere, programs were enacted at the national level even though pockets of intense local opposition remained, so all participants to the process could not be satisfied. In some cases, physical barriers to success in the form of Japan's high population and industrial concentration and limited availability of resources were a factor preventing complete issue resolution. Finally, in some cases, the responses and actions of foreign political actors prevented full resolution of particular controversies or problems.

An example of policy solutions which involved partial compromises accompanied by lingering problems was Japan's decision to have a limited defense establishment in the early 1950s. Initially, some conservative politicians advocated a strong defense establishment, while others preferred a limited defense effort accompanied by a security alliance with the United States and emphasis on economic development. The latter group led by then Prime Minister Shigeru Yoshida won; but because some conservatives have always favored higher levels of military effort, there has always been a lingering difference over defense policy inside the conservative party. These differences have periodically erupted in internal party debates. Meanwhile, opposition to the security policy solutions of the 1950s from the leftist parties was a frequent source of intra- and extraparliamentary protest for over twenty years after the early-1950s decisions were made. In a somewhat similar style of issue resolution, education and police administration were partially recentralized in a series of reverse course policies after Japan regained its sovereignty in 1952. The decisions satisfied nobody fully: some administrators and politicians would have gone further, and some political groups were indisposed to accept any abandonment of the local autonomy principle. Likewise, at a much later point, Japan's responses to overseas pressures to limit exports of steel, color televisons, automobiles, and other products left some ministries and some industrial circles disgruntled and unhappy.

It should be obvious from the above examples that some compromise solutions are satisficing but not really satisfactory or complete resolutions of political differences. This is the nature of political decision making in all governments. But it does suggest areas of limitations in governmental capability to resolve problems and issues completely. Physical considerations may place similar boundaries on governmental solutions. Japan has a very large population in a country small in area and with severely limited space for residential, farming, and industrial uses — actually about one fifth of the nation's territory. Limitations in usable space have contributed to astronomical inflation in land prices, shortages of adequate housing, deficiencies in public amenities such as water supplies and sewage systems, crowding of roads and unacceptable levels of pollution.

Japan's resource dependency and most recently its extreme vulnerability to curtailment of overseas supplies of petroleum have meant that solutions to mineral resource needs and energy problems also have so far been only temporary and partial accommodations to basic problems. Even though the Japanese government has promoted energy conservation with some success, and reliable overseas supplies of minerals and fuels have been avidly sought along with alternative domestic sources of energy, no real solutions of Japan's permanent vulnerability in these areas have been achieved, because of both the immensity of the problem and the unpredictable nature of overseas political environments. Indeed, the foreign environment has been a major uncontrollable factor in Japan's long-term concerns for economic viability with regard to the perennial need for raw materials and fuel imports as well as to the related need for access to free export markets to generate the foreign exchange needed to pay for necessary imports.

In certain policy areas Japan has been successful in achieving solutions which were acceptable at the level of national politics, only to be met by extreme resistance in particular local areas. The search for alternative energy sources through development of nuclear power plants, expansion of transportation infrastructure, and development of new regional industrial centers have all been met by strong local opposition in many areas in recent years. In some instances projects were delayed for years as a result. Japan's new Tokyo International Airport project at Narita is a case in point, as was also extension of high-speed railway projects in some areas. Often the national government has prevailed in the long run, but only after tremendous delays, and some projects were even considerably modified to accommodate local resistance.

Japan's government record in conflict resolution and problem solving is reasonably similar to that of other industrialized democracies. Presumably some degree of failure or delay and even limited success is typical of governmental problem solving in any complex, pluralistic society. These limitations to absolute success are a cost which must be paid in order to have open political systems with adequate opportunities for participation and representation by parties and groups with diverse interests and opinions.

The failure in Japan to resolve some problems over long periods of time probably can be viewed in a similar vein. There have been some problems and issues in Japan's recent experience where intense opposition and conflict led to governmental procrastination over a long period, while in some instances no real problem resolution was forthcoming. In two areas — constitutional revision and enhanced police powers — political opposition was so great that no resolution of the issue was possible. In the case of proposed constitutional reforms, the conservative party lacked the necessary two thirds of total Diet seats needed to make amendment a feasible alternative after the early 1950s. Institutional barriers and the configuration of political power were the constraints in this issue area. Elsewhere, other combinations of forces inhibited conflict solutions. Thus, the Police Duties Bill of 1958 was withdrawn after strong opposition party, media, and mass movement resistance. In the controversy over relations with Communist China as well, resolution of conservative-leftist confrontations was delayed for up to two decades until external events favored shifts in this critical policy area. Internal conservative party fragmentation was also a factor in this delay, since some conservative party groups wanted relations with mainland China, while others were strongly pro-Taiwan. This internal split, plus deference to American policies, led the conservative political leadership to postpone some decisions (or to decide not to decide) for many years before attempting a rapprochement with the mainland, even in the face of continuous and strident opposition party pressure for better relations with the People's Republic. It is undoubtedly axiomatic that democratic political systems cannot resolve basic political cleavages of the dimension of the China issue easily or quickly. But this means that governmental capabilities are lesser in this area, and that a great deal of political resources may be spent in fights over such issues of perpetual combat.

CAPABILITY AS STABILITY AND ADAPTABILITY

Ideally a political system must meet many kinds of expectations. Citizens of democratic societies hope that their opinions will be represented by their governments and that politicians will respect their needs in making policies. Governments must also have authority to extract sufficient resources and regulate critical areas of behavior which are a threat to public safety or preservation of general values. If governments choose to direct the economy toward certain established goals, they must also have the authority to do this. Moreover, political systems should be able to resolve major conflicts in a satisficing way and meet basic general societal needs as they emerge.

Democratic governments ideally should also be stable — succession should follow established routines rather than occur by coups d'état, and institutions should provide basic channels for political decision making rather than be the object of frequent manipulation by political leaders and parties bent on shaping institutions to suit their own purposes. Legislatures should work as responsible deliberating bodies unhindered by threats from the streets or the military. The party system should be sufficiently institutionalized and/or amenable to compromise so as to produce stable governing coalitions. In addition to providing for stable succession and leadership, and stable institutional frameworks, political systems should be able to absorb change in incremental ways. Political systems must be adaptive as well as stable.

Stable government is necessary for an economy to develop — indeed this may have been the most vital contribution of government to economic development in Japan. Stability is similarly vital in providing for a secure life, as the experience of many newly emerging nations have demonstrated in a negative sense. If there are regular means for succession and stable leadership coalitions, viable institutions, and reasonably consistent arrays of partisan alternatives, public and private economic planners can make estimates about future outcomes and business trends in an environment where a number of important parameters are certain. Other economic factors being equal, long-term investments can be undertaken with some expectation of gain, contracts can be written with the expectation that money supplies and values will not run wild as a spin-off of political instability, and a variety of supportive institutions and regulations which affect the economy can be expected to behave in predictable ways. Individuals throughout society can also live in the security that officials will behave in a predictable fashion, and that their own economic activity and general behavior will not be rewarded with arbitrary imprisonment or worse.

Yet for all of the virtues of stability and continuity — many of which have become more obvious as the result of the highly negative consequences of instability in weakly institutionalized nations in recent years — countries must also be able to adapt to new circumstances. Institutions should be able to meet new problems even where this stimulates institutional change. In effect, nations should be able to adapt to new economic situations, new arrays of popular preferences, new external environments, and new societal needs; and in some cases institutional changes may be the best way to meet these challenges. Indeed, change may in itself carry the seeds of stable performance in some situations, as rigid and uncreative responses could otherwise create societal pressures for revolutionary solutions.

By and large, Japan's postwar political system has been remarkably stable, particularly insomuch as it began in some senses as a new regime after wartime defeat and extensive changes in governmental institutions. By most of the measures of stability — stable and institutionalized succession, effective and stable leadership coalitions, responsible and reasonably viable legislative processes, and a reasonably stable party system — Japan's postwar experience has been salutory, especially in the years after the mid 1950s. Yet there have still been important pockets of instability, and these need to be examined carefully since they could be the forerunner of future problems in governmental consistency in Japan. Also, some of the sources of stability in Japan must be probed further.

The first prominent area of stability in postwar Japanese politics has been the basic governmental institutions themselves. While leaders of the conservative movement fought among themselves and with the opposition parties for several years over constitutional reform, the areas of proposed constitutional revision discussed most frequently in these debates were not very broad. Much of the postwar institutional framework was accepted as legitimate by all mainstream political parties. And importantly, the processes and rituals provided for by the new constitution and related laws were accepted by-and-large, in itself a major indicator of the stable institutionalization of critical governmental procedures. Prime ministers were chosen in the prescribed ways from among politicians in the Diet, the executive provided responsible leadership in the sense that major policies were submitted to the Diet for debate and discussion, and the Diet itself solemnly went through the motions of parliamentary government, except for occasional misuses of procedures and physical violence in the 1950s and 1960s. Bills were debated in committee and plenary sessions, and despite the contention that the Diet was something of a rubber-stamp body which ratified bureaucratic inputs rather than acting as an ideally functioning parliament, in reality the Diet was more active in the earlier postwar years than was believed and became even more so in the 1970s.

One factor contributing to the stability observable in Japanese national government since World War II may be a general cultural tendency toward institutionalization of processes and a conventionalist attention to precedent, detail, and protocol. As in other aspects of capability, it is easy to infer that the Japanese tend to place great emphasis on institutions and organizational efforts in all areas of social activity, and that this general cultural tendency spills over into politics. Yet this conservative and organizational bent in Japanese culture did not rule out sudden changes in governmental format and extreme instability in top-level decision making and succession processes in earlier periods of Japanese history, with the 1930s being the most recent example; consequently, we cannot see culture alone as a source of institutional stability, even though it may have been a contributing factor.

A more central explanation of the success of postwar institutions lies in the fact that all political parties have basically accepted them. However much some conservatives longed for a partial return to the past, conservative leadership generally followed the rules. The same is true for the opposition parties. The opposition often provoked distasteful scenes of fistfights on the Diet floor and other pseudocomic, pseudosad examples of violations of parliamentary dignity, aided and abetted by the rigidity and skullduggery of conservative governments. Yet the opposition groups always returned to the fold in carefully orchestrated reconciliation scenarios by which Diet processes were normalized. Despite temporary breakdowns and unseemly behavior in the Diet, both the government parties and the opposition groups kept parliamentary government going.

Secondly, the long-term dominance of Japanese politics by the conservative movement and the extension of this trend into the post-1955 reign by the Liberal Democrats was in itself a source of stable government. Although conservative dominance was the source of opposition frustrations which moved Diet processes to the brink of collapse on many occasions, conservative and later

Liberal Democratic hegemony removed Japan from the perils frequently associated with coalition government in parliamentary systems. Coalition government is not always bad, but when a party system is sufficiently fragmented and ideologically polarized, there may be rapid coalition and cabinet turnover and resulting parliamentary and governmental immobilism. Thus, while provoking the opposition to parliamentary and street violence on many occasions, the conservative camp's hegemony in postwar Japan provided a reasonably stable framework of power in executive selection processes and parliamentary politics.

Thus, Liberal Democratic and conservative dominance has carried Japan through a period of critical institutional development and transtition and has insulated the political process during this era from the potentially destabilizing effects of ideological polarization. The conservative movement was dominant in the 1950s and 1960s by virtue of its often discussed traditional modes of vote mobilization and a benevolent system of unequal apportionment. Conservative hegemony in turn precluded participation in government by parties with which the conservatives could have never cooperated (at that time) and which could in some cases not have cooperated among themselves because of extremely rigid and polarized ideological commitments and mutual distrust. Meanwhile, as the Liberal Democrats have slowly lost support at the polls as time has passed, the increasingly fragmented opposition camp has shown much greater moderation in its beliefs and, in several important cases, demonstrated an ability to work cooperatively in local government coalitions, some of which included even Liberal Democratic participation. Indeed, local mayoral and gubernatorial coalitions in Japan have been marked by their variety of combinations, and by a surprising element of cooperation between parties which have not yet shown an ability to form coalitions at the national level.[10]

Lest the emphasis on the contribution to stability of conserva-

---

[10] There have been many coalitions in local politics in Japan, especially since the early 1970s. For example, between 1974 and 1977 there were between 242 and 311 local mayoral coalitions which included various combinations of the opposition parties (and at times the Liberal Democrats). See Takashi Tsumura, *Kakushin Jijitai* (Tokyo: Kyoikusha, 1978), p. 70. But at the national level, the opposition camp has generally been unable to form long-term coalitions for purposes of electoral success, and discussions of parliamentary coalition possibilities have focused as much on incompatibilities between parties as possibilities of compromise.

tive and Liberal Democratic rule be seen as a unique combination of harmony and strength, it is important to note that internally the conservative parties have carried the seeds of extreme instability even though this has not produced total calamities in recent years. Specifically, the most prominent source of incipient instability in Japanese politics over the past three decades — with the exception of isolated examples of terrorism, a ritual of frequent mass protests, and fisticuffs in the Diet in some periods — has been intra-Liberal Democratic factionalism itself. The Liberal Democratic tendency toward factional squabbles over internal party matters, including succession to the prime ministership, has produced a low-grade political drama and has probably been a major delegitimizing force in shaping a political culture of distrust. This factional infighting has brought the ruling movement to the brink of fracture and the government to the brink of collapse on several occasions. The Liberal Democrats have operated frequently just like a fragmented multiparty system: succession solutions have been delayed for months, and parliamentary initiative immobilized in some periods as the result. Given the traditional workings of group attachments and intergroup tensions in Japanese politics, probably much the same would have happened if the Japan Socialists had come to power or will happen if they come to power in the future. It is necessary to observe, therefore, that if Japanese cultural practices promote acceptance and legitimacy of institutions and processes in some senses, and therefore encourage stable government, other aspects of Japan's cultural tendencies, namely the formation of factions and the eruption of intense interfactional rivalries, bears in itself important dangers for stable government.

Japanese government, meanwhile, has shown itself adaptable and reasonably creative in the face of the challenges it has received during the postwar era. There have been many crises, or near crisis situations, including postwar reconstruction, security in a bipolar world, resource and energy dependency, foreign trade competition, a structural recession and growing obsolescence in some industries, expanding infrastructural needs, demands for more amenities, and internal discord, such as was manifested in the many riots and demonstrations of the 1950s, the mammoth antisecurity treaty movement of 1959–60, and more recently waves of citizen antipollution and antiregional industrialization movements and isolated acts of terrorism. These crises have been met and handled in a more or less satisfactory way. Massive urbanization has also occurred with related changes in life-styles and social organization without causing major social disruptions. Even though urbanization and its companion stresses and problems were a major factor in the emergence of thousands of local political protest movements and were probably the most important factor in party system realignments, they were not a source of general social or political breakdown. How much this adaptability is a tribute to the resilience of Japanese society and how much it speaks for the inherent stability and successful policies of Japanese governments is hard to say. But this is the way things have worked out. It is significant that there have been few institutional changes in Japanese government as the result. New social needs have been approached mainly by creating more public corporations and allocating more budget or FILP monies for social programs for newly important groups of needy persons, such as the aged. New political alignments reflecting social change have altered Diet processes. But these challenges and stimuli to change have not been met with radical institutional reformatting or dramatic shifts in governmental styles.

One final, critical comment on the stability of the Japanese political system is in order. Students of voting behavior in other countries have argued extensively that the stability, indeed at times the rigidity, of voting preferences was governed either by social group attachments or by psychological attitudes of support for particular political parties. As noted in the discussion of Japanese voting behavior, neither traditional social group interpretations nor party identification theories afford a complete explanation of Japanese voting behavior and its tendencies to be extremely stable in some districts of the country. Rather, traditional styles of political mobilization and their modern organizational counterparts in the form of union and other group efforts to build and maintain voting blocs provide a better explanation of stable voting where this has occurred than the traditional sociological and psychological explanations. Remarkably stable and consolidated voting blocs appear as bulwarks of conservative party dominance in the most rural parts of Japan's less urbanized prefectures, and in these districts the sources of both long-term conservative hegemony and electoral stability can be seen. At the other end of the electoral pole lie Japan's expanding urban and surburban areas, where party fortunes are more fragile in the aggregate and across time. In the rural setting, voters are highly mobilized by traditional vote gathering techniques, and they may also express support as members of farm groups and conservative party identifiers. In the metropolitan districts, there appears to be a great deal of image and mood voting, a factor which contributes to more volatile voting patterns in the cities and suburbs. Since the urban areas have steadily increased in overall importance, and rural districts are both dwindling in population and increasingly penetrated by urban life-styles and opportunities for industrial employment, Japan's voters may not provide the kind of stable support in the future that has occurred at critical points in the past. Indeed the fact that currently 40 percent of the Japanese electorate either expressly do not support a political party or answer they "don't know" what party they would support serves as an eloquent indicator of the themes that have been noted as well as suggesting the degree of potential volatility existing in the contemporary voting public.

JAPANESE POLITICAL PERFORMANCE: PAST AND FUTURE

The review of Japanese government and political system capabilities has argued that Japan has had a reasonably legitimate political regime even in the face of an ambivalent political culture, that governmental authority has been sufficient for some purposes even though extractive capability is an emerging problem, that most recurring problems and needs were partially solved, and that government was stable and adaptive in the face of a number of important challenges. Japanese government was also a creative instrument in promoting economic growth or at least contributed to a general environment which encouraged economic growth. While we have not praised Japan as a superior political system in the way that some Japanophiles and futurologists have been prone to do, we have felt that on balance much good could be seen in the postwar political experience.

Will Japanese politics in the future continue to be fairly legitimate, reasonably stable, and more or less successful? This is remarkably hard to say, as we are at this time in a period of important transition in Japan and in the rest of the world which ha vital implications for these very questions. Liberal Democrati and conservative rule, the dominant feature of postwar Japanese politics, still hovers more or less at the margins even though the conservative forces did do better in the spring 1980 House of Representatives and House of Councillors double elections and the 1983 House of Councillors poll than in earlier contests, and have improved their position in opinion polls in the early 1980s over that of the previous decade. But while conservative rule has continued after the December 1983 House of Representatives elections, buttressed by an intra-conservative coalition between the Liberal Democrats and the New Liberal Club, the decline of Liberal Democratic voting support in this election and the Party's failure to obtain a simple majority indicate the continuing fragility of its capability to maintain its traditional pure hegemony in Japanese politics. Also, Liberal Democratic governments are facing a relatively bleak array of policy problems currently and will continue to face them for some time. The Japanese population is "aging" much more rapidly than other national populations as a spin-off of affluence and improved health care, just at a time when budgets seem increasingly inadequate to meet the costs of an expanding social security system. Combined with this pressure on Japan's fiscal viability is a growing concern in some quarters that Japan should expand outlays on defense, accompanied by an apparently strong resistance to increased taxes from Japan's corporate sector and opposition parties. Just how future Japanese governments can work their way out of this dilemma remains to be seen. In addition, the past solution of expanding revenue bases through rapid economic growth seems out of the question for the near future, as the international environment is presently less favorable to the growth of Japanese exports than was the case earlier. Moreover, the domestic stimulus from first-time purchases of televisions and appliances, automobiles and new homes, will not occur again. While this does not mean that Japan is facing fiscal collapse now or in the near future, the momentum of economic growth has changed dramatically, just when new demands for revenues are occurring. No easy political solution is visible, and no Japanese government attempting to provide solutions for this basic problem will presumably come out unscathed.

The other sobering thought in addition to the question of future fiscal solvency is the simple fact that Japan has yet to experience a truly major crisis in the postwar era, except perhaps the traumas of the immediate postwar reconstruction era. There has been no major depression such as the one that made a major contribution to undermining civilian rule and terminating Japan's first experiment with democracy before the outbreak of World War II. And since the end of the early postwar reconstruction period, Japan has thus far been remarkably free of the costs and consequences of war and preparation for war. This has meant that military demands on fiscal resources have been minimal, and governmental demands for societal cooperation have been far smaller than has been the case in some other political systems. The postwar Japanese political system has experienced a series of middle-range crises, most of which have been handled in a satisficing way, i.e., with pockets of societal frustration and political opposition but no significant radical opposition to existing political formats. We cannot say for sure that a depression or war, should they occur, would be met with the kinds of reasonable capabilities and moderate successes which have been the hallmark of Japan's political experience in the three decades of experience covered in this book. Yet the successes in the past in providing the framework for economic development and growth coupled with the institutionalization of the postwar political structure and conservative political stability over the past three decades suggest that the Japanese political system will survive in the years ahead.

Index